Charles M. Russell

Charles M. Russell

THE LIFE AND LEGEND

OF AMERICA'S COWBOY

ARTIST

John Taliaferro

LITTLE, BROWN AND COMPANY

Boston   New York   Toronto   London

FIRST EDITION

The author is grateful for permission to include the following previously copyrighted material:

All personal papers and letters of Charles M. Russell and Nancy Russell from the Britzman Collection,
Taylor Museum for Southwestern Studies of the Colorado Fine Arts Center, Colorado, and the C. M.
Russell Museum, Great Falls, Montanna. Reprinted by permission.

Quotes by Archie Douglas, Jake Hoover, Bill Bullard, B. M. Bower from the Montana Historical Society.
Reprinted by permission.

Excerpt by I. F. "Finch" David from *The Bill Arnold Collection of the Works of Charles M. Russell*.
Copyright © 1965. The Pemberton Press. Reprinted by permission of Maureen Jenkins.

Quotes by Joe DeYong from the C. M. Russell Museum, Great Falls, Montana, and the National Cowboy
Hall of Fame, Oklahoma City, Oklahoma. Reprinted by permission.

Excerpt from "A Few Words About Myself" by Charles M. Russell from *Trails Plowed Under*. Copyright
1927. Doubleday Publishers. Reprinted by permission of Charles Griffin Cale, Trustee of the Estate of
Charles M. Russell and Nancy C. Russell.

Excerpts from interviews by J. Frank Dobie reprinted by permission of the J. Frank Dobie Library Trust,
Texas Commerce Bank, Trustee.

Library of Congress Cataloging-in-Publication Data

Taliaferro, John.
    Charles M. Russell : the life and legend of America's cowboy
artist / John Taliaferro. — 1st ed.
      p.   cm.
    Includes bibliographical references and index.
    ISBN 0-316-83190-5
    1. Russell, Charles M. (Charles Marion), 1884–1926. 2. Artists —
United States — Biography. I. Title.
N6537.R88T36 1996
709'.2 — dc20
[B]   95-45795

10 9 8 7 6 5 4 3 2 1

MV-NY

Published simultaneously in Canada by Little, Brown & Company (Canada) Limited

Printed in the United States of America

FOR JACK AND AUDREY

CONTENTS

ACKNOWLEDGMENTS

I cannot imagine completing this book without the guidance and encouragement of Brian W. Dippie, professor of history at the University of Victoria, British Columbia, and the foremost authority on the life and art of Charles Russell today. I approached Dippie in 1992 to warn him that the thudding and gasping he would soon be hearing on the wind were nothing more than the sounds of a tenderfoot's first forays into a domain that Dippie had explored and mapped so assiduously over the past three decades. Not only did Dippie welcome me to Russell country, he generously steered me to some of the hardest-to-find, and certainly the richest, nooks of research and truth. Numerous observations and assumptions in my narrative derive directly from Dippie's scholarship, for which I am immensely grateful.

I am likewise indebted to a number of institutions, though, of course, it is their human representatives whom I must thank specifically. My respect and appreciation go to Rick Stewart, Paula Stewart, and the staff of the Amon Carter Museum in Fort Worth, who took me in for weeks at a time while I sifted through Nancy Russell's estate papers. Like Brian Dippie, Rick Stewart was extraordinarily generous with his research on Russell, particularly the material he brought to bear in his brilliant book, *Charles M. Russell, Sculptor.* Thanks also to Cathy Wright and Kathy Reynolds of the Colorado Springs Fine Arts Center for lending the estate papers to the Amon Carter in the first place, and for then allowing me access. I am one of the privileged few to have examined this mother lode, and if nothing else, my book is testimony to its great breadth and depth.

I salute the Montana Historical Society, its library and staff. Among the numerous rewards of writing a book about Montana, one of the greatest has been the opportunity to associate with such warm and wise professionals as MHS's Dorothea Simonson, Robert Clark, Brian Shovers, Rebecca Kohl, and Charles E. Rankin, editor of *Montana: The Magazine of Western History.* Freelance researcher Jana Maier was of great service as well.

My good fortune continued at the C. M. Russell Museum in Great Falls, where curator Elizabeth Dear led me nimbly and patiently through the Russell house, studio, collection, and archives, and showed me everything I had hoped for and more. At the National Cowboy Hall of Fame in Oklahoma City, curator Don Reeves gave me liberal rein with the Joe DeYong papers. A spirit of sharing and cooperation seems to be contagious throughout the Western-art community. Both Joan Carpenter Troccoli of the Gilcrease Museum in Tulsa, Oklahoma, and Peter Hassrick of the Buffalo Bill Historical Center in Cody, Wyoming, threw open the doors of their awesome establishments. The Harry Ransom Humanities Research Center at the University of Texas at Austin is a trove of global import, though I value no holding more highly than the papers of hometown historian J. Frank Dobie; his notes from a lifetime of research on Russell were heaven-sent.

My research assistant in Austin, Kathleen Rice, gave me a terrific boost in the early days of digging.

It would be almost rude to categorize the following people as sources, though they were indeed enthusiastic in that role. I prefer to think of them as hosts who shared their lives as well as their knowledge. In St. Louis, I learned my way and took sustenance from Ward Parker, Lyle Woodcock, Sarah Glasgow Willcockson, and Kate Berger, in between valuable sessions at the Missouri Historical Society, the St. Louis Mercantile Library, the St. Louis Public Library, and the Richardson Memorial Library at the St. Louis Art Museum.

In Great Falls, my quest was advanced by Russell Edwin, Joe and Beth Wolff, Harry Mitchell, William Bertsche, Ethel Calvert, Ike Kaufman, and especially Julianne Ruby of the Cascade County Historical Society.

My trip to Glacier Park and the haunts of Frank Linderman was facilitated and enriched by Sally Hatfield, Linderman's granddaughter; Beth

Dunagan, librarian at the George C. Ruhle Library at park headquarters; and last but far from least, Van Kirke Nelson, who ensured access to Bull Head Lodge.

I spent an inspirational, invaluable day with Joan and Dale Stauffer in Tulsa, and benefited greatly from their spadework on the Russells. I had comparable interludes with Ginger Renner in Paradise Valley, Arizona; Harry Carey, Jr., in Durango, Colorado; William Mackay at the Lazy EL Ranch in Roscoe, Montana; Barbara Twiford, Utica, Montana's resident historian and keeper of the flame; and Brian Sindelar, who drove me over hundreds of unpaved miles in the Judith Basin and painted me a grassroots portrait of how the Big Sky must once have looked.

In California, I was greeted by Charles Griffin Cale, trustee of the Russell estate; Frank and Dee Repetti, owners of Trail's End; Carol Sandmeier, director of the William S. Hart Museum; and Harold Davidson, Edward Borein authority nonpareil. I must also thank the Margaret Herrick Library of the Academy of Motion Picture Arts and Sciences; the Southwest Museum, keeper of Charles Lummis's papers; the Los Angeles County Natural History Museum, keeper of William S. Hart's papers; the Santa Barbara Historical Society; and the Los Angeles Public Library.

Never was I more out of my depth than when I ventured into the realm of science and medicine. My hat is off to the Mayo Clinic for sharing Charlie Russell's records and to Dr. Stephen Clark of Austin, Texas, for interpreting Charlie and Nancy's medical histories. Mary Lovey Wood, also of Austin, led me through the fascinating thicket of Russell's handwriting and made his learning disorder plain as day.

Indelible thanks to my editors, Roger Donald, Amanda Murray, Anne Montague, and my remarkable agent, Esther Newberg.

And finally, my heartfelt gratitude to Jack Russell of Oceanside, California, who helped me get acquainted with a man he never knew well enough himself. Mr. Russell died in California in January 1996, just before this book went to press; he was seventy-nine. It was never my intention to take a father's story away from his son. Rather, my hope had been to give a good part of it back to him.

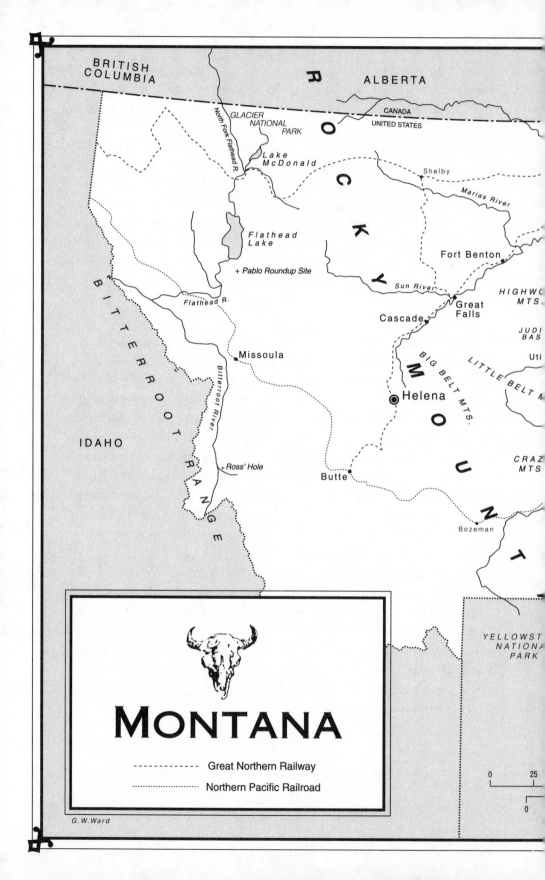

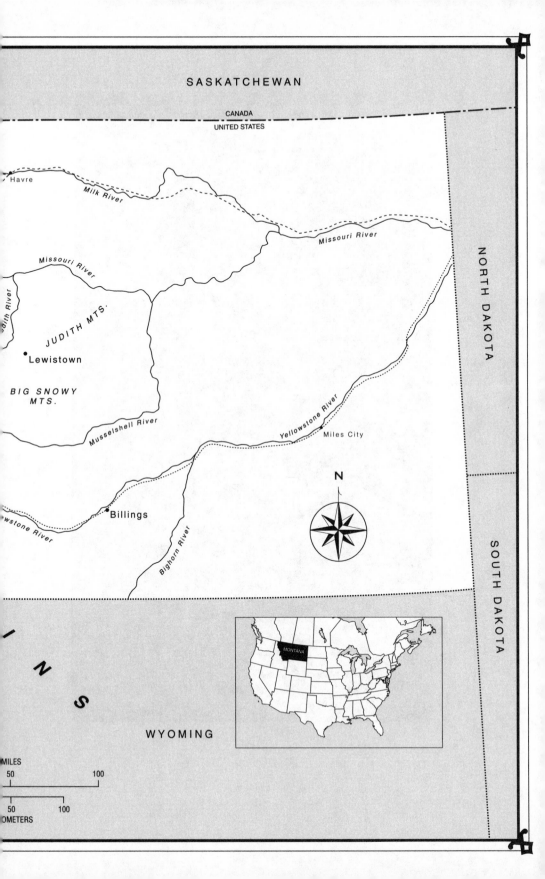

SASKATCHEWAN

CANADA
UNITED STATES

Havre

Milk River

Missouri River

Missouri River

Judith River

JUDITH MTS.

Lewistown

BIG SNOWY
MTS.

Musselshell River

Yellowstone River

Miles City

NORTH DAKOTA

SOUTH DAKOTA

N

Yellowstone River

Billings

Bighorn River

I N S

WYOMING

MONTANA

MILES
50   100

50   100
OMETERS

Charles M. Russell

INTRODUCTION

S MOKE SPOILED CHARLIE and Nancy Russell's view in August 1926. A forest fire had begun on the north fork of Montana's Flathead River and foraged eastward over the Apgar Mountains to the shores of Lake McDonald. For several days, the Russells had feared they might have to evacuate Bull Head Lodge, the lakeside log cabin where they had spent the past twenty summers. But at the last moment, the wind shifted. Flames that destroyed a neighbor's place, just down the beach, stopped mercifully short of the Russells'. Bull Head was safe for the time being, though Charlie and Nancy were socked in, and doubly gloomy.

The horizon had always been special to them. They had built Bull Head Lodge on a slope at the south end of the lake, a hundred feet from the water, facing the sunrise. Morning light filtered through a screen of cedar, tamarack, and hemlock that grew nearly to the water's edge. A footpath led from the lodge's uncovered front porch down to the narrow shore, where a deadfall provided a natural bench. From that front-row seat Charlie, Nancy, and their long parade of summer visitors had habitually enjoyed one of the most spectacular panoramas in North America.[1]

Lake McDonald is a mile-wide, ten-mile-long gouge, the track of an ancient glacier, which, in its patient maceration, had dug a lake nearly five hundred feet deep. When the sun is high, the water approaches a deep turquoise. When the air is still, the timbered ridges on either side of Lake McDonald are reflected on its surface in a most faithful way. Up the lake, to the north, lies McDonald's mountain origin. Early promoters of the area had dubbed this pocket of the Rockies, now part of Glacier National Park, "America's Switzerland."

As seen from Bull Head Lodge, the view is ecclesiastic. The lake is the center aisle of a grand cathedral. As the aisle proceeds northward, it passes between gothic pulpits rising four thousand feet above McDonald's waters: Stanton, Brown, and Gunsight peaks. Finally, several miles farther north, the eye is drawn to a magnificent, God-made apse, at the rear of which is a massive, scalloped, thousand-foot altar of bald limestone. Today this altar is called the Garden Wall. But before whites ever came to the region, centuries of determined Native Americans had made their way up the steep face and had given the route a more spiritual name. It was known as Going to the Sun, a prehistoric path that reached to the Continental Divide and the other side of the world.[2]

Charlie Russell had painted this view occasionally over the years. The paintings were usually quick landscapes in watercolor, different in subject matter and mood from his usual action scenes of Indians or cowboys. Charlie and Nancy liked to set out salt along the shore for the deer, who would repay the kindness by posing in the foregrounds of Charlie's intermittent salutes to water, mountain, and sky. More often, though, Charlie and Nancy would simply sit on their log bench and admire. "There are some things Ma Nature won't let man copy," Charlie liked to say.[3] Often, too, Charlie and Nancy had little view to enjoy; the weather at Lake McDonald was famously fickle.

Clouds and smoke, though, were two different things. One was unavoidable, the other ominous — especially in the summer of 1926. This would likely be Charlie's last season at Bull Head. His health had been poor for years: he was pestered by a bad back, bad digestion, bad teeth, and a goiter that had been growing steadily for a decade. The previous winter, while in California, Charlie had complained of shortness of breath. In May, when he, Nancy, and their nine-year-old son, Jack, had returned to Montana, the family physician, Dr. Charles Coulter, and their trusted osteopath, Dr. Edward Edwin, had agreed that Charlie ought to go to the Mayo Clinic in Rochester, Minnesota. Modern medicine — modern anything — unsettled Charlie. But finally he had agreed to go, though only after Doc Edwin had promised to stay by his side throughout the ordeal.

The goiter operation on July 3 was a complete success — not that it mattered. From the tests done before and after surgery, doctors had discovered that Charlie's heart was a shambles. Blame the goiter, or blame a lifetime of bacon and Bull Durham; either way, the Mayo Clinic measured the rest of Charlie's life in months. He knew it, and so did Nancy, though neither dwelled on the grim truth. Back at Bull Head on August 6, Nancy wrote a wishful fib to wealthy patron Malcolm Mackay at his ranch in Roscoe, Montana: "Charlie is improving every day, not very strong but very happy and I am quite sure he will be a great deal better."[4]

Nancy had Charlie smoking cubeb cigarettes, an herbal tobacco substitute.[5] She called a halt to the merry house parties, with guests from New York, St. Louis, and California swooping in on the train and filling every spare bed and porch for four or five days at a time. No more dressing up like Indians and hamming it up for the camera. No more model-ship building and match-racing on the lake. And no more picnics to the mountains of Glacier Park. Riding was already a thing of the past. Charlie for the most part had quit horses three years earlier, after an accident on the way home from the Jack Dempsey–Tommy Gibbons title fight in Shelby, Montana. Now he got around by car or, at Lake McDonald, by boat.

Two of the few visitors that summer were Charlie and Nancy's neighbors from Great Falls, Josephine Trigg and her mother, Margaret. The Triggs were like family. Nancy called Margaret "Mother," a surrogate for her true mother, who had died when Nancy was a teenager. Josephine was the children's librarian in Great Falls, and she and Charlie shared a love of knights and ladies, gnomes and fairies, and all things medieval and English. Margaret and Josephine had come to do what they could for Charlie.

A photo taken that summer of Charlie, Nancy, Josephine, and Margaret shows them standing in a swatch of sunlight in the side yard of Bull Head. Even in black and white, Charlie appears sallow and spent. He wears his customary sash, boots, and dark, double-breasted suit coat. But his shirt collar is spread wide so as not to constrict his healing neck. In his sixty-two years, Charlie had posed jauntily for hundreds of pictures and had painted himself dozens of times more. But in this shot, he gives off no manly spark. The women are the angels who will escort him over the pass to the other world.

Still, it was a rare day that Charlie did not make something, even if only a doll out of bark or a bear out of clay. He completed a number of important sculptures in 1926: *The Range Father,* depicting a horse chasing a wolf; *The Bug Hunters,* of a bear and her cub on a log; and *Secrets of the Night,* in which an owl sits on an Indian's shoulder. According to Indian lore, the owl possesses special medicine; as a night creature, it has the power to see into the Shadow Land, where spirits go after death. In *The Spirit of Winter,* another sculpture completed that year, a gaunt, hollow-eyed Indian figure stands wrapped in a heavy cloak, a trio of snarling wolves girding his legs. It is, unmistakably, apocalypse in bronze.

That year, Charlie had paintings to complete as well. He had promised his friend Con Kelley that he would paint a panel to go over the fireplace at Kelley's hunting-and-fishing lodge. Kelley was then chairman of the Anaconda Copper Company, and he and Anaconda represented everything Charlie loathed: the rape and scarification of the old West. But the two men were also soulmates, sharing a love of the backcountry and the camaraderie of a hunting camp. Besides, Nancy never let Charlie turn down a deep-pocketed client over philosophical differences.

There was one other project needing completion. The previous February, on their annual trip to New York, the Russells had met Harry Maule, an editor with the publishing house of Doubleday, Page. Nancy had sent Maule a copy of *More Rawhides,* a collection of Charlie's cowboy yarns. At first Maule had said Doubleday was interested in issuing some sort of "big folio" of Charlie's artwork. Eventually he had agreed to publish a collection of illustrated stories, a grander version of *More Rawhides* and its 1921 predecessor, *Rawhide Rawlins Stories.* By summer, Charlie had committed, with Nancy negotiating, to provide thirty thousand words and fifty drawings. The deadline was October.[6]

The book for Harry Maule was something they both wanted. The unspoken issue was posterity. Nancy worshiped "the Bitch Goddess *success,*" as Charlie's nephew Austin Russell would unflatteringly describe the compulsion.[7] Charlie, meanwhile, pretended not to give a damn about fame, but had never known a time when he was not the center of attention. And for all his affected philistinism, Charlie was a book-lover, a lifelong reader, and the idea of his own nationally circulated volume struck his fancy. Will James's *Cowboys North and South* had been a recent best-seller, and Charlie knew that his stories beat James's for humor and authenticity, not to mention illustrations. Clumsy as Charlie was with spelling and syntax, he had nonetheless found a way to talk his stories onto paper. The book he and Nancy had in mind was a combination of the two *Rawhides* with some other bits and pieces mixed in.

In early September, Harry Maule appeared in person at Lake McDonald, fresh from a pack trip in Glacier Park. Charlie's physical condition worried him, and when Maule returned to New York, he wrote Nancy, suggesting the book be postponed till the following year. Nancy would not hear of it. On October 8, she wrote Maule to tell him that the stories and drawings for the book, which she and Charlie had titled *Trails Plowed Under,* were complete and on their way.[8] As an introduction, Charlie submitted "A Few Words About Myself," a piece lifted verbatim from *More Rawhides.* In its new context, it read like a final testament:

The papers have been kind to me — many times more kind than true. Although I worked for many years on the range, I am not what the people think a cowboy should be. I was neither a good roper nor rider. I was a night wrangler. How good I was, I'll leave it for the people I worked for to say — there are still a few of them living. In the spring I wrangled horses, in the fall I herded beef. I worked for the big outfits and always held my job.

I have many friends among cowmen and cowpunchers. I have always been what is called a good mixer — I had friends when I had nothing else. My friends were not always within the law, but I haven't said how law-abiding I was myself. I haven't been too bad nor too good to get along with.

Life has never been too serious with me — I lived to play and I'm playing yet. Laughs and good judgment have saved me many a black eye, but I don't laugh at other's tears. I was a wild young man, but age has made me gentle. I drank, but never alone, and when I drank it was no secret. I am still friendly with drinking men.

My friends are mixed — preachers, priests, and sinners. I belong to no church, but am friendly toward and respect all of them. I have always liked horses and since I was eight years old have always owned a few.

I am old-fashioned and peculiar in my dress. I am eccentric (that is a polite way of saying you're crazy). I believe in luck and have had lots of it.

To have talent is no credit to its owner; what man can't help he should get neither credit nor blame for — it's not his fault. I am an illustrator. There are lots better ones, but some worse. Any man that can make a living doing what he likes is lucky, and I'm that. Any time I cash in now, I win.[9]

Charlie never saw the published book. On the night of October 24, he collapsed in his Great Falls house and died within minutes. The Mayo doctors had given him six months, possibly twelve or twenty-four. He had lasted only three.

Doubleday, Page took a year to publish *Trails Plowed Under,* Russell's death only enhancing its interest. The smart set's oracle, *Vanity Fair,* was one of many periodicals to applaud: "If you have ever loved the West, if there is any loyalty in you for the finest page that was ever turned in American history, then this authentic collection of yarns and pictures of the old-time cowpuncher is your book. It is boisterous, crude and honest; it smells of leather; it leaves you feeling as good as a month with a pack-outfit through Wyoming."[10]

Trails Plowed Under has been in print almost continuously since its initial publication in December 1927. But for all the book's endearing flavor, it will always be overshadowed by Russell's art. Beginning with his boyhood sketches and ending with the unfinished oil, *Father DeSmet's First Meeting with the Flathead Indians,* which was on his easel the day he died, he left behind an estimated four thousand paintings, watercolors, drawings, and sculptures. No one has ever counted, or even located, them all.[11]

Western art has always been about documentation and romance. Charlie Russell combined the two. He lived a cowboy life during the glory years of the open range in Montana, and because of his eagle eye for detail and capacious memory for anecdote, he is credited with chronicling the passing of the West. At the same time, Russell the romantic was seeing only the West he chose to see — a vision shaped by the Leatherstocking tales and dime novels he had read as a boy, and a world-weariness triggered by the closing of the frontier and the uncertainty of a new century. Russell flourished as an artist between the mid-1880s and the early 1920s — arguably the most dramatic period of change in his country's history. His world was altered by automobiles and airplanes; electricity, telephones, and motion pictures; immigration, urbanization, and incorporation; unionism, populism, and panics; jazz, Cubism, Cuba, and world war. It was as if an entire nation was molting, and Charlie Russell had become a symbol, conservator, and champion of the hirsute past.

In many ways, he was the right person in the right place at the right time, and his impact was huge. After the death of Frederic Remington in 1909, Russell became America's ranking Western artist. Where once he had given away hasty drawings to friends, saloonkeepers, and prostitutes, he eventually became the darling of American royalty. Douglas Fairbanks and MaryPickford, Andrew Mellon, and various kings of copper, oil, and rail bought his work and sought his company. His paintings hung in the Montana Club in Helena and the Duquesne Club in Pittsburgh. His twenty-five-foot-wide picture *Lewis and Clark Meeting Indians at Ross' Hole* was commissioned for the House of Representatives in the Montana capitol. California millionaire Edward Doheny, in the throes of the Teapot Dome scandal, paid Russell $30,000 for a frieze he mounted in his Los Angeles mansion.

Much of the success of Russell's art must be attributed to his appealing personality. He balanced manners with mischievousness, passion with self-effacement. He moved easily among men, boyishly among women. At the lowest and highest points of his career, Russell never knew enemies. As the "Cowboy Artist," he was received as an exemplar of Theodore Roosevelt's "strenuous life": Take a man of good stock, expose him to hard work and hardship, and soon an even better man will shine through.

The lionizing of Charlie Russell only escalated after his death. Nancy Russell, who survived him by fourteen years, oversaw memorial exhibitions of his work, commissioned a biography (never completed), attempted one herself, and compiled *Good Medicine,* a volume of Russell's illustrated letters. Today Russell's statue stands in the National Statuary Hall in Washington, D.C. His log-cabin studio in Great Falls is a museum. A national wildlife refuge bears his name, as do a high school, a motel, and a credit union. His art has appeared on three postage stamps, the most recent commemorating the Montana centennial in 1989. And his famous buffalo skull, the identifying mark he scratched on his artwork, now appears in the corner of every Montana license plate. Ask most Montanans about Charlie Russell and they would have you believe he just rode over the hill a minute ago. He is, in short, the patron saint of the Big Sky.

But as with most idols, his image has been polished smooth by the years. Told over and over by schoolkids, dude ranchers, and museum docents, his life story is now immutable gospel: Young Charlie runs away from home to become a cowboy, first lives with a mountain man, soon rides with the big roundups. According to hearsay, Charlie slips into Canada and takes up housekeeping with an Indian maiden. Ultimately, though, our hero returns to Montana, where he is roped and branded by Nancy; she guides him from saloon to salon; before long, he is rich and famous. By formula, he is kin to Wister's Virginian and L'Amour's Sackett; to suggest otherwise would be blasphemy in most Western camps.

But the greater sin would be to reduce Russell's life to bunkhouse vulgate. In reality, his life was rife with contradiction and complexity. His appreciation of Indians and his efforts to help them did not keep him from making Indians the brunt of off-color jokes and smutty pictures. The fact that he arrived in Montana too late to observe the great Indian buffalo hunts did not stop him from painting dozens of pictures of them. Nor did his love of campfire and chuck wagon stop him from settling in Montana's first modern city, Great Falls, and selling art to the nation's most conspicuous robber barons. He was a man of his time, and a man out of time. Which is not to say that he was two-faced or that there was ever more than one Charlie Russell. Rather, he was the sum of many parts.

This, then, is the story of his originality, his mortality, his irony, his charm, and his art. Furthermore, it is the story of his world — both his imprint on it and its imprint on him. "Myth is the Mother of Romance and I am her oldest son," he once wrote to Josephine Trigg.[12] His own history is about dreaming and coming of age; about love, loss, and memory. It is, in short, the profile of an American, as genuine and deserving of fresh exposure as the West itself.

And as with all stories, Russell's is an exercise in interpretation. At least a dozen reminiscences of Charlie Russell have been written over the years. The primary aim of their authors seems to have been to tell a savory, sentimental tale, giving loose rein to facts and context. (Russell himself took liberties in relating his autobiography.) Such embellishment has necessarily thrust Russell into the company of, say, Daniel Boone and Buffalo Bill Cody: figures whose flamboyant myths are now inseparable from their verifiable histories. Even when myth can be discerned from reality, the latter cannot be conveyed without also hefting the former.

Two human sources in particular were invaluable in preparing this book. The first, Austin Russell, was Charlie's nephew, son of older brother Bent Russell. Austin not only has provided insight into the roots and chemistry of the extended Russell family, but from 1908 till 1916 he lived in Great Falls, where he observed the most intimate details of Charlie and Nancy's comings and goings, which he recorded in his memoir, *C.M.R.: Charles M. Russell, Cowboy Artist,* published in 1956, thirty years after Charlie's death.

The other invaluable observer was Joe DeYong, Russell's only protégé and in some respects a surrogate son. As a teenager, DeYong was stricken by meningitis while working on the set of a Tom Mix Western. The illness left him deaf; DeYong then threw himself into art, eventually leaving his Oklahoma home to be near his idol, Charlie Russell. Off and on from 1916 till 1926, the last ten years of Russell's life, DeYong was a presence in Russell's Great Falls studio and house, as well as at Bull Head Lodge. Because DeYong could not hear, he and Charlie often communicated by handwritten notes, many of which survive. And because DeYong outlived Charlie by nearly fifty years, he carried the Russell torch well into the second half of the twentieth century.

And finally, an introductory note on Nancy Cooper Russell. After 1926 she never made her home in Montana again, save for summer visits to Bull Head Lodge with Jack. Instead she chose to finish out her years in the house she and Charlie had begun building in Pasadena, California, just weeks before his heart attack. She lived comfortably, though somewhat somberly, on the income from sales of Charlie's remaining bronzes and paintings until her death in 1940. She was buried next to Charlie on the outskirts of Great Falls.

As a generalization, it is fair to say that those who loved Charlie Russell tarred his wife with commensurate calumny. Many of Charlie's friends never forgave her for taking their easygoing cowpuncher comrade away from them and therefore maligned her in the interviews they granted to the subsequent procession of Russell hagiographers. Was she bourgeois, headstrong, manipulative? Perhaps so. But a woman criticized at the turn of the century for being aggressive and businesslike deserves to be cast in a better light today. Nancy Russell was smart, devoted, and, like her husband, multidimensional and entirely human. A fair and factual reappreciation of her is also long overdue. Let this be Charlie's story, but let it be Nancy's as well.

2

ST. LOUIS

I T CAN BE SAID that the character of Charlie Russell was shaped
by Montana and that he in turn helped to shape the character of that
territory and state. But first, foremost, and forever he was a product of St.
Louis, Missouri. He was born there on March 19, 1864, Charles Marion
Russell, third child of Charles Silas and Mary Mead Russell.

In 1864, St. Louis was a cosmopolitan trading center of nearly two hundred thousand people. Not even the Civil War could stanch its expansion.
By 1870, St. Louis had puffed itself up to fourth-largest American city. The
Russells were one of many enterprising families who adjusted well to the
accelerating growth. Money mattered in mercantile St. Louis, but roots
counted even more, and the Russells had both.

While still in its first century, St. Louis had learned to be snooty. The
original settlers were the French traders Pierre Laclède and René Auguste
Chouteau, who in 1764 located their post and residences on the west side
of the Mississippi, sixteen miles below the debouchment of the Missouri.
There they prospered as masters of a river trade that covered half the con-
tinent. They and other early Creoles were considered the aristocracy of St.
Louis long after the Spanish took over the territory in 1762 and even after
April 30, 1803, when the Louisiana Purchase delivered the territory into
American hands.[1]

The Russells arrived in the first American wave, which surrounded,
without displacing, the Creoles. Thomas Jefferson's $15 million acquisition
not only doubled the size of the continental United States and attached

the West to the newly formed republic, it also made St. Louis the new belly button of America. Sheer force of gravity ensured that every drop of water — not to mention beaver pelt and buffalo robe — in a half-million-square-mile area would eventually flow to or past the wharves of St. Louis. It was the leaving-from place and the coming-back place, and depending on one's perspective, a symbolic portal separating bollixed civilization and pastoral purity, past encumbrance and imminent prospect. Through most of the nineteenth century, St. Louis was a Western caravansary, as fantastic as it was magnetic.[2]

The Russells felt the pull. Their line was English, their spirit American. Though their footprints have grown faint, it is known that they had once lived in Rockbridge County, Virginia, and that the family of Joseph Russell headed west to Tennessee sometime after the Revolutionary War. Three of Joseph's sons continued on to the Mississippi River in the first years of the nineteenth century. One of the three, young Joseph, settled on the eastern bank, near present-day Alton, Illinois. The other two, James and William, ferried across the Mississippi to newer country. James, the grand-father of Charles M. Russell, settled in Cape Girardeau, Missouri, where he married, taught school, and edited a newspaper. William went even far-ther, buying land in the Grand Prairie just beyond St. Louis. The year was 1805.

James Russell's wife died in 1808, and he decided to move again. In 1811 he bought his brother William's land on the outskirts of St. Louis for $5,000. His new bride, Lucy Bent, helped with the purchase, and a hundred of the 432 acres were deeded in Lucy Bent Russell's name. Oak Hill, as the tract was called, would remain in the family for the next 120 years.

It was choice land. The soil was good, and water was available from a creek the Russells soon dammed. James and Lucy built their house on a slight rise amid oaks and walnuts, and began growing produce for the mar-kets of St. Louis. They raised livestock and fowl; they bottled their own wine. Like many Missourians, they owned slaves.

There were other riches in the earth of Oak Hill, specifically coal and clay. The story holds that James Russell was on the verge of selling Oak Hill, probably around 1820, when he happened to notice a freshly eroded gully on his property. Looking more closely, he discovered a dark color in the dirt. He abandoned his plan to sell Oak Hill and began mining coal. Along with fruits and vegetables, fuel was soon being delivered by the Russell wagons to the residents of St. Louis. Other mines opened near Oak Hill, and the area became known as the Gravois Diggings. Then when the coal began to peter out, James Russell discovered a rich layer of clay underneath, which proved even more lucrative.[3]

For all his good fortune, little else is known about James Russell, except that he was enterprising, diligent, and a somewhat less than dominant patriarch. In the grand scheme of things, he was eclipsed by his wife, Lucy, who was, after all, a Bent.

The Bents were already legendary by the time James married Lucy.[4] The first to arrive in America was John Bent, who located in the Massachusetts Bay Colony in 1638. Silas Bent, a great-grandson, served as a Minuteman in the Revolution and, according to family lore, may even have participated in the Boston Tea Party. After the war, Silas, like his counterpart in Russell ancestry, was drawn west. In 1789, he sold his farm in Massachusetts and took up land in Ohio. His son Silas Jr. — Charlie Russell's great-grandfather — followed a similar urge and pushed up the Ohio River to land near Wheeling in what is now West Virginia. There he studied law and went to work for the Surveyor General of the United States. Presently he was advanced to the title of Deputy Surveyor General and given the Herculean task of platting terra incognita, the Louisiana Purchase.

Silas Jr. moved to St. Louis in 1806, just in time to witness the return of Lewis and Clark from their two-year journey to the Pacific. He did well at his new job, and in 1813, President James Madison promoted him to judge of the Supreme Court of the Missouri Territory. Over the years, he sired eleven children, most notably, from the point of view of this narrative, Charles, Lucy, and William. Lucy, as has been mentioned, married James Russell, who begat Charles Silas Russell, who begat Charles Marion Russell. Meanwhile, Lucy's brothers Charles and William Bent were begetting an entire chapter in American history.

When the first steamboat reached St. Louis in 1817, the Missouri fur trade was already in full swing. Charles Bent, ten years older than his brother William, was the first to take advantage of the improved access to the interior. In 1822, he joined the Missouri Fur Company and traveled as far as the Dakotas and maybe as far as the lower Yellowstone River. In 1827, eighteen-year-old William Bent accompanied Charles upriver, then overland across the South Pass of southern Wyoming, finally wintering with other trappers and traders at one of the fabled rendezvous camps on the Green River. By 1829, the Bent brothers were helping to open the 775-mile-long Santa Fe Trail, which followed the Missouri to Westport, then across Kansas to the Arkansas River, upstream into southern Colorado, and finally on a dry trail south into the Mexican outpost of Santa Fe.

If the Missouri River knit the Northwest to the rest of the country, then the Santa Fe Trail connected the Southwest. Charles Bent, in partnership with French trader Ceran St. Vrain, was a principal architect of this linkage. In 1833, brother William established Bent's Fort at the confluence of the Arkansas and Purgatory rivers, a critical way station and trading center on the Santa Fe Trail. In Taos, at the far end of the trail, Charles opened a store and married a Mexican woman. William, in a more radical break with convention, took a Cheyenne bride.

When the United States seized New Mexico in 1846, Charles Bent was named its first governor. In the uprising that ensued, a mob of Mexicans and Indians murdered him while he was helping his family flee through a hole in the wall of his adobe house. His body was mutilated and his scalp tacked to a plank.

William, in turn, had his own adventures. In 1849, rather than give Bent's Fort to the U.S. Army, he burned it to the ground and built a second compound downstream. His disdain for the federal government was amplified by his sons George and Charles. When the Civil War erupted, they both enlisted on the Confederate side. Charles soon left the Army, however, and joined his mother's people, the Cheyenne. George had been captured in Mississippi and imprisoned, and then joined his brother's warrior society, the Dog Soldiers, shortly after gaining his freedom.

Charles and George Bent lived as full-bloods. They rode in buffalo hunts; they took the scalps of their Indian enemies; and they witnessed the depredations of whites upon the Cheyenne people. Both George and Charles fought on the Cheyenne side at the infamous Sand Creek Massacre of 1864, in which more than four hundred Indians died, many of them women. Ironically, their other brother, Robert, was a scout for Colonel John Chivington's cavalry at the time and witnessed the atrocity from the white side of the skirmish line.

After Sand Creek, the blood never left Charles's eye. The following year, he and a band of Dog Soldiers overran a stage station, killing one white outright, then slowly vivisecting another. Quickly he became one of the most wanted, and hated, outlaws on the plains. His family would have nothing to do with him. At one point Charles even plotted to kill his father; fortunately William Bent was away when his bloodthirsty son came calling. Finally, in 1868, Charles Bent was wounded in a fight with a band of Pawnee, caught malaria, and died. The renegade's cousin Charles Marion Russell was four years old when Charles Bent met his end.

The Bent boldness was also evident in Charles and William's sister Lucy. She had married James Russell when she was twenty-one and he nearly twenty years older. She bore him four children — Julia, John, Charles Silas, and Russella — before he died in 1850. Suddenly, at the age of forty-five, she had full responsibility for Oak Hill. By all indications, she did not miss a step.

Lucy gathered her four children around her after James's death. Her second son, eighteen-year-old Charles Silas, was apparently away at college; some accounts say Yale, but this cannot be verified. He had not finished his first year when his mother summoned him home and set the family to the task of running Oak Hill. During the next twenty years, Lucy would quietly become one of the leading businesswomen of the region. Under her executive leadership, the family expanded its Oak Hill Fruit Company, increased production of the coal mines and clay works, and subdivided and developed the hundred acres of the original property that were in her name. In her will she passed authority for the various businesses to her son Charles and son-in-law George Ward Parker.

Charles Silas Russell married Mary Elizabeth Mead in 1858. She was two years younger than her husband and universally described as pious, warm, and devoted. Her portrait shows a well-proportioned woman with blue eyes, a strong chin, narrow lips, and brown hair pulled gently back. She sits holding a pair of opera glasses, her gaze assuredly focused.

The Meads were a creative family. Edward Mead, Mary's father, was a silversmith of considerable skill who came to St. Louis from upstate New York in 1837 and established himself as a "Manufacturer of Silver and Maker of Indian Trinkets." Medallions, brooches, hair ornaments, and arm bands were standard trading stock for the entrepreneurs who bartered with the tribes of the plains, upper Missouri, and Southwest. Mead also sold jewelry and watches to well-to-do whites and built a good reputation in the city.[5] In the peerage of the times, his daughter and Charles Silas Russell were a proper match.

In the first two years of their marriage, Charles and Mary had a daughter, Susan Mead, and a son, Silas Bent. Their third child, Charles Marion, was handsome and "as blonde as a Swede."[6] Chas, as he was usually called so as not to be confused with his father, inherited his mother's blue eyes and his father's broad face and solid physique. He also had his father's high, expressive forehead; the slightest lift of the eyebrows and the Russell face was a map of quizzicality. Charlie was followed by three more brothers, Ed, Guy, and Wolfert. (Mary Russell lost two other babies before they could be christened.)

Though Charlie Russell would later insist that he had been born at Oak Hill, in fact the family was living in the heart of St. Louis at the time.[7] Despite C. S. Russell's active role in the Russell family's mining and produce business, for the first eleven years of his marriage he chose to dwell in the city and list his profession as "watches & jewelry," "jewelry and silverware," and "successor to E. Mead & Co." Not until 1869, when his mother's health had begun to flag, did he move his family to Oak Hill. Charlie Russell was five years old.

A lot had changed since C. S. Russell's father had first settled Oak Hill. Poor city drinking water and a series of cholera epidemics in the 1840s had thrust residential growth south and westward, away from the waterfront. Whereas Oak Hill had once been a rural plantation, by the close of the Civil War it was effectively a suburb of St. Louis. The Russells welcomed the development around them, enjoying the best of both worlds. Even after C. S. Russell had moved his family to Oak Hill, he continued to maintain a business address downtown, and the family traveled back and forth often.

At Oak Hill, Charlie lived the life of a restless scamp. He and his copious cousins — his aunts Julia and Russella and uncle John also had houses at Oak Hill — roamed at will. Charlie got his first horse, Gyp, at eight. He and his band of town-and-country kin would ride their ponies across the fields and down the dirt lanes, ruthless Indians intent on kidnapping and scalping their sisters' dolls in the woodlot.

Yet there was more to Oak Hill than ponies and pranks. In 1866, Charlie's father and his uncle George Ward Parker had established the Oak Hill Fire Brick, Furnace Tile and Gas Retort Works. In 1871, the name became the Parker-Russell Mining and Manufacturing Company. St. Louis was built mostly out of brick, and by 1870 there were eighty-five brickyards in the city. Oak Hill clay, though, was special. According to one sales brochure,

James Russell's discovery was "highly silicious, of very high fire-proof qualities, remarkably free from iron and other impurities and differ[ed] from all
the rest of the Missouri clays." It was ideal for making the bricks and tiles
used in blast furnaces and rolling mills. As America entered the steel age in
the latter half of the nineteenth century, Parker-Russell boasted that it had
become "the largest works [of its kind] in the West." The company's plant
filled an entire block.

Young Charlie had complete run of the belching, bustling complex that
bore his name. He knew his way around the beehive-shaped kilns; he was a
regular at the company-owned store, where he cadged sweets and listened
to the yarns and ditties of the Welsh and German laborers. It was here that
he first observed how the other half behaved. "Charlie was very democratic," according to his sister Sue, "and took keen interest in the people of
the nearby mining village." Above all he was a good mimic, and learned to
reproduce the "oddities of pronunciation in a very amusing way."[8]

Showing off was part of his nature. He liked being the center of attention, even demanded it. Years later, Charlie wrote to a friend in Montana,
recalling a typical boyhood episode of monkeyshines. He and the other
Oak Hill boys had been afoot one day, their arsenal limited to a solitary
muzzle-loading rifle, doubtless a relic either purloined from a gun cabinet
or entrusted to one of the older boys. In his notoriously erratic hand, Charlie described what happened when one of the bigger kids finally allowed
him a turn:

> When he loded for me I remember how the rod jumped clear of the
> barel[. H]e spent five or more minutes tamping the loade then handing
> the gun to me said thair that would kill a tiger an I think it would if hed
> been on the same end I was[.] My game was crows[.] I climbed to the
> top of a rail fence to get cleane range. [A]nd then as the Books say for
> an instant my hawk eye mesured the glistening barrel then the death
> like stillness was broken by the crack of my fathfull wepon and I kept it
> broken with howls for quite a while.[9]

This tale endures as typical Charlie Russell: in a gang of his peers, taking
a pratfall, and stealing the show with a winsome, self-deprecatory flourish.
Whether in a roundup camp, a saloon, or a drawing room of waistcoated
gentry, he never acted much differently. All the world was his stage. He

stored up stories, memorized inflections, laid in minutiae as kindling for his imagination. And when it came time to hold forth with his own narratives — in words or in art — Charlie, if not always hero, victim, or even witness of the actual event on which the story was based, always knew how to shine as the teller.

In 1876, when Charlie was twelve, Oak Hill was incorporated as part of St. Louis proper, making Charlie a city dweller in deed if not decorum. In his celebrity years, he always led interviewers to believe that he had been raised on the perilous fringe of civilization. Never did he describe the scrubbed stoop, high ceilings, and fine china of the Russells' manor-style house. Nor did he mention that directly across Oak Hill's northern property line was one of the most refined botanical gardens in the United States. To visit Tower Grove Park is to instantly reject any buckskin version of Charlie Russell's boyhood.

Tower Grove's patron, Henry Shaw, had been an astute and decisive trader who made a small fortune provisioning St. Louisans during the early boom years of fur trading and lead mining. Smitten by the Royal Botanic Gardens he had visited in England, Shaw worked unceasingly for three decades to create a comparable horticultural preserve in St. Louis. In 1859 he formally dedicated 760 acres as a grand garden and park (now the Missouri Botanical Gardens and Tower Grove Park).[10]

Tower Grove was the site of picnics and Sunday gatherings for the best families of St. Louis. It was also where Charlie Russell often rode his horse. One account has him incurring the wrath of Henry Shaw for riding through some of the park's orderly flower beds. Another describes Charlie posting through the park, dressed in English riding boots, cream-colored suit, and red necktie.[11] In his own mind, Charlie may have been Kit Carson — a famous acquaintance of his Bent uncles — on the trail of dangerous renegades, instead of a member of the St. Louis aristocracy out for an afternoon's recreation.

His parents did their best to civilize him. Mary Russell ran a lively but strict household. The "laws of the Russells and the Meads" — that was the family code, a play on the Old Testament's "laws of the Persians and the Medes."[12] Mary read to her children from the Bible, and the Russells were members of Holy Innocents Episcopal Church, which was built on land bequeathed by Lucy Bent Russell.

Mary Russell also encouraged her children artistically. She had inherited her father's talents and passed them on. Numerous tales survive of Charlie's precociousness, though some are likely apocryphal: young Charlie following a trained bear down the street and returning with its likeness shaped from mud; young Charlie borrowing the wax his sister Sue used to make artificial flowers and effortlessly crafting all manner of creatures; young Charlie meticulously copying a printed picture of an eagle, including the inscription, "Copyright Reserved."[13]

If Charlie got his knack for art from his mother, he got his love of literature from his father. C. S. Russell was a pragmatic, mild-mannered, muttonchopped gentleman, more of a patron than a pioneer. He looked after his business and his family with a steady confidence and few flourishes. His grandson Austin Russell described him as "a healthy optimist who smoked cigars right down to the bitter tip, skewering the tip with a toothpick when it got too short and too hot to hold. He drank whiskey three times daily, and ate whatever he pleased." Also, Austin recalled, "he devoured any kind of book with the same appetite and enjoyed as much as the assembled offspring the boys' books he read aloud."[14]

It would be impossible to overestimate the effect of books on Charlie's development. When Charlie's "hawk eye mesured the glistening barrel," he was cribbing directly from Natty Bumppo, hero of James Fenimore Cooper's Leatherstocking tales. The Cooper novels were sacred texts to Charlie and thousands of other men and boys in the nineteenth century. Even more popular were dime novels. Between 1860 and century's end, two dominant publishing houses, Beadle & Adams and Street & Smith, churned out an endless stream of these pulp serials. Most were Westerns, and the best loved were by Ned Buntline. Buntline's protagonists, Buffalo Bill especially, were rugged, Jacksonian, capable of sudden violence, but morally pure and scrupulous. And in many of the tales, the Western ruffian who saves the day turns out to be a well-bred Easterner who has eschewed his inherited social station for freedom and challenge on the frontier.[15]

Charlie always insisted that he never would have learned to read if it had not been for "yaller-back novels."[16] Along with the Ned Buntline adventures, he favored those by Mayne Reid (*The Scalp Hunters, The Rifle Rangers, The Boy Hunters*) and Harry Castlemon (*Frank in the Woods, Frank on the Prairie, Frank in the Mountains*), which specifically targeted the youth market between the Civil War and century's end. He cherished his copies of these books all his life, and they endure as evidence that Charlie Russell, celebrated for living the "real West," had begun crafting his vision of it long before he ever set foot there.

In Reid's *The Boy Hunters* (1869), the youthful Landi brothers "were the best shots of their age, could ride a horse with any, could swim the Mississippi, paddle a canoe, fling a lasso, or spear a catfish, as though they had been full-grown men. They were, in fact, boy men."[17] In Castlemon's *Frank on the Prairie* (1868), young Frank and his cousin Archie set out across the plains with Frank's uncle and a wizened old trapper named Dick Lewis. Along the way, Lewis — "his long rifle on his shoulder, his powder-horn and bullet pouch at his side and . . . his suit of buckskin entirely new" — opens the boys' eyes to a more wholesome way of life:

"Every thing in them big cities seemed to say to me, 'Dick, you aint got no business here.' Them black walls an' stone roads; them rumblin' carts an' big stores, war sights I never seed afore, an' I never want to see 'em ag'in. . . . It's funny that them ar city chaps don't know nothin' 'bout what's goin' on out here; an' it shows that all the larnin' in the world aint got out o' books."

The sermon sounded a theme — the lost Eden — that Charlie would echo in his art. Scanning the Missouri prairie, trapper Dick laments:

"Things aint as they used to be, youngsters. I can 'member the time when thar was'nt a fence within miles of here, an' a feller could go out an' knock over a buffaler fur breakfast just as easy as that farmer over thar could find one of his sheep. But the ax an' plow have made bad work with a fine country, the buffaler an' Injun have been pushed back t'wards he mountains, an' it won't be long afore thar'll be no room fur sich as me; an' we won't be missed neither, 'cause when the buffaler an' beaver are gone thar'll be nothin' fur us to do."[18]

It was no stretch for Charlie to embrace the Boy Hunters and the Buntline heroes. He had uncles who had been scalped, cousins who had been Indians. Fiction and fact were never far apart in Charlie's imagination, and he learned to poach across the line with a clear conscience. The story of Old Brit is a good example.

Charlie's uncle William Fulkerson had settled on the eastern bank of the Mississippi. Like Buffalo Bill, Fulkerson had been a Pony Express rider, and then had headed off to fight for the Confederacy on a black horse named Old Brit. As the tale goes, Fulkerson was wounded at Chickamauga and lay exposed on the battlefield. Then, miraculously, through the smoke and din of battle, he spotted Old Brit. The riderless horse responded to his familiar whistle, and Fulkerson was able to remount and ride to safety. Later Brit was wounded — shot and then cut with a saber — but each time managed to pull through. After the war, William Fulkerson rode his faithful steed home to Jerseyville, Illinois. The horse lived well into Charlie's lifetime. Whenever Charlie, his brothers, and cousins came to visit, they could see Brit's many scars with their own eyes — proof that what their uncle had said was true.[19]

Charlie never forgot Old Brit. Years later, when as a green hand in Montana he bought his first horse, he gave it a history almost as quickly as he gave it a name. The pinto Monte had begun his years as a Crow buffalo pony — or so Charlie said. Then one night the pony was stolen by Calf Rope, a Blackfeet warrior. But in making his getaway, Calf Rope was killed. As was the Indian custom, a fellow warrior, Bad Wound, shot the pinto so that Calf Rope's spirit would not have to "walk to the sand hills" of the afterlife. Miraculously, the pony survived Bad Wound's bullet and was thenceforth called "ghost horse." No Indian would ride him, for his medicine was strong, and soon Bad Wound sold the ghost horse to a white boy newly arrived in Montana: Charlie Russell. Charlie owned Monte for twenty years and immortalized him in "The Ghost Horse," one of the stories in *Trails Plowed Under*. In Charlie's presentation, Monte's past was real — certainly as real as that of a war-scarred nag on an Illinois farm.[20]

CHARLIE'S MEMORIES OF his formal education are not nearly so vivid. It is extremely difficult to piece together his academic record, partly because he often switched schools and partly because he was frequently absent. He and his siblings and cousins attended the Oak Hill School near home, though it is not clear for how long. Despite the strong influence of the Russell name, he was shown little favoritism. His early teachers treated him like a dunce; they whipped him and made him sit in the corner. Charlie responded by playing hooky. He would recruit a friend, they would stash their books and lunch pails in a culvert, and then they would spend the day exploring the raucous riverfront or the city's burgeoning mule market.[21]

At some point, probably after 1876, Charlie left the Oak Hill School and began attending the Clinton School in downtown St. Louis. One of his chums, Archie Douglass, the son of a prosperous lumber manufacturer, recalled in a letter to Charlie's widow a half-century later:

> There was a carriage that each morning brought the children from Oak Hill to the city for school. . . . One season, the horse races caught our fancy, and Charlie, [brother] Ed and I played hooky so we could go to the races. Our absence from school continuing for a week. Saturday of that week, Charlie and Ed went to their father's office to get their weekly allowance, and instead, received instruction to go home and stay there, until he came home in the evening. Mr. Russell had received a note from the Principal at his office about the boys absence from school. I was with the boys at the time, and when we got out of the office, a consultation was held and the Russell boys decided they would not go home, but go West. I secured my mother's grocery book, and by this means furnished them with things to eat. These articles, with some clothing, were put in a sack and carried in front of the rider, on Charlie's pony. The other two, a boy named Hughes going along, walked. The idea being to take turns riding. I rode with them to the outskirts of the City. That night Mr. Russell and Mr. Hughes came to my house to learn the wherabouts of the boys, but I knew nothing. During the night Ed became sick, so they took him home, and all three slept in a hay cave, as they were afraid to go into the house.[22]

Charlie's truancy and poor academic performance were a source of consternation to his parents. They themselves were precise, orderly, and urbane. Letters and handwritten documents of C. S. Russell reveal a fastidious penmanship and an obsessive attention to detail. He passed these traits on to Charlie's older brother, Bent, who would earn a degree in engineering from Washington University. Similarly, the Russells expected Charlie to go to college and either join the family business or take up a comparably respectable profession. Instead, his teachers remonstrated with him for cracking wise and staring out the window.

There was a reason for Charlie's mischievousness and inattention: he had a learning disability. Today, the best-known learning disability is dyslexia, which relates to reading. But clearly Charlie never struggled with reading. His particular bugbear was writing. He never got the hang of spelling, punctuation, grammar, or syntax. The clinical term for his disability is dysgraphia.

Dysgraphia reveals itself most explicitly in handwriting. Charlie's cursive writing is controlled and really quite legible; however, his block lettering is abominable. Language pathologists say that a problem with basic block lettering often stems from a fundamental deficiency in motor planning; something in the brain is preventing the person from translating words into shapes. A person with this sort of learning disability has difficulty not only with handwriting, but with overall orderliness and completion of tasks.[23] While Charlie could draw a perfect horizon of mountains and sky, he could not for the life of him write a horizontal sentence. Random spelling and anarchic capitalization are also typical of someone with this learning problem. Charlie might spell a complicated, polysyllabic word correctly, then miss an easy one. He could handle "insomnia" or "answering," but then might transpose the letters in the preposition "of," so that it appeared "fo." Punctuation was entirely beyond him.

Charlie's excruciating attempts with pen and paper are described best by his friend and protégé Joe DeYong:

> Charlie would grip the ink bottle in his left hand, and with right grasping the pen almost like a weapon he would sit staring unseeingly at the rim of darkness beyond the circle of light cast by low stand-lamps on the table before him . . . and then, as the first beads of sweat appeared on his forehead, he would suddenly commence to write a single sentence: slowly, carefully shaping every word, seldom did his mind produce more than a single sentence at a time, sometimes two; very seldom three in a row. It might take him an hour to write half a page — or, when the ideas were slow in coming, he might lay a started letter aside until a day or two later.[24]

Other aspects of Charlie's behavior support the conclusion that he had this disability. Although he was nearly as famous for his impromptu storytelling as he was for his art, the thought of giving a prepared speech —

which would require organization and structure, or even a prepared script — sent him into a cold sweat. This is clearly the subtext of a 1922 letter that Nancy Russell wrote to the president of the University of Montana. "[I]t would be impossible [for Charlie to give a lecture at the university]," she apologized. "I am not sure that you are acquainted with him, but if you are, you understand how shy he would be if placed on a platform; but, if sometime you are having an informal reception or gathering where he could be among you all without appearing to stand out alone, I feel sure he would be glad to visit you and the students."[25]

Many of Charlie's friends, patrons, and fans have insisted that Charlie's poor writing was simply an affectation; down-home argot was all the rage, thanks to Mark Twain, Alfred Henry Lewis, and other novelists of the day. Likewise, Charlie's decision to quit school is often regarded as a time-honored American urge, in the tradition of his fellow Missourian, Tom Sawyer. There can be no doubt that the West beckoned Charlie from his earliest childhood onward. But it is just as true that he was driven toward the frontier by his disability, an unruly force that he compensated for, covered up, and never fully understood. Even Charlie's later fascination and facility with Indian sign language must be seen in light of his learning disability. Sign language has no spelling, no tenses, no punctuation, no traditional syntax. It was a perfect language for Charlie; that it was also the language of the buffalo hunt, the tepee, and the warpath made it all the more attractive.

MARY AND CHARLES RUSSELL may not have discerned what was wrong with their son, but they were quick to perceive what was right. To their credit, they indulged his passion for art. He drew in the margins of his schoolbooks and doodled characters in church. He filled a sketchbook with imagined scenes of the frontier, which he captioned "The bear trapped," "face to face with a ute," "Chased by wolves," "A bad fall," and "Crow indian in ware dress."[26] His sister Sue recalls that when Charlie was twelve he sculpted a knight in armor. Their father had it cast and entered it in the St. Louis Agricultural and Mechanical Fair, which drew thousands of visitors each year. The fair featured the art of local collectors and awarded prizes for best drawing, engraving, sculpture, carving, oil, watercolor, and glass. Charlie's entry won a blue ribbon. The next year he made a horse and rider jumping a fence; it too won a prize.[27]

His parents also exposed him to the talent of other artists. Over the years, St. Louis had grown to be more than a gateway for trappers and hunters. A number of fine painters had either lived in St. Louis or had passed through the city on their way west, among them Alfred Jacob Miller, John Mix Stanley, George Catlin, Karl Bodmer, John James Audubon, Charles Deas, and George Caleb Bingham. Even if Charlie glimpsed little of their work as a boy, he nonetheless sensed the special esteem that St. Louis reserved for the artist-adventurer.

One artist whose work young Charlie Russell did view repeatedly was Carl Wimar. Wimar was born in Germany in 1828; when he was fifteen his family emigrated to the United States and settled among the growing German community in St. Louis. In 1851, he returned to Germany to study painting at the acclaimed Düsseldorf Academy, which had become a magnet for American painters in the mid–nineteenth century and, quite unwittingly, set a standard for Western American painting that is still in vogue today.[28]

The man who pulled Wimar (as well as the future Hudson River School painter Albert Bierstadt) to Düsseldorf was the German-American artist Emanuel Leutze, whose *Washington Crossing the Delaware* (1851) was arguably the most popular, and most revered, painting shown in this country in mid-century. The Düsseldorf style, as exemplified in Leutze's *Washington,* was based on discipline of form and detail, with an emphasis on dramatic moments. Nature was awe-inspiring; accordingly, man's role in confronting nature — Washington versus the ice floe, frontiersmen versus "savages" — was heroic.[29] By the time Carl Wimar had finished his training in Düsseldorf in 1856, he was grounded in realism, yet steeped in romance. In a studio far from Missouri, he had painted *The Captive Charger* (Indians stealing a cavalry mount) and *Attack on an Emigrant Train* (settlers in a covered wagon fight off Indians). In each, the sky is saturated, the landscape untrammeled, the Indians musclebound, and the composition perfectly, Germanically balanced. In 1858, Wimar finally got to see the West of his imagination, traveling by steamboat up the Missouri as far as Montana. Yet the sketches he did on the river and the paintings and engravings he produced from them in subsequent years — especially the buffalo-hunting scenes — still honored the principles drilled into him in Europe.

Wimar's work was hard for Charlie to miss. It hung in the parlors of St.

Louis's prominent families, and in 1862 Wimar completed a series of murals for the St. Louis Courthouse. Charlie never met Wimar, who died only weeks after completing the courthouse commission. But forty years later, Charlie could still imitate Wimar's anatomically flawed buffalo and "merry go round hosses." He meant no harm by his parody and throughout his life maintained the highest regard for this seminal figure in Western art. "I have always liked his work," Charlie wrote Wimar's biographer in 1907, "and think he knew the Indian." And in a note to Joe DeYong, he paid Wimar the ultimate compliment: "I wish I could paint like he did."[30]

As a youth, though, Charlie would not take instruction from anyone. The best reckoning is that he received only three days of formal training in his entire life. His sister recalls that he "yielded to persuasion and entered the Washington University Art School [the St. Louis School of Fine Arts] — but objected to going back to first principles, drawing cubes etc., so he gave it up after a lesson or two."[31]

Washington University, which in those days was located in downtown St. Louis, began offering in the 1870s a series of extension programs in fine and applied art. The standard method of teaching life drawing was through the use of plaster casts, and at least one of the university programs was amply stocked with "accurate copies of the finest of the renowned Elgin Marbles from the Royal Academy of London." Charlie was not impressed. One story had him daring his teacher to draw a picture of an Indian, scoffing at the instructor's effort, then quickly dashing off a sketch of his own "that'd scalp you." He then fled the classroom.[32]

The Russells made one final attempt to keep Charlie on an academic track. After the Christmas holidays of 1879, they put him on a train with his good friend Archie Douglass and sent him to the boarding school Douglass was attending back East. Bent Russell had gone away to a series of schools; maybe a change of scenery would work for Charlie, too.

Burlington College was located on the New Jersey side of the Delaware River, north of Philadelphia. The facts that the campus had originally been a beautiful estate and that the town had been the boyhood home of one of Charlie's idols, James Fenimore Cooper, were little consolation. Burlington College was a military school. Charlie lasted less than three months. No transcripts survive of his short time there, but all accounts concur that he performed dismally in the classroom. For good behavior, boys were allowed to take the boat into Philadelphia on weekends;

Charlie walked guard duty. He reportedly swapped drawings of Western scenes for other boys' homework; when caught, he walked more guard duty.

Archie Douglass recollects that Charlie was simply marking time at Burlington: "Charlie's father told him that if he would go East with me to school for six months, that at the end of this time, he would let him go West."[33] If the pact was real, Charlie breached it. He left Burlington sometime in the late winter. Shortly before his sixteenth birthday, March 19, 1880, he was en route to Montana Territory. According to family memory, his frustrated parents hoped that a few months of hard labor on a ranch would shatter Charlie's dime-novel fantasy of the West. Or perhaps it was an expression of their ultimate exasperation. Let him go — they had tried everything else.[34]

Whatever the logic behind this final parental ploy, Charlie simply hit the end of the latest tether and did not stop. He never attended school again, and never again considered St. Louis home.

3

MONTANA

THE TRIP WEST, which a generation earlier would have stretched to many months, took barely a week. In mid-March 1880, Charlie boarded the Wabash, St. Louis & Pacific express at Union Depot. Twenty-four hours later he was in Omaha to catch the Union Pacific bound for San Francisco. By then in its eleventh year of transcontinental service, the Union Pacific was boasting "Luxurious Palace Day and Sleeping Coaches." The train rolled across the Nebraska plains, following the ruts of the Oregon Trail along the Platte River into Wyoming Territory. Soon Charlie was crossing historic South Pass, repeating the route the Bent brothers had taken more than a half-century earlier. Three, possibly four, days after leaving St. Louis, he stepped down onto the platform in Ogden, Utah, the jumping-off point for Montana.[1]

Charlie had not been alone during the fifteen-hundred-mile trip. His traveling companion was Willis L. W. "Pike" Miller. Little is known of Miller, his background, or how he came to be acquainted with the Russell family. He was not one of the many old-timers Charlie kept in touch with in later years. Nor was he a social peer of Charlie's parents. An 1876 directory lists him as a porter at the Park Hotel in St. Louis. In subsequent years, he shifted between clerkships at a law office and dry-goods wholesaler. Some-how by 1880 he had invested in a small ranch in the Judith Basin of Montana Territory. Sketchy as Pike Miller's identity may be, he looms large in the life of Charlie Russell for the simple reason that he gave the unruly youth his first job.[2]

Charlie may have felt he was charging into a virgin land, but this was not entirely so. The first white men to set foot in Montana were the Vérendrye brothers, French fur traders who in 1742 may have ventured as far west as the Yellowstone River. Sixty-two years later, Lewis and Clark passed through the same country on their way west, and again on their way home.[3]

Through most of the first half of the 1800s, the region that is now Montana was the unquestioned domain of Indians. Sioux, Cheyenne, Crow, Assiniboine, Blackfeet, Nez Percé, Pend d'Oreille, Kootenai, Gros Ventre, and Flathead peregrinated and pitched camp according to a vague but time-honored map of homelands, hunting grounds, and buffer zones that stretched from the steep, wet forests west of the Continental Divide northward to the muskeg sumps of Great Slave Lake and east and south across the short-grass prairie. In the fifty years following Lewis and Clark, whites stepped gingerly: trappers cautiously worked the watersheds; traders built forts, easily shuttered, readily abandoned, on the bluffs of the Missouri and its tributaries; priests attempted missions, as much at the mercy of their Indian hosts as of the Almighty. Montana was not a true home for these whiskered men; they were simply making a tenuous foray into a bountiful though harsh hinterland. That is, until gold was discovered.

Montana gold was found as early as 1850, the year after Sutter's Mill in California. But the lid did not blow till 1862, with the strike at Grasshopper Creek, in what is now southwestern Montana. Bannack was the mean and motley boomtown that sprang up alongside the creek; an estimated $5 million in gold was taken out in the first year. A series of other strikes, with their attendant "cities," soon lit up the mountainous western part of Montana. Alder Gulch became Virginia City; Last Chance Gulch became Helena. Congress recognized Montana as a territory on May 26, 1864, the year of Charlie Russell's birth.

It was gold that finally turned Montana white. Miners ignored treaties and moved into sacred Indian lands, and presently the military was ordered to protect the interests of the intractable adventurers. The Sioux and Cheyenne victory over General George Armstrong Custer on a Yellowstone tributary called the Little Bighorn in 1876 only escalated the persecution of those tribes. Similar pressure by Idaho miners forced Chief Joseph's Nez Percé into a running skirmish that covered half the territory, finally ending in surrender in the Bear Paw Mountains of Montana, just south of the Canadian border, in 1877. Joseph's concession, "I will fight no more forever," resonated profoundly.

By 1880, there were many reasons to go to Montana, and three ways to get there. The first was horseback or afoot, but harsh terrain made this approach perilous; besides, one had to travel light over the long trail. The more popular conveyance was still steamboat, up the Missouri, more than two thousand miles from St. Louis to Fort Benton. From Benton, known as "the innermost seaport in the world," one could follow one of many overland trails that sprayed south and west to the mining camps, north to the trading posts of Canada, or east to the cattle ranges of the high plains. The third way to get to Montana was by train.

At Ogden, Charlie and Pike Miller boarded the Utah & Northern, a spur line then inching north to the mining camps of western Montana. Severe weather had stymied construction that winter, but by March, the U&N had scaled 6,870-foot Monida Pass, and its narrow-gauge tracks had advanced a total of 300 miles to a temporary terminus at Red Rock, Montana. From here the two Missourians proceeded by stagecoach to Helena, another 150 miles to the north.

Every aspect of Charlie's trip to Montana is now encrusted in myth. While few of the accounts of his journey can be verified, at least some bear repeating as lessons in legend-craft. "At the top of a rise," Austin Russell claims, "the stage stopped to blow the horses, and the passengers got down to stretch their legs; and there, back from the road and under a clump of bunch-grass, Charlie found his first buffalo skull, bleached chalk white and with the nose bones split but the horns still on."[4] Another account has Charlie riding up top with the stage driver. "Where you from, Bud?" the driver reportedly asked the greenhorn. From Missouri, Charlie replied. "My Gawd, boy, not so loud!" he whispered. "Don't for the life of you tell nobody in Helena y'u be from Missoory. Why they got a tree there in the gulch what they're hangin' people from Missoory on right along jus' as fast as they find 'em."

What Charlie encountered in Helena was undoubtedly real — and the second rude awakening of his journey. He had lit out for the pristine frontier, only to discover that railroad tracks had arrived ahead of him. Now on the streets of Helena he came face to face with a group of Indians who were not the noble savages he had expected.[5] The United States government had by then pushed Montana's Indians onto reservations, except for

Sitting Bull's group, which had fled across the international border and did not surrender until 1881. Because tribes were no longer free to hunt buffalo or steal one another's horses (some did anyway), they were relegated to farming (which they hated and often refused to do) and government rations. Some of the Indians Charlie encountered in Helena, having collected their handout, were undoubtedly drunk; others were simply dispirited. It had been a particularly hard winter, and many of the Indians were sick, starving, or both.

After St. Louis, Helena seemed like a rat's nest. Though it had become the territorial capital in 1875, the city was still rough and unkempt. Fires had swept through the shanties and wood-frame businesses of Main Street in the early 1870s, and the Panic of 1873 had taken the starch out of the city's early pretensions of grandeur. Even so, Helena was still the territory's fastest-growing entrepôt. Of the nearly forty thousand Montanans recorded in the 1880 census, more than six thousand lived in and around Helena, with more arriving every day. Billings, Great Falls, and Missoula were virtually non-existent in 1880; Butte and Fort Benton were Helena's only rivals in size and commerce. And though Helena still had no charter, no paved streets, and no sewer, it did boast nine hotels, two banks, fifteen lawyers, ten doctors, and two undertakers. Saloons, brothels, and opium dens outnumbered all of these and were the boomtown's true measure of prosperity.

Helena was a place where deals were made and schemes hatched. It was the place to provision for a trip, grubstake a claim, or finance a herd. You could meet the right people in Helena, and some others besides. And not every Montanan was a cowboy, prospector, or mountain man. Most were newcomers like Charlie, dreamers looking for the main chance.

One of the first men Charlie met was Colonel Shirley Ashby, a well-to-do Virginian who, with fingers in freighting, real estate, and insurance, was one of Helena's men to see. Ashby recalls meeting Russell:

> He had arrived in Helena with Miller, a man I had some previous acquaintance with and meeting me I invited them to my place to lunch. I really had not seen as green a looking boy as Charlie Russell was that day he came to my house. After we had lunch Miller said that Russell had an idea that he could draw some and might become an artist. He turned to him and said: "Charlie show Mr. and Mrs. Ashby what you can do." He took a piece of black

wax from his pocket and made a little horse which we kept for years.[6]

Though Ashby remarked that "Charlie's hair was too long and I thought he needed shearing," he knew of the Russell family's good standing in St. Louis. There is some evidence that Ashby had done business with Parker-Russell.[7] Charlie may even have had a letter of introduction. What is clear is that he arrived in Montana not as a chip tossed into a torrent of hustlers and heathens, but as a well-connected young man protected by a far-reaching safety net. In the future he would deny this, but he knew that if his grip ever slipped, he would probably land softly.

Charlie and Pike Miller stayed in Helena a week or so, long enough to buy provisions, a wagon, and a four-horse team.[8] The route to Miller's sheep ranch in the Judith Basin was lumpy and circuitous. The two-hundred-mile wagon track Charlie and Miller followed led south along the Missouri River, then east through the snowcapped Castle and Crazy mountains. Three weeks after leaving Helena, they stood atop Judith Gap and took in a view that had changed little since the arrival of the first humans ten thousand years earlier.

The Judith Basin is a generous bowl, fifty miles in diameter, 2 million acres total, once the bottom of a great inland sea. As Charlie descended from Judith Gap for the first time in the early spring of 1880, he was set afloat in a sea of grass — brown and dormant, but still thick and dominant — with not a single tree or fence to dam his view. At every quarter of the compass stood mountains — not peaks that loomed like exclamation points, as they did farther west in the bigger ranges, but snowy, far-off ellipses at the end of a long, wavy paragraph of prairie. And the sky: this land, for all its expanse, was a footnote to the opus of blue overhead.

The Judith Basin takes its name from the Judith River, which runs in a northerly direction, contributing to the Missouri just south of the Bear Paws. The explorer William Clark, perhaps feeling a twinge of home-sickness, named the river for his sweetheart back in Virginia, Julia (Judy) Hancock. The Lewis and Clark party had reached the mouth of the Judith on May 29, 1805. On the north side of the river, the explorers discovered "the remains of 126 Indian lodges which appeared to be very recent date." A couple miles farther up the Missouri they soon came across "the remains of a vast many mangled carcases of Buffalow which had been driven over the precipice of 120 feet by the Indians."9

The buffalo hunters had probably been Piegan, the southern- and easternmost of the three Blackfeet tribes: Bloods, Piegan, and Blackfeet proper. Blackfeet were wanderers by nature and necessity.10 Having acquired the horse sometime in the early eighteenth century, they became matchless raiders and hunters. So central was the buffalo in the tribe's diet and culture that the Blackfeet seldom ate fish, though they lived among one of the most abundant upland fisheries in North America.

By the middle of the nineteenth century, the Blackfeet were the most formidable tribe of the northwestern plains and, as such, were the last tribe living south of the Canadian border to negotiate a treaty with the United States. In 1855, in a grove of cottonwoods near the mouth of the Judith, the Blackfeet Nation signed a pact that gave them exclusive right to virtually the entire northern half of Montana east of the Rockies. But it was only a matter of time before friction and bloodshed eroded the pact, and in 1873 the Blackfeet (and Gros Ventre and River Crow) consented to give up their land between the Musselshell and Missouri rivers. Judith Basin was up for grabs.

After the withdrawal of the Indians, buffalo were the next to go. Adventurer William Pickett wrote that as he topped Judith Gap heading southward on a trip in 1878, he met a herd of five thousand buffalo migrating north into the basin. A year later, however, the picture had changed drastically. The first gold mines opened on Yogo Creek, a feeder for the South Judith. In 1879, Yogo City was "building up rapidly."11

Though Yogo had all but played out by 1880, whites had finally begun to outnumber Indians in the area. That year, the trading post of Reed's Fort opened for business on the site of present-day Lewistown. The old Carroll Trail, the freighters' route from the mouth of the Musselshell to Helena, had given way to a better stage route from the Missouri. Also in 1880, the Army established Fort Maginnis on the northeastern edge of the basin, and the enterprising Nald Barrows built a stagecoach stop near Judith Gap, midway on the route between Fort Benton and the Yellowstone. Barrows christened his store, post office, and hotel Ubet. Utica, another stagecoach stop twenty miles to the north, served as a way station for traffic in and out of Yogo and became the hub for a new group of speculators: the stockgrowers.

Herds of livestock were not new to the Montana range. Small numbers of sheep and cattle had been driven in from Oregon and the south to supply the mining camps. And in 1866, Nelson Story, a flinty Texan, had driven a herd of six hundred cattle up the trail from Dallas to the Gallatin valley near Bozeman.

The first man to bring a large quantity of cattle into central Montana was Granville Stuart.[12] One of the early gold prospectors in the Beaverhead valley in the 1860s, Stuart then went into the cattle business; built up one of the biggest herds in the Northwest; married an Indian; founded the Montana Stockgrowers Association; roused a group of his fellow ranchers — "Stuart's stranglers" — to lynch a fraternity of recidivist rustlers hiding out in the Missouri Breaks; and ultimately retired to Butte, where he became city librarian and wrote a two-volume memoir. This last accomplishment provides, among others things, a portrait of the Judith region as Charlie Russell would have first seen it.

In April 1880, the same time Russell was arriving in Montana, Stuart left Bozeman and traveled east down the Yellowstone valley with one objective in mind: to find the best possible grazing land in the territory. Near the Little Snowy Mountains in the Judith country, he encountered what proved to be the last of the buffalo. Then crossing into the basin, he described "billowy hills covered with green grass. . . . The soil of the basin is very deep and fertile." The lack of cover was Stuart's only big concern — and a portentious one, as a winter not too many years off would prove. Despite the magnificent terrain, he noted, "This is a cold bleak region and there are snow drifts still under banks and in ravines." The date was May 19.

Stuart eventually selected a site on Flat Willow Creek between the Judith Mountains and the Little Snowies, east of the Judith Basin. "This is an ideal cattle range," he wrote in his journal, noting matter-of-factly that none of the land had been surveyed and "the only way to hold it is by occupying it." By the end of the summer of 1880, Stuart (with two financial backers, Andrew J. Davis and Samuel T. Hauser) had five thousand head of DHS-branded cattle on the range. Many more herds followed.

The 1880s were a boom time for the livestock industry not only in Montana, but in the entire West. Between Appomattox and 1888, an estimated 10 million head of Texas cattle were driven up the trail, most to railheads in Kansas. But many herds, beginning with Nelson Story's, plodded through to the new ranges farther north. In 1867, an estimated sixty-seven thousand cattle grazed in Montana Territory. By 1880, there were more than half a million head eating Montana's free grass; by 1885, the number approached a million. And though history would mark this the golden age of the American cowboy, it was also the age of the golden fleece. In 1875, there were five cows for every sheep in Montana; by 1881, sheep outnumbered cows comfortably and stayed in the majority until after World War II.

AND SO CHARLIE RUSSELL received one more rude awakening in his quest to become a Westerner. Upon arrival at Miller's ranch, located two miles from Utica on the Judith River, Charlie was put to work tending sheep. Sheepherding required a different set of skills from cowboying, not that Charlie had any experience in either branch of husbandry. Sheep could not be left alone; they were more vulnerable to predators, weather, noxious plants, and one another. Let a band of them wander out of sight, and they might drift into a steep coulee, the followers piling on top of the leaders till nearly the whole mob suffocated. Sheepherders, consequently, had to dedicate long, lonely, alert hours to their animals, and bear the stigma of eccentricity bestowed on them by cowmen. "Sheep herders that had no other interest except herding sheep often became queer and sometimes not infrequently went crazy," asserted one early appraisal of the central Montana sheepman. "Cowboys would not associate with a sheep herder. A sheep herder was below a cowboy."[13]

No calendar ever recorded how long Charlie tolerated his enrollment in this lower caste. "I did not stay with Miller long as the sheep and I did not get along at all well," Charlie told the *Butte Inter Mountain* in 1903 "so we split up and I don't think Pike missed me much, as I was considered pretty ornery."[14] Charlie, consumed with sketching and modeling, had apparently misplaced the band of sheep he was assigned to watch.

But even as he was failing at his first job, he strove to dress the part of the seasoned plainsman. Sometime during his stint with Miller, Charlie bought his pinto Monte, the purported "ghost horse," for $40.[15] In some quarters, pintos have a reputation for being temperamental, but Charlie did not seem to care. He had not simply bought a stout pony with a blaze down its nose and a blotched neck and belly; in his own mind, at least, he had tapped into the Indian world. And to his artist's eye, the color contrast of a pinto's markings was especially dazzling.

Charlie's other signature purchase was a buckskin shirt with elaborate scroll beadwork on the sleeves and front. Aboard Monte, in his new shirt, he cut a dashing figure. Years later Charlie painted a watercolor portrait of his young self in the Judith Basin. He titled it *When I Was a Kid*. It shows a round-cheeked Charlie riding a pinto pony down a steep mountain trail, cigarette pressed casually between the fingers of his free hand, rifle across his saddle, and long blond hair falling from underneath a broad-brimmed hat. He might have painted the portrait from memory or an old photograph — or he might even have lifted his self-image straight from the pages of *The Boy Hunters*. In the Mayne Reid novel, one of the young heroes "wore a hunting shirt with fringed cape, handsomely ornamented with beads, . . . a belt fastened . . . around his waist, from which was suspended his hunting knife" and "deerskin leggings . . . with moccasins upon his feet."[16] In the self-portrait, Charlie wears nearly all of these. He had finally assumed the role he had been dreaming of since early boyhood.

In those first Judith years, Charlie was surrounded by men trying on a new life. "Our section of Montana was socially in a state of flux. The trader, hunter, and trapper were in evidence, but their day was waning; the farmer had not yet appeared. Sheepmen and cattlemen were driving their herds into the country, but neither their costumes nor their customs were then standardized," recalled John Barrows, who was a boy about Charlie's age when his father opened the stage stop of Ubet. His neighbors were "mostly eastern men," Barrows explained. The town of Utica was named after the upstate New York home of its founder, Joseph Cutting. Jack Waite, partner to Pike Miller, had come west from Penn Yan, New York. The Barrowses themselves were Wisconsin people. "I think," said Judith woolgrower E. P. Chandler in a letter to his mother, "we have an exceptional neighborhood, a class of educated eastern men with western push and energy."[17]

There was a strong St. Louis connection as well. Living not far from the Miller place were the Edgars. William and Elizabeth Edgar were from old St. Louis families, their roots nearly as deep as the Russells'. The Edgars and the Russells saw each other socially and attended the same church; Mary Mead Russell's sister had even been a bridesmaid in the Edgars' wedding. William Edgar had shifted his investments from one speculation to another: cotton, mining, and, in 1879, Montana ranching. He spent the winter of 1879–80 in Montana and returned with "glowing accounts of the beauties & opportunities of the new country."[18] He urged his friends to move there with him and give it a go. The Russells listened raptly and sent Charlie, knowing that the Edgars would keep an eye on him.

⌇

CHARLIE HAD A KNACK for locating guardian angels: Pike Miller, the Edgars, fellow cowboys and artists, and finally Nancy, his wife. But one of the most important mentors of all was a man named Jake Hoover. Charlie's movements and whereabouts after quitting his sheepherding job are not very clear. There are two different versions of this interlude in his life, but in both, Jake Hoover plays a central role.

Part of the problem with sorting out the Hoover years is that Charlie apparently embroidered the facts. "I was fifteen years old, a pilgrim, when I first met Jake Hoover, and a man never needed a friend worse than I did." So begins a story Charlie gave to the Great Falls High School yearbook in 1918. By stating his age incorrectly, he cast a shadow on his testimony. Still, this was how Charlie saw his Judith initiation:

Jake was still a young man, but he had spent many years in the mountains; a hunter, trapper, prospector, and an all-around mountain man. I had come to Montana a few months before with a man much older than I was, and we did not get along well together. He did not understand a boy's nature and was not backward about telling me that I was no good. He finally told me that I could not live in Montana, but he didn't call the turn, for I'm here yet and still living.

One day I quit him and went to a man who had promised me a job herding horses, but when I reached the stage station, which was near the present town of Utica, I found that my supposed friend, the man whom I had just left, had beaten me out of the job by telling the station man that I wasn't worth my grub. The station man said that he did not want a kid of that sort around, so there was nothing for me to do but drift. All I owned in the world was a brown mare and a pinto pony. I rode the pony and used the mare to pack my bed, which was very light. With no money or grub, life did not seem joyful, and I felt mighty blue, but leaving the stage station I rode a short distance up the Judith river and made camp. While I was wondering where my next meal was coming from, a rider with several pack horses appeared and made his camp on the river near mine. I recognized him as Jake Hoover, whom

I had seen several times. After getting his packs off he strolled over to my camp and looked it over.

As I remember him then, Jake Hoover was of medium height, with thick, curly brown hair which he wore quite long, a mustache and several months' growth of beard. His eyes, gray and deep-set, saw everything at a glance. He was seldom afoot, but when he walked, travelled with his toes out. He wore a light, soft hat, blue flannel shirt, duck pants and boots. His spurs were short shanked, with broad heel bands. He never used a cartridge belt, but instead a plain leather strap on which hung a knife scabbard holding two butcher knives. His cartridges were always carried in a pouch either in his pocket or hanging under his belt. His gun was a .44 Winchester rifle which he packed across the saddle in front of him in a horn sling, but in a game country he carried it loose in his hands. His gun and cartridges were both kept slick with bear grease, and he could empty a Winchester faster than any other man I ever knew, never taking it from his shoulder once he started shooting.

After surveying my camp, Jake asked: "Where do you keep your grub?"

"I ain't got none," I answered.

Then I told him my troubles. He listened until I was through, and while I was talking I couldn't help feeling that he would be my friend.

"Well," he said, "if you want to, you can come with me, but trade that mare off as soon as you can." He explained that mares were a nuisance in the mountains because they would lead horses out of the country.

Jake was a skin hunter, but not wasteful, as he sold his meat to the few scattered ranchmen that live along the Judith river. He had just got rid of a load of deer and elk meat, and was now returning to his mountain home on the South Fork of the Judith.

Early next morning we broke camp and started for the mountains.[19]

As easy as that, or so the story goes, Charlie's initiation as a true Montanan was under way. His parents (and parental surrogate Pike Miller) could carry Charlie only so far. It took a mountain man to escort him through the portal of manhood — just as the old trapper Dick Lewis, "his long rifle on his shoulder, his powder-horn an bullet pouch at his side," had guided dime-novel hero Frank across the prairie.

Jacob Hoover was all that Charlie said he was: a man of action, a man on the fringe. Born in Iowa, he had arrived in Montana in 1866, at the age of eighteen. After knocking around the gold camps and working for a cattle outfit, "in 1871 I went to the Judith Basin," he recounted. "I trapped and hunted over the whole country and went down the Missouri River on a steamboat to Bismarck. On my return . . . I joined the stampede to the newly discovered gold mines at Yogo."[20] Yogo was actually known as Hoover City for a while — but only because Jake Hoover had been elected recorder of mines, not because he himself had made a big strike. This was the story of Hoover's life: always in the right place at the right time, but never able to cash in. By 1880, Hoover had built a low-ceilinged, two-room log cabin in Pig Eye Basin, where the South Judith escapes the Little Belt Mountains.

"Well," said Charlie in the *Butte Inter Mountain,* "I lived with Jake about two years." Or did he? In the popular version of Charlie's life — the version he helped perpetuate — he is the borderer's apprentice, a "meat-skinner, packer, and camp-tender for Jake Hoover." But in an interview six months before his death, Hoover stated: "My fondest recollections are of my old homestead shack in Pig Eye Basin. . . . That was the place where I first met Charlie Russell, the famous artist, a stripling boy, fourteen [sic] years of age. In riding the grub line he was a frequent visitor of mine for weeks at a time."[21]

"Weeks at a time" does not equal "about two years." Which is not to diminish the importance of Charlie's contact with Hoover. Indeed, the experience was seminal, paramount. But as with so many chapters in Charlie's version of his early life, he blended firsthand experiences with borrowed memories. The history he painted from this palette was always believable — nothing conspicuously overblown or out of place — but impressionistic nevertheless. And he was notoriously bad with dates.

Most likely Charlie whiled away the Hoover years as a wide-eyed dilettante. His nickname was "the Buckskin Kid" or simply "Kid Russell," though even Charlie's consistently sycophantic protégé Joe DeYong acknowledges that these monikers were patronizing and somewhat sarcastic.[22] Charlie himself admitted to being spoiled in those days. The truth was, he had not come to Montana with career ambitions. A job herding or camp-tending was, in his youthful eyes, not the swapping of sweat for livelihood that it was for most men. It was raw sensation, which he craved.

Jake Hoover did not expect too much of his sidekick, and he did not count on Charlie to bring in any game. One of the great quirks of Charlie's Western personality was that he never actually hunted. He owned a variety of pistols and rifles over the years, but, boyhood blunderbussing aside, he rarely discharged them. Even so, he relished the ritual of hunting trips. In later life, he marked a fall hunting trip indelibly on each year's calendar. He loved to join a group of friends, trail a string of packhorses into wild country, set up camp, and fill his pores with woodsmoke. He savored the taste of wild game as much as he admired its physical beauty. "No other man alive knew the anatomy of our native animals as he did," wrote Frank Linderman, a perennial hunting partner of Charlie's. "[H]e never once failed to sketch the bodies, heads, legs, eyes and ears of deer, elk, bear, mountain sheep, or goats as soon as the animals were dead. . . . [But] inordinately fond of their meat as he was, I never knew him to kill a deer, elk, or any other animal."[23]

If he did not hunt, how then did Charlie earn his keep during his purported two-year stint with Jake Hoover? Charlie freely confessed that he was not much of a cook, at least in those days. Once when Hoover was away hunting and Charlie was alone in the Pig Eye Basin homestead, Charlie looked up to see a large, well-armed Indian in the cabin doorway. He was hungry and demanded food. Charlie did not dare explain what a lousy cook he was, and proceeded to tear into the camp provisions. Fortunately the visitor was not picky; he stuffed himself with Charlie's repast, then left. Austin Russell recalls, "When I was a boy I had for years a pen-and-ink sketch on brown wrapping paper . . . which Charlie sent home in a letter — Charlie, with his hair on end, tossing flapjacks and burning bacon, and the Indian with the rifle across his knees, sitting there watching him. The caption: 'Plenty good breakfast.' "[24]

In all probability, Charlie's main job for Hoover was nothing more than house-sitting. During the long stretches when Hoover was away, either hunting or delivering meat, Charlie's responsibility was to feed and water the livestock. We know Hoover had chickens because Charlie tells about angering the rooster to the point that it attacked Hoover when he got home. We know Hoover had a pig because one of Charlie's very best stories is "Jake Hoover's Pig."

It seems that Jake Hoover acquired a pig to vary their diet of wild game. But as the pig fattened and the day for butchering neared, Jake discovered that he had grown quite fond of it. So he asked Charlie to slaughter the animal. Charlie refused. They went back and forth, neither willing to do the dirty work. Finally Jake grabbed his rifle and climbed the hill behind the cabin. Minutes later a shot rang out and the pig fell dead. Jake had done the deed from behind a tree, believing that anonymity would somehow ease the pain for victim and executioner alike.[25]

Above all, Charlie was good company, a trait that would open countless doors throughout his life. Jake Hoover was twice Charlie's age in 1880; the life of a single man in the mountains was lonely, no matter how stoic the stereotype may have been. Hoover simply liked having Charlie around. While he expected Charlie to do certain chores, he also allowed him to laze about and indulge his compulsion to draw. Scraps of paper, cracker boxes, barrelheads — Charlie covered everything in sight with sketches. Here was a life-study class superior to any studio with its copies of the Elgin Marbles.

While with Hoover, Charlie began to lose some of his rich-kid cockiness. Besides learning how to shift for himself in rough country, he gradually acquired the subtle etiquette of camp life. Charlie came to appreciate what men expect of one another, and what men should expect of themselves. Chief among these lessons was the law of self-effacement. "We lived in an era of story telling," John Barrows explained. "Long evenings were passed in recounting stories of personal experiences or in relating stories we had heard from others. There was one inflexible rule: the narrator could tell of his misadventures, but was not allowed to tell of his exploits. He could tell about the heroism of others, but was careful to avoid bragging. He did not want to be nicknamed 'Windy.' " Charlie took the lesson to heart, and from then on, according to Joe DeYong, it was Charlie's "total lack of arrogance . . . that earned him a genuine open handed welcome wherever Chance led him."[26]

Plenty of accounts confirm that Charlie did not spend his entire time under the tutelage of Jake Hoover. One of the most vivid recollections of the social life of the Basin is provided by James Bollinger, a judge from Davenport, Iowa, whose father-in-law was a financial backer of S. S. Hobson, one of the early Judith ranchers. For several summers, a group of well-to-do Davenporters visited Hobson, camping near Jake Hoover's place in Pig Eye Basin, fishing for trout and hunting grouse and deer. One of the treats, Bollinger related, was meeting Charlie Russell:

Now Charlie was . . . very amusing then as always. Kept the place in uproar all the time. At night he would come in, flop on his belly, and paint a water color in the very sight of all assembled. When the Gilmans started home he gave each of the girls two or three of his sketches, apiece. And Mrs. Gilman asked him what she should send him. He said, "I need paints and brushes and paper for my sketches." And upon her return [to Iowa] she filled the order generously.[27]

From this point of view, life in the Judith resembled a Gilded Age lark. Jake Hoover's place was not simply a rawhide redoubt; it also happened to be a popular tourist spot. Anna Williams Lee, who visited her sister in the Judith in the 1880s, corroborates:

> One of the entertainments proposed was a trip to the Belt Mts. to the camp of Jackie Hoover, the guide of those parts. My sister chaperoned the party of seven, four going horseback and three in the big wagon carrying the supplies. Sitting around the camp fire one evening, some one asked Charlie to "draw something." He went through all his pockets and said "I have nothing to draw on." My sister ripped out the satin hat band from her hat and said "take this."[28]

With his art, charm, good looks, and good name, Charlie did nearly as much courting as camping during those first years in Montana. The visiting girls were titillated by his frontier dress and mannerisms, but his roughness came with references, and his impecuniousness was immediately recognized as an affectation by anyone who knew his lineage. Charlie, for better or worse, came across as a romantic. It only made sense that he would fall deeply in love.

She was Laura "Lollie" Edgar, daughter of the St. Louis Edgars. The Edgar place was a half-mile east of Utica. In 1880, Lollie's father had filed a 160-acre homestead claim and had spread a band of sheep across the unclaimed Judith Basin land that surrounded it. In the spring of that year, he sent for his wife and twelve-year-old daughter in St. Louis. "Our tent was pitched by a spring & a shelter of small logs was built around three sides of it," Lollie wrote. "Here my mother & I lived . . . while our house was being built. . . . That summer is one of my memories that I cherish. Our house was finished just as the first snow came."

Though their parents knew each other well, Charlie and Lollie had never met until that summer in Montana. Even then, Charlie did not pay the little girl much notice on his visits to the Edgars. Charlie was at an awkward stage, tooling his new image, and Lollie too was at an awkward age, just growing out of girlhood. Nevertheless, she recalled nearly sixty years later, "We were thrown together constantly."

It took absence to make their hearts grow fonder. In 1880–81, Lollie was sent away to school in St. Louis. "I went back . . . a little girl in short skirts & hair down my back," Lollie wrote. "The winter changed all that. I came home with my hair put up & my skirts long. Charlie liked the change & told me so. Where we had been comrades before we became sweethearts."

They made quite a pair. He was fair and sturdy. She was brown-haired, brown-eyed, and slight — barely ninety pounds. She still dressed like a proper St. Louisan. Charlie had affected the dishabille of a plainsman. Still, they had much in common. "We both loved the mountains, the sky & the little river," Lollie reminisced. "We rode long hours over the hill & built our castles in the air."

When they were not out exploring the Judith Basin, Charlie was wooing her with his artwork. He drew pictures of the Edgar ranch, Indians, horses, wildlife, and Lollie herself. He was never without his art materials. "His cake of ink & small paint brush was always in his pocket. He did have some water color paper, but he painted on anything that was at hand. A piece of wrapping paper or a blank page of a magazine. . . . I do not remember of ever seeing him paint from a model of any kind. He always worked from memory or inspiration."[29]

Charlie's appeal derived not just from his knack for entertaining with art and stories. He had a certain don't-give-a-damn quality mixed with "rock-solid honesty" that drew people to him. In the early stages of his courtship of Lollie, he would ride up to the Edgar ranch, jump from Monte, remove his hat, coat, and spurs, but leave his chaps on. "Finally," according to one of the Edgars' neighbors, "Lollie's curiosity got the best of her, and she asked Charlie what the reason was. With much embarrassment, he explained that someone had stolen his pants, and he hadn't been able to afford a new pair, so in the meantime he had cut out a piece of horse blanket, and sewn it in the seat of his chaps."[30]

As much as his appearance might have tickled Lollie, it nettled her father. His daughter was too young; Charlie, his blue bloodline aside, was too irresponsible. "I don't think either of us ever had a practical thought," Lollie admitted. "We were sure our romance was the most beautiful thing that ever happened & it would never die."

At first none of the grown-ups took Charlie and Lollie's togetherness seriously. But then after spending two winters in Montana with her parents,
Lollie went back again to school in St. Louis. Charlie followed her, staying
for much of the winter of 1883–84. When both returned to Montana in
the spring, William Edgar tried to keep them apart. "His objections were
natural," Lollie stated in hindsight. "Charlie was hardly supporting himself
& I was still in school. Of course like all young people we saw each other in
spite of objections. Where before we had ridden for miles we now walked
or visited when we could."

In the end, the romance simply faded. The Edgars went back to St. Louis
in 1884 and sold their sheep ranch the following year. This time Charlie did
not chase Lollie. By then he was a grown man of twenty, fully immersed
in the rugged life of roundups and the open range. Lollie was just sixteen,
her dark brown eyes turned in an entirely different direction.

In 1890, Lollie Edgar married Robert Blackwell Whittemore. The
Whittemore parents knew the Edgar parents, as they both had known the
Russells, and all their children ran together in a privileged social set in-
formally known as "the Club." The Club went to lectures and parties together — and, to show their voguishness and daring, occasionally "roughed
it" at well-catered, closely chaperoned camps in the Missouri countryside.[31]
Had Charlie stayed in St. Louis, this might have been his world, just as Lollie
Edgar might have been his girl. But he hadn't, and she wasn't. "I did not
see Charlie [from 1884] until just before my wedding," Lollie recalled. "We
were both a little sad."

Many years later — long after Charlie had met and married Nancy, long
after he had made a name for himself as an artist — he wrote a poem to
a friend, lamenting the passing of better days. "The West is dead," he declared. "You may lose a sweetheart, but you will never forget her."[32] He
was, of course, eulogizing the open range, the windblown life of the cowboy. But once upon a time there had been another sweetheart, and she
had wrenched his emotions as sharply as any prairie horizon or mountain
sunset ever did. Assuredly Charlie grew more sentimental the older he
got. Yet if it is true that his art and worldview were saturated with steadily
increasing doses of nostalgia, then that first tincture of melancholia dates to
the time in the Judith when Lollie Edgar touched his heart.

4

"LAST OF FIVE THOUSAND"

COMING FROM MONEY, Charlie never really thought about it. His mother and father sent him occasional drafts, but he was too stubborn to solicit their donations openly. Once he had bought Monte, plus a second horse, his expenses were minimal anyway. When he did find himself in need, the kindness of cohorts and strangers proved ample. Jake Hoover and the Judith ranchers were good for meals, and Hoover may have paid him a few dollars now and then for helping out. Charlie's credit was apparently accepted at the general mercantile in Utica. A ledger entry under his name for October 1, 1882, records "boots, gloves and meals, $14." Other entries show he had developed new, adult habits: "cigaret papers, 25 cents," and on July 13, 1882, $18.25 for "saloon account."[1]

Having arrived in the spring of 1880, Charlie stayed in Montana through the following winter. The story is told that his parents sent him the money to come home that first winter, but that he turned them down or squandered the money or, in one version, gave it away.[2] Clearly he did not go home, for when Lollie Edgar mentions that she was sent to school in St. Louis for the winter of 1880–81, Charlie is notably absent from her recollection.

But the wayward son was back in St. Louis for at least part of the winter of 1881–82, eager to show off his new self. He was a hardened five-foot-ten, 160 pounds. His face was sunburned, his shoulders thick, his hands rough. His talk was different too — not just in the repertoire of stories he told to his transfixed kin, but in the easy way he unraveled them. His enthusiasm for Montana was so contagious that when he left home again in the spring of 1882, he was accompanied by his eighteen-year-old cousin from Illinois, Jim Fulkerson.

The journey was even easier this time. The Northern Pacific Railroad, its westward progress having been stalled at Bismarck, Dakota Territory, for years, was now reaching up the valley of the Yellowstone River. Charlie and Jim were able to ride the new line as far as Billings, then a brand-new town, located 120 miles southeast of the Judith Basin. The bad news was that Jim Fulkerson had taken sick.

For all the sadness Charlie Russell expressed in his life — grief over the loss of the open range, mourning for the plight of the Indians — he seems to have registered the loss of friends and relatives with a clipped Anglo-Saxon stolidity. In 1901, Charlie wrote to an old friend, listing the demise of some old cronies: "Pat Rily was killed while sleeping of [f] a drunk at grass range . . . Charly Bowlegs was killed at Dupuyer, while playing car[d]s . . . Panhandle Jack killed at Gild Edge by a saloon man . . . Frank Harstel bushwhacked at his ranch on warm spring creek while pealin potatoes for supper. . . . Al Malison killed by a falling horse while cutting out on the beef round-up on the Mirias range."[3] Perhaps it was his early exposure to grief that made it hard for him to express it freely.

Jim Fulkerson "died of mountain fever at Billings two weeks after we arrived."[4] In later years, Charlie never used more words than these to describe the event. He and Jim had been lifelong chums. Charlie had shared Jim's stories of Old Brit; Jim, in turn, had acquired Charlie's passion for Montana. But this was no dime novel; they were alone in a raw railroad town, and as soon as Charlie realized how grave his cousin's condition was, he telegrammed the Fulkersons in Illinois, who boarded the earliest possible train for Billings. Meantime, Charlie summoned a doctor, who applied a poultice to Jim's face that succeeded only in blinding the boy. When Jim finally died, most likely in great agony, his parents took his body back to Illinois. Charlie, shaken but resolute, pushed on to the Judith.[5]

Again he was broke. And again he was succored by strangers:

When I pulled out of Billings, I had four bits in my pocket and 200 miles between me and Hoover. Things looked mighty rocky. There was still quite a little snow, as it was April, but after riding about 15 miles I struck a cow outfit coming in to receive 1,000 dougies for the 12, Z and V outfit up the basin. The boss, John Cabler, hired me to night wrangle horses. We were about a month on the trail and turned loose on Ross Fork, where we met the Judith roundup.[6]

In the two years since Charlie had first arrived in the Judith, the country had continued to fill with ranchers and their stock. The assumption was that a land that had carried hundreds of thousands of buffalo could handle an enormous quantity of domestic livestock. In a typical July in the days before cattle and sheep, the grass in the Judith reached haunch-high to the buffalo, elk, and antelope that grazed there. The hillsides, benches, and riparian areas were covered with a mixture of hardy grasses that created a reliable, year-round pantry. Some greened up earlier in the spring, some did better in times of drought, some grew back more quickly after grazing, some cured better on the stem for winter consumption. Together they achieved a nutritious balance, and in those early years, the Judith could produce nearly two thousand pounds of feed per acre.[7]

The Judith Basin's greatest natural blessing is that, although a dry country, it is not as *high* and dry as the rangeland immediately to the south. The center of the Judith is 3,500 feet above sea level, nearly 2,000 lower than most of Wyoming and Colorado. Texans who drove herds up the trail beyond the railheads of Kansas quickly realized that by pressing farther north, they reached a better climate, one so hospitable that cattle fattened on northern grass were worth twice as much as their stringy Texas counterparts.

The 1870s and early 1880s had been relatively wet years in the West; the Montana range, with its diminished buffalo herd, appeared unusually healthy. The fact that most of the land was, if not exactly free, then nearly so made the picture even more attractive. All one had to do was pay a small homesteading fee and then "prove up" 160 acres (or, after a succession of later legislative acts, as many as 640 acres). But a homestead was really just a pinprick on the map in those early years, a base from which to broadcast one's livestock onto the tens of thousands of unclaimed acres nearby. "I worked for a cow outfit," recalled Charlie's friend Con Price, "that run twenty-five thousand cattle and three or four hundred saddle horses to handle the cattle with, and they didn't own one foot of deeded land."[8]

For the moment at least, it was a stockgrower's dream come true. The population of the United States had doubled between 1850 and

1880, with the vast majority of newcomers living in Northeastern cities. (The Homestead Act had been designed to draw immigrants westward; ranchers, however, preferred to view them as distant consumers, not nagging neighbors.) With the Northern Pacific near completion, Montana beef, lamb, wool, and horses could be delivered to Eastern markets quickly and economically. At the same time, another lucrative market had sprung up much closer to the point of production. With the Indians now starving on reservations, government beef contracts, representing millions of pounds, waited to be filled.

Those who could not see opportunity when it dangled in front of their faces had only to read James S. Brisbin's *Beef Bonanza,* subtitled *How to Get Rich on the Plains.* Brisbin was an ex–cavalry officer who boasted years of experience in the West (though he chose not to dwell on his less-than-noble association with Custer in the days leading up to Little Bighorn). "When I visit the Eastern States," he exclaimed,

> it is a matter of astonishment to me to learn how little is known of the advantages, resources, and interests of the West. . . . Every one East seems to think the days for speculation are over, and they regret a hundred times a year they had not been fifty years sooner. To the discouraged let me say, be of good heart and go West, for what has been occurring in the East during the last two hundred years is now occurring in the West, only with tenfold more rapidity.9

Brisbin specifically touted Montana, where "grazing cannot be excelled."

Stoked by hyperbole, interest in the northern range caught fire. Most speculators had two things in common: vaulting optimism and absentee ownership. Pike Miller was, for the most part, an absentee owner. Granville Stuart's original backers, Hauser and Davis, were absentee. Louis Stadler and Louis Kaufman, who would soon loom large in Charlie's life, were butchers living in Helena. Bay State was from Boston. Continental Land & Cattle was out of St. Louis. Theodore Roosevelt was perhaps the best-known outsider; his ranch was just across the Montana line in the Badlands of Dakota Territory. For all the emphasis he put on Western values, Roosevelt was only an intermittent visitor.

The bug spread overseas as well. Blue-blooded Europeans brought heraldry to the husbandry boom, and no one had a larger interest than Scottish and English investors. "The Scotch, who are supposed to be one of the most thrifty races on the globe," Scotsman John Clay observed, "are on the other hand the most speculative." In 1882 they led a charge that in the next two years would put more than 20 million acres of Western rangeland under foreign control. "The year 1882 saw cowpunching in all its glory with a color of carmine around it. It was fashionable," explained Clay, who worked for Scottish interests in California, Wyoming, and Montana. "The drawing rooms buzzed with the stories of this last of bonanzas, staid old gentlemen who scarcely knew the difference betwixt a steer and a heifer discussed it over their port and nuts."[10]

The price of cattle and sheep rose as investors bought up herds to stock the range. As they stocked and as their cows and ewes bore calves and lambs, they recorded the increase in account books kept thousands of miles from their ranches.

THE JUDITH ROUNDUP of 1882 began in May and lasted most of the summer. Because the range was unfenced and because livestock were not fed from haystacks in the winter months, the herds foraged far and wide from autumn till spring. The job of gathering and sorting a herd by owner and then branding, castrating, and earmarking the year's calf crop took a lot of men and even more horses. Each cowboy needed anywhere from six to ten mounts; the ones he was not using were held nearby in a herd, usually called a remuda, or cavvy — from the Spanish *caballada*. The various herd owners chose one boss to oversee the entire roundup; the roundup boss held rank over the foremen of each outfit; foremen, in turn, gave orders to their respective cowboys. Low man on the totem pole was the night wrangler, or nighthawk, of the horse herd.

Horace Brewster, boss of the Judith roundup, was the man who gave Charlie his big break. Neither ever forgot the other. In 1916 Brewster became one of the first rangers in Glacier National Park, and he visited Charlie and Nancy Russell often over the years. In 1926, as a final gesture of friendship, Brewster rode horseback in the cortege that carried Charlie's body to the graveyard. The day of the funeral, he recalled the spring of 1882, when he first set eyes on Charlie Russell:

We had more than 400 horses . . . in our remuda, and Pete Vann [Van] was the horse wrangler. Pete was tryin' to keep awake all day and couldn't make it on the night herd. I talked with S.S. Hobson, representing some of the owners there, and he said I would have to send to Helena or Billings to git a man, unless I took a kid that was livin' with Jakie Hoover up in Pig Eye Basin. I told 'em to send him along, and Russell showed up one morning at camp. . . . He had 50 cents in his pocket and looked like he needed a job. I kinder took to him and put him on as horse wrangler. He had never herded, so I sent Charley Colthay of the B-D outfit to show him how to wrangle.[11]

Much to Brewster's surprise, Charlie got the hang of nighthawking quickly. Though considered menial, the job was crucial. One or two riders, depending on the size of the remuda, were sent out after supper. The night wrangler's task was to keep several hundred mounts together without benefit of fences or help from sleeping comrades. Come daybreak, he was expected to deliver a watered, fed, and rested herd to a makeshift corral near the chuck wagon. Once each cowboy had roped and saddled his horse for that day's work, the watchman's work was done. He shaded up as best he could and tried to get some sleep. Charlie's first shifts as nighthawk contrasted dramatically with his sheep-tending days with Pike Miller. If anything, he was too conscientious, holding the horses so tightly that they could not spread out to graze. Still, Horace Brewster said in his eulogy four decades later, "I'd rather ride 'em hungry than hunt 'em."

Charlie nighthawked for the next eleven years. He worked the calf roundups in the spring and summer and the beef roundups (when the grass-fattened stock was shipped) in the fall. At some point in his early wrangling days, perhaps 1883, Charlie had his photograph taken. In it, he is wearing his fringed buckskin shirt, woolly chaps, and boots. Hanging loosely around his waist is a cartridge belt with holster; his gun drapes just below a slightly dipped right hip, gunslinger style. Charlie has crossed his arms across his chest and pushed his broad-brimmed hat back on his head. If this is a hammy, boardwalk pose, his severe expression does not belie it. His jaw is set and his eyes stare down all comers, as if to say, I, Kid Russell, am the real thing.

And he had the stories to go along with the photograph. As related by Joe DeYong years later,

there'd been several night herders killed in the Judith by Indians one summer & [Charlie's] outfit was camped in a spot where war parties crossed between two buttes. He was night hawk & had some bunch quitters necked together [a wild horse roped to a tame one]. And along in the night he was sure he saw a man on foot at the head of one horse. He was afraid to go close but did & found it was just another horse tied to the first one & standing head on so he looked thin.

The laugh was on Charlie, but it was not without redeeming benefits. Charlie got to represent himself as the courageous rider in harm's way. Most likely Indians had not killed any of his fellow nighthawks, but a little fib was allowed in a story that gigged only the teller. De Yong continues:

Also another time [Charlie] was night herding beef when he heard Indians singing — a bunch rode out of a coulee in the moonlight but stopped singing when they saw the cattle. The Chief [De Yong's nickname for Charlie] kept still & the Indians went on.

He told of another time when he and a bunch of cowpunchers up on Milk river got some whiskey & went to an Indian camp. The Indians had three lodges made into one big one. They all got drunk & the Chief went to sleep. When he woke up his friends had left & those Indians were dancing to beat the devil. One with a Henry rifle was just foaming at the mouth and shooting into the fire as he danced. The Chief was scared so he pulled up some tent pegs & rolled out quietly. It was very dark & he got up to run to his horse & hit the limb of a tree which knocked him down & he thought he was shot. He layed still a long time then crawled to his horse & got away.[12]

Though his credentials as a nighthawk became well established, Charlie did not soft-pedal his shortcomings. When in "A Few Words About Myself" he admitted to not being much of a rider, he was not simply being modest. "No," an old-timer told cowboy author-illustrator Ross Santee, "Charlie wasn't a good roper or a good bronc rider; didn't seem to be particularly interested in acquiring either knack. Many's the time when a steer broke out of a holdup I've seen Charlie set his pony, never make a move when he could have had a throw."[13]

As with hunting, Charlie was plain timid. "I think one thing that kept him from cowboying more was he was afraid of strange horses. He couldn't ride a horse that bucked very hard," revealed Ballie Buck, a respected Montana cowboy. Another old-timer, C. J. Ellis, concurred: "He was the most scared fellow I ever saw when there was the least chance of any one getting hurt. If a fellow got throwed off a bucking horse Charlie would actually turn white."[14]

Indeed, if Charlie had debuted with any roundup other than the Judith, he might never have found work at all. Beginning in 1879, stockgrowers had begun dividing themselves into roundup associations: Judith, Flat Willow, Shonkin, Maginnis, Moccasin, Bear Paw, to name the most prominent. Given this expansion, there were not enough seasoned hands to go around, and no roundup was without its share of green remittance men. "Rich men's sons from the East were nothing new as far as I was concerned," stated Teddy Blue Abbott, one of Charlie's lifelong friends. "The range in the eighties was as full of them as a dog's hair of fleas."[15]

The Judith roundup was an extreme case. Lacking "the leaven of Texas men, who gave tone to the other roundups," John Barrows explained, "the Judith roundup was spoken of derisively. In 1881, when the Judith roundup was first organized, they built all of their corrals with a snubbing post in the center." (He is implying that the Judith cowboys could not saddle their horses without first tying them firmly to a post.) "This created a situation comparable to . . . [one in which] the Brooklyn Dodgers equipped their infielders with bushel baskets to trap hot grounders."[16]

To make such a team, all Charlie had to do was perform his night-wrangling duties tolerably well. His congeniality around the bed ground and campfire took care of the rest. The men slept in blankets covered with a waterproof canvas tarp, called a sougan. Sometimes they were fortunate enough to have tents. They ate from a chuck wagon: beans, bacon, fresh beef, and thick coffee. Alcohol was strictly forbidden in camp. Nearly everyone smoked, generally roll-your-own Bull Durham or Climax tobacco. Work, eat, sleep — there was little time or energy for much else. But spread across a day's regimen was a web of joshing, griping, and jawing for jawing's sake. This was the only part of cowboying that Charlie ever truly mastered.

While there were those who found fault with his riding and roping, nobody ever had a bad word to say about his personality. He got to be "the most popular kid on the range," Horace Brewster attested. "I've known him . . . in sun and shade, and he was sure for his friends. . . . He never swung a mean loop in his life, never done dirt to man or animal in all the days he lived."[17]

C. J. Ellis recalled one chilly fall roundup:

> Charlie and I figured if we spliced our sougans and he used them in the day and I used them at night we would have a fine warm bed and still not be crowded. Now I wonder if eating out of the same frying pan, drinking out of the same coffee pot, sleeping in the same bed and swapping strings [of horses] will answer how well I was acquainted with him! You ask what kind of man he was? . . . I'll say this — he was straight as string.[18]

In those days, cowboys did not all wear similar clothes, but even amid the motley frontier garb, Charlie stood out. In addition to his elegantly beaded buckskin shirt, he had begun wearing a long woven sash. Beyond flamboyant, it was downright outré. This kind of sash was the signature adornment of an ethnic group known as Métis, or "mixed breed." They were the descendants of French voyageurs and Cree Indians whose original homeland was on the Canadian plains of present-day Manitoba. Migrating westward after losing a protracted pushing match with the white Protestant (Métis were Catholic) regime in Ottawa, a small colony, including their leader Louis Riel, had settled in the Judith Basin.[19] Whether Charlie meant it or not, his decision to wear a Métis sash was a bit like a college boy wearing a beret in solidarity with an exiled underground.

But Charlie could get away with most anything, and the pranks attributed to him are legion. "He would have played a practical joke on his grandmother if he had had a chance," C. J. Ellis said. Mostly it was kid stuff: smearing ripe cheese in a man's boots so he would think his feet were rotting, or reflecting sun off a glass onto a fellow's bare skin so he would think he had been stung by a hornet. But Charlie's creativity made even the silliest pranks more pointed and their enactment somehow more forgivable. The result, said John Barrows, was that Charlie became the "privileged jester of the Judith roundup."[20]

One morning Charlie arrived in camp after a long night of horse-herding and discovered Bill Bullard, his day-shift counterpart, dead drunk. Charlie decided to have some fun with this colleague who had literally fallen down on the job:

He rustled an old buffalo skin with the horns on it and placed Bill's head on it for a pillow. He arranged it so that a horn turned up on each side of Bill's head just above his ears. He then arranged a pair of hairy chaps around his neck like a scarf and called the boys to see his handi-work. . . . Charlie was so proud of his work of art, that after the riders had all gone he got out Bill's gun and a shoe awl and drew on the lock plate of the gun the most perfect picture of Bill, with Buffalo horns, a hairy neck and chest, that could be drawn, blending Bill's image into the buffalo head perfectly.[21]

Many of Charlie's comic antics were not lampoons so much as they were celebrations of the quirks of daily life. Often the horses the cowboys rode were barely broken, which could turn the near-simultaneous roping, sad-dling, and mounting of several dozen horses into a bona fide rodeo. It was a nuisance, not to mention dangerous, to be thrown. Even to "pull leather" — grab the saddle horn to stay aboard — was a blow to a cowboy's pride. As off-duty night wrangler, Charlie was guaranteed a front-row seat for these diurnal dustups. With a few deft strokes of pencil or charcoal, he would dash off a lighthearted sketch of a gyrating bronc. He memo-rized individual horses, brands, and riders, and he became fluent in the body language of man and beast. Even in the early sketches, when his compo-sitions were corny and his perspectives flat, he instinctively knew how to measure the weight and angle of a boot in a stirrup, the bow of a horse's neck, and the flip of a saddle skirt.

Charlie's favorite subject was a tempestuous scene in which a snuffy horse has crow-hopped through the cow-camp kitchen, kicking over kettles and coffeepots and ruining the meal. Later in life, Charlie would paint this scene numerous times in oil and watercolor, calling it variously *Bronc in Cow Camp, Camp Cook's Trouble,* and *Bronc to Breakfast.* As the rider in each tries to get control of his horse, cowboys skitter out of the way while the cook charges with carving knife or, in some cases, shovel. In at least one of the versions, Charlie painted himself seated in the background, a plate of food in his lap, a crease of a grin on his face.

"At camp and elsewhere," recalled old-timer Al Andrews, "his habit of drawing on the wagon covers, on poker chips and playing cards never failed [to] arouse wonder and admiration of the rest of the gang." Frank "Doc" Nelson, who insisted he had been the inspiration for *Bronc to Breakfast,* described a time in Martinsdale in the early 1880s: "Monroe 'Beaver' Nelson, my brother, rode in for provisions for the cook. Russell took a fancy to his riding outfit. He picked up a piece of wrapping paper and drew a sketch of him which was a photographic likeness. He asked me if I wanted [it]. . . . I took it and put it in my pocket, intending to send it home. However, I forgot about it and it was soon worn out."[22]

Such stories multiplied as Charlie grew more famous; so many people claimed to have ridden with him or received artwork from him that he jokingly calculated "there must have been a thousand Cowpunchers on the Judith roundup that I never saw." Yet despite the early kudos from his peers and the obvious pleasure he got from his efforts, Charlie still did not take his art very seriously. In 1886, he was twenty-two years old and still nighthawking, "an easy-going, friendly humorous youngster, who followed the line of least resistance," as one friend pointed out.[23] If he was a touch complacent, it was a condition born of complete contentment. The future was not something he dwelled upon.

Yet contentment did not dull his senses. As fully as Charlie had immersed himself in the roundup life, he was always perspicacious, though graciously so. John Barrows observed that Charlie had a knack for straddling the distinct classes of "chivalry and shovelry." That did not mean he resorted to condescension or put on airs. "He was always 'aboveboard,' and in all ways 'open to the sky,' " Joe DeYong insisted. " 'His lodge,' to use an Indian simile, 'had but one door,' which always faced the rising sun." Still, Charlie had the option of stepping away, returning to St. Louis whenever he chose, and he exercised it with regularity. Roundup work was seasonal, after all; ranchers typically paid only one or two hands through the winter.[24]

In 1885, Charlie arrived back in Montana with his brother Ed, two years his junior, and his second cousin Chiles Carr, eight years older. Charlie gave Ed the tenderfoot's rush, but also introduced him to the good families around the Judith Basin. The Russell brothers' joint calling card seems to have been a banjo. For one reason or another, Charlie never mentioned his musical flair in the autobiographical recaps he gave to reporters in later years. But those with independent recollections of Charlie and Ed Russell saw a banjo in the picture. Ed and Charlie both played, recalled Eliza Walker, whose family moved into the Judith in 1882. Lollie Edgar remembered later that Charlie "always carried his Banjo with him. He knew all the popular songs."[25]

Chiles Carr made an entirely different impression. Like the Russell boys, he came with fancy references; his reputation, however, was considerably more tarnished. Carr had lived at home and worked for his father's iron-works throughout his early twenties, though less than diligently. His silver spoon got in the way of hard work, and apparently so did the bottle. His family hoped that a stint in Montana would snap him to attention or at least remove him from public scorn. In the summer of 1885, Carr filed a homestead claim on 160 acres along the Judith River, five miles from Utica and nearly next door to Pike Miller's original sheep ranch. Carr announced that his new ambition was to raise horses.

Charlie's own whereabouts and ambition at this time are less clear. At least one account has him filing his own homestead claim and building his own crude cabin. If this is so, no record of the filing exists. More likely he was simply bunking with cousin Chiles and others in between his so-cial sashays and seasonal wrangling duties. Assuredly, Charlie was not the homesteading type.[26]

AROUND 1882, CHARLIE began painting with watercolors — his first tentative steps into color. He did a number of night scenes, perhaps because darkness forgave his heavy hand. *A Dream of Burlington* depicts a booted and buckskinned figure, presumably Charlie, lounging before an open hearth with hat brim pulled over his face. Smoke from his cigarette makes a dream cloud in which a column of military figures stand at attention. In another watercolor, a similar figure sits by a campfire, smoking alone; in yet an-other, Charlie stands amid a clutch of older men — perhaps one is Jake Hoover — who are seated in front of a fireplace. It has since been given the title *Telling Some Windies.*

He also favored hunting and riding scenes. Many of these efforts were still quite rudimentary: a single rider and horse in profile or a lone coyote on an empty plain. But because the medium of watercolor required greater effort and therefore suggested greater permanence — more so than pencil-drawing, anyway — Charlie began to pay closer attention to the techni-cal matters of composition, perspective, and depth of field. He learned to tie together the central elements of a painting — cowboys roping a steer, for instance — by positioning them in a triangular or diamond-shaped arrangement.

Over time, Charlie became partial to certain settings and subject matter simply because he was able to make them work compositionally. Two hunters hide their horses behind an elevated outcropping and take aim at a group of antelope on the flat below them; in the far distance are a series of buttes. Another favorite is a laconic derivative of the bronc-to-breakfast theme: a rider enters a roundup camp, men seated or lying about, saddles and gear in the foreground, chuck wagon as backdrop. Or three antelope stand in profile, a jackrabbit running from the sagebrush in front of them, mountain peaks in the distance. Charlie did versions of all these subjects over and over again. Sometimes he drew Indians behind the outcropping; other times, stagecoach robbers. Sometimes the cowboys rope cows, other times wolves or grizzlies.

Storytelling is the primary goal of all these compositions. But a constant, underlying theme is space, vast Western space. Charlie's horizons are always miles away. One of his favorite techniques was to elevate the hunters (or Indians or outlaws) above their surrounding landscape. This gave them monumental, heroic stature and created a grand vantage point for the central figures as well as the viewer of the painting. Similarly, by dividing the near details and remote background of a painting with, say, a gully, he succeeded in telescoping vast expanses within the frame.

Another of his tricks was to busy up his foregrounds with rabbits, brush, or a buffalo skull. He began drawing or painting the familiar horned skull in the foreground of his work as early as 1882. (Carl Wimar had done the same thing in the 1850s.) By 1887 Charlie had adopted the buffalo "bull head" as part of his official signature, much as a stockman simplifies a more complex image into a brand. Iconographers have pounced on these bones as symbols of a fleeting frontier. But while the skull was intended to strike a sentimental chord, it was there also to sling the eye, by means of efficient Düsseldorfian mechanics, to the far, miles-away recesses of the composition. One is inevitably drawn to the horizon in Charlie Russell's paintings — to the mountains, buttes, badlands, and saturated sunsets. Yet it is the fullness of his skull-cluttered foregrounds that gives his pictures their sweep.

Charlie's progress was catch-as-catch-can. His early exposure to fine art had given him a rudimentary sense of form. He followed up in Montana by studying, idly or ambitiously, the popular periodicals of his day: *Leslie's Weekly, Harper's Weekly, Harper's Monthly, Century,* and the workingman's favorite, *Police Gazette*. These carried the work of commercial illustrators such as Howard Pyle, Edwin Abbey, A. B. Frost, and eventually Charles Dana Gibson and Frederic Remington. Charlie used their structure and subject matter as training aids, which gave him the courage to attempt more difficult artistic terrain. Certain tricks he picked up readily, but even he acknowledged that he was a bundle of undeveloped talent. He could not draw faces, for instance, and never did get very good at them. His horses had personalities, but too many of his humans had the same expression, and apparently the same parents. Portraiture he rarely attempted, and never with much success.

Charlie also struggled with color. In his early work, the Judith Basin is invariably brown and black; highlights are swallowed up by their drab surroundings; everything seems in shadow. The reason is that Charlie had only a primitive notion of how to mix paint. But mix it he did, till it turned to mud.

Nevertheless, he persisted. In 1885, James Shelton, a Utica saloonkeeper, commissioned Charlie to paint a picture to hang behind the bar. Utica had grown since its founding five years earlier. It now had a hotel, general store, post office, and blacksmith shop. Shelton felt it was high time his place had some class. Charlie had no studio, so his patron invited him to paint in the back of the saloon. This was scarcely a hardship; by then Charlie was a regular customer. The real challenge was not work space, but materials. In 1885, oil paints were still an unfamiliar medium to Charlie; undaunted, he forged ahead with house paint on a pine board, six feet long and eighteen inches high.[27]

The mural is in fact three pictures, a triptych revealing all of Charlie's potential and all of his shortcomings. On the left side of the panel a group of Indians in the foreground are shooting at a wagon train circled below them; white puffs envelop their gun barrels, and one Indian is falling from his horse. In the right-hand scene a trio of antelope are lured into shooting range by two Indians concealed in the distance. Dividing the two wing pieces, within a black-rimmed circle, a group of elk converge in a high-mountain park. Charlie's colors are murky, and his compositions pat. But as barroom decoration, the images are thrilling; they evoke a time before white men ruled the Judith. And each scene, however primitive, would have inspired a skein of associative yarns from the moistened throats of Shelton's regulars.

As Charlie's confidence grew, he dared to undertake more complex images. In 1885, the same year as the Shelton saloon commission, he completed another large oil, this one on canvas for rancher Jesse Phelps. *Breaking Camp,* as it is now called, is a horizontal view (eighteen by thirty-six inches) of the Judith roundup of that spring. Snowcapped peaks mark the horizon, a buffalo skull the foreground. But the real achievement of the painting, other than the fact that it is Charlie's first major oil on canvas, is that he succeeded in packing twenty-five of the roundup's riders into the frame. This was obviously the point; Charlie wanted to include everyone and wanted everyone to be recognizable. The resulting assemblage of men sitting, roping, saddling, mounting, riding, and bucking owes more to folk art than fine art, but it was received by the connoisseurs of Utica as a tour de force.[28]

So pleased was Charlie with his accomplishment that he submitted the painting to an exhibition in St. Louis the following year. Apart from the boyhood sculptures his father had entered in the St. Louis fair, *Breaking Camp* was his first work to be shown outside Montana. But unlike the early sculptures, *Breaking Camp* won no ribbons. In fact, Charlie's contribution drew no particular acclaim at all. The St. Louis Exhibition was mostly an occasion to show off regional manufactured goods, from Goodyear galoshes to Anheuser-Busch beer. The art exhibit proper was choked with the predictable mawkishness of hobbyists. Regardless, it was a significant event in Charlie's life: he had shown he was ready and willing to break out.

CHARLIE WAS STILL night-wrangling the year *Breaking Camp* was shown. Despite his increased momentum as a painter, it is impossible to say how his art career would have progressed had history not overtaken him that following winter. Charlie played a minuscule role in the events of that season, but as a keen witness he ensured that the disaster known as "the Big Die-up" would never be forgotten.

In so many ways, the die-up was a tragedy waiting to happen. There were even those who had predicted it. "Overstocking may cause little or no harm for two or three years," Teddy Roosevelt wrote in the fall of 1886, "but sooner or later there comes a winter which means ruin to the ranches that have too many cattle on them; and in our country, which is even now getting crowded, it is merely a question of time as to when a winter will come that will understock the ranges by the summary process of killing off about half of all the cattle throughout the Northwest."[29]

Even so, nobody was ready. The winter of 1885–86 had been mild. Cattle had little trouble finding forage, and in the spring the herds were healthy and the calf crop good. But lack of a winter snowpack also meant that the range was poorly watered come summer.

In the days of the buffalo, not so long past, when a vast herd had depleted a range, it simply migrated. The exact opposite happened in the Judith Basin in 1886. When the existing cattle were nubbing down the hillsides and creek beds, no effort was made to move them to new range or to market, for that matter. Thanks to the railroads and the recent bonanza of investment, the glut of cattle on the Chicago stockyards had driven the price of beef down, from $4.70 per hundredweight in 1883 to $3.90 in 1885. Stockmen preferred to hang on to their herds, hoping that prices would bounce back. Meanwhile, columns of lanky Texas longhorns continued to flow up the trail. In the summer of 1886, at least a hundred thousand additional head of cattle were pushed onto the Montana range, a good portion of them spreading across the Judith country. It was simply a case of not enough range to go around.[30]

Teddy Blue Abbott was riding for Granville Stuart's DHS outfit when the calf roundups began in June 1886:

> Our outfit branded at Fritz's Run corral about three miles from the ranch, and the girls would ride over to watch us. . . . [Y]ou would see damn fools like Teddy Blue and Perk Burnett wrestling calves and cutting ears, blood flying in every direction, down on the ground in the dusty old corral, with a white boiled shirt on, and twelve-dollar California pants. Light-gray ones, too. We were all hoping that when the branding was over, we'd get to ride home with one of the girls.

But the girls had to wait a long time, because with the range so heavily stocked, one roundup seemed to blur into another. Abbott reports that the DHS roundup started

> at the mouth of Elk creek on Flatwillow and the whole Moccasin roundup joined us. Besides, the A Bar sent a rep wagon from the Musselshell and reps from the Big Dry and other ranges. It sure made a

big lot of men and horses, wagons, etc. . . . We worked the Flatwillow and Maginnis range when the whole Judith Basin roundup showed up on Bear creek so we had three roundups working together. It was the most men I ever saw on one roundup. . . . The cow business was in its glory and the boys sure did wear good clothes and ride good horses.[31]

Little did they realize they were dressed for a funeral. On May 23, Judith rancher H. P. Brooks observed that "the land now is all desert. We had no rain this spring and there is little food for stock." Summer is always a dry season in Montana, but in July 1886, the territory received less than half its usual meager allotment of rainfall. August was better, but by then even a normal amount of moisture was too little too late. Fort Benton recorded a temperature of 110. Grasshoppers, whose eggs do best on dry ground, covered the bunchgrass with a cacophonous enthusiasm matched only by their appetite. An acre produced barely a quarter of the feed it had a decade earlier. Many of the cattle were in poor condition by first frost. The best hope was that winter would be mild again.[32]

The signs indicated otherwise. Lincoln Lang, a neighbor of Teddy Roosevelt, reported that the beaver were stockpiling "abnormal quantities" of saplings; that the bark on young cottonwoods was of "unusual thickness and toughness"; that native birds were oddly restive throughout the fall; and that the fur on wild animals was especially thick. In November, Teddy Blue Abbott spotted "the first white owls I have ever seen." The weather they portended was called *kissin-ey-way-o,* which is Cree for "it blows cold." In translation, at least, it was the understatement of the century.

The first front hit the third week of November. "[T]he banana crop is a failure," the Miles City newspaper announced waggishly on November 20. But soon no one was cracking wise. "When it began to snow softly one evening in November," Lincoln Lang wrote in his memoir,

we paid little attention to it, regarding it as the usual wet snow storm of late fall. But by night the temperature had dropped below zero, the wind had increased to a gale . . . the air [becoming] literally filled with dry, swift-driving ice dust, rather than snow, which, impelled by the frigid blast, finds every crevice, and coldly burns the skin where it strikes. It finds its way into your nostrils and thence to your lungs, rapidly chilling you through and paralyzing the senses to a point where you lose all sense of direction, where you begin to wander around helplessly in circles to become at length an easy victim of the Nemesis that is upon you.[33]

More storms followed in December. A foot and a half of snow fell between Thanksgiving and Christmas. What little hay ranchers had stored they fed to their horses. Meanwhile, cattle drifted from the stubbled and frozen high ground into the sheltered but drifted coulees, where there was no food but willows.

The first chinook arrived the second week of January. This warm southwesterly wind can raise the temperature sixty degrees in half a day. A January chinook is a drippy, roof-shaking halftime show to winter's siege; a March chinook is often the sign that spring is just around the corner. This particular chinook, however, had a tail that cracked like a whip. "The latter part of January it started a chinook — just enough to melt the snow on top," wrote Teddy Blue Abbott. "But it turned cold, and on February 3 and 4 the worst blizzard I ever saw set in. The snow crusted and it was hell without the heat."[34]

The chinook had succeeded only in sealing the ground with a layer of ice that cattle hooves could not penetrate. Henry Bierman, a freighter who was able to coax his team from Utica to the Musselshell in January, reported "the worst sight of a lifetime: cattle everywhere, bawling for feed. For three or four days they would go down the river, then turn and go up again, eating everything they could get hold of. . . . Dead cattle lay everywhere." H. P. Kennett stated on January 29 that his cattle were "now as poor as they are at the end of a hard winter & we do not know what is coming. . . . I do not think we can get out no matter how the weather clears away."[35]

The rest of the winter seemed like one long storm. The U.S. Signal Corps recorded twenty-five days of snow in February. On January 31 the temperature in the Judith Basin dropped to nearly 30 degrees below zero, and the mercury barely bobbed above zero until early March.

There was little that men could do. With neither fences nor feed, cattle set their own course. They wandered into towns, eating the tender plants in yards and seeking shelter from the wind behind houses. Many simply piled into the coulees and starved. Others turned their backs to the north wind and walked south; when spring finally came, ranchers studying the carcasses stacked along their drift fences identified brands of ranches hundreds of miles away. "The cowpunchers worked like slaves to [keep their herds] in the hills," Teddy Blue Abbott attested,

> but as all the outfits cut their forces down every winter, they were shorthanded. No one knows how they worked but themselves. They saved thousands of cattle. Think of riding all day in a blinding snowstorm, the temperature fifty and sixty below zero, and no dinner. You'd get one bunch of cattle up the hill and another one would be coming down through the deep snow that way; you'd have to fight every step of the road. The horses' feet were cut and bleeding from the heavy crust, and the cattle had their hair and hide wore off their legs to the knees and hocks. It was surely hell to see big four-year-old steers just able to stagger along.[36]

To keep from freezing to death himself, Abbott wore two pairs of wool socks, moccasins, overshoes, two suits of heavy underwear, pants, overalls, chaps, a heavy shirt, a blanket-lined coat, a sealskin cap, and mittens on top of gloves. Cowboys wore masks to protect their faces and blackened the skin under their eyes to prevent snow blindness. Sometimes they would stand in a bucket of water to form a protective shell of ice over their boots.

Even indoors they were none too cozy. A typical winter cow camp was a low-slung, cramped, windowless log cabin with a sod roof and open fireplace. Cow-camp diet was long on coffee, bacon, and bannock (unleavened bread cooked in a skillet); canned tomatoes and canned milk were luxuries that never lasted long. Cowboys slept in crude bunks; an outhouse was less important than a lean-to in which to stable their horses. In the depth of winter, daylight did not arrive till after 7; darkness fell by 5. The only light, Charlie's Rawhide Rawlins commented, "was coal-oil lamps or candles — sometimes [we] were forced to use a 'bitch,' which was a tin cup filled with bacon grease and a twisted rag wick."[37] A man spent most of his waking hours outdoors on horseback, fighting numbness and the futility of it all, with only lice and ripe cohorts to come home to.

But the hardest part of the hardest winter in memory was passing the bad news on to the owners, the capitalists ensconced in Helena, Fort Benton, Cheyenne, St. Louis, Omaha, New York, London, and Edinburgh. A cowboy, unaccustomed to paperwork, did not know where to begin when it came to describing the Big Die-up. Fact was, he could only guess at the losses.

Fact was, too, nobody really knew exactly how big the herds had been at the start of winter. The early 1880s had been "flood tide," John Clay remarked. Because it was difficult to count the actual livestock on the range, "book count" had to suffice. Range bosses were notorious for padding calf-crop sizes and underestimating winter losses as a way to explain dramatic herd growth to their superiors. The old joke among cowmen was that no matter how bad a winter might be, "The books won't freeze."[38]

Except this time they had. In the meanest days of the winter of 1886–87, when it became obvious that conditions had progressed far beyond severe, cowmen on the range began to calculate the carnage, quietly but honestly; guesses of a 10 percent loss increased to 40, then to 60, then 90. Then they entertained the unthinkable. No man knew exactly how many head of cattle he'd had in his herd, but whatever that number had been — fiction or fact — by February the thought loomed that every last beast might perish.

Charlie Russell spent some or most of that winter in the Judith Basin, holed up with Jesse Phelps, owner of *Breaking Camp*. (Ed Russell had returned to St. Louis the previous year.) Phelps's ranch, the OH, was on the south side of the Judith River, a mile or so east of Utica. Besides looking after his own stock, Phelps kept an eye on a herd belonging to Louis Stadler and Louis Kaufman, the Helena butchers. Like so many other successful Montana entrepreneurs, Stadler and Kaufman had jumped into the cattle business with great enthusiasm. Their herd was estimated at five thousand head, branded with a −R (Bar R) on the right hip.

The story of Charlie and the Bar R herd has long since become legend. One version of what transpired comes from Charlie himself. On August 6, 1926, less than three months before Charlie's death, someone sat him down at Lake McDonald and had him dictate the following to a stenographer:

The winter of '86 and '87 all men will remember. It was the hardest winter the open range ever saw. An awful lot of cattle died. The cattle would go in the brush and hump up and die there. They wasn't rustlers. A horse will paw and get grass, but a cow won't. Then the wolves fattened on the cattle. . . . Now, I was living at the OH Ranch that winter. There was several men there and among them was Jesse Phelps, the owner of the OH. One night, Jesse Phelps had got a letter from

Louie Kaufman, one of the biggest cattlemen in the country, who lived in Helena, and Louie wanted to know how the cattle was doing, and Jesse says to me: "I must write a letter to Louie and tell him how tough it is." I was sitting at the table with him and I said: "I'll make a sketch to go with it." So I made one, a small water color about the size of a postal card, and I said to Jesse: "Put that in your letter." He looked at it and said: "Hell, he don't need a letter; this will be enough."[39]

Without ceremony, Charlie had just dashed off the most famous painting of his career, on the bottom of a box of paper collars three inches tall, four and a half inches wide. He limited his palette to gray and black. He drew a single steer, Bar R branded on its right hip, standing shank-deep in the snow. The steer's horns are crooked and its eyes hollow. Its backbone and every rib are vivid black stripes. Its tail has been chewed to a nub, and the probable chewers, two gray wolves, lurk just at the corner of the sketch. For once, the horizon is indefinite; the forlorn steer stands lonesomely in a miasma of storm. The end cannot be far off.

As Charlie finished the watercolor, he wrote a title underneath, the glibness of which was like a rinse of vinegar over raw flesh. *Waiting for a Chinook,* he called it, and then in the lower left-hand corner he drew the outline of a buffalo skull and jotted his initials, CMR.

It is generally believed that the picture was sent with not even a sentence of explanation to accompany it — and with no indication, besides Charlie's initials, who had painted it. This seems farfetched. A cartoon — a slightly sarcastic one, at that — would have required at least a footnote of sober exegesis, though none survives today.

The most vivid corroboration of the incident comes from a letter written ten years later by Finch David, a cowboy whose family had arrived in the Judith about the same time as Charlie. David claims,

[I]t Was the latter part of Feb or early March of spring of 1887. Warmed up some. and I Was out looking for some of My Fathers cattle that had escaped from our pasture. and I called in on these Batchelors. . . . and as Was one of the first Warm days for Months All of them Was out in the door yard enjoying the Sunshine. I went in doors and Russell Was sitting at a table a drawing or painting. I walked up. and asked what are

you painting Russell. he Replerd. Saddler & Kauffman who oun the
—R Brand just Wrote doun to Jesse phelps asking how the winter Was.
and what was the probable loss of stock. Russell said. I am makeing
this picture for Jess to send to them. show them how things are. I tried
to look at the picture and Russell turned it a Way from Me and said.
I will soon Be done then you can look all you Want to. finely he Was
done and turned picture to Ward Me saying Now you can look. I did
look. and I laughed so hearty that the Men out doors hollered in saying what the joke. I said come in and see what Russell has done. they
came in and looked the picture over. and considered it a great joke . . .
on the old jews as We called them. . . . Russell held up the picture and
said I wont sent it to them. it is too Raw and I dont want to hurt their
feelings. . . . the oarther boys joined Me. And urged him to send it to
them. they told him same as I did, saying the old jews are good sports
and will just laugh.⁴⁰

Finch David may have been no more reliable than he was literate. But even
if it is hard to accept the firsthand particulars of his story as anything but
the vulgar and prejudiced elaboration of a Russell crony, there is something
about his account — the jocular atmosphere, particularly — that has the
ring of possibility. One thing is certain, however: Stadler and Kaufman did
not laugh when they saw the sketch.

Charlie vouched that when Louis Kaufman received the picture, "he got
drunk on the strength of the bad news."⁴¹ Kaufman and Stadler were not
the only investors drowning their sorrows that spring. The question was not
who got hurt, but how badly. Soon after receiving *Waiting for a Chinook,*
Kaufman began showing it to friends and business acquaintances around
Helena. Eventually somebody — no one knows who — added a second
caption to the little sketch: "Last of Five Thousand." Kaufman reckoned he
had lost his entire herd.

Actually, he had not. Enough survived so that Stadler and Kaufman survived, and they stayed in the cattle business for years to come. Others, however, were not so resilient. When a kind chinook finally did arrive in early
March, the worst fears were realized. In his memoir of his youth on the
northern plains, the novelist Wallace Stegner describes the first thaw after a
killing winter as "carrion spring," with its own smell: "not really rotten and
not coming from any particular direction, but sweetish, faintly sickening,

sourceless, filling the whole air the way a river's water can taste of weeds." But in the spring of 1887, the water in many creeks was undrinkable. Too many carcasses lay rotting; for anyone who stopped to think, it was an ironic reprise of the buffalo slaughters of ten years earlier. A conservative estimate of the cattle loss in 1887 is 210,000; a gloomier guess is 360,000, or 60 percent of all the cattle in Montana Territory.[42] The gallows gag went that some owners suffered losses as high as 125 percent.

Clearly the hardest hit were the herds of newly arrived Texas cattle. Longhorns, such as the steer in *Waiting for a Chinook,* were typically hardy, nearly feral animals, having survived on their own in the brush along the Mexican border. But the long walk from Texas had made these already lean beasts even leaner, and most were not prepared for a Montana winter of even moderate hardship. "Just to show the loss," wrote Teddy Blue Abbott,

> we had branded by actual count 10,000 DHS calves on the Flatwillow and Maginnis roundup in the spring and fall of '86; this meant, as we estimated, 40,000 cattle. On the spring roundup of '87 not 100 year-lings showed up, and on a rough count there were only 7,000 cattle all told, mostly steers and dry cows, and these were cattle raised on the Montana range. Double-wintered Texas steers in the Big Dry country [east of Judith Basin] got through in the best shape of any cattle in the state, but the loss on trail cattle that had just come into the country was 90 per cent.[43]

As the bad news poured in, and the rising stench tested the gorge of the knottiest cowboys, the steer in *Waiting for a Chinook* took on a synecdochic celebrity, the way a solitary poster child can speak for a whole famished subcontinent. Soon everyone in Helena had seen the little watercolor, and many more had heard it described. And nearly everyone knew the identity of its creator: the "cowboy artist," Charlie Russell. "Within twelve months past," declared the *Helena Weekly Herald* on May 26, 1887, "the fame of an amateur devotee of the brush and pencil has arisen in Montana, and nurtured by true genius within the confines of a cattle ranch, has burst its bounds and spread abroad over the Territory." Charlie not only had a calling, he now had a following as well.

5

CANADA AND BACK

THE PERIOD OF unlimited, free grass had lasted barely ten years. The need for winter feed and for fences to control herd movement and size, plus the encroachment of the farmer-homesteader, dictated a new approach to ranching. "A business that had been fascinating to me before, suddenly became distasteful," Granville Stuart wrote in his autobiography. "I wanted no more of it."[1] Neither did Teddy Roosevelt, who abandoned the Badlands to renew his political career in the East. A good many of the corporate speculators, especially the foreign ones, folded their tents as well.

Everything had been better before. That was the nub of it, from the cowboy perspective: the land had been more abundant, the game more bountiful, the water sweeter, the grass greener, the sky bluer. "Like all things that happen that's worth while," Rawhide Rawlins remarked, "it's a long time ago."[2]

Charlie Russell, who had been chasing a dream all his life, now had a rationale for not reaching it. His honey-coated hinterland had been buried — by the weather, by the plow, by time itself. Charlie perceived his new duty to be the sentimental documentarian of the Old West; he would bottle the past before it vaporized.

The year of 1887 was a productive year for him. *Waiting for a Chinook* had attracted the most attention, but it was by no means his best work. That winter, he had begun another commission for James Shelton of Utica. The painting, an oil two feet high and four feet wide, is now known as *Cowboy Camp During the Roundup*. The subject is the same as *Breaking Camp,* but even more encylopedic. Again Charlie's primary aim was to shoe-horn in as much minutiae as possible: the painted log buildings of Utica in the background; a stagecoach approaching from the east; twenty or so tents and roundup wagons filling the middle ground. All told, nearly fifty men and perhaps a hundred horses dot the rest of the canvas like ants in an ant farm. A dozen of these cowboys are recognizable, if not by their faces then by their chaps, hats, saddles, and "horse jewelry"; Charlie had produced a Who's Who of the Judith roundup. Even Jim Shelton can be seen standing in the doorway of his establishment, a wee speck in a white shirt.3

That summer, Charlie began showing some of his work in Helena. Jesse Phelps brought *Breaking Camp* to town and allowed it to be exhibited in Hundley & Preuitt's general store on Main Street. That same month, an-other store, Calkins & Featherly's, exhibited several new works: an oil show-ing the breaking up of an Indian camp; a watercolor of deer in a mountain landscape; and another watercolor of two Indians hunting antelope. Both of Helena's weeklies took an interest. The *Independent* commented:

> Russell has chosen a line of business that, with a little more training
> in his art, and with so wonderful a conception of the odd and peculiar
> glimpses of life in the west, places a fortune in his hands. Such pictures
> as he is painting and selling at $10 to $25, coupled with the story of his
> life, would create a rage in the east and his work would sell for figures
> that would astonish him.4

One person who saw a bargain in Charlie's work was T. W. Markley, a visitor from Washington. The *Herald* reported that Markley bought the antelope-hunting oil and that he was so enamored of Charlie that he offered to stake him to art school in Philadelphia.5 But Charlie's appeal was that he had not gone to art school. "Cowboy" excused his lack of polish as "artist," just as "artist" excused his lack of skill as "cowboy." Rarely was his art reviewed without some colorful details of his life on the range being woven in. His shortcomings were always forgiven. And the rumor never died that he was about to leave for Philadelphia or Paris or Italy or St. Louis to hone his considerable native genius by studying with the masters. He never did, of course, but it was a way for the locals to suggest that their man was only a lesson or two shy of joining the ranks of Michelangelo.

For all the encouragement, Charlie was still not ready to forsake the familiar, downscale life of the range. He passed most of the summer of 1887 night-wrangling in the Judith Basin and, according to one account, doing a little wolfing. Stockmen hated wolves; where once they lived in symbiosis with the buffalo herds, they now preyed on calves, lambs, and the weak fringes of a livestock herd. After 1886–87, the wolves were fat and emboldened. Ranchers retaliated by lacing dead cattle or sheep with strychnine, then waiting for the wolves to feed on the bait. That summer Charlie and a cohort named Billy Page camped awhile on Warm Spring Creek and worked at reducing the wolf population; that fall he joined the roundup once again.[6] It is not known whether he went home to St. Louis for Christmas, but by February 1888 he was in Helena.

Charlie had grown more devil-may-care as he began his ninth year in Montana, and the saloon became a second home. He had nicknames for booze — sheep dip, brave-maker, joy juice — and even after he had sworn off drinking later in life, he made no apologies for his years with the bottle. "Whiskey has been blamed for lots it didn't do," he averred, but in his case it did its share.[7] Many of his humorous yarns involved not just drinking, but heavy drinking, falling-down binges, and crippling hangovers. One tale especially, "Night Herd," first published in *More Rawhides,* has the ring of autobiography. A night wrangler — "I ain't givin' his name 'cause he's married, and married men don't like history too near home" — has been given the night off and heads for town.

It ain't long before my hoss is at the rack, and I've joined the joymakers. They're sure whooping her up, singin', and I get a little of that conversation fluid in me. I'm singin' so good I wonder why some concert hall in Butte don't hire me. The bartender is busy as a beaver — the piano player's singin' "Always Take Mother's Advice; She Knows What Is Best for Her Boy." And, of course, we're all doin' that. I've heard that song where a rattlesnake would be ashamed to meet his mother. But whiskey is the juice of beautiful sentiment.

A little while before I become unconscious, I'm shaking hands with a feller that I knowed for years but never knowed he had a twin brother. The last I remember, I'm crawling my horse at the rack. Then the lights go out. When I wake up I'm cold as a dead snake, and I'm laying on my belly in the middle of the herd.[8]

The real shock comes when he discovers that he has passed out in the town dump. The steers are "nothin' but stoves, tables, boxes," and Charlie's protagonist has "a taste in my mouth like I had supper with a coyote."

Was this just a bad night, or did Charlie — the wrangler with the coyote breath — have a problem? His friend John Barrows has suggested that Charlie "was nearly spoiled by his addiction to drink."9 This is impossible to substantiate, and even those who testify to Charlie's bingeing say he was never a difficult drunk, though he was apparently no gentleman after he'd had a few. Decades later, saloon regulars still chuckled as they recalled the wax model Charlie made for them of an Indian chief wearing a hat over his erection. And Charles Holmes, a cowboy who knew Charlie in his drinking years, described him fondly as one of the foulest-mouthed men he ever knew.10

Alcohol was merely the stimulant, however, and not the root of Charlie's licentiousness. Part of his profligacy stemmed from his urge to cultivate an image diametrically opposed to his St. Louis patrimony; an even bigger portion sprang from a fundamental passion for place and time, for life and art. Granville Stuart's wife, Allis, new Charlie through her nephew Bob Stuart, a boon companion of Charlie's in the 1880s and early '90s. Mrs. Stuart recalled:

[I]n those days they were both about as worthless as that sort of life made them. . . . [B]oth youngsters loved everybody and everybody loved them and though they both turned out fine men, they lived every minute of a twenty four hour day. Some of them are not stories of any Sunday School boys but there was never anything dishonest or disgraceful. They were just healthy young boys living the colorful life of their time, and enjoying every minute.11

Much of that enjoyment was found in the company of women whose virtue was negotiable. In Helena, where Charlie spent much of his time when not in the Judith, a demimonde of at least half a dozen sporting houses lined Wood Street, employing nearly a hundred girls in all. By 1887, the city fathers had tried to crack down on these establishments, only to have several of the more nimble madams open "variety theatres." At such places, men could sit with the "actresses" in curtained balcony boxes, buying drinks and whatever else while the entertainment proceeded onstage.12

Numerous customers have vouched that they noticed Charlie's drawings pinned to the walls of brothels, though the consensus is that they were presents to his favorite girls, rather than direct payments for services rendered. "Charlie's gifts to the girls," wrote nephew Austin Russell,

> were little pictures, brightly colored, even pictures of posies, red roses in full bloom and ferns and stuff, painted on big wooden sugar scoops and other inappropriate articles, all meant to hang up on the wall. . . . The ladies treasured them, as is proved by the fact that twenty years later, when I was living with Charlie, suddenly, without warning, there would appear a wooden shovel, platter, scoop, butter barrel or what not, each with its faded little picture, and each accompanied by a middle-aged intensely respectable woman — they all married in the end — who wanted Charlie to touch it up.[13]

The most famous of Helena's red-light emporia was the Coliseum Theatre, run by one of the West's most celebrated proprietors, Josephine "Chicago Jo" Hensley. A commemorative poem began: "There was music in Jo's hurdy-gurdy, / The polka and waltz in full swing; / Where with full bosomed girls of the dance hall / Gambler, miner, cowboy, and judge had their fling."[14] Indirectly, Chicago Jo was the spark that sent Charlie on his next great educational adventure.

In early 1888, Charlie was in Helena, enjoying a wastrel's winter. He batched in a shack with several other cowpunchers and painted from time to time. On Washington's Birthday, he and Phil Weinard, a cowboy and part-time vaudevillian, dressed as Indians and attended a masquerade ball. Weinard played a brave, Charlie his wife. "We took first prize for best costume, 1st prize for best sustained character," Weinard wrote fifty years later.

> I danced a war dance while Charlie beat on a tambourine. . . . We made such a hit I had the corner of my blanket filled with artificial flowers the ladies threw at us. When it came to giving us the prize some of the judges, thinking we were real Indians, hesitated saying a real Indian could not sustain an Indian character. As we had one prize I refused to take another. All sorts of people invited us to dinner and many wanted a photo.[15]

The photo that survives shows Weinard sitting on a stool, feathers in his hair, a rifle on his knee. Charlie is seated cross-legged in a dress with a mossy black wig on his head, looking more like a Hasty Pudding trouper than a Native American. Still, he enjoyed the role. In years to come, one of Charlie's favorite amusements was to dress in Indian getup — selected from his extensive collection — and act out Indian hunting scenes in the woods behind Bull Head Lodge.

In Helena, Phil Weinard was in the midst of another drama. He had fallen for Chicago Jo's niece Mary, who worked part-time as Jo's maid. Jo did not disapprove of the couple's intention to get married, but did object to Weinard's plan to take Mary away to a ranch in Canada. She was counting on them to help her run a new, improved (and legitimate) theater, scheduled to open the Fourth of July.

Weinard and his sweetheart could not wait, and enlisted Charlie as their accomplice in a roundabout plot. Weinard had been promised a job on a ranch near High River, Alberta, just across the Canadian line. Earlier in the winter, he had told Charlie he would take him along. Weinard would not go back on his promise — but first the elopement. The scaffolding for the new Coliseum apparently reached just under Weinard's window. "Charlie used to come about midnight," Weinard recalled, "to receive parcels of clothes . . . through my bedroom window, which Charlie would take home and deposit into a trunk I had there for the purpose. In this way I got most of my affiances clothes out of the house."

On May 16, they were ready to fly. Weinard and his girl had arranged to be married by the Episcopal minister at 7 A.M. sharp. Charlie was to be the best man. But he had spent the night at Auntie Fats, one of Helena's brothels, and awoke late with a hangover. Weinard was forced to enlist a hack driver as a stand-in. Once the vows were exchanged, he put his new wife on a train for Minneapolis, where she was to stay for several days before joining him in Alberta. Charlie finally surfaced later that morning. By noon they were in the saddle and headed north.

Much has been made of Charlie's trip to Canada. In the Russell gospel, it is the equivalent of a full-immersion baptism, validating him as a Western artist who had crossed over — not just to another country, but to another plane of awareness.

Charlie never claimed to have had a transcendental experience, but he did allow that he had gone native: "In 1888 I went to the Northwest Territory and stayed about six months with the Blood Indians. In the spring of 1889 I went back to the Judith, taking my old place wrangling." This statement, given to the *Butte Inter Mountain* in 1903, contains chronological errors. Charlie did not stay six months; in fact, he stayed half that time. And he did not stay through the winter of 1888–89; in fact, he left Canada in August of 1888.

The trip seemed like a good idea at the time. Charlie had just spent a lazy, boozy winter in Helena, with the prospect of returning to the Judith for another summer of night-wrangling on a depleted range. By contrast, the western plains of Canada were still sparsely settled and largely unfenced in 1888; most people were not even sure of the exact location of the international boundary. Clearly, too, Charlie saw the trip as an opportunity to learn more about Indians. Francis Parkman, whose *The Oregon Trail* (1847) Charlie had all but memorized, had sought out Indians to live with on his trip to the plains in 1846. Charlie's ambition was not much different. "My Indian study came from observation and by living with the Blackfeet in Alberta. . . . I don't know much about them even now, they are hard people to 'sabe.' "[16]

But the urge to understand the Indian was strong. By the mid-1880s, as soon as the American public was assured that its indigenous population had been suppressed, genocidal hatred gave way to a sudden wave of nostalgia for "the noble savage." A variety of well-meaning whites flocked to Indian homelands throughout the West, poking into lodges, taking down oral histories, and buying up "artifacts" — sometimes the only assets that stood between Indians and starvation. Museums and magazines took a keen interest. Ethnologist Frank Hamilton Cushing was the first to seriously appraise the material culture of the Southwest Indians, living among the Zuñi from 1879 to 1884. Historian George Bird Grinnell traveled the upper Missouri documenting Blackfeet life and values. Photographer Edward Curtis would soon begin his three-decade endeavor to catalog every tribe in North America. There were others to come, many of whom Russell would meet: Frank Bird Linderman, James Willard Schultz, Roland Reed.[17]

A new generation of artists had also discovered the American Indian. The first wave had been "explorers," who traveled as keepers of visual records on the first surveys of the Western unknown: George Catlin, Karl Bodmer, Alfred Jacob Miller, John Mix Stanley, Seth Eastman, Paul Kane, and even Alfred Bierstadt and Thomas Moran.[18] Now came a tamer flock, who embarked almost as tourists but returned as "experts" on the West and its natives. Joseph Henry Sharp, who would later befriend Charlie in Montana, made his first painting trip to New Mexico in the spring of 1883. George de Forest Brush traveled to Wyoming in 1884 to observe the Crow and subsequently published an article and illustrations in *Century*. He might as well have been studying specimens behind a glass:

> All that Rembrandt asked of the human figure was that it might exhibit light and shade; he never looked for pretty people, but found in this aspect of things a life-work. It is not necessary that an Indian learn to spell and make changes before we see that his long locks are beautiful as he rides against the prairie winds. . . . A really handsome squaw is rare, but there are more superb and symmetrical men among them than I have ever seen elsewhere, their beardless faces reminding one always of the antique. . . . It is when we detach them [Indians] from all thoughts of what we would have them be, and enjoy them as part of the landscape, that they fill us with lovely emotions.[19]

Charlie may have missed the Brush article, but was likely to have noticed several by Frederic Remington. In April 1887, *Harper's Weekly* had sent Remington to the Blackfoot reserve in Alberta.[20] His articles and illustrations appeared in the fall of 1887 and the winter of 1888. Perhaps inspired by — and somewhat jealous of — Remington's work, Charlie submitted his own Indian painting to *Harper's*. Much to his surprise, it was accepted.

Caught in the Act is a winter scene depicting the hard times of the previous year. A group of starving Crow have shot a range cow and are discovered by two cowboys while in the act of butchering the animal. The picture is clearly sympathetic to the plight of the Indians and is by far Charlie's most sophisticated work up to that point. Unlike his other panoramas of the period, this painting defines a precise narrative moment and conveys a palpable tension — dramatic and compositional — between the two parties. When *Caught in the Act* appeared in the May 12, 1888, issue of *Harper's* (Charlie's first piece in a national publication), its accompanying caption stated the obvious:

> The starving Indians, with their savage faces, are even more grim from hunger. The gaunt, sore-backed horses are humped by the cold. There

are the scurvy dogs that, wolf-like, are snarling as they scent the blood-drops in the snow. Mr. Russell has caught the exact dreariness of it all — the long stretches of the plain, that mournful aspect of a winter scene in Montana.

Meantime, Charlie rode off to Canada on his gelding Grey Eagle, leading Monte as a packhorse. Two other men accompanied Charlie and Weinard: B. J. "Long Green" Stillwell, a gambler whom Weinard describes as "a confederate attached to the theatre," and a cowpuncher friend of Charlie's who was going only as far as Great Falls. The three-hundred-mile trip to High River took Charlie, Weinard, and Stillwell nearly two weeks. When they could not find ferries across the swollen rivers of northwest Montana, they were obliged to swim their horses. The nadir of the trip came one morning when the men awoke to find that the corpse of an Indian child had fallen from its burial place in a cottonwood tree and landed squarely in their campsite.[21] The high point for Charlie was an encounter with a pair of Mounties who were escorting three captive Blood Indians, presumably horse thieves. Charlie painted the scene later that year, stressing the misery of the Indians and the rigidity of the Mounties.

The ranch where Weinard had a job was on Mosquito Creek, twenty-some miles outside High River. No jobs were waiting for Charlie and Stillwell, so they lived off Weinard, who found them a vacant log cabin to stay in at High River. "[N]either one had a dollar when we left Helena. I financed the whole trip," Weinard griped, "paid the duty on the horses, and left them blankets and camp outfit."[22]

From here on, the story takes on artificial flavoring. Blame Charlie for being vague, and downright misleading, about his doings and whereabouts in his own accounts of the time. Blame Nancy Russell, who, in her introduction to *Good Medicine,* Charlie's posthumous book of illustrated letters, suggested once again that Charlie had stayed in Canada through the winter of 1888–89. And blame the corps of mythmakers who have filled in the chronological gap with hokum they simply wished was true.

Purportedly, Charlie and Stillwell loafed around High River the summer of 1888, then split up in the fall, Stillwell heading back to Montana, Charlie to the Indians. Charlie's cabin was near five different Indian reserves: Stoney, Sarcee, Blackfoot, Piegan, and Blood.[23] One account has Charlie being invited by the Blood chief Black Eagle to join "the lodge of his red brothers" for the winter. Other versions give the Blood chief's name as Sleeping Thunder or Young Louse. One unreliable account claims that during his time with the Bloods, Charlie

> hunted with the men of the tribe, and listened by the fire of their lodges to the tales of war and hunting. . . . He learned their traditions and the meaning of the symbols and emblems they used on their dress ornaments. Charlie became, in fact, one of the tribe. He let his hair grow long and, because his cowboy outfit had worn out, adopted much of the Indians' garb. . . . Sleeping Thunder urged his friend to forsake the path of the white man and to marry one of the Indian women. This was no fantastic proposal, for there were many instances in the early days, of white men "goin' Injun."[24]

Charlie had his own version of his Canadian sojourn. Writing to fellow cowboy Charlie Joys in 1892, Charlie congratulated his friend on his recent marriage:

> I never expect to be that lucky. I expect if I ever get married it will be to [t]his kind [he had drawn a picture of a squaw wrapped in a Hudson's Bay blanket] as there is a grat many fo [of] them here and I seem to take well among them[.] I had a chance to marry Young louses daughter he is blackfoot Chief [.] It was the only chance I ever had to marry into good famley but I did not like the way my intended cooked dog and we broke off our engagment[.][25]

Historians should have smelled an obvious windy, if for no other reason than that the Blackfoot have never been dog-eaters. Charlie did know an Indian named Louse, however. Apsinkas, whose name means White Louse but who was called Louse or sometimes Ab, was a Blood who lived in his own camp, not on any reserve. He was a diehard; he dressed in traditional garb and still lived in a tepee. Charlie befriended him, and it seems likely that Apsinkas's family was the main focus of Charlie's "Indian study." It mattered that Apsinkas spoke some English, because Charlie spoke no Indian languages. Phil Weinard had begun teaching Charlie some sign language on the ride from Helena, but his vocabulary was still rudimentary, at best.

It mattered, too, that Apsinkas had a teenage daughter, whom Weinard has described as "a very handsome girl." Her name was Pokinaki, which translates as Small Long Woman. Weinard insisted that nothing serious happened between Charlie and the fair daughter, but others are not so sure.

"Goin' Injun" was something Charlie understood and, to some extent, approved of. Of course, his great-uncle William Bent had been a "squaw man," and Granville Stuart and many others he had met since coming to Montana had married Indians. The entire Métis culture that Charlie had come to appreciate was the result of mixed marriages. "Most folks don't bank much on squaw-men," Charlie wrote, "but I've seen some mighty good ones doubled up with Indians."

The prurient appeal of Indian women was something few in Charlie's crowd denied. Impoverished and starving, wives and daughters often were driven to selling their bodies to whites to stay alive. "Charlie was like most of the Cow Pokes," his friend Con Price attested. "[W]e all visited Squaw Camps and as white women were scarce a Pretty little Squaw looked good."[26] For all the credit Charlie has been given for his progressive sensitivity to Indians, it must also be remembered that Indian pornography was one of his trademarks. The only erotica of Charlie's that survives today — *Cowboy Bargaining for an Indian Girl, Joy of Life,* and *Anticipation/Exasperation* — are anatomically vivid paintings of cowboys procuring and mounting Indian women.

Yet libido and curiosity notwithstanding, it cannot be true that Charlie ever "lived" with the Bloods or married an Indian maiden. Perhaps he did enjoy a brief tryst, but there is evidence that art commanded a generous amount of his attention in Canada as well. The owner of the cabin in which Charlie and Long Green Stillwell were batching was an English rancher named Charles Blunt, who happened to be a hobby painter and generously provided Charlie with paints and canvas. Charlie painted *Canadian Mounted Police Bringing in Red Indian Prisoners* for Blunt. He also did a sketch of Apsinkas and several landscapes with wildlife.

After three months, Charlie and Stillwell decided they had had enough of Canada and its diversionary pleasures. The two had been living on charity, though they could have found work on a local hay crew. Weinard had given them a grizzly-bear skin, which kept them warm — until they sold it. For food, they hooked trout in the creek, but still "dam near starved to death," Stillwell recalled.[27] Another hardship was thirst: with the Northwest

Territories under prohibition, liquor was in scarce supply. In early August, Weinard stopped by the High River cabin, only to discover that Charlie and Long Green had pulled out. Charlie's token of thanks to their host was a series of sketches, including his portrait of Apsinkas, left tacked to the walls of the cabin.

By early September Charlie was back in Montana. The *Helena Weekly Herald* for September 27 reported:

> C.M. Russell, the cowboy artist, has returned to Helena after several months' absence on the range, where he no doubt secured subjects for more of his characteristic paintings. Mr. Russell, we understand, is seriously considering the propriety of going to Europe to perfect his talent in the noted art schools of the old world. . . . Under such cultivation, Mr. Russell's exceptional talents would doubtless bring their fortunate possessor name and fame as an artist.

If Charlie was contemplating European study, he did not follow through. He had taken his trip to a foreign land. After a stopover in Helena, he headed back to the Judith Basin and joined the fall roundup. The winter of 1888–89, when he was later thought to have been with the Bloods, he actually spent in St. Louis. Nellie Glasgow, a belle of one of the old downtown families, wrote in her diary on January 19, 1889, that she had gone to an affair at the home of Ann Clendennin and "saw 'the Club' there," including Sue Portis (Charlie's married sister), Bent Russell (who later married Ann Clendennin), and Charlie.[28] His summer of socializing with the Indians had not kept him from reentering the holiday whirl of his hometown.

Yet the winter had not been devoted wholly to tea dances, either. In March, Helena businessman Russell B. Harrison, son of President Benjamin Harrison and secretary of the Montana Stockgrowers Association, had purchased an interest in the popular national weekly *Frank Leslie's Illustrated Newspaper*.[29] Keen to have better coverage of Western topics, he apparently influenced the editors to take a look at Charlie's work, and on May 18, *Leslie's* published a series of drawings. The group was captioned "Ranch Life in the North-West — Bronco Ponies and Their Uses — How They Are Trained and Broken." In seven sequential sketches, cowboys hunt, capture, rope, saddle, and break a group of wild horses. Beneath Charlie's signature has been added the name of journeyman illustrator J. H. Smith. *Leslie's* had cleaned up Charlie's hand and made its own montage out of his work to fit the newspaper page, a small indignity compared with the value of the exposure.

Charlie continued to lean on other illustrators for tricks of the trade. Very rarely did he take an easel into the field or paint from a live model in the studio. Most of his art, for all its conscientious realism, came from his memory, his imagination, or, more often than he ever acknowledged, from looking at photographs and reproductions of other artists' work. In this last respect, no one loomed larger than Remington.

Today Remington and Russell are often regarded as the Tweedledum and Tweedledee of Western art. More accurately, though, they are opposite sides of the same coin. Frederic Sackrider Remington was born in 1861 in Canton, New York.[30] Like Charlie, he came from a well-to-do family and fought shy of a traditional career in business. Instead, he studied art at Yale. Taking a small inheritance, he went west, to Kansas, in 1881, and — another parallel — dabbled in sheep raising. He too took a liking to saloon life and became a heavy drinker. Eventually he returned east and threw himself into serious art studies, learning from such masters as William Merritt Chase, Kenyon Cox, and Alden Weir.

Remington's career as an illustrator took off after a series of his drawings on the military campaign against Geronimo appeared in *Harper's Weekly* in 1886. He was a hail-fellow-well-met in the clubs of New York; he had the advantage of Yale connections; plus, as the writer of many of the pieces he illustrated, he could invent, inflate, and promote his own persona. Though he never lived in the West after his short sojourn in Kansas and though his obesity — he was five-foot-nine, three-hundred-plus pounds — made it difficult for him to sit a horse, he held himself forth as a seasoned cowboy and Indian scout. "He draws what he knows, and knows what he draws," wrote *Harper's Weekly,* failing to add that Remington created most of his Western work in studios on the Hudson and St. Lawrence rivers.

Beginning in 1887, Remington's work was hard to miss. Dozens of illustrations appeared in *Outing* and *Youth's Companion,* in addition to *Harper's Weekly,* including the series on the Canadian Blackfoot. Teddy Roosevelt had specifically requested Remington as illustrator for *Ranch Life and the Hunting Trail,* Roosevelt's accounts of his adventures in the Badlands, which were first serialized in *Century* in 1888, then appeared in book form the same year. Remington's "Horses of the Plains" appeared in the January 1889 issue of *Century*.

Over the years, Charlie took "inspiration" from more than a dozen works by Remington. At some point in 1888, Charlie got hold of a copy of George William Sheldon's book *Recent Ideals of American Art,* which included an engraving of Remington's award-winning *Return of a Blackfoot War Party.* It is a winter scene in which a group of warriors exultantly approach their village, waving scalps, firing rifles, and towing two barefoot captives. That same year, Charlie painted *Going Into Camp,* which shows a line of Indians plodding single-file down a snowy trail. In content and composition, the similarities to Remington's piece are too great to be coincidental. The position of the lead rider's horse in each, the upraised quirt, the feather in the fur hat, the striped Hudson's Bay capote all bespeak the blatancy of Charlie's larceny.[31]

It is possible that Charlie undertook his version out of territorial spite. Who did Remington think he was, painting Charlie's Blackfeet? More to the point, who did Remington think he was, painting the West in such a savage light? There lay the grudge, and there lay the difference between the two. Over and over, Charlie would appropriate Remington's subject matter and designs down to the most minute cock of a rifle or snort of a pony. But he always injected a different mood and message. Remington was in many ways terrified by the West and its boundless physicality. Indians were depraved fiends; whites were always innocent victims or plucky heroes. Where Remington's Blackfeet were thugs dragging home hostages, Charlie's were a bedraggled but brave family struggling through a tough winter. Or when Remington painted a circle of horses fighting off wolves with their hooves, he succeeded in conveying only grisly violence; in Charlie's version, the put-upon horses are making a valiant stand to protect their helpless colts. To Remington, a rider turning in his saddle to shoot at his pursuers is *A Fugitive;* to Russell, a man in the same situation is an honest soul fleeing to safety. Where Remington assigns heartless cunning, Charlie sees a more honorable instinct. And though Remington had better command of color and was a superior draftsman, in his Western work at least he strove to communicate only militancy, danger, and dread. Charlie's untrained hand was forever guided by sympathy.

Unquestionably, Charlie owed a great debt to Remington — and not

1. Mary Mead Russell (*Britzman Collection, Taylor Museum, Colorado Springs Fine Arts Center*)

2. Charles Silas Russell (*Britzman Collection, Taylor Museum, Colorado Springs Fine Arts Center*)

3. Charlie, age three or four (*Collection of Ward Parker, St. Louis*)

4. Kid Russell (*Britzman
Collection, Taylor Museum,
Colorado Springs Fine Arts
Center*)

5. Judith roundup, CMR
seated third from left
(*Britzman Collection,
Taylor Museum, Colorado
Springs Fine Arts Center*)

6. With Phil Weinard, Helena, 1888 (*Britzman Collection,
Taylor Museum, Colorado Springs Fine Arts Center*)

7. Nancy Cooper Russell
(*Montana Historical Society*)

8. Charlie and Nancy, Lake McDonald (*Britzman Collection, Taylor
Museum, Colorado Springs Fine Arts Center*)

9.

10.

11.

13.

9. In the log-cabin studio, Great Falls (*Britzman Collection, Taylor Museum, Colorado Springs Fine Arts Center*)

10. Great Falls house and studio (*National Cowboy Hall of Fame and Western Heritage Center*)

11. Central Avenue, Great Falls, Park Hotel at right (*Montana Historical Society*)

12. Nancy at her desk, Great Falls (*Britzman Collection, Taylor Museum, Colorado Springs Fine Arts Center*)

13. Joe DeYong, sign-talking (*National Cowboy Hall of Fame and Western Heritage Center*)

14. Bull Head Lodge (*Britzman Collection, Taylor Museum, Colorado Springs Fine Arts Center*)

15. Charlie in Indian garb and greasepaint (*Montana Historical Society*)

16. With Sarcee Indians, Calgary Stampede, 1919 (*Montana Historical Society*)

17. With Jack Russell,
    Great Falls (*Britzman
    Collection, Taylor
    Museum, Colorado
    Springs Fine Arts Center*)

18. With Austin Russell, Lake McDonald (*Britzman
    Collection, Taylor Museum, Colorado Springs Fine Arts
    Center*)

19. With Will Rogers,
    Hollywood
    (*Britzman Collection,*
    Taylor Museum,
    Colorado Springs Fine
    Arts Center)

20. Trail's End, Pasadena
    (*Britzman Collection,*
    Taylor Museum,
    Colorado Springs Fine
    Arts Center)

21. Funeral procession,
    Great Falls (*Montana*
    Historical Society)

simply because of the Remington pieces he mimicked. More than any other artist of the nineteenth century, Remington spurred public interest in Western art. He helped create a market, and though counterfeit himself, he did establish authenticity — Charlie's strong suit — as a sine qua non for the fledgling genre.

IN THE SPRING of 1889, Charlie was back in the Judith to "subdue the erratic broncho and chase the nimble and elusive calf," in the words of one local paper.[32] But the pace of his life was quickening. He seemed to be drinking even harder, painting more intensely, and pulling up stakes more frequently.

At the end of the 1880s, more and more stockmen were pushing their herds farther north to get away from homesteaders and to take advantage of the better grazing between the Milk River and the Canadian border. Charlie followed the work, spending less time in the Judith country. From 1889 to 1893, he took roundup jobs in and around the Bear Paw Mountains, and others near the towns of Big Sandy and Chinook. He spent part of one winter back with Jake Hoover. Betweentimes, he drifted between Lewistown, Helena, Cascade, and Great Falls.

But even as his range was expanding, his hold on it felt precarious. In October 1889, Charlie's cousin Chiles Carr was thrown from his horse and killed. Despite his reputation as a ne'er-do-well, Carr had stuck it out on his Judith Basin ranch; he had commuted his homestead entry to a cash purchase in July, paying $200 for his 160-acre patent. Three months later he was dead. His horse may simply have stumbled in the dark; some speculated that Carr had been drunk. Whether a victim of bad luck or bad judgment, Chiles Carr probably had not lived life that much differently from his artist cousin.[33]

Charlie went home to St. Louis again that Christmas, where Carr's tragedy was quickly overshadowed by a more pressing worry. All through the holiday, Charlie's youngest brother, Wolfert, lay ill with typhoid. Finally, on December 29, six days shy of his nineteenth birthday, Wolfert was dead as well.

First Jim Fulkerson, then Chiles Carr, and now a brother. Youth was no guarantee of life. Two years later the message would be impressed on Charlie's soul one more time. His closest brother, Ed, after spending part of

1885 and 1886 in Montana, had tried prospecting in Nevada. Finally tired of gallivanting, he had settled down in St. Louis, taken a position at Parker-Russell, and announced his engagement to a local girl. The wedding was not to be. In May 1891, he caught pneumonia and never recovered. He was twenty-four years old. Despite the cumulative shock of losing two brothers and two cousins, Charlie rarely mentioned them.

It was as if he had transferred his notions of life and loss to a broader, more metaphoric plane. By the end of the 1880s, his favorite artistic subjects were set: cowboys riding cantankerous horses with various degrees of success and mishap; cowboys roping wild animals, not limited to cattle, with various degrees of success and mishap; buffalo (sometimes hunted by Indians, sometimes migrating peacefully); Indians in a bunch studying the horizon (looking for other Indians, buffalo, white men's latest intrusion); Indian domestic life (breaking camp, doing chores, debating, courting, grooming, teaching). He painted these over and over, often with only slight variation, and not just to lean on a compositional crutch. These images were like melodies; he knew them by heart, just as he had memorized the landmarks he put in so many paintings: the Missouri River near Fort Benton, the Judith Basin, and Square Butte, south of Great Falls. He could always fall back on a buffalo hunt (he did nearly fifty) or perhaps another group of Indians approaching a wagon train, a steamboat, railroad tracks, prospectors. In 1890, Charlie's most prolific year as a painter thus far, he completed *Bronco Buster, Roping a Wolf, The Buffalo Runners, Wild Meat for Wild Men* (another buffalo hunt), *The Silk Robe* (squaws treating a buffalo hide), and *Indians Hailing Immigrants.*

The other significant event of 1890 was the publication of *Studies of Western Life,* an inspiration of Ben Roberts, a saddlemaker friend of Charlie's in Helena. Roberts's shop was just across from Stadler and Kaufman's butchery. A year or so after Louis Kaufman had tired of showing *Waiting for a Chinook* to friends, he gave it to Roberts, who displayed it on his wall, where it remained, collecting fingerprints and grime, for the next twenty-five years.34 Roberts (who was never a very successful saddlemaker) got the idea to have it reproduced and eventually was printing *Waiting for a Chinook* postcards by the thousand.

Roberts's next brainstorm was to sell a booklet of a dozen Russell illustrations: *Cowboy Sport* (wolf roping), *Hands Up* (stagecoach robbers), *Close Quarters* (two whites attacked by Indians), *The American Buffalo, The Horse*

Wrangler, Bronco Busting, and several other cowboy and Indian scenes. Printed in Brooklyn and copyrighted by Roberts, *Studies of Western Life* was an attempt to cash in on Charlie's rising fame as the Cowboy Artist and the general public's steadily mounting interest in the Wild West. On the cover is a reproduction of *Waiting for a Chinook* along with the rakish 1883 photo of Charlie wearing buckskin, woolly chaps, and a six-gun. Inside, though, the Roberts-Russell collaboration (even with a text by Granville Stuart in a later edition) lacked the zip of a good dime novel, and there is no evidence that Charlie ever made any money on the project. If nothing else, he had shown a willingness to let others promote his personality as a way to promote his art.

For Charlie was reluctant to push his career himself. In April 1891, the magazine *Nature's Realm* called him "[o]ne of the best animal painters in the world," but lamented that he "prefers to round up a herd of cattle or cut out a steer, rather than paint. Only his absolutely leisure moments are employed in this occupation. It is a pity that one so gifted and enjoying such exceptional opportunities . . . should not be willing to place himself in the way of securing a world-wide reputation."[35]

Charlie defended his recalcitrance. "I have tirde [tried] several times to make a living painting but could not make it stick and had to go back to the range," he wrote to a friend. "I expect I will have to ride till the end of my days but I would rather be a poor cow puncher than a poor artist."[36]

He seemed actually to enjoy being poor. In February 1891 he had been commissioned to decorate the vault door of the Bank of Fergus County in Lewistown. Wilford Johnson, who later managed a rival bank in the same town, recalled: "Charley was in Lewistown, trying to get through a hard winter. He was broke, had been drinking rather heavily and was desperately hard up. He tried to borrow some money in the bank and was turned down. Then, either he or the banker conceived of the idea of his putting an adornment on the two iron doors." It took Charlie six hours to paint a cowboy watching over a grazing herd. According to legend, he promptly gave his $25 fee to a fellow cowpuncher who needed it to buy new boots.[37]

In times of poverty Charlie knew he could lean on Ben Roberts. After Roberts had married and settled in the town of Cascade, Charlie was welcome to sleep and paint in the shack behind Roberts's house. It was here that Charlie drew a pair of pictures, now called *Contrast in Artist's Salons.* In the first he shows himself in the Cascade shack, dressed in boots and

Métis sash. He sits on a crate before a tiny easel, painting a picture of a man on horseback. His paint box and saddle are strewn on the floor; an Indian, wrapped in a blanket and holding a long pipe, watches in wonderment as Charlie leans toward the canvas. The second drawing is subtitled *My Studio as Mother Thought*. It shows a priggish artist in cravat, quilted smoking jacket, and handlebar mustache. His studio is decorated with a Victorian lamp and Japanese parasol. The painting on his easel is of a shapely Egyptian woman with an urn balanced on her head. In place of an Indian observer, a lady in high collar, billowy sleeves, and feathered hat sits on a fancy divan, coyly observing the artist's handiwork.

By juxtaposing the two scenes — one a jolly self-portrait, the other a sharp parody — Charlie was signaling how far he had come since leaving home. While his art might not please anyone beyond a few natives, it was what he enjoyed doing. The temptation to adopt local vernacular to win local acceptance had been impossible to resist, observed friend John Barrows. "In Charlie's case he made virtue of necessity."[38]

In the fall of 1891 Russell received a professional proposition from "Pretty Charlie" Green, a bartender at the Brunswick saloon in Great Falls. Green presented him with a contract "as long as a stake rope," Russell recalled. Green would pay him "$75 a month and grub," nearly twice the average wage of a cowboy. In return, Russell had to paint from six in the morning until six at night, the proceeds from all sales going to Pretty Charlie. He gave the deal a try, but soon threw in the towel. "I argued that there was some difference in painting and sawing wood," he said, "so we split up and I went to work for myself."[39]

For Russell, the winter of 1892–93 was a repetition and exaggeration of all the winters that had gone before. His pockets were predictably empty. He had sold some paintings in Great Falls, but while one newspaper article reported that the pictures had "brought ready customers before the paint was dry," he rarely got more than $15 to $25 apiece. By the time he and six of his fellow cowboys had settled into a cabin in Chinook, they had only $175 to last the winter. They called themselves the Hungry Seven.[40]

It was an extreme time — drinking, whoring, stealing chickens, pleading for credit. Charlie had always been a popular person to winter with, as he usually had some trickle of income (from art and perhaps the occasional package from St. Louis) and an unwavering willingness to share. At one point, the Hungry Seven took an entrepreneurial notion to open a saloon, except they managed to give away whatever spirits they did not consume themselves. "[M]y booze parlor dident last long, fourteen days I think," Charlie recollected in a letter many years later. "[I]t was like the life of a butter fly short but [a] verry merry one."[41]

Maybe it was the booze or the missed meals or the drafty, lice-infested winter shacks. Or maybe Charlie was feeling old and anxious. Whatever the cause, his jovial personality was beginning to show a sharp edge. He and his cohorts took to hanging around the Chinook train depot. The cowboys would play practical jokes — mostly harmless — on the newly arrived homesteaders, drummers, and dudes as they stepped onto the platform.[42] They would warn of renegade Indians nearby or simply rattle the "honyockers," "scissorbills," "nesters," and "pumpkin rollers" with their hostile glances. The aim was always to make the greenhorns squirm.

The population of Montana had nearly quadrupled since Charlie had arrived in 1880, many of the newcomers drawn by the promotions of the Northern Pacific and its recently completed competitor, the Great Northern Railway. Charlie's resentment toward the bib overalls and bow ties increased proportionately. Foreigners were the easiest targets, and no group was considered more incongruous than the Chinese.

In 1893, Charlie completed a pair of painted wax models, *The Poker Game* and *Not a Chinaman's Chance,* inspired by Bret Harte's immensely popular poem "Plain Language from Truthful James" (1870), otherwise known as "The Heathen Chinee." The poem is about a cardsharp named Ah Sin; its most memorable stanza admonishes "That for ways that are dark / And for tricks that are vain, / The heathen Chinee is peculiar." In the first of Charlie's two models, a cowboy, an Indian, and a Chinese are seated on the ground playing cards. From the upturned cards and the looks on the faces, it is apparent that the Chinese is winning and the two losers think they've been cheated. In the second model, the cowboy has his six-gun stuck in the Chinese's ribs; the Chinese has his hands up, and his eyes are bugged out in distress; the Indian leans toward the cowboy in a gesture of approval.

The alliance forged between cowboy and Indian in the models is telling. Charlie never sugarcoated the role cowboys had played in displacing Indians ("They've been living in heaven for a thousand years, and we took it away from 'em for forty dollars a month").[43] But as more and more settlers poured into Montana, he painted fewer scenes of open combat between whites and natives. To his way of thinking, the open-range cowpuncher was fast becoming an endangered species, just as the buffalo-chasing Indian had felt the pinch of civilization a generation earlier. Charlie elaborated in a letter thanking Teddy Blue Abbott for a photo Abbott had sent of himself:

> [W]henever I look at the picture my memory will drift back over trails long since plowed under by the nester to days when a pair of horse ranglers sat in the shaddoes of thair horses and wached the grasing bunches of cyuses. . . . I remember one day we were looking at a buffalo carcus and you said Russ I wish I was a Sioux Indian a hundred years ago and I said me to Ted thairs a pair of us[.] I have often made that wish since and if the buffalo would come back tomorrow I wouldent be slow shedding a brich clout [breechcloth] and youd trade that . . . ranch for a buffalo hoss and a pair ear rings[. L]ike many I know, your all Injun under the hide and its a sinch you wouldent get home sick in a skin lodge[.] Old Ma Nature was kind to her red children and the old time cow puncher was her adopted son.[44]

Even so, the time had come for the son to leave the fold. When the beef roundup was over in the fall of 1893, Charlie climbed aboard a stock train headed for the slaughterhouses of Chicago. His job was to walk along the tops of the cattle cars with a long "punch pole," prodding cattle to keep them from lying down or trampling one another. This trip was the last time Charlie ever tended a herd; or, as he told the *Butte Inter Mountain,* he "never sung to them since."

Strangely, though, in later years, whenever Charlie alluded to his trip to Chicago he never mentioned his real purpose for going. The train ride was indeed a turning point, and not just because of the life he was putting behind him. Charlie was going to the Columbian Exposition — the Chicago World's Fair — a grand celebration of Columbus's discovery of America and a cocky assertion of the country's achievements since 1492. In among the thousands of exhibits were three of Charlie's paintings. Once again, Charlie had been granted a small part in one of the great pageants of his time. America would never be quite the same after the fair, and neither would its Cowboy Artist.

6

THE WHITE CITY

CHARLIE HAD TO have known all about the World's Fair long before his train pulled into Chicago's Union Stockyards in late September of 1893. Since the fair's opening in May, more than 10 million people, from European royalty to Midwestern farmers, had visited Chicago, and journalists had spent many more millions of words in their overreaching bids to describe and critique the seven hundred acres of lagoons, promenades, and exhibition halls. The Columbian Exposition was the biggest extravaganza of its kind ever, anywhere.

"I remember that morning well," Charlie later wrote of his arrival in Chicago. "I was armed with a punch pole[,] a stock car under me loded with grass eaters. I came from the big out doores and the light smoke and smell made me lonsum." He did not say how long he stayed at the fair or which exhibitions he saw. In a Rawhide Rawlins story inspired by the 1893 trip, he mentions, "The minute I hit the burg, I shed my cow garments an' get into white man's harness. A hard hat, boiled shirt, laced shoes — all the gearin' known to civilized man."[1] These, however, are the only details he lets slip.

Perhaps Charlie spent the time in a drunken fog, as was the case with Rawhide Rawlins's trip to Chicago: ". . . I was unconscious, an' wasn't in shape to remember. . . . [W]hen I come to, my hair's sore an' I didn't know the days of the week, month or what year it was." Or perhaps the fair was just another one of the many interludes that did not fit into his increasingly public, determinedly un-citified persona.

Four hundred years after Columbus, Chicago had spared nothing in vaunting its own arrival as the new plexus of a modern, muscular republic.[2] At the suggestion of Frederick Law Olmsted, the designer of New York's Central Park, city fathers had turned a South Side mudflat into an agora of neoclassical excess. A swamp became a stately lagoon, with Venetian gondolas coursing its radiant canals. The Court of Honor, as the fair's central buildings were named, was a confectioner's dream of Beaux Arts domes, arches, colonnades, courtyards, and statuary. Indeed, the edifices were quite nearly confection, made not out of marble but a concoction of plaster of Paris, jute, and cement. The entire complex was painted white to suggest a utopian purity and quickly took the name "the White City."

Nearly four hundred more structures sprawled outward from the Court, all showcasing the latest advancements of discipline or region. There were buildings for Manufactures, Agriculture, Electricity, Mines, Art, Liberal Arts, Transportation, and Fisheries. Machinery Hall alone covered seventeen acres and claimed to be the largest structure on earth. There was a women's pavilion, and each state had its own building, as well as its own "day" at the fair. The Midway Plaisance was a riot of cultural folkways and architectural styles, including a Chinese bazaar, a Moorish palace, a tropical village, Smithsonian-style displays of craftwork, and the sideshow tent of the dancer Little Egypt, whose special skill aroused keen anthropological interest, particularly among male visitors. The fair's restaurants could feed seventeen thousand people at one sitting. As Paris had topped off its exposition of 1885 with the Eiffel Tower, Chicago erected the first-ever Ferris wheel — 260 feet tall, holding sixty people in each of its thirty-six cars.

Many visitors did not know where to begin, then ended up by rushing from hall to hall in a mad attempt to gulp in everything. Hamlin Garland, who would become America's celebrated son of the Middle Border, pushed his mother through the grounds in a wheelchair:

> Stunned by the majesty of the vision, my mother sat in her chair, visioning it all yet comprehending little of its meaning. Her life had been spent among homely small things, and these gorgeous things dazzled her, overwhelmed her, letting in upon her in one mighty flood a thousand stupefying suggestions of the art and history and poetry of the world. . . . At last utterly overcome she leaned her head against my arm, closed her eyes and said, "Take me home. I can't stand any more of it."[3]

One can imagine Charlie similarly befuddled by the latest inventions, just as one can picture him in a convenient beer garden, poking fun at the gimcrackery and winning friends with his clever Western know-nothingism. On some level, though, he was proud of his small part in the show.

The Montana pavilion was a one-story Romanesque building that bragged of the state's mineral opulence while honoring its frontier spirit. The state motto, "Oro y Plata" (Gold and Silver), was inscribed in large letters to the left of the main entrance. A huge sculpted bull elk stood atop the arched vestibule. Inside, the central rotunda was "decorated with the heads of buffalo, elk, bear, and other animals indigenous to the state," reported *The Book of the Fair*. Amid the taxidermy and various displays of fruits, "feminine handiwork," and mining might, a variety of artwork told the story of Montana. "Among the paintings most admired," the guidebook stated, "Russell, 'the cow-boy artist,' entirely self-taught, has several subjects selected from incidents of his life, [such] as 'The Bucking Broncho,' 'The Buffalo Hunt,' and 'The Indian Tepee.' "[4]

Charlie was in distinguished company. Everywhere he turned he saw more art — at least a thousand pieces by masters from around the world. Grand sculptures decorated the grounds, the grandest being Daniel Chester French's *The Republic,* which stood in the formal central basin of the Court of Honor. In the galleries, Charlie got his first glimpse of Japanese art, which had become all the rage in East Coast circles since the Centennial Exhibition seventeen years earlier. He also had a chance to study European masters, including Rembrandt, Vermeer, and Velázquez. He undoubtedly took a close look at the several hundred works by his fellow Americans.

American art had changed significantly since the time of Carl Wimar. In the Düsseldorf days, painting and sculpture had employed "literal imitation." At their most ambitious, they celebrated "nobler actions, elevating ideas, inspiring sights."[5] Hence the grandiose landscapes of Frederick Edwin Church and Alfred Bierstadt and the romantic narratives of Wimar and Emanuel Leutze. But by the 1890s, grandeur and fussy documentation were giving way to forces of immediacy. "Hitherto historical painting has been considered the highest branch of art; but, after all, see what a misnomer it was," wrote the American artist Childe Hassam in 1892. "The painter was always depicting the manners, customs, dress and life of an epoch of which he knew nothing."[6]

The new ideal was Impressionism, imported from Europe. It elevated the commonplace and played down obsessive detail and heroic sweep; it was about light and mood, a day at the beach, a rainy avenue, and it was fully in evidence at the World's Fair. In Chicago, the author of *The Book of the Fair* complained, "we search in vain for anything that reminds us of the stirring episodes of our national history." Instead, the fair had been crashed by Mary Cassatt's mural *Modern Woman;* fresh portraiture by William Merritt Chase; eleven canvases by Thomas Eakins, including two surgical scenes, *The Agnew Clinic* and *The Gross Clinic;* six paintings and fifty-nine etchings by James McNeill Whistler; fifteen oils by Winslow Homer, including *The Gale;* plus emotion-filled efforts by the rest of the new American peerage: Hassam, George Inness, John Henry Twachtman, Alden Weir, and John Singer Sargent.

Charlie knew how to seize the moment in his own art, but he still considered himself in the old school: accuracy, detail, and action took precedence over the frivolousness of art for art's sake. His taste ran toward Henry Bush-Brown's immense plaster *The Buffalo Hunt,* though the piece, given prominent display at the fair, doubtless drew Charlie's niggling criticism as well. In 1889 Bush-Brown had been so fastidious as to import a buffalo, an Indian pony, and a Blackfeet model to his upstate New York farm to pose for the piece.[7] The completed work was dramatic and magnificent in every respect — except that as the buffalo charges under the rearing pony, the Indian prepares to drive an arrow into the animal's left side. Charlie would have been quick to inform passersby that, for reasons of balance and maximum effectiveness, a right-handed buffalo hunter always shoots into the right side of his prey.

With equally critical scrutiny, Charlie studied the Western scenes of Henry Farny, De Cost Smith, Worthington Whittredge, George de Forest Brush, and Frederic Remington — all of them Easterners, all of them thriving in a genre he claimed as his own. Even if he did not like everything he saw, he now knew what he was up against.

TWO OTHER ASPECTS of the Columbian Exposition would go a long way toward defining Charlie Russell's world. One was a speech that few people heard; the other was an event that was not allowed on the fairgrounds at all.

Under the slogan "Not Matter, But Mind; Not Things, But Men," fair organizers had planned a rambling colloquium, with conferences and lectures scheduled throughout the six months of the exposition. One of the speakers was a hardworking Wisconsin scholar by the name of Frederick Jackson Turner. The paper he presented the night of July 12 (well before Charlie's arrival in Chicago) was titled "The Significance of the Frontier in American History."[8]

Turner, in effect, was intellectualizing many of the things Charlie had been expressing in his art. Both men equated frontier with freedom. And they both felt that the disappearance of "free" Western land was somehow un-American. Turner had based his speech on a four-page government pamphlet, *Extra Census Bulletin No. 2; Distribution of Population According to Density: 1890*. Along with a map indicating different population densities across the United States, the pamphlet included the statement: "Up to and including 1890 the country had a frontier of settlement, but at present the unsettled area has been so broken into by isolated bodies of settlement that there can hardly be said to be a frontier line." This would be the linchpin of Turner's thesis and one of the most repeated lines in American history.

Turner posited a democratic "germ," with the frontier as the petri dish in which the Jeffersonian model of democracy thrived and evolved. "American social development has been continually beginning over again on the frontier," he wrote. "This perennial rebirth, this fluidity of American life, this expansion westward with its new opportunities, its continuous touch with the simplicity of primitive society, furnish the forces dominating American character."

But the whole process by which the frontier fomented democracy hinged on one condition: free land. Without it, Turner declared, there would be no impulse to go west; without it, the Jeffersonian model might implode. If in "the crucible of the frontier the immigrants were Americanized, liberated, and fused into a mixed race," then what sort of unruly polyglot would America become now that the immigrants, though homesteading, were swallowing the remaining free land and obliterating the "line" of frontier? If the germ of democracy could not reproduce, would the American character turn cannibalistic, decadent, rancid?

Turner did not venture a guess in his lecture, choosing instead to finish on a neutral note. "And now," he said to his audience, "four centuries from the discovery of America, at the end of a hundred years of life under the Constitution, the frontier has gone, and with its going has closed the first period of American history."

Few people took notice of the speech, since Turner's remarks offered none of the dazzle that emanated from the fair's other diversions. Not till months later, when the speech was published by the State Historical Society of Wisconsin, did the significance of "Significance" begin to emerge. Theodore Roosevelt took it to heart, and other scholars and statesmen followed. Although some of them picked at Turner's premise of a frontier "line," they all acknowledged that he was onto something important. The lecture soon became a central document of the zeitgeist. Without a frontier, the republic was now on shaky ground. While closing a chapter in American history, Turner had opened a brand-new one as well.

Several blocks down the street from Turner's lecture hall, outside the fairgrounds proper, William F. "Buffalo Bill" Cody was putting his own spin on Western history.[9] Unlike Turner's speech, the daily performances of Cody's "Wild West Show" were extremely well attended. Cody's version of evolution was more compelling. His troupe of sharpshooters, cowboys, and Indians reenacted "Epochs" (which, according to Cody, had "their existence in fact"), beginning with Indians meeting pilgrims, then a buffalo hunt and attacks on settlers, and finally a bombastic reprise of Custer's Last Stand.

Buffalo Bill had ridden for the Pony Express, fought in the Civil War, driven a stagecoach, and hunted for the Kansas Pacific Railroad. It was in this last job that he earned his nickname: he boasted that he had once slain 4,280 buffalo over an eighteen-month period. In 1869 he was installed as a latter-day Leatherstocking by Ned Buntline in the dime novel *Buffalo Bill, The King of Border Men!* In 1871, his fame grew even more when he guided General Philip Sheridan, General George Armstrong Custer, and Grand Duke Alexis of Russia on a gentlemen's buffalo hunt. That same year, Cody appeared (as himself) in his first stage performance. But the event that launched him into superstardom was the battle of the Little Bighorn.

Shortly after hearing of Custer's demise, Cody went west, vowing revenge. Soon he was back in the theater, reenacting the encounter in which he allegedly had taken "The First Scalp for Custer." In 1882, when Cody began his Wild West shows, he played the role of Custer's stand-in. He even looked a bit like the fallen hero, down to the buckskins, long locks, and signature flourish of whiskers under his lower lip. The grand finale to Cody's program was the battle of Little Bighorn. For a couple of years, he even recruited Custer's nemesis, Sitting Bull, as a participant — proof that Cody's depiction was honest, authentic, living history.

Charlie Russell, like so many Americans of his generation, had subscribed to the Buffalo Bill myth since early childhood. Chicago was his first chance to see the golden-maned hero in person, and he would not have passed it up. Nor would it be his last encounter with Buffalo Bill. On a trip to New York in 1907, Charlie finally got to make the acquaintance of the aging performer. "I was down at Madison Square gardon the other day an met Cody," Charlie wrote home. "[H]e's lost most of his hair . . . but his back locks are still long. [T]he show was good real cowboys an Indians."[10] Charlie's close encounter did not diminish his esteem. Two of his liveliest paintings in later years were *Running Buffalo*, also known as *Buffalo Bill and Grand Duke Alexis Hunting Buffalo* (1918), and *Buffalo Bill's Duel with Yellowhand* (1917).

WHEN ALL WAS said and done, it was evident that Charlie had acquired a new set of bearings in Chicago. He had witnessed the power of art, the state of the nation, and the history of the West, and he sensed how they all came together. If he had still been considering more seasons as a dollar-a-day wrangler, he abandoned that idea now. Before heading back to Montana, he made another trip home to St. Louis. While there, according to some accounts, he received a significant commission from local steel magnate William F. Niedringhaus.[11] It is likely that the Parker-Russell Mining and Manufacturing Company supplied firebrick for the Niedringhaus furnaces, and certainly the two families knew each other socially. The Niedringhauses had jumped on the cattle craze in the 1880s and established the N Bar N ranch in Montana, where Charlie had worked for at least one season.

So the Russell-Niedringhaus link was indeed strong, and it may well be true that William Niedringhaus asked Charlie for some paintings. But the assertion by some that the commission was a turning point in Charlie's career — that it was the boost that persuaded him to pursue art full time — does not quite wash. For one thing, most of the paintings that wound up in Niedringhaus's collection were not completed until 1896, two years after their purported commission. Upon Charlie's return to Montana later that fall, he probably worked on several pieces for Niedringhaus, but it seems unlikely that this patronage was a critical springboard. It may have been one factor, but his experience at the Columbian Exposition had already opened his eyes to his potential as a professional artist.

Back in Montana, he set to scratching out an existence with his brushes. He drifted between Helena, Great Falls, and Cascade. In the fall, he had an exhibit in the window of the C. K. Wells bookstore in Helena. In Great Falls, saloonkeepers Bill Rance of the Silver Dollar and Albert Trigg of the Brunswick were good for a place to sleep and work. Trigg, an erudite Englishman, even acted as an agent of sorts for Charlie's work. When in Cascade, Charlie batched with old cowboy crony Con Price and could count on a meal with Ben Roberts and family. The local justice of the peace offered his courtroom as an occasional studio.[12]

But even while Charlie tried to throw himself into his work and friends, he could not shake the feeling that he had lost his footing. He turned thirty in the spring of 1894, and his own fear of growing up and growing old seemed to be echoed wherever he looked. Despite the dazzle of the Chicago fair, deep in the American gut was a sense that the nation's course, however inspiring in its ambition and achievement, was somehow out of control. Charlie felt it as acutely as anyone, and bluntly or obliquely, the message informed everything he did thenceforth.

Every quick step forward seemed to be a chance for the nation to stumble. The 1890s saw the arrival of skyscrapers, elevators, motion pictures, and a hundred new financial behemoths called (not sarcastically) "trusts." But in the Panic of 1893, more than six hundred banks failed, great railroads went bankrupt, and an army of the nation's unemployed marched on Washington. Americans were flocking to cities, which provided the amenities of electricity, restaurants, and vaudeville. But cities also meant graft, prostitution, tenements, and a contagion of atrophy that rendered Americans decadent and soft.

In the Gay Nineties, pessimism was as fashionable as bicycles, ragtime, and straw hats; prejudice kept pace with the rising population.[13] Up until 1890, the vast majority of new Americans hailed from northern or western Europe, but in the 1890s, the demographics of immigration shifted radically: suddenly the wave was from the Austro-Hungarian Empire of southeastern Europe ("bohunks"), or they were Italians, Poles, Greeks, Syrians, Chinese, and Russian Jews. These "depraved dregs" and "alien breeds,"[14] as they were called in jingoistic circles, were blamed for such events as the Haymarket riot of 1886, the Mafia riots of 1891, the Homestead and Coeur d'Alene strikes of 1892, the Pullman strike of 1894, and the general corruption and dilution of American stock.

Looking for a new hero, preferably a throwback, the nation settled on the cowboy. Theodore Roosevelt was chiefly responsible for this abrupt enshrinement. His belief in a "strenuous" cowboy lifestyle was an echo of Turner's thesis: The frontier was where America must turn to cure its effeteness and unify as a race. "All honor must be paid to the architects of our material prosperity, to the great captains of industry who have built our factories and our railroads," Roosevelt told a men's club in Chicago, but, he quickly added,

> [M]ore important than any, are the cowboys. . . . They are smaller and less muscular than the wielders of ax and pick; but they are as hardy and self-reliant as any men who ever breathed — with bronzed, set faces, and keen eyes that look all the world straight in the face without flinching as they flash out from under the broad-brimmed hats. Peril and hardship, and years of long toil broken by weeks of brutal dissipation, draw haggard lines across their eager faces, but never dim their reckless eyes nor break their bearing of defiant self-confidence.[15]

Roosevelt's message took on a life of its own. If social Darwinism called for the survival of the fittest and if the West was the crucible of the New World, then the cowboy — the Anglo-Saxon cowboy — was the element that could not be ground down or amalgamated. This at least was the role contrived for him by the nation's most reactionary pundits, particularly Frederic Remington and Owen Wister.

The two had met quite by coincidence in Yellowstone National Park in September 1893 (just as Charlie Russell was preparing to leave the Montana range).[16] Remington was by then a veteran journalist and illustrator in the

West on assignment for *Harper's Monthly* and *Harper's Weekly,* while Wister was a tourist, with only one published Western story to his credit. Nonetheless, they had much in common and struck up a deep and complex relationship.

Wister and Remington's first collaboration was in 1893, with Remington illustrating Wister's second published story, "Balaam and Pedro," for *Harper's Weekly.* As their friendship progressed, Remington, whose career as a writer was not keeping pace with his illustrating, began suggesting story ideas to Wister. Since the success of his "Horses of the Plains" in 1889, Remington had been gestating another anthem to the West, this one on the rise of the cowboy. In the end, he persuaded Wister to write the piece and fed him all his notes. "The Evolution of the Cow-Puncher" appeared in *Harper's Monthly* in September 1895.

In "Evolution," Wister asserts that the Anglo-Saxon bloodline is a master race. He allows that its superiority may have lost its edge on the East Coast, where the ground is "debased and mongrel with its hordes of encroaching alien vermin, that turn our cities to Babels and our citizenship to a hybrid farce." But, he says, the West has provided a fresh start. "[T]o survive in the clean cattle country requires a spirit of adventure, courage, and self-sufficiency; you will not find many Poles or Huns or Russian Jews in the district." Contrarily, when an English nobleman got a whiff of the West,

> the slumbering untamed Saxon awoke in him, and mindful of the tournament, mindful of the hunting-field, galloped howling after wild cattle, a born horseman, a perfect athlete. . . . Destiny had tried her latest experiment upon the Saxon, and plucking him from the library, the haystack, and the gutter, set him upon his horse; then it was that, face to face with the eternal simplicity of death, his modern guise fell away and showed once again the mediaeval man. It was no new type, no product of the frontier, but just the original kernel of the nut with the shell broken.

After Roosevelt's *Hunting Trips of a Ranchman* (1885) and *Ranch Life and the Hunting-Trail* (1888), "The Evolution of the Cow-Puncher" was the first significant glorification of the cowboy in the mainstream press. Pulp fiction had already nurtured the myth, but the *Harper's Weekly* text, accompanied by Remington's illustrations, was a manifesto for a new American self-image. It helped explain Roosevelt's Rough Rider approach to the Spanish-American War (1898); it set the stage for Wister's colossal best-seller *The Virginian* (1902); and it helped cast the heroes of the first Western movies (1903). The cowboy had happened along at a convenient time. Now he was a character for the ages.

≫

FOR CHARLIE, THE sanctification of the cowboy cut two ways. Like the World's Fair, it was part distraction, part inspiration, and he wasn't sure where he stood. He belonged in the West, but he wasn't from the West; he had been a cowboy, but he wasn't exactly one anymore; he was an acclaimed artist, regionally anyway, but still not an accomplished or successful one. To add to his worries, his mother had died.

Mary Mead Russell had always kept a special place in her heart for Charlie. She had spoiled him constantly when he was a little boy and had been a pushover for his jokes and shenanigans. While correspondence between Charlie and his family is conspicuously rare (one suspects that letters were lost, lifted, or sold after the death of Nancy Russell), still his mother had a way of keeping in touch. When Charlie was back and forth between Cascade and Great Falls, Mary Russell corresponded with Ben Roberts's wife; presumably she'd had sympathetic sources in the Judith Basin before that.[17]

There is no record of where Charlie was on June 18, 1895, the day of his mother's death, or whether he made it home to the funeral on June 20. It is safe to say that he was devastated. John Barrows recalled running into him in Cascade around this time: "He was discouraged that day, and for more than an hour we sat in the shade of Ben Roberts' store and talked of his problems. . . . He was getting nowhere, the range cattle business was dead. [H]e was about as pessimistic as anyone ought to be."[18]

With the blues came the bottle. In September 1895, Charlie was in Great Falls, drinking too much. "How could he help it," Austin Russell explained, "when every old-timer who came into town immediately looked up Charlie Russell — and every new-timer wanted to be introduced? And every introduction meant the stranger buying Charlie a drink, Charlie buying back, anybody else who happened in buying for both of them, and they reciprocating, and so on and so on." Long after Charlie had mended his ways, he continued to suffer for his excesses. Austin reports that Charlie was prone to the shakes — "his hand jumping so that he couldn't draw" — which scared him badly.[19]

Surprisingly, though, neither the drinking nor his black moods seemed to stem his artistic urge. Quality may have suffered at times, but Charlie never stopped creating. His fellow tippler Bill Rance even remembered Charlie modeling with clay as an antidote to the whirlies.

> At night, Charlie'd lay in bed with his hands hangin' down close to the floor. Pretty soon he'd bring up some little animal he'd made. When I'd get tired, I'd say, "Aw, hell, Russ, forget that stuff. Let's get some sleep." But I don't think there was a mornin' when we got up in that room in the back end of the Canary Block that there wasn't some kind of little animal settin' under the edge of the bed.[20]

If anything, 1894 and 1895 saw a significant increase in output. In 1894, Charlie did a series of seven watercolors to illustrate *How the Buffalo Lost His Crown,* a sort of Blackfeet "Just So" story written by John Beacom, an officer at nearby Fort Shaw. In March 1895, one oil and five watercolors were included in the "Historical Art Exhibition of Works by St. Louis Artists of the Last 50 Years" mounted by a St. Louis art society called the Palette. (The show also included nine oils by Carl Wimar and one by George Caleb Bingham.)[21]

Many of Charlie's paintings in these two years were solidly in the cowboy mainstream, including *Bronco Busting,* a watercolor of his longtime friend Bob Thoroughman; *Bested,* an oil depicting the bloody aftermath of an open-range shootout; *Attack on the Mule Train,* a rare (and primitively executed) example of Indians threatening whites; and *A Quiet Day in Chinook,* in which a fun-seeking phalanx of cowboys gallops through town, scaring the wits out of dogs, chickens, and a Chinese laundryman.

Indian pieces outnumbered all of these. Charlie painted Indians in battle (*For Supremacy, Indians Attacking*), but devoted even more attention to the calmer, day-to-day activities of Native Americans (*Indian Women Crossing Stream, The Marriage Ceremony*). He was intent on preserving the details of Indian garb and equipage for posterity, down to the packing of a travois and the beadwork on a moccasin. But beyond his attachment to ethnological minutiae, he was striving to convey the innate dignity and grace of the race. *The Defiant Culprit,* also called *Sioux Torturing a Blackfoot Brave,* depicts a lone captive, stripped to the waist, but with chin up and chest out, his fate soon to be decided. It has been suggested that the scene may have been inspired by a similar picture that appeared in Edward S. Ellis's book, *The Indian Wars of the United States* (1892),[22] but the spirit Charlie invokes is straight out of James Fenimore Cooper. Charlie seems to have committed to canvas his version of the capture of the warrior Uncas in *The Last of the Mohicans.* "The form of Uncas dilated," Cooper wrote, "and his nostrils opened, like those of a tiger at bay; but so rigid and unyielding was his posture, that he might easily have been converted, by the imagination, into an exquisite and faultless representation of the warlike deity of his tribe."

Ever since his sojourn in Canada, Charlie had spent more and more time on buffalo pictures. The buffalo hunt had been an American icon for nearly a century, and Charlie had joined the fraternity in 1890 with *Wild Meat for Wild Men* and *The Buffalo Runners,* both oils. In 1894, he did two more, both of a single Indian mounted on a white horse about to drive an arrow into the right side of a galloping bull. One clearly mimics a painting by Titian Ramsay Peale, the other a painting by Carl Wimar.[23] From a practical standpoint, Charlie was simply availing himself of convenient models; from an egotistical standpoint, he was proving that he was every bit as good as the masters who had gone before.

His paintings *are* better than Peale's and Wimar's in these instances. Charlie succeeded in duplicating the quirks of buffalo anatomy perfectly — the angle of the neck, the rise of the hump, the length of the legs. In years to come, he would grow downright adamant on the subject, taking Wimar to task and lecturing Joe DeYong on the dos and don'ts of this very exacting subgenre.[24] Getting it right was Charlie's way of making up for never having seen it in real life. And regardless of the latest trends in art, he was still determined to give his West its romantic due.

ROMANCE TOOK ON new meaning in October 1895. With the death of his mother four months earlier, Charlie found himself in an emotional vacuum. Ever since his puppy love for Lollie Edgar, his only amorous encounters had been short-lived assignations with available women. Now came Mamie Mann.

Her Christian name was Nancy, and her father's surname was Cooper.

But everyone called her Mame or Mamie, and because she had never known her father, James Albert Cooper, she used her mother's maiden name. In 1895, she was a virtual orphan, barely seventeen years old, who had been living with the Ben Roberts family in Cascade for the previous year, helping Lela Roberts with the cooking, cleaning, and three young children.

Charlie never wrote down his memories of first meeting Mame. She, however, wrote several drafts, the most colorful of which turned up after her death. In a way, her introduction to Charlie is the best possible introduction to herself:

Mrs. Roberts (this was the Roberts home) had told us she had known Mr. Russell in Helena, when he first came to Montana in 1880. Mrs. Roberts and I are getting the supper on the table, when Gorham, the ten-year old boy came bouncing in with, "Oh, Mother, he's here!"

Then, we heard voices; that of Mr. Roberts and the stranger. They were coming near the back door. There was a jingle of spur-rowels, on the steps, then a call, "Leila [Lela], here's Charlie!" and Mrs. Roberts went to meet him.

They came in and were introduced in that clean, spacious kitchen. The table was covered with a red and white cloth, a wood fire in the cook-stove, the biscuits were ready to be put into the oven, supper was to be served in fifteen minutes.

Our cowboy guest took his stetson off his very erect, blonde head and said, "I'm glad to meet you," and shook hands with all of us, even the baby. Then, taking off his spurs, he said, "I'd like to wash."

On a bench near the back door was a wash-pan, soap and a pail of water, hanging on the door a roller-towel. He was told to help himself, while we put the supper on the table.

There was something different about this man. He took off his coat, a double-breasted blue serge, hung it on a chair-back, turned very square shoulders and straight back to me and walked over to the wash-bench. He was very little above average height and weight. His high-heeled riding boots covered small arched feet, his riding breeches were snug-fitting of heavy blue army cloth. In fact, they were Northwest Mounted Police pants, I learned later. They were held up by a wonderful bright colored French half-breed sash that clung just above the hip bones. The sash was wound around twice, the ends twisted and turned into a queer flat knot and the long fringe tucked into his hip pocket, a gray flannel shirt unbuttoned at the throat with a neck tie hanging loosely. It was worn just because a tie was supposed to be part of a civilized man's dress not that it was needed or wanted by him. His face, with its square jaw and chin, large mouth, tightly closed firm lips, the under protruding slightly beyond the short upper, straight nose, high cheek bones, gray-blue deep-set eyes that seemed to see everything but with an expression of honesty and understanding. In time I came to know that he could not see wrong in anybody. He never believed anyone did a bad act intentionally, it

was always an accident.

His hands were good-sized, perfectly shaped with slender long fingers. He loved jewelry and always wore three or four rings. They would not have been Charlie's hands any other way. Everyone noticed his hands, it was not the rings that attracted but the artistic, sensitive hands that had great strength and charm. When he talked he used them a lot to emphasize what he was saying, much as an Indian would do.

As he washed, I was watching him as closely as possible without being observed. While he was drying his face, there seemed to be a chance to take a good look from boots up. When my eyes reached his head, he was drying one side of his face and peeking out of one corner of the towel at me. He laughed and I almost dropped the plate of fried ham.

"The potatoes burned and will you please get the quince preserves in the cellar way?"

Mrs. Roberts saved me in my great confusion by asking me to do the things I knew I should.

There must be a gun hidden away somewhere in that sash but it could not be seen though I tried my hardest because it was not there. This was not a gun-man but a gentle, lover of nature. We all learned this as the years passed.

At the supper table in the soft light of the coal oil lamp, he talked. We could see the play of laughing wrinkles on that Indian-like face. He looked like a white Indian and had us fascinated with his stories of real life.[25]

Charlie had never met anyone as attentive as Nancy.

7

NANCY

THOUGH CHARLIE WOULD be celebrated for his American-
ness, it was Nancy who, out of necessity rather than a sense of adventure, embodied the American qualities of self-sufficiency, ingenuity, and
tenacity. Charlie was a quick study; Nancy was a true bootstrapper.

When Charlie and Nancy met, then married, most of his friends shook
their heads and wondered aloud how the pair of them ever fell into double
harness. The answer was simple: They needed each other. Though their
ages and backgrounds were disparate, they found themselves occupying
the same rung at the same time: Charlie had chosen, for whatever reasons,
to climb down the social ladder; Nancy, for the usual reasons, was determinedly climbing up it. This congruence created a strong bond, even while
their diametric urges made for potential conflict. Completing the formula
was another, not insignificant, ingredient: honest-to-goodness love. Theirs
was a good marriage; they made each other, and they made each other
happy.

Nancy's people were Irish, and like the Russells, the Manns had made
their way to Virginia before the Revolutionary War.[1] They too fought
redcoats and Indians and pushed westward across the Appalachians to
Kentucky. Their home was called Mann's Lick, which became Mannsville,
named for Nancy's great-great-grandfather, Moses Mann. Name and pride
were about all that was left by the time Nancy Bates Cooper entered the
world on May 4, 1878.

By the standards of the day, James Albert Cooper was a no-account. He had married Texas Annie Mann in 1877. He was nineteen, his bride two years younger. Within a year he had deserted her. Would he have stayed if he had known she was pregnant? Or was that why he fled? The upshot was that Nancy had a fatherless childhood. Texas Annie lived on her father's farm, coaxing a subsistence from the tired ground. Then when Nancy was eight, her mother married a first cousin, James Thomas Allen, who farmed nearby. Two years later, half-sister Ella Carrie Allen was born.

There was little to keep Thomas Allen in Kentucky. Family holdings had been so splintered through the generations that not much land or legacy was left to go on. "The atmosphere wasn't so good down there" was all Nancy ever said about her Kentucky childhood.[2] By contrast, the West shone brightly. In the summer of 1890, Thomas Allen put himself, his wife, daughter, and stepdaughter on a train bound for Montana. Their new land of milk and honey was the devil's den of Helena. By the early 1890s the boom was bygone; the big gold strikes had long since petered out, and Last Chance Gulch, always a hard place to keep body and soul together, was now grasping for whatever comes after a last chance.

Thomas Allen deposited his family in a mean rental house and hit the road. Some say he drank; clearly, he did not strike it rich. Back in Helena, his family was living hand to mouth. One account says Texas Annie took in sewing and washing. Others speculate — with no hard evidence — that she may have sold a more personal service in order to feed herself and two daughters.[3] Whatever it took, it took too much. In September 1894, Texas Annie died of consumption, leaving behind sixteen-year-old Nancy, six-year-old Ella, and a missing husband. With the help of neighbors, Nancy saw to her mother's burial. When the news of Texas Annie's death reached Thomas Allen, he appeared in Helena and collected his only blood, Ella; Nancy he left to shift for herself.[4] She had little schooling, scant wherewithal, and few prospects.

For a time, she was most likely taken in by one of the neighbors as a house girl. Then sometime in 1895, Ben Roberts's wife, Lela, received a letter from a woman named Biggs, a friend in Helena, telling her she knew of a girl who could help her around the house. Mrs. Biggs had feared the teenager "was beginning to run with the wrong crowd." Mrs. Roberts already had an Indian girl named Josie Wright working for her, but with three young children, she said she could use two more hands. And so Nancy came to Cascade on the train.

The Robertses could not pay her much, but at least she had a home out of harm's way. Lela Roberts helped Nancy refine her cooking and housekeeping skills and doubtless improved her manners as well. In later years, Nancy never wanted the Roberts family to speak of her as having worked for them. Nor did she freely mention her mother, father, or stepfather. Hebe Roberts Sheridan, one of the children Nancy helped raise, could only say later that Texas Annie Allen "was not all that she should have been."[5]

To an unsophisticated mother's helper in Cascade, Montana, a visit from Charlie Russell was a special occasion. Not that he was princely or obviously rich. It was not like having a prosperous young rancher to supper or an up-and-coming politician. But Charlie had star quality, and as Nancy made clear in her unfinished manuscript, he had considerable style. Perhaps she had seen him around Cascade once or twice. And perhaps he had seen her.

The match was unlikely, to say the least. Charlie was thirty-one years old. He had been around, known all sorts of women. Not the type of fellow you would fix up with a seventeen-year-old whom you had recently saved from Sodom. But as two of Charlie's closest friends, the Robertses knew his good side — his gentleness, his love of family.[6] Too, they could see that he was adrift, sleeping in lofts and back rooms, drinking too much. A bright, cheery, sensible girl might be just what Charlie needed. Certainly the Robertses did nothing to keep them apart.

Charlie and Nancy were both natural flirts. When he chose to radiate his charm — part Huck Finn, part Lancelot — he could melt women and men with equal effect. An audience was all he needed. Nancy had her own winsome ways, but the result was the same: Most anything she ever set her mind to, she got.

She had the grit of an urchin, but there was nothing slight about her. She stood five-foot-seven (three inches shorter than Charlie); portraits of her as a young woman reveal a certain babyishness: large, soft hands, full lips, round cheeks, honey-brown hair, and big blue eyes beneath a pudding-smooth brow. Overall, she possessed a certain plump voluptuousness that came across more through body language and the temperature of her expressions than in any bundling of hair or rise of bosom. She was sexy in an innocent way. And it was her very innocence that made her so effective. She could be coy, kittenish, buttery, bitchy, obsequious, obdurate — arsenal enough to vanquish nearly any human.

Given the time, the terms, and the terrain of the courtship, Charlie did not stand a chance. At least that is what many of his friends thought. Fred Barton, an old acquaintance, claims he once told Charlie "that I firmly believed that Nancy had suggested marriage and that he was too damn polite to say no. He did not contradict me, but merely smiled and said nothing."[7]

Most every opinion of Nancy, however, must be taken with a grain of salt, especially those offered by Charlie's friends from his bachelor days. Later in their marriage, Nancy would acquire the sobriquet "Nancy the Robber," because of the high prices she was able to get for Charlie's artwork.[8] But for most of the old-timers, that was not the theft that mattered. When Charlie met Nancy, she had robbed them of his company. In retaliation, they never gave her an even break, and they never forgave her. Years after Charlie's death and hers as well, his friends continued to cast her in the harshest possible light. The testimony against her is rich and, seen a certain way, is a fair measure of her presence and strength. Charlie had indeed met his match, and he seemed to enjoy being caught between Nancy and his old saloon cronies.

In 1895 Cascade was a simple town of two hundred on the banks of the Missouri River, surrounded by the undulant grazing land of Chestnut Valley. Lela Roberts's father, Thomas Gorham, had anticipated the route of the Great Northern Railway and established a homestead in its path. He sold a right-of-way to the railroad, opened a combination store and post office, and became the seigneur of Cascade, dying there in 1891. His store then became Shepherd & Flinn's, where Ben Roberts, erstwhile saddlemaker, worked as a clerk. By then the town proper boasted two churches, two blacksmith shops, two hotels, and one livery stable. Even today, Cascade is quiet and idyllic, the Missouri River a sparkling blue-green as it edges past cottonwood-lined banks and a cluster of modest frame houses. As a setting for romance, its appeal remains obvious.[9]

Charlie conducted his courtship of Nancy entirely in Cascade. He spent less and less time in Great Falls, more and more in a makeshift studio behind the Robertses' house, where he finally set to work on the commissions for William Niedringhaus. The inspiration for one of the watercolors, *A Piegan Flirtation,* is not hard to guess. A young Indian girl, wearing braids and a colorful dress, approaches the water with an earthen jug under her arm. A befeathered brave on a white horse interrupts her evening chore. In response, she has demurely tucked her chin into a fold of her blanket.

A similar pas de deux occurred on the banks of the Missouri between the autumn of 1895 and the summer of 1896. Evenings, or whenever Nancy was not needed by Lela Roberts, she and Charlie strolled along the river, getting to know each other. There were more invitations to supper, and often Charlie lingered well after the Robertses had retired to bed. Hebe Roberts and her brothers Gorham and Vivian were tucked away in a room above the parlor. "There was a big fireplace downstairs," Hebe related nearly fifty years later. "Vents in the floor allowed the warm air to go up and heat a bedroom over the living room." Night after night, the three little Robertses sneaked out of bed and pressed their faces to the grate. There by the light of the fireplace, they could watch Charlie and Nancy, squished into a red-plush chair, nestling and nuzzling.[10]

Old habits died hard, however, and from time to time during his year-long courtship of Nancy, Charlie would catch the train into Great Falls. His drinking buddies, including bartender Bill Rance, ribbed him fiercely about his new distraction. To show he was serious about Nancy, Charlie told Rance and the rest of the crowd that he had left his horses Monte and Red Bird in her care. "That settles it," Rance purportedly exclaimed. "A man don't give a gal his hoss — not a man like Russ anyhow — 'less he's plumb locoed 'bout 'er. He'll have to marry the gal now to git his hoss back."[11] But even with Charlie's fate foretold, Bill Rance went on record against the match, a position that made him persona non grata around the Russell house for the next thirty years. A typical prank was for Rance to call Ben Roberts on the telephone and report that Charlie was too drunk to make the train, too drunk even to come to the phone.[12]

Charlie, though, was never too drunk to make it back to Cascade to see Nancy. And even if he had tried to hide his boozing from her, it would not have worked. Once before their marriage, he poured off the train with a friend, Jack Coates. "Charlie's voice was very husky and I said, 'Oh, you've taken cold!' " she recalled. In fact, Charlie and Coates were three sheets to the wind. "Coates smiled and looked at this guilty party of his, who said, 'I guess I must have slept near an open window or in a draft.' " Nancy didn't buy his alibi for a minute, but let him off the hook. "The truth of the matter was [Charlie and Coates] had not slept and did not remember how they got to Cascade."[13]

But she did not cut him any slack when it came to a proposal. Nancy was a rock-ribbed negotiator, in love as in business. The story is told that Charlie initially suggested that they simply live together, without getting married.[14] There is no telling how intimate they had become at this point, and no telling what Charlie thought of her "reputation." Perhaps as an experienced sporting man, he thought he could get his goods at a discount. A kinder spin on the exchange is that he was simply too bashful to come right out and ask for her hand. ("Nancy, don't y'u want to throw in with me" is the conjectured troth.) She pressed for specifics, and in the end, he had to spit it out. He wanted her to marry him. In that case, her answer was yes.

Nancy was a nervous bride-to-be. The wedding was set for September, and as the day approached, her health broke. She had apparently had some sort of breakdown and been sent to Great Falls for rest and treatment. Of the few letters Charlie ever wrote to Nancy, several are from August 1896. "Dear Nancy," he wrote on August 20, "I reached home all ok and every one was glad to here that you were better I hope you got your tooth bruch all right." Then three days later (and two weeks before their wedding day): "Dear Mamie . . . We are getting along all right but we all miss you verry much and you know I do but I am so glad you are in good hands[;] you must not come back till you are well and strong."[15]

Friends attempted to warn Charlie that he was getting defective merchandise. Austin Russell, who did not arrive on the scene till years later, insists that Great Falls doctor John Sweat even tried to disrupt the wedding plans. " 'Dont marry that Mann girl,' " Austin has Sweat saying. " 'She's a nice little girl, an she's pretty, but she's got a bad heart — she'll be dead inside three years.' "[16]

Of course Nancy lived much longer than three years. Yet the doctor's caveat had a basis in truth: Nancy did have a bad heart. As a child, she was nagged by frequent sore throats. Most probably she suffered from chronic strep infection, which in those days took the name rheumatic fever.[17] If allowed to persist, rheumatic fever can damage heart valves (and it did in Nancy's case, as her autopsy in 1940 revealed). At the time, the only known cure was extended bed rest. Intermittently throughout her life, she was beset by headaches and fainting spells and driven to her darkened bedroom in a state of exhaustion; part of Charlie's morning ritual was to bring her a glass of hot water with lemon as a tonic for her throat and "condition." She always bounced back, but it was mostly willpower, rather than natural stamina, that drove her through the world.

Nothing could keep her from her wedding. It took place in the Robertses' parlor at 8 P.M. on September 9. Charlie had bought a ring at a jewelry store in Great Falls. Lela Roberts had made Nancy's blue wedding dress. "The day we were married," Nancy recalled, "Charlie had only $15.00. He gave $10.00 to the preacher who tied the knot and $5.00 to the fellows around town to keep them from chivareeing us."[18] Nancy made the wedding cake and Charlie cranked the ice cream. The brief ceremony was witnessed by the Roberts family, the minister's wife, and two others. No one from the bride's or groom's family was present. Interestingly, on the marriage license, Nancy recorded her father's name and gave her own name as Mamie Cooper, a legal recognition of her jumbled past. In its one-paragraph announcement, the *Great Falls Tribune* described her as "one of the most popular and most estimable young ladies of Cascade."[19]

Charlie was as submissive as he was pleased. He sketched himself being lassoed by a Cupid riding a horse with a big heart branded on its hip. The term he liked to use for his condition was "necked," referring to the cowboy technique of breaking a wild horse by tying it to the neck of a tame horse until the undisciplined bronc has learned to behave. "[I]ts the onley way to hold a bunch quitter," Charlie elaborated to fellow cowboy artist Ed Borein on the occasion of his friend's marriage.

> [A]nimals are easier found in pairs than alone[.] A he bear has no home till he ties to a lady[.] The wolf is a drifter intill the she one of his kind shows him the cave under the rim rock[.] The mules in the pack trane would leave the trail and scatter, but thairs a differnt shaped track in the trail a head. [I]ts the hoof marks of the lady hoss that leads her long eared lovers to camp. . . . Im hoping the tie rope will never choke ore break.

He could reel off the metaphors endlessly to mask his mushiness and to frame his respect for the opposite sex. If being "necked" was better than living "lonsum," then it was because women had it all over men. "It's the women that make the men in this world, I heard an educated man say once," Charlie wrote in *More Rawhides,*

> an' it's the truth that, if a man's goin' to hell or heaven, if you look in the trail ahead of him you'll find a track the same shape as his, only smaller; it's a woman's track. She's always ahead, right or wrong, tollin' him on.

In animals, the same as humans, the female leads. That ain't the exact words this educated man uses, but it's as near as I can interpret, 'n' it's the truth. If you ever run buffalo, you'll notice the cow-meats in the lead. With wild hosses the stallion goes herdin' them along, snakin' and bowin' his neck, with his tail flagged. From looks you'd call him chief, but the mares lead to the water-hole they've picked out. An' I believe, if all women were squaws, the whites would be wearin' clouts to-day.[20]

Necked, mated, and married, Charlie and Nancy moved into the studio behind the Robertses' house. "Our weddin' trip was a hundred yards to that one-room shack — an' we walked," Charlie joked. He had spent about $75 fixing it up. Nancy described it as a twelve-by-twenty-four room with a "small lean-to kitchen" at the back. "The room was wainscoted and he had tried to paint it light blue but was not very handy with that kind of paint and brush so he gave up the job to a halfbreed Indian who was doing odd jobs around Cascade."[21]

The furnishings were spare. Charlie's relatives in St. Louis, who had never met Nancy and had scarcely a clue as to what sort of home they were making for themselves, sent such essentials as silver berry spoons, after-dinner-coffee spoons, and a bonbon dish. Charlie's sense of decor leaned much more toward tepee living. He hung Indian relics on the walls. In a corner, Nancy recollects, he put a willow backrest covered with "a buffalo calf robe decorated on the skin side by Indian drawings . . . picturing some incidents in Charlie's life. He had used this robe in his bed for years so it was worn quite thin but together with an Indian blanket thrown on the floor against the back rest [it] made . . . a comfortable place to sit and recline as [we] were short of chairs."[22]

Their church-mouse straits helped knit them together more tightly. Nancy continued to work for the Robertses for small wages, while Charlie painted on a homemade easel in their little house. He had not made much money in 1896, except for the Niedringhaus watercolors. "Things had gone very much awry with Charlie's work after we were married," Nancy wrote. "He had no [new] orders for pictures and no chance in Cascade to meet buyers. [But our] credit was good, so we were eating regularly. Life was not too serious."[23] For the fun of it, Charlie dressed Nancy up as an Indian and painted her as an Indian odalisque, leaning against the willow backrest in front of the painted buffalo robe. He continued with his native themes in

Indians Discovering Lewis and Clark (emphasizing an Indian perspective) and *A Doubtful Guest,* a nostalgic re-creation of a meeting between Charlie, Jake Hoover, and an armed Indian. None of these sold for significant sums.

Still, Nancy and Charlie managed to get by. In Nancy's hindsight at least, their first Christmas together may well have been their happiest:

> Our first Christmas, with no money to spend, an no place to spend it if there had been. . . . We both needed lots of things, and among those we wanted most were warm slippers, as the shack-home of ours was not very warm except in summer, so I bought for Charlie a pair of felt slippers and made a slipper bag out of black broadcloth and worked his initials with red silk on one side and mine on the other, put the slippers in the case and hung it by his sock which he hung up for Santa Claus. My stocking was in another place to give plenty of room for Santa to get around. At four in the morning, there was no more sleep for us — it was Christmas morning! Our first Christmas, trotting in double harness!
>
> I stepped out and got my stocking and crawled back into bed. I found some nuts, an orange and just the same kind of little hard, bright colored candies we had always had as children, and way down in the toe of my stocking I found a $5.00 bill and one package revealed to me a pair of felt slippers, the exact mates (only smaller) to those I had given my cowboy husband.
>
> We were happy over that Christmas with nothing more than I've described because the happiness came from within. Charlie was as pleased as if he had received a million dollar gift. The simple things in life always did thrill him, no one could live near him without taking on some of that child-like joy from little things.[24]

Yet as cozy as Cascade was that first year, it meant a dead end for Charlie's career unless he could reach a broader market. Perhaps inspired by the success of Remington and no doubt egged on by Nancy, he wrote his first piece of fiction, "Early Days on the Buffalo Range." It appeared, along with two full-page illustrations, in the April 1897 issue of *Recreation,* one of the new magazines cashing in on the nation's faddish passion for the outdoors and the strenuous life. Charlie threw everything he had into his story; he even dared to write the piece in the first person, though he set it seven years before his birth. "Early Days" is a straightforward salute to the era when Indians and buffalo ruled the plains and a remarkable demonstration of Charlie's acquired knowledge of Indian lifeways. He described the garb of the Indian buffalo hunters down to the last feather. He threw in bits of Indian vocabulary. He recounted the hunt as if dictating a manual. Yet his melancholy closing says as much about his own life as it does about that of the Indians:

Many years have passed since then. I am now an old man, and have watched the advance of civilization, but can't say I have welcomed it, when I look at the half starved, ragged Indian of today, standing on some street corner, or at some railway station trying to sell polished buffalo horns. These are the least remnants of that mighty throng which has vanished from the earth. They have left nothing to tell the tale but a few scattered bones. A feeling of sadness comes over me as I think of the once great herds. They are both "have beens."[25]

No record of his fee for this story remains, but he could not have made much more than $30 — the amount he had earned a month earlier for three illustrations used in *The Story of the Cowboy,* a nonfiction book by well-known Western writer Emerson Hough.[26] Even when Charlie was lucky enough to sell original paintings, the take was measly. For several years he had been sending his completed work to a middleman in Butte. Charles Schatzlein, proprietor of a paint, wallpaper, and picture-framing store, also sold original art and was Charlie's first real dealer. The best Schatzlein could get for smaller watercolors was, again, $10. A large oil went for $75 — a pittance in the opulent copper capital.

Still, the exposure Schatzlein gave Charlie eventually paid a dividend. In May 1897, editor William Bleasdell Cameron passed through Butte, talking up another new outdoor magazine, *Western Field and Stream,* which he had begun publishing the year before in St. Paul. "I walked into the lobby of Butte's principal hotel," Cameron reminisced half a century later,

to find myself staring at some pictures on the walls, pictures which . . . topped anything . . . I had ever before seen. In vivid and revealing action, they were compositions illustrative of the fast-disappearing lawless West and the picturesque characters who made up its population — Indians, cowpokes, trappers, prospectors, traders, Chinese, gamblers and "bad" men generally. . . . [T]he thing that most impressed me was their fidelity to truth — the sureness evident in all the work of the artist. Here was no bungling or timidity. On the contrary, he had woven in the very fabric of his canvasses the impress of his own striking and original individuality. They were largely reflections of his own wild young life. . . . Moreover they somehow conveyed to the arrested observer a sense of the hidden joy and satisfaction that the expression in color of his genius brought to their creator.[27]

Cameron went out of his way to track down the possessor of this "hidden joy." Charles Schatzlein directed the editor to Cascade, where he met Charlie, "a well set-up young fellow in shirt sleeves, of medium height, with blue eyes, straight blond hair and the unmistakable garb of the cowpuncher." Charlie quickly sized Cameron up as well and invited the magazine man back to his house-studio to watch him paint. On the easel was *Bronc in Cow Camp.* Cameron was enthralled — by the painting, Charlie's character, the entire setting — and rattled off his pitch. He planned to move the magazine to New York soon (where it would become *Field and Stream*). "That was where the money was," Cameron told Charlie, "and where the men who had it and liked to adorn their residences with fine pictures were ready to pay for them. With [Charlie's] talent it was a shame that he should be painting such splendid canvasses and selling them locally for just enough to buy his daily bread. Once these men of wealth had seen what he could do with paint, there wouldn't be banks enough to hold all his money."[28]

Cameron did not propose paying Charlie a kingly sum himself; what he offered instead was exposure. Initially Cameron suggested that Charlie paint twelve oils to be used as frontispieces for *Field and Stream*. But by the time the contract had been signed in September, the deal was for "twenty black and white oil paintings about 24 by 18 inches in size each and twenty pen sketches about 12 by 8 inches each, composing a pictorial history of western life." For this group, *Field and Stream* would pay $15 per painting and $50 total for the pen sketches. "If it was true that he would receive from his magnificent work a mere trifle," Cameron rationalized, "on the other hand . . . he would become known to thousands who had never before heard of him." As a bonus, the contract promised to print a special run of the paintings Charlie supplied and advertise them in the magazine. Furthermore, *Field and Stream* pledged to publish the paintings and sketches in two separate books, assigning Charlie one-third of the profits.[29]

Field and Stream did move to New York, but within a year Cameron had quit in a huff over money. Charlie sent a number of pieces to the magazine, including *Keeoma* (Indian odalisque), *Before the White Man Came* (Edenic Indian tableau), *Caught Napping* (a moose-hunting scene), and *A Friend in Need* (a Russell staple in which a hunter saves his buddy from a bear attack). At least four were made into prints and advertised at fifty cents apiece or three for a dollar. They did poorly. The magazine also ran several stories under Cameron's byline that had all the flavor of Russell yarns, suggesting that Cameron, like the editor at *Recreation,* had not only cleaned up Charlie's prose but had appropriated it outright.[30]

For all the increase in attention, Charlie's lot was not much improved by the end of 1897. He still was not earning a great deal more than he had as a wrangler and seemed to care less whether his pockets were empty or full. When it came to business, Austin Russell remarked, Charlie was "dog-ignorant."[31] Nancy, on the other hand, was champing at the bit as she watched Charlie turn out painting after painting, with little to show for his toil. Within a year of their marriage, she had moved them from their shack in bucolic Cascade to a proper house in booming Great Falls, where she set about improving their financial position.

The new house was a four-room rental on Seventh Avenue North — north being the "good" side of town, but Seventh not one of the best avenues. The house was cramped and the basement leaked. Ever a Spartan, Charlie bragged that the cellar would make a great place to raise ducks in the summer and a good one for ice-making in the winter.[32] The dining room was his studio.

Soon Charlie began turning out work at a rapid clip. With quantity, however, came erratic quality. *Lewis and Clark Meeting the Mandan Indians* is an elaborate composition, painstakingly painted. Charlie adapted scenes from the Lewis and Clark journals throughout his life, and almost always from the Indian perspective. In the Mandan painting, Clark, clad in buckskin, is reaching to shake the hand of a bare-chested chief, whose people are gathered around him. At Clark's side is his black servant, York, who fascinated Charlie, as well as the Indians. In the background can be seen the Missouri River and the white men's boats. The painting, though, is full of anachronisms and other lapses in adroitness.[33] By their dress and tepees, the Indians are clearly not Mandan at all, but Blackfeet. (This explains why the name of the painting was later changed to *Captain William Clark of the Lewis and Clark Expedition Meeting with the Indians of the Northwest*.) What is more, the Blackfeet clothing and accoutrements are from a much later time.

Other aspects of the piece expose Charlie's appropriative haste as well. The figure of Clark is more statue than flesh, suggesting that Charlie lifted the form from another source. And in the foreground he has placed a hunch-backed, gray-headed crone, whose clichéd form also appears in several other pieces, as if ordered up from Central Casting. Charlie apparently had become attached to the character of the crone ever since reading Parkman's description in *The Oregon Trail:* "Except the dogs, the most active and noisy tenants of the camp were the old women, ugly as Macbeth's witches, with their hair streaming loose in the wind, and nothing but the tattered fragment of an old buffalo-robe to hide their shrivelled wiry limbs."

If Charlie was expedient in paintings such as *Lewis and Clark Meeting the Mandan Indians,* he was just as capable of tossing all notions of time and economy out the window. "If left to himself, Charlie was not very practical; he would devote just as much care to things not meant to sell," Austin Russell observed.[34] He would make little dolls out of bark and moss, consume hundreds of hours carving and rigging model sailboats, decorate store windows, or add elaborate sketches to the margins and endpapers of borrowed books. It was a way to procrastinate, to be boyishly contrary.

In late 1897, Charlie accepted a commission to decorate dozens of menus for a special Christmas supper at the Park Hotel, Great Falls's posh hostelry. He did a separate watercolor for every one, borrowing from his inventory of tried-and-true images. His total pay for the 125 little gems was $20. Many of the dinner guests ended up leaving their customized menus on the table, to be swept up with the crumbs.[35] Nancy was never able to suppress Charlie's Christmastime magnanimity — he virtually shut down his regular work around the holidays to make little cards, drawings, dolls, and all manner of clever, and often intricate, lagniappe for friends and their children. But never again would she allow him to be roped into illustrations at sixteen cents apiece.

Soon after settling in Great Falls, Charlie painted a watercolor of a Missouri steamboat whose upstream progress had been stalled by a herd of buffalo crossing the river. "When finished," Nancy wrote, "it was a beauty and should bring a good price" — especially since it was a commission for the mayor's wife. Nancy's recollection of the transaction is characteristically sunny:

> Charlie hoped she would pay $25.00. We needed hay for the horses and I wanted a new cook stove. So, I asked if I couldn't deliver the picture.
>
> "Now, Mame, if you ask more than $25.00 for that picture, she won't take it and we need the money."
>
> Our lady saw the beauty of the picture and was much pleased.
>
> "How much does Mr. Russell want for it?"
>
> With a choking feeling, I said, "$35.00."
>
> "Just wait and I will get you a check."
>
> Glory be! I had $10.00 toward the new cook stove. When I gave Charlie that piece of paper, he got as much of a thrill out of it as he did when handed a check for $30,000 in 1926.[36]

Charlie always pretended to be embarrassed by his ever-escalating prices. He claimed that the amount being asked — whether $100 or $10,000 — was too high. He told a *New York Telegram* reporter in 1925, "The worst fight [Nancy and I] ever had was in 1897 when she asked $75 for a canvas, which I thought highway robbery — and got it. I was willing to sell it for $5, but she insisted we had to eat." But in fact he was quite proud of her and quite relieved to turn over the pocketbook and other worldly affairs to her. "We are partners," he said to the *Telegram*. "She is the business end and I am the creative. . . . She lives for tomorrow and I live for yesterday; so it is the combination which brings things today."[37]

It was a testimonial he never tired of giving. On a visit to Minneapolis in 1919, Charlie found himself cornered by a reporter and asked about Somerset Maugham's *The Moon and Sixpence,* which had just been published and was all the buzz among highbrows. One of the morals of the story, at least in the opinion of the inquiring Minneapolitan, is that the bourgeois institution of marriage inhibits the higher passions of art and expression. Charlie's eyes must have rolled skyward when he was asked to compare himself to the zealot antihero of a novel he had never read. "Should Genius Marry? Yes, Says Cowboy Artist" was the headline tacked over Charlie's response in the next morning's paper:

> "I know nothing of this socalled modern school of artists who think themselves divine. Their art means nothing to me. I can make nothing

out of their pictures. Much less can I understand their philosophy [the reporter surely has spruced up Charlie's diction] which considers marriage a hindrance to a career. Why, say, I wasn't getting more than $5 or $10 for a picture when I met Mrs. Russell and I didn't have any reputation east of Great Falls, Box Alder [Elder] creek or any of the other localities that I was punching in. Today I have a home, a son, a wife who thinks a lot of me and whom I think a heap of. . . . I don't lay any claim to being a genius, but I will say my wife has been an inspiration to me in my work. Without her I would probably have never attempted to soar or reach any height, further than to make a few pictures for my friends and old acquaintances in the west. I still love and long for the old west, and everything that goes with it. But I would sacrifice it all for Mrs. Russell. . . . It's a fifty-fifty game with us and I never felt that domestic relations were in any way a hindrance to my career."[38]

If anything, the only hindrances to his career, and Nancy's well-being, were social. The undertow of the Great Falls saloons was stronger in 1897 than it had been when Charlie had first passed through their doors seven years earlier. Now, as then, he did not resist the largesse and diversion of that culture. Nancy, meanwhile, received no such welcome from Great Falls society. In her entire life of achievement, it was the only nut she never truly cracked.

8

GREAT FALLS

G REAT FALLS HAS always been the least Western of Montana's
cities. From its founding, it embodied and promoted everything
Charlie Russell detested about progress and modern living — none of
which deterred him from residing there for the latter half of his life or
inhibited him from eventually becoming the town's leading citizen.

In the bid to be Montana's first twentieth-century city, Great Falls had no
rival. Helena and Butte had grown up around mining claims. Fort Benton
was a glorified boat landing and wagon depot. Miles City was a cow town.
Billings was a train stop. For all their latter-day spit-shine, these other urban
upstarts were never quite able to remove all the dirt from their boots. Their
main streets followed clogged gulches or funneled livestock from trail to rail.
They had purpose, but they had little vision. They enjoyed prosperity, but
they were never quite prepared for it. By contrast, Great Falls was designed
to be different, as its nickname "Electric City" implied. Its citizens were
grateful for a past that contained neither "boot hill nor hangin' tree."[1]

The falls were indeed great. They posed the biggest hindrance to river
navigation that Lewis and Clark faced in their entire journey to the Pacific.
The mildest drop-offs were five feet, the severest nearly twenty times that.
All told, in a ten-mile stretch of roiling mayhem, the Missouri River fell
more than five hundred feet. Descending the steep bluffs along the river,
Lewis was intoxicated by the roar, the rainbows, and the "perfect white
foam which assumes a thousand forms in a moment." The overall spectacle,
he said, "was the grandest sight I ever beheld."[2]

The Great Falls, as Lewis and Clark designated the largest cataract on their map, remained just as they had found them for most of the remainder of the nineteenth century. Military roads and railroad surveys steered clear of the impassable gorge the Missouri had cut through the high plains. Trappers paused here, forty miles upstream from Fort Benton — and forty miles closer to the Blackfeet stronghold — but ventured no permanent settlement. In 1880, the year Charlie Russell arrived in Montana, the town of Great Falls was still little more than a twinkling in the eye of a Yankee speculator named Paris Gibson.

Gibson arrived in Montana in 1879 as one of the early stockgrowers near Fort Benton. He had read Lewis's descriptions of the Great Falls and vowed to explore the area for himself. "Although I had traveled much over Northern Montana and the country between the Missouri River and the Yellowstone," Gibson wrote, "I had never seen a spot as attractive as this and one that at once appealed to me as an ideal site for a city."3

By the end of 1882, Gibson had enlisted the backing of his Minneapolis friend James J. Hill, whose Great Northern Railway was reaching across the top of the nation toward the Pacific. Hill's main trunk would not pass through Great Falls, but impressed by the potential of the falls and the abundance of coal nearby, Hill agreed to construct a branch line connecting Butte, Helena, and the spot Gibson had picked for his new town.

The town site was a blank page awaiting the grid of human enterprise. Streets were surveyed precisely north-south, avenues east-west. Each thoroughfare would be a generous eighty feet wide, except for Central Avenue, which would be ninety. Twenty-foot-wide alleys bisected each block, and each block was divided into fourteen lots, fifty feet by a hundred feet. To turn harsh prairie into shady neighborhoods, Gibson saw to the planting of more than five thousand trees and laid out four hundred acres of park. Out of modesty or bet-hedging, James Hill would not let Gibson call his creation Hilltown, so in 1883 it became Great Falls.

By 1886, only a couple hundred adventurous souls had relocated there, some of them still in tents. Central Avenue consisted of five buildings and "scarcely a foot of sidewalk." Stage drivers on the route from Helena to Fort Benton would jerk a thumb toward Gibson's settlement. "Pity, isn't it?" they would say to their passengers. "Poor old man, gone crazy, thinks he's founding a city on this 'ere buffalo bench." But Gibson was quick to stare down the skeptics. "Young man," he would say, "we have a hundred people now, but before you have reached middle life it will have a hundred thousand."[4]

All the ingredients for a metropolis were present. No railroad hyped homesteading more vigorously (or more self-servingly) than the Great Northern. Its stops across Montana were named Glasgow, Tampico, Malta, Harlem, Zurich, Havre, Kremlin, Inverness, and Dunkirk — and the mix of immigrants the Great Northern delivered to their platforms was nearly as exotic. Great Falls was poised to be the western hub for these Italian, Bohemian, Russian, Slavic, and Scandinavian newcomers, and when their homesteads dried up or were hailed out, as happened to so many, Great Falls was one of the cities they fled to for wages and one more try. Given the presence of labor, power, and transportation, Gibson's dream of building "the Pittsburgh of the Great Northwest" was anything but a crapshoot.

Gibson and his fellow boosters, incorporated as the Great Falls Water-Power and Townsite Company, went to elaborate lengths to rank Great Falls above every other mill town in the United States. Because the Missouri dropped in a succession of falls — and not all at once — its force could be captured, released, captured again, and so on. Great Falls bragged that "the combination of the natural advantages gives a total power over twice as great as Niagara."[5]

With the completion of the first dam, Great Falls was well on its way to becoming a company town. Lumber and flour mills were driven by the falls, and the railway was a steady, significant employer. But the biggest boon for Great Falls was the completion of the Boston & Montana copper smelter in 1890. Ore came by train from Butte and was crushed by direct waterpower. After the Black Eagle Falls dam was built, the plant could be driven by electricity, allowing the new process of electrolytic smelting. By 1892, the B&M smelter employed a thousand workers.

The smelter brought more than growth and a blue-collar workforce. It also brought cosmopolitanism, or at least its veneer. The Boston & Montana Company, as its name half-suggests, was owned and financed by Easterners. Its engineers and supervisors came from New England, with advanced degrees and stylish wives. True, Great Falls would never be defined by the plump plutocracy of Butte, with its copper kings. Great Falls was a town of managers, not owners. Still, what it lacked in lucre, it made up for in decorum. The town that Charlie and Nancy Russell moved to in 1897 not only had telephones, electric lights, and electric streetcars, it also had unwavering social pretensions.

As the century drew to a close, Great Falls society became as regimented as the Romanesque tiers of the city's Grand Opera House or Paris Gibson's plats.[6] The B&M's top managers lived on Smelter Hill, across the river, surrounded by gates. Laborers lived in the Little Chicago section or on the south side of Central Avenue, which was also the location of the tenderloin; better-paid smelter employees tended to live in Boston Heights. But as Great Falls filled out and reached urban adulthood, the "good families" all settled on the near north side; Fourth Avenue North was *the* street. Here lived the doctors, the newspaper publisher, the successful merchants, the bankers, lawyers, judges, and the city's patriarch, Paris Gibson.[7] The architecture was regionalist — that is, it expressed the styles of the regions where homeowners had once lived: Arts and Crafts, Queen Anne, gingerbread Victorian, New England colonial. Some houses were stone, some clapboard; some had maids' quarters, most did not.

In Great Falls, all the citizens knew where they fit in; if they did not, their neighbors had subtle ways of reminding them. Women of standing joined — rather, were invited to join — the Twentieth-Century Book Club, the Shakespeare Club, the Browning Club, the Tuesday Music Club. The most exclusive sorority was the Maids & Matrons, which convened regularly for luncheons, teas, and self-appreciation. No Maid, Matron, or Maid/Matron aspirant was ever seen in public without hat and gloves. Men joined clubs, too, sometimes for business, sometimes for poker, often taking care of both at the same time. Husbands of the Maids & Matrons, though not active in any organized way, comically referred to themselves as "Mutts & Muttons."[8]

Even the saloons in Great Falls came to be stratified. The ultimate measure of a man was not whether he drank, but whom he drank with. During the Russells' time in Great Falls, the dominant watering holes were the Maverick, the Brunswick, the Silver Dollar, and the Mint. The latter two would draw the lion's share of Charlie's patronage. The capacious Mint, with its solid mahogany fixtures and backward-running clock that had to be read by looking in the plate-glass mirrors around the main room, catered to a noisy "lunch-bucket" crowd. The cozier Silver Dollar, directly across Central Avenue, with its coin-inlaid floor and doorway, drew Great

Falls's "quality drinkers." Part of the attraction at both was the collection of Russell originals on the walls.9

Charlie was never one to dwell on Great Falls's hierarchical subtleties. Nancy, on the other hand, became an avid, though frequently frustrated, student of the game. Even before the Russells had left Cascade, she had made sure that their names and movements were recorded in "Spray of the Falls," the *Great Falls Tribune*'s society column. There are no equivalent clippings, however, documenting how Great Falls society received her. All that remain are the children and grandchildren of that era, who suggest that Nancy Russell's attempted entry into Great Falls society was met with a collective cluck of disapproval. Neither her gumption nor earnestness could redeem her humble roots. Despite the pride derived from being Mrs. Charles Russell, it galled Nancy no end that the world loved him better. Particularly in the early Great Falls years, she hated to have to share her husband with a town that thought so little of her. She always preferred him at home, working — to support them, of course, but also to keep him from "the bunch."

Charlie held the middle ground as best he could. He did it by splitting his day in two. Each morning he would rise before dawn, fix his own breakfast, and set to work by 6. At noon he would wash his brushes and eat the lunch Nancy cooked for him; the room in which he painted at the Seventh Avenue house faced west and was no good in the afternoon light anyway. So after a short digestive nap, Charlie would saddle Monte and disappear downtown for several hours.10 Nancy had her own ritual. As he rode off, she would stand at the door with two fingers held in the air: Two drinks, Charlie, only two drinks.11

Charlie's art at the time reflected his domestication, but it could be stubbornly atavistic too. While he was inclined to paint *Indian Hunters Return* (1900) of men bringing meat to their families or *The Picture Robe* (1899) of a brave and his mate nesting in their tepee, he directed a larger portion of his work at the saloon trade. For the Mint, Charlie painted a large oil, compositionally as busy as the roundup scene he had done for Shelton's saloon in Utica in the mid-1880s. *The Hold Up* depicted "Big Nose George" Parrott's infamous stickup of the Deadwood, South Dakota, stage in 1880.12 Anyone who followed the pulps was familiar with the outlaw's escapades: how Parrott and his gang had terrorized the Black Hills, were captured while robbing a Union Pacific train, then lynched in Wyoming. Charlie leaned heavily on a J. H. Smith illustration that had appeared in *Leslie's* and had his friend Con Price model for Big Nose George. But instead of painting familiar locals as the robbery victims, Charlie chose stereotypes of the time: the weak-kneed preacher, the bearded prospector, the hungover gambler, the pajama-clad Chinese, the beak-nosed Jewish peddler. Every Mint customer knew someone of their ilk and ethnicity. *The Hold Up* was a lasting conversation piece.

Marriage did not entirely stifle Charlie's bawdiness either. His cow-camp humor — "innate, sometimes lusty, always infectious," according to Joe DeYong — played well in barrooms, where women were not permitted.[13] His interest in the personal habits of the opposite sex extended beyond mere aesthetics. *Indian Maiden at Her Toilet* (1899) is a tender depiction of a fully dressed Indian woman braiding her hair. But *Indian Maiden Braiding Her Hair,* done the year before, is considerably more erotic. In it the woman is sitting by the water, a blanket covering her knees, but with her pubic area exposed. Her hair hangs to the side, revealing bare breasts.

For the Silver Dollar saloon, Charlie painted a series of four watercolors intended to tickle more than the funny bones of many customers. The first painting shows a cowboy seated in the shade of his horse, watching over the herd; the second shows the cowboy on horseback in a downpour; in the third the cowboy is seated on the edge of a prostitute's bed as she pulls off his boots; and in the final scene he is back on the range, grabbing his privates and dancing a tortured jig, a bottle of therapeutic elixir on the ground beside him. The titles of this moral montage are an apparent spoof of a well-known ditty of the day: *Just a Little Sunshine, Just a Little Rain, Just a Little Pleasure, Just a Little Pain.* It has often been speculated that Charlie mined his own medical history for the last panel.

The saloon patrons who liked the *Just a Little* quartet got an even bigger charge out of a watercolor that eventually bore the scholarly title *Cowboy Bargaining for an Indian Girl.* A young cowboy stands before a tepee, haggling with a seated Indian. The cowboy holds up one finger, offering one dollar for the Indian's daughter; the poker-faced father counters with two fingers. Meanwhile, the daughter stands nearby, eyes averted, her blanket pulled snugly about her.

Charlie depicted the result of a similar cross-cultural exchange in *Joy of Life,* a watercolor completed about the same time as *Just a Little* and *Cowboy Bargaining.* In later years, *Joy of Life* hung in a case the size of a modern-day jukebox or phone booth. The contraption was an early peep show. Saloon customers could peer into the box at a seemingly innocuous painting of an Indian brave guarding the door of his tepee. Off to one side, a cow pony and cow dog wait obediently. After the peeper deposited a coin in the slot, the tepee door pivoted open mechanically, affording a view inside the tent. Therein was revealed a cowboy in flagrante with the brave's daughter (or wife, perhaps). The details of their missionary coupling are as explicit as any illustration in *The Arabian Nights*. The punchline to this randy entanglement is delivered when, after glimpsing the indoor intimacy, the viewer takes a closer look at the rest of the painting and discovers that the cowboy's faithful dog is proudly displaying his own arousal.

It is hard to imagine how Charlie could have produced these risqué whimsies without getting caught, and censored, by Nancy. But somehow he did. She spent the rest of her life trying to retrieve them, but Bill Rance of the Silver Dollar, and then Sid Willis of the Mint, who bought them from Rance during Prohibition, never relented.

Rance was a Canadian, an ex-Mountie, who graduated from barkeep to proprietor. Joe DeYong recalls him as "free-wheeling, high-dealing." Rance's obituary describes him as an "authority on mixed drinks," a sports enthusiast, and a boulevardier rarely seen without a gold-headed cane.[14] Sid Willis was less colorful, more distinguished. Born in Arkansas (where he went to school with Will Rogers's wife), he first came to Montana in 1888 and had gone on to become sheriff of Valley County in northern Montana. In Great Falls, he went to work at the Maverick saloon; he then took over the Mint and later parlayed his popularity as a publican into stints as state senator and United States marshal.[15]

Charlie never renounced Rance, Willis, or his other drinking friends. Nor did he ever turn his back on the various clerks, tradesmen, laborers, cowhands, and children who greeted him as he made his rounds. As a little girl, Frances Longeway Flaherty sat on the fence in the front yard of her home on Third Avenue North every afternoon, waiting for Charlie to ride by. He always had a kind word, and recalling the effect of that sunny recognition eighty years later, Mrs. Flaherty chirped, "I nearly burst my buttons."[16] Memories that preserved little else over the course of decades still held clear pictures of Charlie's smile, gold rings, hand-rolled smokes, and sash. They remembered Monte and a later horse, Neenah, tied to the rail on Central Avenue or to a utility pole behind the Silver Dollar. They

noticed when Charlie was out of town; his return was cause for minor celebration. "It wouldn't be long until there was a group of men around him,"
one regular recalled. "When people saw Charlie on the street . . . they just
gravitated to him."[17]

Whether he had had two or a few on his afternoon rounds, he always
made it home in time for supper. This was a bargain with Nancy he never
broke. Evenings at home had their own pattern. Frequently he would pencil a sketch of the painting he planned to start in the morning. Often, too,
he would read. His library was long on Western history and travel; in particular, he pored over the writings of Lewis and Clark and other Missouri
River travelers who had come before his time. He also read popular magazines, novels, and books on Africa, Russia, and India. Although he was far
from an intellectual, he was constantly improving his mind and expanding
his knowledge of the world. Nancy, despite her unflagging commitment
to self-improvement, did not share his catholic inclinations.[18]

The first years in Great Falls were hard ones, and it is no wonder Nancy
begrudged Charlie his long afternoon recesses. The *Field and Stream* commissions paid poorly, and the hodgepodge of other illustration work did not
command much more. In 1899, he illustrated *Then and Now,* the memoir
of Robert Vaughn, who had helped Paris Gibson found Great Falls. Charlie also began doing steady business with the local W. T. Ridgley Printing Company. (Will Ridgley was married to Josephine Trigg, daughter
of Brunswick saloon owner Albert Trigg.) In 1899, Ridgley's firm compiled reproductions of twelve of Charlie's pen sketches in a bound volume
and sold separate prints for framing. Ridgley also published *Rhymes from
a Round-up Camp,* a Russell-illustrated collection of cowboy doggerel by
Charlie's friend Wallace Coburn of the Circle C ranch near Malta. A sample:

> Over the prairie the cow-boy rides,
>   As a modern knight he stands alone,
> Always ready with heart and hand,
>   A typical prince of the western zone.
>
> No other land can claim his like,
>   He's a native American, born and bred,
> A product of God's noblest land,
>   The land for which his fathers bled.[19]

Charlie's best paintings during this period were buffalo-hunt scenes. The worst were uncharacteristic clichés of Indians surrounding a wagon train or a group of dismounted plainsmen, firing from behind their horses in a desperate stand. But even while Charlie's commercialism was unabashed and despite Nancy's successes at upping his productivity and prices, he was not yet making a good living. If he was not worried, his father was.

Charles Silas Russell was running out of sons. Guy Russell, Charles and Mary's fourth son, five years Charlie's junior, had never been well. He had epilepsy, and his family had tried a variety of treatments for his seizures, all of them in vain. In the spring of 1898, Guy was a patient at the Baptist Sanitarium in East Alton, Illinois. On May 12, he wandered away from the hospital; the next day his body was found washed up on the bank of the Wood River. Suicide was ruled out. The local paper speculated that Guy Russell had been "in a spell of mental aberration, and [had been] seized with an epileptic attack in crossing the river." He had not yet reached his twenty-ninth birthday.[20] The news was withering to C. S. Russell, who had lost a wife and two other sons in less than a decade. His thoughts turned to his surviving children: Sue and Bent were both married and living in St. Louis, but his sandy-haired namesake was away in Montana.

In the summer of 1898, C. S. Russell made his first trip to Great Falls. Ed Russell, Jim Fulkerson, and Chiles Carr were the only family members to have visited Charlie before then, and all three were dead. No one in the family had ever met Charlie's bride. "The St. Louis Russells," nephew Austin joked, "feared Charlie had married a squaw, a halfbreed or something."[21]

Nancy proved to be a welcome surprise. "There was a question in the minds of the family and seeing the girl was the only way to settle it," she wrote in her memoir. "I guessed I passed inspection as Father always made me feel I was really and truly his daughter."[22]

After re-bonding with Charlie, and having been smitten by his diamond-in-the-rough daughter-in-law, C. S. Russell returned to St. Louis and set about helping the newlyweds in whatever ways he could. He began pushing Charlie's work in St. Louis, and through connections persuaded the well-regarded New York art dealer William Macbeth to take four of Charlie's watercolors.[23] C. S. Russell even began boning up on art technique; at one point he wrote to urge Charlie to consider working from live models, his advice based on a book he had just read about art in England.

Father Russell's love took material form as well. In November 1899, with Nancy's consent, he had a suit made for Charlie in St. Louis. At Christmastime, he sent Charlie and Nancy a package of canned goods and candy. "Tell him I will help him if he gets hard up. Will be glad to do it," Mr. Russell wrote to Nancy, and soon he forwarded a Parker-Russell Mining and Manufacturing dividend check for $500.[24]

Money was also forthcoming from the estate of Mary Mead Russell, and as soon as the weather broke that spring, Charlie and Nancy began building a new house on the corner of Thirteenth Street and Fourth Avenue North.[25] Contractor and neighbor George Calvert, who had built Charlie his first decent easel, set to work erecting a two-story frame with clapboard siding and steep, shake-shingle gables. The house was decidedly modest compared with some of its neighbors; Nancy herself called it a "cottage." The first floor consisted of a small front hall, dining room, bathroom, kitchen with maid's room, and parlor running across the front of the house; a steep stairway led to three small bedrooms and tiny water closet upstairs. Stylistically, the first floor was a sort of Arts and Crafts knockoff, with dark paneling and woodwork. The second floor was more like a New England farmhouse, the bedrooms squeezed under the gables and the windows too small and too few to let in much sunlight.

Charlie and Nancy moved in at the end of the summer. The *Tribune* ran a flattering photo of Charlie, arms crossed, necktie loose, and cowboy hat tipped back on his head. "Charley in His New Home" declared the two-column headline; by 1900, a last name was unnecessary. The text expressed a similar familiarity:

> Charley Russell, the famous cowboy artist, whose splendid works have won renown over the world, has finally concluded to settle down for all time to come. . . . The new residence will make a pretty and comfortable little home, and a little barn in the rear will hold Charley's famous calico horse [Monte] that the artist has refused $7,000 for on various occasions.

The conclusion of the article reads more like a bachelor-party ribbing than a society-page notice and reveals as much about Charlie's public jocularity as it does about his private life:

Charley is devoting his time at present to arranging the hot house and caring for the splendid growth of hay in the back yard [an inside joke about lawn-mowing, no doubt; the backyard was not meadow size], and as long as Mrs. Russell watches him, he performs his task with ease and apparent pleasure. As soon as she retires for a moment from Charley's view, the artist mounts his pegassus [sic] and hies away down town to see the boys.[26]

The Russells' choice of lots had not been in any way random. The Triggs lived three doors down. Although portly Albert Trigg was a saloonkeeper, somehow the Russells, especially Nancy, never considered him a peer of Sid Willis, Bill Rance, or George "Cut Bank" Browne of the Maverick. The difference was that the Triggs were English — in their blood, their speech, their comportment. Though they had lived in Canada and then Michigan before settling in Great Falls, they had not discarded or played down their European sensibilities. Even Josephine, though born in the United States, never entirely lost her family's British accent.

The Trigg family proved to be a strong social influence on the Russells; they sensitized Charlie to his own Anglo ancestry, culminating in his trip to England in 1914, and Margaret Trigg provided Nancy with an informal course in table-setting, parlor protocol, and feminine fare-thee-well. The tie between the two families became so close that Nancy called Albert and Margaret "Father" and "Mother." Charlie and Josephine (who eventually divorced Will Ridgley) were like surrogate siblings; their relationship was so close that rumors still fly about their secret feelings for each other. When the Russells were in Great Falls, scarcely a day passed that they did not visit with the Triggs.

Nancy's education took another leap in the spring of 1901, when she and Charlie paid a visit to St. Louis — Nancy's first trip out of Montana since her arrival in Helena as a young girl. They stayed with Charlie's sister, Sue Portis, and her husband, Tom, a lawyer, in downtown St. Louis. Austin Russell, son of Charlie's brother Bent, remembered the gathering of the clan vividly. "This was Charlie's first exhibition: he exhibited his wife." Apparently the refined St. Louisans approved of Nancy, but according to Austin, "were shocked by her English, which was worse than Charlie's, and amused by her clothes and by her ignorance of everything they thought important." They gave her good marks for her adaptability, however: "A girl that age is like water; pour her into a pitcher, no matter how convoluted, and she takes the pitcher's shape with effortless ease."[27]

At times, however, Nancy did slosh over. The most comical faux pas occurred during her first-ever elevator ride. As the car ascended, she reportedly grabbed herself around the midriff and blurted, "Oo! my stummick!" Such anatomical specificity was considered gauche in St. Louis in those days.

Charlie did his own share of shocking. His very appearance lifted eyebrows around town. In an era when gentlemen wore vests and suspenders, Charlie went vestless and held his trousers up with a sash. At a time when smoking cigarettes was considered lower-class, Charlie puffed away in public without inhibition. He never carried a handkerchief; instead, let the world know that he snorted cold water up his nose, in imitation of a horse's toilette. When Sue and Tom Portis took Charlie and Nancy to the opera, Austin reports, "Charlie escaped at the first intermission and didn't come back." When he rejoined Nancy and the Portises at the theater door later on, he told them that he had spent the interim at a nearby carnival watching a sideshow performer bite the heads off live snakes.[28]

The newspapers liked everything about Charlie. After describing examples of his art hanging at the Portis house and at a local gallery, the *St. Louis Post-Dispatch* recapped Charlie's now-mythic hegira through the Judith Basin, his ordeal during the winter of 1887, and his sabbatical on the Blood reserve. Above all, the writer was transfixed by Charlie's physical charm:

> He is cast in [a] powerful mold. There is an amplitude of shoulders that tempts womankind to admire. There is a leonine head closely cropped and well set upon a neck like a Dorian column. The face glows with perfect health. It is frank and inviting. It is a face full of power as well. The features are large and suggest the strength and more of the nobility that he has stolen from his Indian friends and transferred to canvas. Deep-set, penetrating blue-gray eyes have a direct gaze. . . . A square, massive chin bespeaks decision.[29]

CHARLIE RETURNED TO Great Falls and buckled down. He did some very strong work that year and the next, including three oils of Indian action, *The Horse Thieves, Counting Coup, Trouble Hunters,* and several buffalo-hunt scenes. In 1902, he traveled to the site of the Custer massacre and the following year did a watercolor of the 1876 battle — again from the Indians' perspective.[30]

All of these splendid pieces were completed without the benefit of a decent place to work. Even in the new house, he had to commandeer the dining room as his studio, filling the hall, parlor, and upstairs with the smell of turpentine and paint and forcing Nancy to serve all their meals in the kitchen.[31] He needed a proper studio.

The best account of the studio's genesis comes from Nancy's introduction to *Good Medicine:*

> After the cottage home was finished and furnished, Charlie said, "I want a log studio some day, just a cabin like I used to live in."
>
> That year, 1903, the studio was built on the lot adjoining the house. Charlie did not like the mess of building so he took no more than a mild interest in the preparations. Then, one day, a neighbor said, "What are you doing at your place, Russell, building a corral?"
>
> That settled it. Charlie just thought the neighbors didn't want the cabin mixed in with the civilized dwellings and felt sure they would get up a petition to prevent our building anything so unsightly as a log house in their midst. But way down in his heart, he wanted that studio. It was the right kind of work-shop for him, but he was worried at what he thought the neighbors would say, so said he would have nothing to do with it.[32]

For lack of better timber, Charlie was obliged to build the studio out of telephone poles. Telephone service had begun in Great Falls in 1890 with 137 customers and had expanded rapidly over the next decade. As with all things mechanical, Charlie was slow to subscribe. Even after he allowed Nancy to have a phone installed in the house, he approached it "with hesitation and handled it with caution — even a scowling suspicion, as though it might jump out and bite him," Joe DeYong recalled.[33]

It followed, then, that the notion of a log cabin made of telephone poles would be every bit as perturbing as the broader issue of neighborhood approval. Charlie refused to go near the studio, according to Nancy, until one evening Albert Trigg came over and said:

"Say, son, let's go see the new studio. That big stone fireplace looks good to me from the outside. Show me what it's like from the inside."

Charlie looked at me kind of queer. The supper dishes had to be washed. That was my job just then, so Charlie took Mr. Trigg out to see his new studio that he had not been in. When he came back into the house, the dishes were all put away.

Charlie was saying, "That's going to be a good shack for me. The bunch can come visit, talk and smoke, while I paint."[34]

Forever after, he called it his "shack." It was one room, twenty-four by thirty, with the stone fireplace at one end, and a narrow porch whose roof was soon strewn with elk horns in the custom of an old-time cow or hunting camp. Because cabins are notoriously dim, Charlie had a skylight installed in the roof. He furnished the room with the most rustic stools and benches and carpeted it with buffalo and bear skins. Over the years the studio became more and more cluttered with Charlie's personal museum of cowboy and Indian gear. An inventory prepared after his death lists more than three hundred items, including moccasins, shields, bows, arrows, travois, breechcloths, beads, medicine bags, coupsticks, cradleboards, pipes, Indian saddles, Western saddles, packsaddles, bridles, quirts, spurs, and an arsenal of old guns.[35] These were useful props for Charlie's art, but on another level they were sacred mementos, each with its own magical story. To enter Charlie's studio was to step far away from Electric City. Too, it was like entering a young boy's playhouse: toys everywhere, and civilization kept out.

Much of what is known about Charlie's studio habits comes from Joe DeYong, who began sharing the log studio years later. When fully engrossed in his work, Charlie was a man who had left the here and now. His "employment of . . . certain mental processes," DeYong wrote, "verged on a combination of clarevoyance [sic], self-hypnotism and, possibly, spiritualism. . . . [A]t least there is no other way to account for, or describe his ability to reach back into earlier time and temporarily lose himself in order to visualize the types, dress and activities of the peoples of those remote times."[36]

Nancy called Charlie's absorption "the Great Silence." In the studio, with the morning sun beginning to seep through the skylight, Charlie would throw himself into the project of the moment. Sometimes he would work out an idea with pencil and paper, "sketching with the freedom of a cartoonist." Often he would make a model of his subject from beeswax or clay, using the touch of a finger to program his painter's eye. But even without a model, he had the ability to visualize any subject in the round. When the time came to start the actual painting, he fairly leaped to the task — "no procrastination, no mental shadow boxing, no rig a ma roll . . . of warming up exercises," DeYong noted. "[H]e simply knew what he wanted to do and went at it!" Typically he sat on an old, backless kitchen chair.[37] When a cigarette was not stuck between his lips, a paintbrush or two took its place.

Charlie developed different routines to keep his momentum up and to propel himself through trouble spots. "I think its better to work all over your picture [and] not finish one figer and then another. [I]t rests you," Charlie scribbled in one of his studio notes to DeYong. He also preferred to work on two or three paintings at a time; while one was drying, he could press forward on the others. When he stalled, unsure how a figure should look, he would remove his shirt and study his own anatomy in the mirror.[38] On the rare occasions when his muse deserted him, he would wander across the alley to the firehouse and chat with the firemen. Or he would practice rope tricks in the yard. Sometimes he would flee entirely. "Often on a frosty morn," recounted DeYong,

> when the work wouldn't go so well, he'd put on a mackinaw, pick up a bridle, pull his hat down & step outside where [his horse] would be stepping about pretty with his neck & tail kinked, blowing mighty scarey. . . . An hour or so later he'd come back, his face red & a light sort of blazing in his grey eyes. . . . He didn't ever say much at such times but you could tell he'd got what he'd gone for — he'd made connections. The work'd go with a swing then, & he'd step back & forth to and from his easel with a quick impatient sort of toss of that long lock of sandy hair that hung down at the side of his forehead. A trick he had when inspiration crowded close — and after a while when he'd stop to build a cigarette, [he would] grin in sort of a shame faced way & sign, "My medicine is strong now."[39]

Charlie was able to concentrate even with other people in the room, which was a blessing. As his work and his whereabouts became better known, more and more visitors came to see the Cowboy Artist in action.

Indeed, the number of people who claim to have visited the studio to watch Charlie paint compares to the number of people who insisted they rode the range with him. Children in particular were attracted to the cabin. (One of the young visitors was Wallace Stegner, who lived in Great Falls in 1920 and did occasional chores for the Russells.)[40] Most reminiscences echo that of L. E. Falk, who grew up down the block:

> If one entered and he did not look up from his work, it was a sign that he was busy and all who knew him would make their exit as graciously as possible. If he laid down his brushes and palette and reach[ed] to his shirt pocket for his tobacco and made ready to roll a cigarette, the gods smiled on the visitor . . . for that meant a most delightful half hour of talk about anything that might be on his mind.[41]

Charlie's old-time roundup cronies were constantly drifting through Great Falls, and Nancy did not have the heart to rebuff all of them:

> One of Charlie's great joys was to give suppers cooked over the fire, using a Dutch oven and frying pan, doing all the cooking himself. . . . There was usually bachelor bread, boiled beans, fried bacon, or if it was Fall, maybe deer meat, and coffee; the dessert must be dried apples. A flour sack was tucked in his sash for an apron and, as he worked, the great beads of perspiration would gather and roll down his face and neck.
>
> [After the meal,] the coffee pot would be pushed to one side, frying pan and Dutch oven pulled away from the fire, and Charlie would get the "makins." Sitting on his heels . . . he would roll a cigarette with those long, slender fingers, light it, and in the smoke, drift back in his talk to times when there were very few, if any, white women in Montana.[42]

A frequent visitor was Con Price, who had ridden with him in the 1880s. Another was Henry Keeton, a Judith alumnus who then lived around the corner in Great Falls; Charlie would immortalize him as Highwood Hank in the first Rawhide Rawlins collection. Yet another drop-in was Pete Van, whose dismissal from the Judith Basin roundup in 1882 for sleeping on watch cleared the way for Charlie's first night-wrangling job. "Pete and I were friends since boy hood in the days when friendship meant more than a handshake," Charlie later eulogized. "Our home was where we spread our blankets. . . . Often the Roof leaked making it wet cold and lonesome, but its discomforts that pans out the good and bad in man."43

The rougher they came, the more he liked having them around, especially in the years of claustrophobic celebrity. One such hard case was Johnny Matheson, the last of the jerkline freighters to ply the route from Fort Benton to the Judith.44 Matheson was one of Nancy's least favorite people, and he frequently tried to time his arrivals to coincide with her absences. Matheson never was entirely housebroken. Even though the Russells' indoor plumbing worked fine, the old freighter still felt more comfortable relieving himself in the backyard.

Charlie always had time for his Indian friend Young Boy. Young Boy was a Cree, a people whose original hunting grounds were the woodlands and plains of Canada, just west of the Great Lakes.45 Along with the Chippewa, with whom the Cree intermarried, the tribe had been pushed ever westward and had ultimately sided with the rebellion of Louis Riel's Métis in their 1876 fight for an independent homeland in Saskatchewan. As a result, neither the United States nor the Canadian government would officially recognize the Cree-Chippewa. They were forced to drift across the northern plains, humiliated and starving. By the turn of the century, a small band of Cree-Chippewa, including Young Boy, were squatting across the river, opposite Great Falls. They survived by selling their remaining possessions, particularly hat racks made of old buffalo or beef bones they had found on the plains. Often they fed themselves by scavenging through the garbage cans in the city's fastidiously planned warren of alleys.

Charlie clearly sympathized with the plight of Young Boy's Cree and saw Young Boy as a tutor of the lessons of the past. Though Charlie resisted using live models for his paintings, on occasion he made exceptions with Young Boy. Young Boy returned Charlie's friendship with gifts of his own, including an Indian shield and other traditional accessories. Young Boy also helped Charlie acquire a new horse. In 1901, Charlie's faithful mount Monte was on its last legs. (The pinto would die two years later on a ranch owned by Paris Gibson; the Great Falls paper saw fit to run an obituary, citing age and indigestion as the cause of death.)46 The replacement Young Boy found was Neenah ("Chief"), a notoriously snuffy bay gelding, especially on cold mornings. Charlie rode Neenah until the horse died in 1919; it was the last horse he ever kept in Great Falls.

In 1902, Charlie hooked up with another wanderer. A native of Newburgh, New York, William S. Hart had spent his childhood in the West — Wisconsin, Minnesota, the Dakotas.[47] Hart encountered Indians, trail drives, even a shootout between a sheriff and two outlaws. Returning east as a teenager, he threw himself into acting. Fame and prosperity came slowly, however. In the second decade of the twentieth century, Hart would become the first cowboy movie star, almost single-handedly lifting the emerging genre from tawdriness to glory; but in 1902, he was slogging across the country in a play called *The Christian*. In February it was booked into the Grand Opera House in Great Falls. The high point of this chilly stopover was a visit to the home of the town's best-known artist. Afterward Hart sent Charlie two photos of himself. "The world is wide," Hart wrote, "but I trust we may some day meet again."[48]

Charlie took four months to respond, handcuffed by his writing disability. "I liked [the photos] verry much," he scratched. "I guess you think Im a long time saying so but you wont have to go far in this letter to find out that writing is no pass time with me its WORK." Here Charlie inserted a nifty drawing of himself in sash and boots, hat knocked to the floor, struggling over a writing table; next to it he added a sketch of a pen, ink bottle, and paper. "I am average on talk but hand me these tools an Im deaf and dum." Like Hart, he signed off with the hope that they would meet again: "Well if you ever drift west which I hope you will an sight the smoke of my camp come and as our red brothers say my pipe will be lit for you."[49]

Hart promptly wrote back a nine-page letter that epitomized the sentiments of all the friends who would ever receive an illustrated note from Charlie: "I shall value it & treasure it always. By thunder! what a genius you are in your art." Then, commiserating with Charlie's complaint that writing was "work," he presumed that it was lack of formal schooling that held Charlie back. "You have had the greatest college on earth to grow up in[,] Nature — Nature which throws back the lie in the teeth of the cramped and cooped up civilization. You were cradled in that great west at a time when the air and water and the ground were free gifts to man and no one had the power to portion them out by measure or weight."[50]

THAT SUMMER OF 1902, the West was stirring the passions of a lot of Americans. In April, Owen Wister had published *The Virginian;* by January

1903, it had been reprinted fifteen times; over the next eight years, presses would turn out twenty-three more editions.[51] Not simply a runaway best-seller, the novel was received as "literature," the first Western to be set on the shelf next to *Pride and Prejudice* or *Ivanhoe.*

Suddenly the West was more than noble; it was downright chic. Rough Rider Theodore Roosevelt was now in the White House. The railroads, along with delivering immigrants to their sod homesteads, were carrying increasing numbers of tourists to hot springs, dude ranches, and newly opened national parks across the West. Wild West shows, especially Buffalo Bill's, were well attended.

Western art had been growing in popularity as well. Frederic Remington was going great guns, having published nearly three thousand illustrations in popular magazines. For more than a decade, Joseph Henry Sharp had been winning acclaim for his paintings of the natives of Taos, New Mexico, and had paved the way for E. Irving Couse, Ernest Blumenschein, Oscar Berninghaus, Herbert Dunton, Maynard Dixon, and an entire school of Southwestern artists. By 1898, Sharp was also making regular trips to the Crow reservation in Montana. And in 1899, Charles Schreyvogel, an unknown German-American raised in New York, won a prestigious award from the National Academy of Design for his cavalry scene, *My Bunkie.*[52]

Now with the success of *The Virginian,* the stampede to stake out the West as a literary and aesthetic genre grew thunderous. Six months after Wister's publication, his good friend Remington published his own novel, *John Ermine of the Yellowstone,* which also sold briskly and then became a Broadway play. Andy Adams's trail-driving true story, *The Log of a Cowboy,* appeared that same year, and the first Western movie, *The Great Train Robbery,* shot in New Jersey and starring Broncho Billy Anderson, riveted nickelodeon patrons and tripped a floodgate of enthusiasm for screen shoot-'em-ups.

One of the more overlooked contributions to the Western rush of 1902–03 was a short story written by an ex-convict who used the pen name O. Henry. "Art and the Bronco" is the tale of Lonny Briscoe, a cowboy with ambitions as a painter. Briscoe has painted an enormous panorama, "a typical Western scene, interest culminating in a central animal figure, that of a stampeding steer, life-size, wild-eyed, fiery, breaking away in a mad rush from the herd [which is] close-ridden by a typical cowboy." The fact that the canvas was so realistic and had been painted by a real cowboy "counted high against faulty technique and crude coloring." After considerable arm-twisting and speechifying, the legislator from Briscoe's remote district succeeds in passing a bill to purchase the picture and hang it in the state capitol. Briscoe, who has ridden his bronc Hot Tamales to town for the occasion, ultimately realizes that he and his painting are merely props in a larger drama of boondoggle and ego inflation on the part of the bill's sponsor. He sees that his work, for all its vividness, is not really fine art after all. O. Henry, in an uncharacteristic ending, has Briscoe ride Hot Tamales up the capitol steps and into the hallway where the picture is hanging. The horse spies the nearly life-size tableau.

> His ears pricked up; he snorted. . . . Did Hot Tamales fancy he saw a steer, red and cavorting, that should be headed off and driven back to herd? There was a fierce clatter of hoofs, a rush, a gathering of steely flank muscles, a leap to the jerk of the bridle rein, and Hot Tamales, with Lonny bending low in the saddle to dodge the top of the frame, ripped through the great canvas like a shell from a mortar, leaving the cloth hanging in ragged shreds about a monstrous hole.

Charlie never acknowledged having read O. Henry's story; it certainly never came up in 1912, when Charlie was commissioned to do an equivalent canvas for the Montana capitol. As proof that O. Henry's low opinion of the emerging genre of Western art was not universal, a correspondent for the *Chicago Record-Herald* hailed Charlie as "the greatest American artist," and in the fall of 1902, art dealer William Macbeth wrote to Nancy asking for more work.[53] "I must frankly say that I like your husbands work better than that of any artist in his field," Macbeth stated. He specifically requested more "action" pictures. Nancy, smelling gravy, replied with a quick assurance — except that instead of $40 for Charlie's watercolors, the price Macbeth had set before, she now demanded more than $100 apiece. Macbeth balked politely: "When Mr. Russell is as well known here as he ought to be he will get much higher prices."[54]

In August 1903, Great Falls writer-photographer Sumner W. Matteson, on assignment for *Leslie's,* visited the Fourth Avenue studio and received a rich dose of Russell medicine. At first he found Charlie as "stolid and indifferent" as an Indian. Eventually, though, the atmosphere warmed up.

"He has a large heart," Matteson reported, "and spreads it on the canvas in a way that makes his pictures breathe the incense of the prairie and glow with tints that only a true Westerner could appreciate." Matteson was likewise impressed by Nancy, pronouncing her "a good type of thorough-going Western woman." He credited her with holding a monopoly on the family's energy and ambition, and "knowing her husband's natural ability . . . she has taken the contract to make good his shortcomings. . . . Their devotion to each other is truly beautiful."[55]

With the climate so fair, and Charlie and Nancy in apparent harmony, the time had come to break out. Quite serendipitously, the path led to St. Louis.

The centennial of the Louisiana Purchase was shaping up to be an even bigger extravaganza than the 1893 Columbian Exposition. Nancy was determined that Charlie's work be included in the fair's immense art exhibition, the purpose of which was to celebrate a hundred years of western expansion. She had begun her campaign a full year ahead. She had written to William Macbeth, asking for advice on the best way to approach fair officials, given the crush of expected entrants. On the same day, she had also written to Charles Kurtz in the fair's department of art; the letter, for all its directness, belied her little fish–big pond trepidation. "Dear Sir," she began,

> I wish to know in what way one goes about it to get a painting in the gallery there at the Fair[.] I write in my husbands intrust and hope you will look at some of his work before you decide whether you have room or not. He is not knowen very well in that part of the country so I have no doubt you will not know what style his work is and for that reason I will be glad to send you a sampel when I here from you and am shure of your address[.] Kindley let me hear from you.[56]

Kurtz wrote back perfunctorily, sending her only a "general circular of information."[57] Her best chance, she figured, was to travel to St. Louis and meet with the fair officials in person. On October 8, armed with several watercolors — including *Roping a Grizzly,* the first painting completed in the new studio, and *Pirates of the Plains,* of a group of Indians — she and Charlie prepared to embark for St. Louis.

Just before train time, as chance would have it, Charlie and Nancy ran into John N. "March" Marchand and Will Crawford, two illustrators from the East. The demand for Western illustration was steady in New York, and they had come to Montana to soak up the scenery and gather artifacts to be used as studio props. They had been guests of cowboy poet Wallace Coburn at his family ranch near Malta. Marchand had seen some of Charlie's illustrations previously, and no doubt it was Coburn who urged the two to pay a visit to Great Falls. As Bill Hart had done the year before, Marchand and Crawford cordially pleaded with Charlie to look them up if he ever decided to try New York. There was lots of work to be had, especially for a guy with Charlie's credentials; they'd show him around.[58]

Charlie's response, though unrecorded, would have been friendly, but predictably noncommittal — that is, if the invitation even registered at all. Nancy, it would soon become obvious, had been listening very carefully.

9

TALL TEPEES

CHARLIE'S HOMETOWN HAD evolved in the twenty-three years since he had left it. Like the rest of America, St. Louis had become a melting pot; a full 60 percent of its residents were foreign-born or had foreign-born parents. The city had six German-language newspapers and only three in English.[1] Even so, St. Louis was still controlled by many of the same families — names such as Chouteau, Clark, and Carr. The downtown circle of bankers, lawyers, merchants, and manufacturers was dubbed the "Big Cinch," for its hold on politics, commerce, and society.[2] "Boodle," the term for back-room graft and influence-peddling, had become standard practice and had drawn the ire of muckraking journalists, particularly Lincoln Steffens, author of *The Shame of the Cities* (1904). "The corruption of St. Louis came from the top," Steffens wrote in the October 1902 issue of *McClure's.* The timing of this humiliating national attention could not have been more awkward. "[T]he fourth city in size in the United States," Steffens said, "is making two announcements to the world: one that it is the worst-governed city in the land; the other that it wishes all men to come there (for the World's Fair) and see it."

For the sake of the city and the fair, St. Louis took steps to straighten up its image. A number of boodlers were sent to jail; a new mayor promised a cleaner "New St. Louis." But in truth, the same people were still in charge in 1903 as in 1893, when Chicago had wowed the world with its fair. Back then, Mayor David R. Francis and a committee of his fellow St. Louis businessmen had vowed to host a fair in St. Louis that would eclipse Chicago's. Toward this end, he and his team formed a corporation in 1899 and set out to raise $15 million in seed money. One of the corporate subscribers was the Parker-Russell Mining and Manufacturing Company; two of the directors of the Louisiana Purchase Exposition Company were Charlie's uncle George W. Parker and Frederick Niedringhaus, whose family owned several Russell paintings. David Francis, who had held stock in Parker-Russell since 1885, was named president of the fair.[3]

Whether Nancy pulled strings is not known, but on November 3 she gained an interview with the chief of the department of art, Halsey C. Ives. He was director of the St. Louis Museum of Fine Arts and had been chief of the Chicago fair's art department ten years earlier. All told, he was responsible for the display of eleven thousand art objects from twenty-seven countries. Between the submission deadline of December 1 and the selection date of March 1, Ives and his staff would choose 3,648 pieces by American artists from a considerably larger pool of submissions.[4] Given such an enormous task, any special attention afforded the wife of Charles M. Russell was precisely that — special.

In the end, Nancy submitted six of Charlie's paintings. Her application lists *Running Fight (Crows & Bloods)*, *The Upper Missouri (in 1840)*, *Roping a Rustler* (in fact, *Roping a Grizzly*), *Pirates of the Plains*, *The Challenger*, and *The Dancing Master*.[5]

Five days after the deadline for submissions, a curious article in the *St. Louis Post-Dispatch* reported that Charlie was busy "modeling a series of studies which he intends to enter as exhibits in the fine arts display during the World's Fair." Illustrating the article was a picture of an Indian on horseback done in wax.[6]

Having failed to submit any models or sculpture to the main fine-arts exhibit, Charlie must have been eyeing the outdoor sculpture competition. But that deadline had passed as well; the winners had been made public, and some statues were already in place — as Charlie had discovered when he inspected the fairgrounds a month earlier. The centerpiece of the fair was a man-made cascade that tumbled into a Grand Basin, an obvious imitation of Chicago's lagoon. Of greater interest to Charlie were the sculptures chosen to decorate paths, pavilions, colonnades, and the Ten-Million-Dollar Pike, St. Louis's answer to Chicago's Midway Plaisance. These included statues of Sioux and Cherokee warriors and famous explorers: Lewis and Clark,

Daniel Boone, DeSoto, Joliet. All of these Charlie probably dismissed for what they were: stiff, classical treatments of unclassical subject matter.

The truly Western pieces were a different story. Four sculptures by Utah-born Solon Borglum were given a prominent place beside the main lagoon. Borglum's *The Buffalo Dance, Cowboy at Rest, The Indian Sage,* and *A Peril on the Plains* were subjects Charlie might well have done himself. Borglum's older brother Gutzon (who would later add Mount Rushmore to his portfolio) was prominently featured as well. His piece *Mares of Diomedes,* of a group of plunging, galloping horses, was chosen for the sculpture court of the fair's central pavilion. Perhaps the best placement of all went to Frederic Remington's sculpture *Cowboys on a Tear.* Four yahooing horsemen, six-guns in the air, announced the entrance to the Pike and set a lively tempo for the entire exposition.[7] "It is very grand but don't interest me much," Charlie wrote dismissively to Albert Trigg after his visit to the grounds.[8] Still, he must have been impressed. There can be no other explanation for why he became so engrossed in modeling that fall in St. Louis and why he publicly stated his aim to have his own sculptures appear at the fair (though he never did submit any).

AFTER THE COMMOTION of entering the fine-arts competition, the pressure was off for a while. Charlie hung some of his work in a downtown St. Louis gallery, but concentrated most of his attention on family. He and Nancy split their stay between sister Sue Portis and brother Bent. Bent had followed a more conservative path than Charlie, becoming an engineer for the city of St. Louis. In his own way, he would garner a snippet of glory at the World's Fair. Ever since the day Laclède and Chouteau had first pulled ashore below the mouth of the Missouri, St. Louisans had accepted muddy drinking water as a fact of everyday life. Without a drastic change, the soon-to-be-completed cascade of the Grand Basin would resemble a boiling pot of gravy. With fair officials breathing down their necks, Bent Russell and his fellow engineers cast about for a solution, finally installing a state-of-the-art filtration system for the entire city. On March 21, 1904, just five weeks before the opening of the fair, a clear, potable liquid began flowing from St. Louis taps. Natives accustomed to quaffing the local gruel eventually identified it as water.[9]

Unlike Charlie, Bent was interested in all the new gizmos. In 1903, only two or three hundred automobiles navigated the streets of St. Louis; one of them belonged to Bent Russell. This may well have been Charlie and Nancy's first intimate exposure to the "skunk wagon," Charlie's pejorative term for the machine whose fuel was especially vile-smelling in those days. He made his disdain clear in an illustrated letter to Bill Rance, knowing it would be passed around among the regulars at the Silver Dollar: "I am here in the smoke of the tall teepees an about the onley excitment I get is dodging [street] cars and automobiles but thats plenty[. O]f course the law enforces them to ring the bell after pasing over a human but I think thats to call the wagon which hauls you to the morgue." In describing a twenty-five-cent taxi ride, he allowed: "Id a give more than that to walk[. B]etwene holding on and staying under my hat I was mighty bussy."[10]

He missed the simpler St. Louis of his childhood, regardless of its water quality. In his letter to Albert Trigg, he said that he had been more impressed by the animals at the nearby zoo than by the fairgrounds. The zoo had a very good collection, he wrote, including "a cyote who licked my hand like he knew me[.] I guess I brought the smell of the planes with me[.] I shure felt sorry for him poor deval." In the end, he found his old haunts "much bilt up" and told Trigg he missed the mountains. "I cant see far enough," he complained.

There was one final burst of excitement during this trip to St. Louis: Nancy heard from her father. The standard story is that James Albert Cooper had seen the profiles in the St. Louis papers that fall and had spied the mention of Charlie's go-getter wife, Mamie Cooper Russell.[11] Out of love, guilt, or a gold digger's reflex, he supposedly had written her in care of the Russell family.

This makes for a wonderfully dramatic turn — like a chapter from a Victorian novel — but it is not an entirely trustworthy tale. While it is true that Nancy first met her father that fall, the reunion probably did not happen with such snug serendipity. For starters, neither of the articles on Charlie to appear in the St. Louis papers during their visit had mentioned Nancy's name. Furthermore, if Nancy had not been aware of her father's existence when she was growing up, as many biographies aver, then why had she used the name Cooper on her wedding license? Answers are not forthcoming, but an argument can be made that Nancy did have some knowledge of her father, perhaps some contact with him, before 1903. At the very least, he could have known of her whereabouts since 1901, for that is when her name had first appeared in the St. Louis paper. The item read: "Accompanied by Mrs. Russell, whom he met and loved at first blush, five years ago, at Cascade, Mont., as Miss Mamie Cooper, a former Kentucky girl, [Charlie] is visiting his father, Charles S. Russell, president of the Parker-Russell Mining & Manufacturing company."[12] Whatever the truth, Nancy hurried to Mr. Cooper as soon as she received his letter.

Cooper was working at a small hotel in Paxton, Illinois, north of Champaign and not far from the Indiana state line. The only extant account of their meeting is a single letter that Nancy wrote to Charlie back in St. Louis:

> I arrived O.K. My Dady meet me at Champaign and took me to his brothers house to stay[. T]hey seem very nice and were very much disapointed at your not coming with me[. W]e have been playing Flinch all evening but it is time to go to bed. . . . I cant tell just how I will be home. . . . I cant leave here till Monday[. T]hey want me to stay[.] I realy must stay[.] I will explain when I see you. Give my love to the folks and lots to your dear self. Your Wife Nancy.[13]

Father and daughter hit it off immediately, and James Cooper was never again out of touch with Nancy. He would live for a while in Great Falls, make frequent visits to Lake McDonald, and eventually marry one of the Russells' housekeepers and live next door to Nancy in Pasadena after Charlie's death. Yet little is known about Cooper's doings between 1878 and 1903; the best that can be said is that he was a jack of many trades. Few people could see any family resemblance. "He didn't look at all like [Nancy]," Austin Russell wrote.

> She was blonde and plump and he dark and thin, but he had the same driving nervous energy, and though the mess he made of his marriage [to Texas Annie Mann] and a lifetime of loneliness had given him an anxious, timid, apologetic look, this timidity never prevented his branching out and trying new things in business and he nearly always made money. . . . It was an enormous release to him to find that he had a daughter and was not, as he had always supposed, entirely alone in the world.[14]

In a way, Cooper had more in common with Charlie than with Nancy. They had a workingmen's rapport. A few days after Nancy's return from

Illinois, Cooper came to St. Louis for a visit. Forever after, Charlie called his father-in-law Coop.

After nearly three months in St. Louis, Charlie and Nancy might reasonably have been tempted to return to Great Falls to recover from the hubbub of family, the city, the gallery exhibit, the fair entry, and the holidays. Some accounts have said that their plan all along was to proceed to New York; others suggest that their decision to continue eastward after New Year's was more impulsive.

There had been no sense in waiting around to see whether the Louisiana Purchase Exposition had accepted him; a decision would not be made until March 1. "Whether or not [Charlie's art] will come up to the technical standard of [the fair] committee and be hung in the great art gallery of that exposition is problematical."[15] So said the *Great Falls Tribune* the day after Charlie left Montana, and it was a fair appraisal. Better for Nancy and Charlie to keep on the move than to sit home that winter, worrying.

NEW YORK WAS twice the shock St. Louis had been. A record cold gripped the East in early January; the streets were deep in snow. Gas explosions, gambling raids, and corruption trials were the talk of the town. A hundred thousand people visited the automobile show at Madison Square Garden, while concerned citizens complained that the installation of asphalt pavement on city streets would be cruel to horses.

The Park View Hotel faced Bryant Park, just off Broadway on Forty-second Street. The New York Public Library was under construction nearby. Unfortunately, Charlie and Nancy had a view of neither landmark; their $12-a-week room looked out on an airshaft. The one good thing about the address was its nearness to 132 West 42nd Street, the studio shared by John Marchand, Will Crawford, and a third illustrator, Albert Levering. They welcomed Charlie with "a hearty Western handclasp, and a kindly friendly smile," Marchand's sister recalled, "and . . . New York lost some of its terrors for the Westerner."[16]

Illustrators were enjoying a golden age.[17] At the end of the nineteenth century, new magazines had joined America's publishing wars, grabbing audience share and advertising dollars not only from the penny-dreadful dailies, but also from such staid journals as *Scribner's, Harper's, Leslie's, Century,* the *Nation,* and *North American Review.* Between 1895 and 1905, nine hundred new magazines appeared; at the top of the heap were the ten-cent monthlies — *McClure's, Cosmopolitan, Munsey's, Collier's, Argosy.* The newspapers responded by adding magazine-style Sunday supplements, which provoked the magazine industry to counter with weeklies of its own. It was a period of frantic one-upmanship and, as it turned out, a unique niche in the history of print. For as fast as the presses rolled, and as splashy as layouts became, the technology to reproduce photographs was not yet widespread. The demand for cartoonists and illustrators was enormous, for both advertising and editorial work, and some of America's best artists did their best work for publications. "The world today wants illustration," announced the great turn-of-the-century author-artist Howard Pyle, "and I, as an illustrator, believe that by nobly satisfying their wants there can be created from them another and vital art."[18]

In the 1890s, New York society illustrator Charles Dana Gibson had turned the heads of an entire nation with his "Gibson girl."[19] Drawn in black and white for *Collier's* and *Life,* she defined a fresh ideal of the American female. Gibson-girl illustrations were tacked on the walls of ladies' dressing rooms and immigrant sweatshops alike. Men worshiped her respectfully; women copied her. The Gibson girl was smart, active, pure, elegant, and commonsensical. Her breasts were small, her carriage erect, her hair swept back, her gaze direct. A photograph could not have created the stir that Gibson's illustrations succeeded in doing.

The potency of illustration was proved even more dramatically in February 1897, when Frederic Remington, working for William Randolph Hearst's *New York Journal,* drove the country to the brink of war with a single drawing.[20] Remington had heard the story of a Cuban woman who had been searched by Spanish detectives. (They had suspected her of carrying messages for insurgents.) His illustration showed three swarthy Spaniards in straw hats surrounding a naked woman. It was a sensational, inaccurate interpretation of the actual events, and it accomplished precisely what Hearst and Remington intended: every red-blooded, mother-loving American was outraged by the unspeakable depravity of those despots across the water. Only the sinking of the *Maine* in Havana harbor a year later had a greater incendiary effect.

Not every illustrator enjoyed the celebrity status of Pyle, Gibson, and Remington, but the camaraderie and energy shared by illustrators was strong indeed. Marchand, Crawford, and Levering gave Charlie a refuge and workplace, and they introduced him around town to other colorful characters. Charlie met Alfred Henry Lewis, author of the popular Wolfville novels; Ernest Thompson Seton, author and illustrator of *The Biography of a Grizzly* and *Lives of the Hunted;* and Bat Masterson, once a gunfighter, now a sportswriter. They took him to the Players, the Gramercy Park club founded by Shakespearean actor Edwin Booth; the membership included Mark Twain and Remington. (Charlie did not meet Twain, who had fallen behind in his dues, but he may well have met Remington, at least in passing. At the very least, Remington was by then aware of Charlie, who, along with Charles Schreyvogel, was being touted in the press as a pesky challenger to his throne.)[21]

Another of Charlie's guides in New York was William S. Hart, who had been hoping to get reacquainted for two years. "I received a card bearing a New York postmark," Hart recalled. "How! I'm in the big camp," was the only message. There was no signature, "just Charlie's emblem, the buffalo skull." Hart dropped by the Forty-second Street studio on several occasions. In those days, the neighborhood was thick with Runyonesque hustlers and hard cases. "Hell was poppin' down below on 42nd Street, seemed like more shots were bein' fired than had been in the Spanish-American war," Hart observed. "Seems like old times" was Charlie's wry response.[22]

Hart took Charlie and Nancy to Far Rockaway beach on Long Island so Charlie could get his first glimpse of the ocean. It was a "cold, cloudy January day," Hart recalled in his autobiography.

> The sea was angry, great breakers were smashing their way high up on the shore. . . . Nancy and I were stomping our feet and blowing on our fingers to keep warm, but Charlie — with head uncovered, his touseled blond mane blowing in the wind — was actually wading through the edge of the breakers.
> "Come out of there, you doggone sage brush cow-waddy."
> "I may never see this crick again, Bill," his voice trailed back through the wind. He put on his hat, as would a scolded kid complying with a reprimand; his feet were in the water, his boots were soaked, but he kept on walking just the same.[23]

The other favor Hart did for Charlie was to hook him up with a reporter.

"We were a pathetic little crowd," Hart described the meeting in his auto-biography. "Nancy was scared; Charlie wouldn't talk, and what I did not know about art did not need to be told. . . ."[24] Eventually, as was usually the case, Charlie defrosted somewhat. "Smart Set Lionizing Cowboy Artist" was the headline above the January 31 profile in the *New York Press*. The stage version of *The Virginian* had opened earlier that month to excellent reviews, and the enthusiasm for real-life cowboys in Gotham was apparently contagious. "[Charlie's] rugged simplicity and his quaint ideas about the people of New York delight those who have met him," the *Press* item read. "Aside from this his work as an artist is highly commended by the artistic set, who see in him a new type of the American painter. . . . Taciturn as a Sioux chief, self-contained and impassive, he is hardly the man to care for pink teas."

For all his reserve, Charlie still managed to regale the interviewer with an account of being surrounded by "a warparty of Piegans" during his trip with Pike Miller, and the usual embroidery on his Canadian sojourn. In the end, though, he scarcely needed to open his mouth; the *Press* writer was able to fill the page with his own imaginings. In Charlie's eyes, he wrote, "the tallest skyscrapers are but modest piles of stone. . . . He will remain a Westerner of the old school to the end, the Westerner who has conquered the bucking cayuse and who has stalled off the night stampede of maddened steers without a thought that the frenzied cattle might grind him to powder beneath their flying hooves."

Such exposure was all well and good, but the trip to New York was more than just a chance to gab and glad-hand. Charlie had not been very productive while in St. Louis. In New York, he claimed he did "consid-erable work." At first Charlie and Nancy had hung some of his paintings in a basement studio they had rented near their hotel. Nancy would collar anyone she could to come by for a look. Charlie would lurk in the back-ground, chain-smoking, as she tried to close a sale. They had few takers, however, and gave up the studio halfway through their stay. Charlie then accepted an invitation from Marchand, Crawford, and Levering to move in with them. They welcomed the chance to soak up the authentic details of his art and stories. He chided them for what he considered an overdependence on models, but overall, he probably learned as much from his studio mates as they did from him. Crawford, one of the best pen-and-ink men in the business, was particularly influential. He worked with the precision of an engraver, but his "shaky" style gave his illustrations an energy that appealed to Charlie.[25]

Though he never admitted it, New York was a bit of a catch-up course for Charlie, as he had spent more time around cowboys than he had around other artists. The barnlike Forty-second Street studio was a far cry from the nearby Art Students League, but for Charlie it was a chance to watch professionals mix colors, discipline their palettes, apply washes, and so on. After his visit to the East, his colors began to snap to attention and his shadows grew less deadly. Even while he was outwardly pooh-poohing high-brow art, his eyes were constantly picking up new methods and ideas. His standards rose accordingly.

Charlie also absorbed a great deal by touring the galleries and museums of New York. The big event that January was the seventy-ninth annual exhibition of the National Academy of Design, which featured paintings by Childe Hassam, Alden Weir, and Charles Schreyvogel among the three hundred–plus entrants. Within days of the opening of the National Academy's exhibit, the National Arts Club created a stir twenty blocks away with its show of work by Robert Henri, Arthur B. Davies, George Luks, John Sloan, William Glackens, and Maurice Prendergast. The bold and often gritty social realism of these six, most of whom had begun as illustrators, was just beginning to transform the New York art community. Soon they would be dubbed the Ashcan School.

One area in which Charlie seemed to need little guidance was sculpting. Whereas painting and drawing were an acquired skill, working with clay and beeswax was an unconscious act for Charlie. He could model a wild animal or a human head without looking — and did so frequently, behind his back or under the table "as casually as a farmer might whittle a stick of wood" for the amusement of friends and children.[26] In New York, perhaps inspired by the Remington statue he had seen at the fairgrounds in St. Louis, Charlie modeled *Smoking Up,* a twelve-inch-tall figure of a cowboy on a spree.[27] Though the horse is rearing, the cowboy sits effortlessly in the saddle, adjusting his balance with a deft shift of hips and stirrups. Draped in chaps, hat, and kerchief, he tugs on his reins with one hand while he points the other skyward, saluting life with his six-shooter. The emphatic O of his open mouth frames a shout that is quite nearly audible. *Smoking Up* was a triumph, as good as anything Charlie ever accomplished afterward, especially considering it had been executed in a Manhattan studio.

At some point, probably after he had completed *Smoking Up,* Charlie was introduced to Charles Schreyvogel.[28] Schreyvogel was three years older than Charlie, the son of German immigrants. He had lived most of his life on New York's Lower East Side and in the German neighborhoods of Hoboken, New Jersey. He had studied in Munich; upon his return to the United States, he began painting portraits of the members of Buffalo Bill's troupe and veterans of Indian wars stationed on Governor's Island. He finally made his first trip west in 1893 and then made several more by 1904, including a visit to the Blackfeet reservation in Montana. By the time Charlie met Schreyvogel, he was a successful, if controversial, member of the New York art community.[29]

Frederic Remington had never forgiven Schreyvogel for the award *My Bunkie* had received from the National Academy of Design in 1899. Remington had spent his career seeking the Academy's approval, with scant success, and he could not hold his temper when the April 19, 1903, edition of the *New York Herald* carried an eight-column-wide reproduction of Schreyvogel's latest cavalry painting, *Custer's Demand.* Below the picture was a photo of Schreyvogel, taken on the roof of his Hoboken brownstone. He stands at his easel in a bowler hat; kneeling in front of him is a mustachioed man in a cavalry uniform, gun drawn. Presumably Schreyvogel had recruited his model from a neighborhood beer hall just minutes before. The accompanying article heaped on the praise, calling Schreyvogel "the Painter of the Western Frontier."[30]

Four days after the *Herald* piece, Remington weighed in with a letter ripping *Custer's Demand* and Schreyvogel's credentials as a Western artist. "While I do not want to interfere with Mr. Schreyvogel's hallucinations," Remington hissed, "I do object to his half baked stuff being considered seriously as history."[31]

Remington prefaced his critique by saying, "I have studied and have ridden in the waste," but of course the pot was calling the kettle black. Over the years, Remington had come to believe the hype promulgated by his publishers, though by the time he wrote his letter to the *Herald,* he was living in New Rochelle, New York, and hiring a compliant Indian to model for him in his driveway. Even so, with righteous indignation he nitpicked *Custer's Demand* not on its aesthetic merits, but for its accuracy. The *tapadero* on a stirrup should have been oblong, not triangular; the stripe on a saddle blanket was wrong; one of the Indians' holsters was an anachronism.

The enormous contretemps that ensued eventually involved Custer's widow and even President Theodore Roosevelt. Elizabeth Custer said she found the likeness "excellent." Roosevelt reportedly told Schreyvogel that Remington had made "a perfect jack" of himself. The ultimate result was more fame for Schreyvogel.

Charlie and Schreyvogel apparently got along, for Charlie came away from their meeting with Schreyvogel's calling card. On the back Schreyvogel had written the name of Riccardo Bertelli, owner of the Roman Bronze Works in Brooklyn.[32] Charlie soon took *Smoking Up* to the Brooklyn foundry to be cast, and thereafter sent many more sculptures to Bertelli for bronzing.

While Charlie was meeting Schreyvogel and other artists or working in the Forty-second Street walk-up, Nancy was pounding the pavement in her role as Charlie's agent, making appointments with book and magazine editors around town. Crawford and the others had tried to give her some pointers on how to approach the profession, but all their advice was "very promptly and most emphatically rejected," according to one friend. She would do it her own way. If New York's men of publishing had expected the Gibson ideal, twenty-six-year-old Nancy Russell of Great Falls, Montana, came as a robust surprise. "Pretty as a young girl," according to Joe DeYong, "Nancy actually became beautiful with the passing years." Those not tempted to flirt were inclined to patronize her. Either way, Nancy had them right where she wanted them. Underneath she had a "shrewdly calculated manner of 'diplomatic-manipulation,' " DeYong, her devoted fan, would later write. Her gloves, "whether suede, buckskin, or velvet, actually contained a pair of brass knuckles." By the time Charlie and Nancy left the East in February, *Scribner's, Leslie's,* and *Outing* had all promised to use Charlie's illustrations. Nancy had also managed to sell at least one painting. The trip had been a success.[33]

CHARLIE AND NANCY arrived home in Great Falls on February 15, 1904, after being away more than four months. Charlie's appearance on Central Avenue "in the latest Fifth Avenue cut of a Tuxedo overcoat" was a major news event. To reassure the old crowd — and perhaps himself — that he had not become citified by his time in St. Louis and New York, he repledged his allegiance to the West. "Yes, I had a fine time," he told the

Tribune. "Everybody was mighty nice to me. As nice as they could be. But the east is not the west. Give me the choice of spending the rest of my life in either New York or Ulm [a community on the Missouri between Great Falls and Cascade] and I would take Ulm."

A throng gathered around Charlie as he stood at the bar, the *Tribune* man scribbling furiously as Charlie picked up steam and tipped back drinks:

The minute you get west of Chicago you can notice the difference in people. You begin to strike westerners again. If you go into a smoking car east of Chicago, sit down beside a man and start talking to him by saying, "This is a fine country through here," he'll mumble "yes" and look the other way. You can't get anything out of 'em. I guess they're afraid you'll spring a shell game on 'em or try to sell 'em a gold brick.

And the style in those New York saloons. The bartenders won't drink with you even. Now I like to have the bartender drink with me occasionally, out of the same bottle, just to be sure I ain't gettin' poison. They won't even take your money over the bar. Instead they give you a check with the price of your drink on it, and you walk yourself sober tryin' to find the cashier to pay for it.[34]

As pleased as Charlie and Nancy were to be back home, the next couple of weeks were uneasy ones, as they waited to hear whether any of Charlie's submissions had been accepted in the St. Louis fair. The announcement date was supposed to have been March 1, and on March 15 Charlie's father finally pressed fair officials for an answer: ". . . I take the liberty of recalling [Charlie's art] to your mind for fear that in the multiplicity of calls on your attention it might have slipped your memory." And in case the head of the fair's art department had forgotten who Mr. Russell and his son were, he wrote his letter on Parker-Russell stationery. Within a week, Charlie was notified that his oil *Pirates of the Plains* had been accepted and would hang in the Palace of Fine Arts. And as a bonus, three other paintings, *The Buffalo Hunt, Roping a Rustler,* and *Running Fight,* would hang in the Montana pavilion.[35]

Through the spring and summer of 1904, Charlie and Nancy took stock of their new circumstances. St. Louis and New York had turned their heads. It was one thing to be the darling of Central Avenue and the *Great Falls*

Tribune, quite another to be saluted by New York's newsmen and smart set. On April 8, Marchand wrote Charlie from New York to let him know that "all the boys ask for you right along."[36] Sumner Matteson's profile of Charlie, based on his 1903 interview, appeared in the March 3 issue of *Leslie's.* Three weeks later, Charlie's watercolor *A Moment of Great Peril in a Cowboy's Life* appeared on the cover. Another Russell illustration, *Navaho Horse Thieves Hotly Pursued by Robbed Mexicans,* made the April 21 cover. (Charlie had never seen a Navajo or a Mexican.) And in August, his first illustration appeared in *Outing.* Three books published in 1904 — *Hope Hathaway: A Story of Western Ranch Life; The Trail of Lewis and Clark;* and *Bucking the Sagebrush* — featured Charlie's work.

More than ever, Nancy saw everything on Charlie's easel in terms of its commercial potential. When he painted *A Rainy Morning in Cow Camp,* a variation on one of his favorite themes, she sent it off to the A. J. Tower Company of Boston, manufacturer of waterproof clothing. The painting testified to the indispensability of slickers on the open range, but Nancy apparently drove too hard a bargain. The Boston firm chose not to use *Rainy Morning* in its advertising, informing Nancy that her price was too high. She had no regrets. Several months later, when the Peters Cartridge Company of Cincinnati approached Charlie about "three strong sketches for use in our magazine advertisements," she again asked for more than the client was willing to pay.[37]

Sometimes, though, the peg was made to fit the hole. John A. Sleicher, editor of *Leslie's,* had bought a Russell oil of three cowboys roping a wolf on the dusty plains. His intent, he said, was to give the piece "a place of honor in my little gallery." He also wanted to use it in his magazine. "Could the picture properly be printed . . . under the caption of 'A Christmas Wolf Hunt in Montana', or something like that[?] This might do for my Christmas number," he wrote Nancy. She chose not to quibble that wolf extermination was hardly a holiday topic. Instead, she sent Sleicher a bill for $200 on an invoice bearing the printed heading "In Account With Chas. M. Russell The Cowboy Artist."[38]

Her confidence bolstered by her new worldliness, Nancy began to show the brass beneath the velvet with greater regularity. On October 14, she lashed out at a Mr. H. Behrens, a disgruntled customer who had visited the Russells in Great Falls. What she still lacked in syntax, she made up for in sheer fury. "From your letters," Nancy scolded Behrens, you would think Mr. Russell had nothing to do but try to pleas you and waist so much time and you look at the work then return same as if you had not ordered it at all dont you know that the style of work you wand does not sell well and when Mr Russell has spent two or three weeks on some thing of this kind then have you return it some thing that is out of his line all to gether which was told you in Great Falls when you were there as for him making you another set of pictures that is impossible. . . . Very truly, (Mrs) C.M. Russell[39]

By the first week in October, Charlie and Nancy were on their way east again. First they intended to visit the World's Fair, then they would tackle New York once more.

The Louisiana Purchase Exposition was less a tribute to a century of western expansion than it was an assessment of a world on the doorstep of the twentieth century.[40] In the Palace of Electricity one could transmit messages by wireless to Chicago and Kansas City or listen to voices being played back on a forerunner of the tape recorder. Electricity not only powered lamps and automobiles, it also introduced the world to fast food: steaks cooked in six minutes, an entire chicken roasted in twelve. In another portent of the gastronomic future, America fell in love with junk food in St. Louis: hot dogs and ice cream cones were huge, if unnutritious, hits.

Visitors could ride a miniature train or the enormous Ferris wheel, the latter having been transplanted from Chicago. Carl Hagenbeck's Zoological Paradise and Animal Circus featured trained lions, tigers, polar bears, and seals; elephants launched themselves gaily down slides into a pool of water. One could visit an "Eskimaux" village, the Holy City of Palestine, the Tyrolean Alps, or Zuñi cliff dwellings. Those who survived a re-creation of the Galveston flood or a deep-sea dive might journey to the Hereafter exhibit on the Pike, where "spectators pass over the River Styx, and visit the domain of his Infernal Majesty . . . after which they pass to the beautiful realms of the redeemed and feast their eyes upon the glories of Paradise." Heaven beckoned from another corner of the fairgrounds as well: the aeronautics concourse, where fair sponsors were offering $100,000 to the builder of "anything that can fly at least one person."

It is hard to imagine Charlie not being drawn to Frederick Cummins's Wild West Indian Congress and Rough Riders of the World, one of the many Buffalo Bill knockoffs touring at that time. The Cummins ads boasted fifty-one different tribes of North American Indians in the show, one hundred cowboys, and three hundred wild horses. And just as Sitting Bull had appeared with Buffalo Bill at the Chicago World's Fair, Cummins featured Geronimo, whom he had sprung from his imprisonment in Indian Territory. The Apache chief spent much of his time selling bows, arrows, and autographs. While taking in the Cummins show, Charlie and Nancy may also have caught the act of another performer of Indian extraction: twenty-five-year-old Will Rogers was a trick roper of great promise.[41]

Charlie likewise took a special interest in the so-called anthropological exhibits. Back of the palace of Forestry, Fish and Game, "housed in tepees and other primitive dwellings . . . [were] most of the aboriginal tribes of the earth," according to the official history of the fair. The list included American Indians, Patagonian Indians, African pygmies, and a delegation of Ainu, aboriginal inhabitants of Japan. Each group was given their own village, where they lived in a semblance of their typical dwellings and observed their indigenous customs, which was sometimes a stretch, but sometimes quite practical. For instance, when sparrows became a nuisance on the fairgrounds, Negrito tribesmen from the Philippines were recruited to dispatch them.

The inherent racism of putting ethnic groups on display like so many sideshow freaks was lost on Charlie and nearly every other fair-goer. His favorite natives were another Filipino tribe, the Igorot. Because the Igorot were partial to dog meat, the St. Louis city pound was obliged to provide them with a ration of twenty animals a week. "[T]hese folks are verry primitive," Charlie jotted to Albert Trigg,

> forging there own weapons an weaving there own cloth but from this sketch [of warriors in breechcloths carrying spears and shields] that the latter industry dos not take up much of thair time as there wasent enough cloth in the hole camp to up holster a cruch[.] An judging from the way they handle the spear . . . if they ever lern to handle the new gun Uncle Sam is liable to have trouble corraling em[. T]heir sirtenely a snakey looking artical and they say they aint sadisfide with no puney suvinire like a scalp but take the hole top peace from the Adams apple up[.][42]

June 14 had been Montana's special day at the fair. Charlie and Nancy were in Great Falls; consequently, they had to read Montana senator Thomas

Carter's tribute to Charlie in the newspaper. "One of the wonders here presented [at the Montana pavilion]," Carter had said,

> is to be found in the exhibits of art, the production of a civilization so young and a country practically in its swaddling clothes. . . . I doubt not that those who may go through these rooms . . . will surmise that some of the pictures are from the brush of Remington, or some artist of like renown. But not so, those who see animals in action, and some of the most captivating artistic work of the age on these pictures will find that an ordinary cowboy from the City of Great Falls . . . is shown to be the peer of Remington, and one of the artists destined to live in the history of art.[43]

The Remington comparison was getting to be an article of faith. Not only did reporters repeat it over and over, but in the context of promotional speeches such as Senator Carter's, hitching Russell to Remington was a way to boost Montana's overall status as a grown-up state. Charlie Russell was a manifestation of Montana's native character, as well as its world-worthy achievement.

But he was anything but the star of the show. The World's Fair galleries were full of big names who vied for the public's attention. The United States exhibited paintings by John Singer Sargent, William Merritt Chase, James McNeill Whistler, Thomas Eakins, Robert Henri, John La Farge, Childe Hassam, John Alexander, George Inness, and Winslow Homer, to name a few. Schreyvogel's *Custer's Demand* was also on hand, as well as works by Western painters Henry Farny and E. Irving Couse.

If Charlie had been intrigued by the outdoor statuary he had seen on the fairgrounds the previous fall, he was doubly fascinated by the smaller sculpture he encountered inside the Palace of Fine Arts. Small sculpture had caught on with the American public in the 1890s, partly because of a resurgent interest in artisanship and partly because the advancing technology of foundries had improved the quality and affordability of sculpture.[44] A significant number of the entries were tabletop size, many of these of wildlife. Sixty-year-old Edward Kemeys, America's ranking sculptor of wild animals, displayed a bronze menagerie of bears, bighorn sheep, and other wild animals that Charlie would later mold himself. It was the largest assemblage of three-dimensional art he had ever seen in his life.

By the time Charlie and Nancy arrived in New York in January of 1905, he was itching to get to Crawford and Marchand's studio and shape his own figures. "I am lonsum to night for my range," he wrote Albert Trigg on January 29.[45] Yet he had to know that, at the age of forty, his range was vastly enlarged.

BULL HEAD AND BUFFALO

NEW YORK WOULD always be a mixed blessing to Charlie. As many visits as he made over the years, he never got the hang of the city; he was afraid of the traffic, frequently lost his way, and considered Gotham "lots wilder than the woolly West." Still, he could never resist the urge to circulate, especially among other artists. On his second trip, he got another chance to meet Frederic Remington, whose art saturated the city that winter. In January 1905, the Knoedler Gallery had an exhibition of nine Remington bronzes; in March, another gallery opened an exhibition of Remington paintings; and just before Charlie and Nancy left the East, *Collier's* came out with an issue devoted entirely to the gouty giant of Western art. In the midst of this Remington outpouring, it is highly likely that mutual friends pressed the two artists together for at least a handshake. Yet the only shred of evidence that the meeting did indeed occur was a polite quote Charlie gave to the *Helena Independent* on March 18: "I like New York; the artists there are princes." Specifically Charlie named Marchand, Crawford, and Remington.[1]

Charlie completed three models while in New York, *Counting Coup, The Buffalo Hunt,* and *War Dancers,* all of which he had cast at the Roman Bronze Works (where Remington also took his models). Tiffany's accepted them for sale, setting a price of $450 each on *Counting Coup* and *The Buffalo Hunt.* The store also carried Remington's bronzes, listing them in the $300 range. The higher price for Charlie's work did not indicate that he had surpassed Remington commercially, however. He did not sell a single bronze at Tiffany's, while Remington sold more than a hundred of *The Rattlesnake*.[2]

If there was a consolation, it was qualitative. Charlie's sculpture was well received by his fellow artists. Moreover, one of the buyers of *Smoking Up*, his bronze of the previous year, had presented the sculpture to President Theodore Roosevelt. Somehow during the casting process, the horn on the saddle had been eliminated, which vexed Charlie no end. When he learned that Roosevelt now had one of the bronzes, his reaction was more one of chagrin than of pride. Surely the ex-ranchman and Rough Rider would notice the goof. Charlie (or perhaps Nancy) promptly wrote the White House a note of apology and explanation, which in turn garnered a personal note of thanks from the President.[3]

THE NEXT BOOST came from an entirely different quarter: a woman whose identity was hidden from the public for years. She was Bertha Bower from Big Sandy, Montana. Using the pen name B. M. Bower to cloak her gender, she wrote Western stories for popular magazines, and in 1905 completed her first novel, *Chip of the Flying U*. She and Charlie both insisted that they had never known each other before *Chip;* in time, after the book had sold widely and brought added fame to Charlie, they became warm friends.[4]

Chip of the Flying U was the first feminist Western. The heroine, Della Whitmore, has come home to her father's ranch, the Flying U, after graduating from medical school in the East. The cowboys have their doubts about this new breed of female; she has lots more moxie than the schoolmarm in *The Virginian*.

Chip is one of the skeptics, but he is not so ornery as his coarse talk and tough hide suggest. He is a cowboy artist, a bunkhouse doodler, and Miss Whitmore becomes his biggest cheerleader. At one point she asks him where he learned to draw so well. "Chip blushed and looked away from her. This was treading close to his deep-hidden inner self." He tells her he has never taken a lesson in his life. " 'I never had a chance, working around cow-camps and on ranches.' "

Like the Virginian, Chip wants to prove that he can be something more. His opportunity comes when, laid up with a broken leg, he completes a painting begun by the multitalented Miss Whitmore, whom he is now in the habit of calling "the Little Doctor." It becomes his master-piece:

> Chip lay back against the cushions and smoked lazily, his eyes half closed, dreaming rather than thinking. The unfinished painting stood facing him upon its easel, and his eyes idly fixed upon it. He knew the place so well. Jagged pinnacles, dotted here and there with scrubby pines, hemmed in a tiny basin below — where was blank canvas. He went mentally over the argument again [she had wanted him to help her finish], and from that drifted to a scene he had witnessed in that same basin, one day — but that was in the winter. Dirty gray snow drifts, where a chinook had cut them, and icy side hills made the place still drearier. . . . A poor, half-starved range cow with her calf which the round-up had overlooked in the fall, stood at bay against a steep cut bank. Before them squatted five great, gaunt wolves intent upon fresh beef for their supper. But the cow's horns were long, and sharp, and threatening, and the calf snuggled close to her side, shivering with the cold and the fear of death. The wolves licked their cruel lips and their eyes gleamed hungrily — but the eyes of the cow answered them, gleam for gleam. If it could be put on canvas just as he had seen it, with the bitter, biting cold of a frozen chinook showing gray and sinister in the slaty sky. . . .

Chip calls his painting *The Last Stand,* as if readers needed any more clues to its "Last of Five Thousand" heredity. Naturally, *The Last Stand* is a big hit, exhibited in the lobby of a Great Falls hotel and purchased by a wealthy land baron. Chip and the Little Doctor kiss on the final page, and Bertha Bower went on to write another sixty-seven books. Till the end, her reviewers and readers referred to her as "Mr. Bower."

When it came to commissioning the illustrations for *Chip,* Bower did not hesitate in her choice. But first she had to get by Nancy, who insisted on $100 apiece for three watercolors. She had Bower over a barrel. The publishers liked Charlie Russell, but would not pay more than $25 for each illustration. In the end, neither Nancy nor New York would back down and Bower had to pick up most of the cost of the artwork herself. She forgave Charlie, but never Nancy. Charlie's wife, she maintained, was the kind of woman who always thought she needed "to help God run the world."⁵

≈

CHARLIE'S ILLUSTRATION WORK continued briskly after his first two trips to New York. He did two more Bower books, eight illustrations for W. T. Hamilton's memoir, *My Sixty Years on the Plains,* and illustrations for the the first two installments of Stewart Edward White's novel *Arizona Nights,* for *McClure's.* Charlie's print and calendar work for Ridgley were steady earners as well, and he owned an interest in the firm. One measure of his commercial exposure was his decision in the fall of 1906 to register his buffalo skull with the United States Copyright Office.⁶

Despite this stepped-up work pace and gadabout schedule, Charlie and Nancy decided to complicate their lives even further. In the summers of 1904 and 1905, they had taken trips to Lake McDonald, a day's train ride west of Great Falls on the western slope of the Continental Divide.⁷ The area was already being talked about as a potential national park, but when the Russells first discovered the lake, it was part of a forest reserve, known only to a few Indians, hunters, trappers, prospectors, and loggers. Writer-naturalists George Bird Grinnell and James Willard Schultz had piqued America's interest in the region in the 1880s, but it took James J. Hill's Great Northern Railway to consummate the love affair. The last rail over the mountains was laid in 1891, and the region was thrown open to vacationers. Charlie and Nancy were among the first.

From Great Falls to Lake McDonald, they took a train north to Shelby, then the westbound Great Northern on to Belton, on the middle fork of the Flathead River. From Belton, they hired a wagon to travel the four miles to the lake. In the early years, one visitor recalled, the road was "a slender ribbon, the trees so close that my father, standing in the open coach, pulled white and brown moss from the trees. . . . The wagon trip was so deep with needles and moss and leaves that the hooves of the horses made only a gentle clip-clop as they sped along."⁸ This path is now the main entrance to the national park at East Glacier.

The small settlement of Apgar had sprung up along the south end of Lake McDonald. Brothers Milo and Dimon Apgar had built a dozen log cabins, which they rented out to tourists. The accommodations were not luxurious by any means — no running water, certainly no electricity. There were still no roads along the lakeshore, but a steam-powered launch plied the lake and delivered passengers to the newly completed Glacier Hotel farther up the east shore.[9] The Great Northern's publicists were quick to tout the wonders of the area. Anyone who visited was entirely smitten, including John Muir, who wrote the best possible advertisement in his 1901 book, *Our National Parks:* "Give a month at least to this precious reserve. The time will not be taken from the sum of your life. Instead of shortening, it will definitely lengthen it and make you truly immortal."

After their first visits to Glacier, Charlie and Nancy bought a small lot a quarter of a mile up the beach from Apgar and contracted to build a log house. They spent the summer of 1906 in the cabin and every summer thereafter. They first thought to call it Kootnaei [sic] Lodge, after the Kootenai Indians who once had paddled the lake and hunted in the surrounding mountains, but then switched the name to Bull Head Lodge, after Charlie's newly copyrighted logo.[10] They marked their landing with a buffalo skull mounted on a prominent tree.

The cabin was thirty feet across the front and twenty feet deep, with a kitchen off the back. Over the years, Charlie and Nancy extended the kitchen wing, added a loft, porches, and finally a combination studio–guest cabin. Until a road was completed, guests were rowed along the shore from Apgar, and then climbed a steep path to the cabin. Their sleeping quarters were cots, their privacy provided by screens placed between the berths. The screens doubled as a guest register and are today preserved as works of art as well as historical documents. Each year's visitors — in 1907, nearly two dozen — signed on the same panel; if they were artists, or even if they were not, they often added a humorous sketch.

It took a hardy temperament to appreciate Bull Head. Food was mostly canned goods. The toilet was a two-hole outhouse forty feet from the back door. The lake, averaging a brisk 55 degrees in August, was the primary bathtub. One of Charlie's cousin Fergus Mead's most vivid memories of his visit to Bull Head was of Charlie "starting a story and keeping going strong all the time he was dousing his face in the lake," pausing only to remove his dentures (his real teeth were gone by 1920) and rinse them in the clear water.[11]

Charlie had endless ways of amusing his guests. He still crafted little gnomes and nymphs out of bits of wood; he used moss for hair, bark and leaves for clothes. "Shopping at Birch and Company," he called it. When

artist Philip Goodwin visited in 1907, he and Charlie drew a series of wildlife scenes in the wet cement of Bull Head's new hearth and became com-
petitive builders of model sailboats. In the evening there were stories by
firelight — cowboy yarns and Indian legends. Many times Charlie would
urge a guest or two to costume themselves as natives, even providing greasepaint and wigs.[12]

The best entertainment, however, was nature itself. On hired horses,
Charlie would lead trips to see the glaciers and other spectacular spots
"whare they make snow." Or he simply found diversion in the goings-on
under and around the cabin. He put salt out so the deer would feed close
by. A favorite trick was to throw a handkerchief across the back of a porcupine; when the porcupine shrugged off the unwanted cloak, it was full
of quills that Charlie would then use to decorate his Indian garb. A chicken
bone in an old tomato can was good for a lengthy sideshow. "Mr. Skunk
. . . will surely work for that chicken bone," Nancy recalled, "but without
much success."[13]

To Charlie, even the pests were pets; he felt that Bull Head was as much
theirs as his. "[O]ne ore two skunks have taken up quarters under the
house," he wrote to a Great Falls neighbor in 1908,

> an seem to like the place[. A]lso a number of mountian [pack] rats have
> mooved in an by the noise they make Iv a hunch my night watches [two
> of Charlie's handcarved gnomes mounted on the porch rail] are sleep-
> ing on gard[. A]s soon as dark comes the new comers goes to work all
> hands[. T]he skunks practice two s[t]eps and barn dances on the porch
> or in the kitchen[. T]he rats dont seem to like our roof [. A]ll night
> long thair bussy making it over occasionaly stopping to gether up tooth
> brushes leaving rocks s[t]icks or old bones in exchange.[14]

Such equanimity was a measure of Charlie's love of nature, but also revealed much about his overall sense of well-being at the time. Life was going
well for the Russells. Charlie was finding time to paint and sculpt, and
Nancy was selling the output at a good clip and a good price. As a result,
they could afford to buy and build Bull Head in 1906; that same year, they
invested in a small ranch in the Sweet Grass Hills, near the Canadian border.[15] Their partner in the deal was Charlie's old roundup chum Con Price.
Price was still a puncher, but, like Charlie, he had cleaned up his act considerably after marrying Claudia Toole, the niece of a Montana governor.

Why Charlie and Nancy bought into the Lazy KY, as the ranch was called, is hard to figure. Perhaps they saw it as a shrewd investment (of $2,500 over two years); Price would live on the place and look after the thirty horses and hundred-plus head of cattle. Or perhaps they saw it as a sentimental gesture. By 1906, the Russells were established city dwellers, and Lake McDonald was hardly a windswept cattle range. At least now they could call themselves cow people without having to bend the truth. As it turned out, though, they scarcely spent any time on the place and finally cashed out at a loss in 1910.

They simply could not be in all the places they wanted to be. In March 1906, at the urging of *Outing* editor Casper Whitney, Charlie, Nancy, and Charlie's father took a trip to Mexico, with the idea of studying and sketching the life and culture of the Mexican vaqueros. For Charlie, this was a trip to the Holy Land; most of the habits, habiliment, and horsemanship of the American cowpuncher were inherited from his Mexican predecessor.

The Russells visited Mexico City and Cuernavaca.[16] The highlight of the journey was a tour of the Chihuahuan ranch of Don Luis Terrazas. Terrazas had begun building his herd as a teenager in the 1840s; by the first decade of the twentieth century he owned more than 6 million acres and controlled another 20 million acres of "public" land. Rough estimates put his cattle herd at half a million head; he also owned a hundred thousand horses and two hundred thousand sheep. At the time of the Russells' visit and up until the Mexican Revolution drove him into exile, Don Luis was the world's ultimate cattle baron.[17]

Charlie was enthralled by the ranch. If one could ignore the obvious feudal oppression — and Charlie could — the Terrazas spread stood as a cowboy paradigm.[18] Applying his usual romanticism, Charlie allowed himself to posture that Chihuahua was like Montana had once been, before the nesters, and more like Montana might have turned out if the nesters had stayed away. "[I]ts shure an old time cow country," Charlie wrote to Bob Stuart, nephew of Granville Stuart, Montana's version of Don Luis. "I travelled from the northe line to within a 100 miles of the ismus an never saw a wire. . . . I ust to think the old time cow punchers were pritty fancy in [Montana] but for pritty these mexicons make them look like hay diggers."[19] Charlie did a number of drawings and watercolors based on his Mexican travels, but none was published in *Outing*.

The following winter, Charlie and Nancy traveled to St. Louis for the wedding of C. S. Russell to Florence Newcomb Davis. The marriage was her second as well. Charlie was pleased that his father had found a new companion. Even after the death of C. S. Russell, Charlie and Nancy stayed in touch with her. After the wedding, Charlie and Nancy went on to New York for their third trip in as many years. One of the draws this time was an exhibit of his paintings at the highly venerated Plymouth Church in Brooklyn, his first show in the East. Plymouth's minister, Newell Dwight Hillis, had admired Charlie's art during a lecture stop in Great Falls the previous year. The Russells did not make it home until May 1907, and they were encamped at Lake McDonald by July. Charlie worked at Bull Head, but not every day and never without interruptions. Somehow, though, his productivity seemed to improve as distractions increased.

Nancy had long since given up trying to get Charlie to write down his stories but sensed there was a good market for them. "Russell was obdurate," explained a newspaper account of their standoff. "He was not sure whether he could paint, but he knew he could not write."[20] In the end, Nancy persuaded him to dictate his choicest yarns to her. The result was a series of stories that appeared in *Outing* in late 1907 and throughout 1908. (All of them eventually wound up in *Trails Plowed Under.*) "Longrope's Last Guard" laments the loss of a fellow night wrangler in a stampede. "How Lindsay Turned Indian" is Charlie's autobiographical fantasy about taking an Indian girl as a bride. The narrator of "Finger-that-Kills Wins His Squaw" mentions more of the same: "When I say marry, I traded her pa two ponies 'n' a Winchester 'n' in accordance with all Injun's law, we're necked all right."

Charlie's paintings of 1907 included two watercolors for the Mint: *Have One on Me,* of a cowboy forcing a teetotaler to have a drink at gunpoint, and *Dance, You Shorthorn, Dance,* echoing the same bully theme. He also did two sensitive scenes of Indian domestic life: *The Beauty Parlor,* depicting a wife braiding her husband's hair, and *Sun Worship in Montana,* of a mother holding her papoose up to the morning sun.

The most memorable paintings of that year, however, are two cowboy oils, *Jerked Down* and *A Quiet Day in Utica.* As more and more time separated Charlie from his cowpunching days, he felt an increasing need not only to preserve the bygone era, but to document his own presence in that chapter of history as well. He had painted a couple of different self-portraits: *When I Was a Kid,* of himself in buckskin riding Monte and accompanied by Jake

Hoover; and another of himself aboard a more recent horse, Red Bird. *A Quiet Day in Utica* was even more specific proof of having "been there." The painting was commissioned by Charles Lehman, then owner of the general store in Utica, for use on a calendar.[21] The scene Charlie chose is of the store and the main street of Utica, exactly as they looked in the 1880s. (He consulted an old photo to prompt his memory.) A practical joker has tied a string of cans to the tail of a dog. The dog has bolted into the dusty street, tangling the string in the hind legs of a passing cow pony. Charlie froze the frame just as the horse explodes under its rider; characteristically, he chose the moment just before chaos turns to calamity. The scene is saturated with the energy of what must have happened seconds earlier and the anticipation of what will inevitably transpire in the next heartbeat. And for those who might doubt that this tin-can prank actually occurred, Charlie painted in a crowd of identifiable witnesses. There is Charles Lehman standing in the doorway of his store. There is Milly Ringgold, the black prospector from Yogo. And there is Charlie, recognizable by his red sash, leaning over the hitching rail, smoking a cigarette.

Jerked Down conveys similar energy and authenticity. Charlie's exposure to his illustrator cronies — particularly the Howard Pyle–trained Philip Goodwin — had begun to pay off. The composition of *Jerked Down* is tried and true but not formulaic, the palette disciplined and lively, the perspective and choice of subject exhilarating. In *Jerked Down,* a cowpuncher has roped a hefty range cow in a dry coulee. Her proportionately stout calf has tripped over the taut lasso — and this is where Charlie has chosen to balance the entire weight of the picture, however precariously. Sagebrush grows in the foreground, mountains rim the horizon, and in the mid-distance another cowboy prepares to hurl his own loop. But all these secondary elements merely accentuate the tautness of the rope stretched across the canvas. The cowboy, his boots buried deep in the stirrups, shifts sideways in the saddle to keep his balance and to add leverage. His left hand grips his reins, while his right controls his dally around the saddle horn, even while his little cow pony is being jerked off its feet. (In a letter to Brown & Bigelow, the prominent St. Paul calendar company that was considering *Jerked Down,* Nancy explained that the horse is an unbroken bronc that has committed the ergonomic sin of turning perpendicular to the tug.)[22] The mother cow, slobber flying, looks belligerently up the obnoxious rope. The rider is looking down it, right into the eyes of his quarry. What will happen next?

Will he let go and lose his rope? Will he hang on till his horse is upended in the coulee? Or will the approaching rider save the day with a second loop? A riot of possibility hangs on the moment.

~

NANCY SUCCEEDED IN selling the reproduction rights to *Jerked Down* to Brown & Bigelow, and just in the nick of time. In early November 1907, Charlie was stricken with severe abdominal pains. The onset of the illness — ultimately diagnosed as appendicitis — was gradual, and Charlie at first tried to beat it without surgery. Con Price remembered that someone told Charlie "to stand on his head and walk on his hands and knees and it would cure him. He said he tried that cure until his hands and knees were so sore he couldn't perform anymore."[23]

Eventually, Charlie consented to have his appendix removed. "When they dressed him for the operating table (he called it putting a set of harness on him)," Price wrote, "Nancy was very much frightened and looked like she might break down under the strain. To quiet her, he began to tell her how simple the operation was and that he didn't mind it at all and started to roll a cigarette, but his hands got to shaking so bad the tobacco all fell out of the paper."

For all the agony and anxiety the appendicitis caused, the changes it triggered were salubrious. Photos taken before the operation show his face beginning to sag and his midriff thickening. He exercised little, chain-smoked, and drank immoderately. Perhaps he had been intending for some time to renounce the bottle. What is certain is that from his appendicitis onward, Charlie was a teetotaler — or in his words, a "buse fighter."[24]

As soon as he had recovered from his surgery, he was back in the bars of Central Avenue, but drinking only Vichy water.[25] To show that he had not forsaken his chums, he drew cheery advertising illustrations for the Mint and Silver Dollar. Meantime, he hinted at his inner struggle in an illustrated New Year's greeting he sent to his friends in 1908. It is a winter scene. Three riders, one with a bottle in his hand, are stopped at a fork in the trail. One route is marked with a sign announcing a temperance lecture; the other has an arrow pointing to "Poker Jakes Palice." The snowy trail to sobriety has one dim set of tracks, while the trail to Jake's is trampled by many hoofprints and littered with an empty whiskey bottle.

"It's the first part of the road that is the hardest," Charlie later reflected on that first winter without alcohol.²⁶ In his case, it was a road he chose not to travel alone. In late January 1908, he visited Chico Hot Springs, a hotel and spa just north of Yellowstone National Park, to commiserate with Johnny Matheson, who had also sworn off strong drink. A photograph taken of Charlie, Matheson, and two other friends on January 27 is a study in dark suits and lockjawed temperance.

Four months later, Charlie accompanied Matheson on one of the freighter's final trips from Fort Benton to Lewistown, until a heavy snowstorm closed the trail. Under similar circumstances in an earlier time, idle hands might have uncorked the wet goods. Now Charlie and Matheson kept from falling off the wagon by sleeping in it. "[W]e had a fine trip," Charlie wrote to Philip Goodwin. "[W]e were snowed in so we dident turn a wheel for three days but we were comfurtible[.] John slept in his cook cart and I in the trail wagon and theres no better snoosing place than a big Murphy wagon with the roar of the storm on the sheets[. N]ature rocked my cradel and sung me to sleep."²⁷

With abstinence, Charlie's painting became infused with newfound energy. *The Medicine Man, First Wagon Tracks,* and *When Blackfeet and Sioux Meet,* all done in 1908, are the fruits of a clear head and a steadier hand. The timing could not have been better. That spring, Charlie signed a five-year contract with Brown & Bigelow. The deal called for him to send a selection of paintings; Brown & Bigelow would pick the ones they liked best and pay $500 for the exclusive right to reproduce them. Charlie could keep all the originals and sell them to anyone he wanted.²⁸ Not only did the contract give his work a huge circulation, it also gave him regular cash flow to complement his intermittent income from direct sales and Parker-Russell dividends. Nancy could now raise the price of his paintings and wait patiently for the big fish to bite.

Nominally, Brown & Bigelow gave Charlie complete freedom to choose his subject matter, but on April 25 a company representative wrote Nancy to suggest that while "I was not going to attempt to tell Mr. Russell what kind of pictures to paint, I am inclined to think we could use a 'cattle' piece and possibly a 'gun fight.' "²⁹ Charlie seemed not to mind such coaxing, for some of the ensuing paintings of roundup hijinks and cow-town gunfire — *Bronc to Breakfast, A Serious Predicament,* and *Smoke of a .45* — fit Brown & Bigelow's bill perfectly.

Charlie kept busy in other ways that first drinkless season of 1908. In

March, he was initiated into the Great Falls lodge of the Benevolent and Protective Order of Elks, the fraternal organization founded, ironically, as a drinking club.[30] The Elks had long since come to eschew secret handshakes, passwords, and Masonesque hocus-pocus. From Charlie's perspective, the club was simply a group of good, decent fellows, including Bill Rance, who all enjoyed one another's company. His brethren still drank but did not expect Charlie to join in. The fact that the elk, noble animal of the Montana high country, was the group's symbol added to his sense of belonging. Four years later, when the Great Falls lodge moved into new quarters, Charlie painted and donated one of his finest oils, a portrait of a bull elk, *The Exalted Ruler* (after the title given a lodge's chief officer).

By July, Charlie and Nancy were at Bull Head Lodge, surrounded by relatives. By September, the screen register bore more than twenty names. Charlie's father and stepmother led a contingent from St. Louis that included Florence's son and Bent Russell's two children, Austin and Isabel. Austin Russell, a serious man of twenty, had inherited a gloomy strain of the family wanderlust. After the summer at Bull Head, he chose not to return home to St. Louis, but took a job with the Great Falls streetcar company — perhaps his twentieth-century idea of wrangling — and later went to work for one of the most conspicuous symbols of the new Montana, the Great Falls smelter.[31]

Nancy's father also paid a visit that summer, along with her half-sister Ella Allen, ten years her junior. Ella and Nancy had reunited two years earlier after nearly a decade apart. When Ella subsequently moved to Great Falls, Nancy and Charlie helped her get her bearings and put her through secretarial school. Ella's relationship with Nancy was cordial, but not particularly close. She eventually married and moved away, ending up in California and Alaska.

After closing up Bull Head in September, Charlie was in Great Falls scarcely long enough to unpack, much less paint for any significant stretch of time. Nothing could keep him from participating in a history-making event under way on the Flathead Indian reservation.

❧

ONE OF CHARLIE'S biggest regrets in life was that he had never seen an Indian buffalo hunt. The remnant bunches of buffalo he had come across in the Judith Basin in the early 1880s served mostly as depressing reminders of better days.

An estimated 30 million to 60 million buffalo had roamed the North American continent in the mid–nineteenth century; by 1900, the total population of buffalo in North America barely exceeded a thousand.[32] The largest single group was the Pablo herd of Montana. According to a somewhat shaky oral history, a Pend d'Oreille Indian named Samuel Walking Coyote had been hunting buffalo near the Milk River and somehow managed to lead a half-dozen buffalo calves across the Continental Divide to the Flathead country. In the early 1880s, two ranchers on the reservation, Charles P. Allard, who was white, and Michel Pablo, of mixed blood, bought the herd, which had doubled in size. A decade after Allard's death in 1896, Pablo's share of the herd approached seven hundred head.

In 1906, the government announced its plans to open the Flathead reservation to homesteading. President Roosevelt, as honorary head of the American Bison Society, encouraged Congress to buy the Pablo herd or at least award it a special grazing allotment on some other patch of federal ground. When the President's plea failed, Pablo quickly struck a deal to sell the herd to the Canadian government for $200 a head. Pablo's agreement with the Canadians called for him to deliver live animals to Alberta — a task easier said than done. Pablo expected to complete his roundup in two years; it took him six.

Charlie Russell had read the news accounts of the first year's effort with great interest. In 1907, four hundred of Pablo's more docile buffalo had been driven to the pens at Ravalli, Montana, and loaded on stock cars. That left nearly three hundred still in the hills; they were the wild ones, made even more ornery by the pestering of Pablo's two dozen Indian riders. In February 1908, Sumner Matteson, who had written the profile of Charlie in *Leslie's* four years earlier, published another Montana piece in *Leslie's*, this one on the Pablo herd.

The story lit a fire under Charlie. "That will undoubtedly be the 'final buffalo chase,'" Matteson announced, "and one well worth crossing the continent to participate in, or at least to witness with binoculars from 'Round Top,' which commands a view of the whole valley." By November 2, Charlie was on the Flathead reservation, ready to observe and sketch. "You must know what all this meant to the artist," Nancy later told a group of Great Falls women. "It was the last time on this continent these wild creatures would ever break their hearts against the cunning of man."[33]

The roundup lived up to its billing as high drama, and for Charlie it had two acts. He spent two weeks on the Flathead reservation in the fall of 1908, then returned when Pablo and his men renewed their efforts the following May. The strategy was the same each time. Pablo had set a trap on a five-hundred-acre horseshoe bend in the Pend d'Oreille (now Flathead) River. Riders dispersed in the hills and drove the buffalo toward two long fences that formed a funnel, the mouth of the funnel being the bank of the river. The buffalo would then have no choice but to swim the river and become trapped in the horseshoe bend, the throat of which had likewise been fenced off. The steep cliffs on the outside bank of the horseshoe provided a natural barrier, as well as a good vantage point for watching the entire circus.

Charlie was officially an observer, not one of Pablo's $5-a-day riders. For the most part, he stuck with the Canadian officials who had come to watch the capture of their purchase, and a small group of reporters, photographers, and observers like himself. They slept in tents by the river; Charlie dressed as he had in his Judith Basin days. And as in the Judith, he was a cordial companion who brought a certain elegant seasoning to the outdoor setting. "He was not a roughneck," recalled photographer Norman Forsyth. "Gathered around the campfire at night he would keep us all entertained . . . and he never ran out of stories."[34] Charlie's cooking was memorable in its own right. His boiled beef had his urbane Canadian companions gagging at the thought of it years later.

Despite the bonhomie of camp, Charlie itched to be closer to the action. One Canadian reporter noted, "Charlie Russell, the cowboy artist, who came to paint and not to chase, has thrown aside his brushes, and is now chafing in his long boots and inquiring about a suitable cayuse."[35]

It took a lot of nerve to wade into the thick of the Pablo roundup, and it was no place for a tenderfoot. These were not range cows accustomed to biannual handling; buffalo had run wild for millennia. If there was something fiercer on the plains than an eighteen-hundred-pound buffalo bull on the prod, then it was a twelve-hundred-pound buffalo cow that had just been separated from her calf. Some buffalo simply ran away from their drovers; others turned and attacked. Horses were gored and knocked off their feet. One bull lifted a Pablo horse and rider on its horns and carried them three hundred yards before dumping them on the ground. Photographer Forsyth was caught afoot on the riverbank as a small herd charged across the river. "[W]e all thought he was a goner," Charlie wrote to Philip Goodwin, "but whin the dust cleared he showed up shy a camra[,] hat an most of his pants[. L]ucky for him there was som seeders [cedars] on the bank and he wasent slow about using one[.]"36

Danger and practicality aside, Charlie was pulling for the buffalo. "I think he rejoiced when outwitted by these grass-eaters," Nancy said.37 In the November 1908 hunt, Pablo had succeeded in corralling 120 animals. "[W]e all went to bed that night sadisfide with a 120 in the trap but woke up with one cow," Charlie wrote Goodwin. "[T]he rest had climed the cliff and got away[. T]he next day the[y] only got 6 and a snow storm struck us and [t]he roundup was called off till next summer."38

The following May, Charlie was back on the reservation, booted, spurred, and ready to play a more active role in the roundup. He got all he bargained for. While trying to force a group of buffalo into smaller pens so they could be loaded on the specially made wagons that would haul them to the railhead, Charlie was confronted by a buffalo bull. The story is told by Newton Mactavish, a reporter for *The Canadian Magazine:*

> Suddenly you hear a pistol shot, and, turning your eyes quickly towards the middle of the field, you see Charlie Russell's pony swinging about and young Pablo leaning from his saddle, smoking pistol in hand, over a big bull that stands quivering as if about to fall. Charlie and Young Pablo had undertaken to head-off this bull, which was running away. Charlie must have run too close, for, as you learn later, the bull suddenly turned and charged. Had Young Pablo not been ready, having anticipated the move, Charlie's cayuse at least would have been a victim. But the bullet from the pistol took effect, and hereafter the camp will have a supply of fresh buffalo meat.39

In the end, Pablo succeeded in delivering seven hundred buffalo to Canada. Ironically, in the middle of his roundup a fickle United States Congress decided to dedicate the portion of the Flathead country right next to Pablo's as a national buffalo preserve. Had the government acted sooner and bought Pablo's herd (instead, buffalo were imported from elsewhere), the entire roundup, which was not officially over until 1913, would have been unnecessary.

Charlie produced several important buffalo paintings in 1909. *The Wounded Buffalo* was clearly inspired by his own close encounter. The oil shows an enraged buffalo cow driving a horn into the side of a frantic Indian pony, whose breechcloth-clad rider is trying to spin the horse out of harm's way. A watercolor, *Pablo Buffalo Drive*, may well have been painted at the actual roundup. Two cowboys, one in woolly chaps similar to those Charlie sported, attempt to haze a bunch of running buffalo by waving their hats and cutting off the leaders. *When "Brother Van" Was Young*, a watercolor gift to Charlie's longtime friend the Reverend W. W. Van Orsdel, recounts a buffalo hunt the intrepid Methodist preacher went on with the Blackfeet in 1873. All three of these paintings show the newfound confidence with which Charlie depicted his favorite subject.

THE SUMMER AFTER the buffalo roundup, Nancy was put in charge of the art exhibit at the Montana State Fair in Helena. A local magazine had griped about the poor quality of the art at past fairs; appointing Nancy as the new maven was a shrewd choice. The 1909 exhibit included several of Charlie's freshest pieces, most notably *When Horse Flesh Comes High*, as well as work by Montana painters Joseph Henry Sharp (who was still working on the Crow reservation) and two lesser lights, Edgar Paxson of Missoula and Ralph DeCamp of Helena. Charlie knew them all, and together they formed the first true nucleus of Montana artists.[40]

Nancy's strong hand as art curator of the state fair belied her underlying fragility. She had never outgrown her headaches and swoons in times of stress and fatigue. In December 1909, she too had to have her appendix out. "[M]y wife was taken sick an the docters found out I had the price so called it appendecitis," Charlie wrote to a Pablo comrade. Nancy was slow recovering, and even after she was on her feet, she and Charlie took their meals at a Great Falls boardinghouse. The trip east they had discussed taking that winter had to be postponed until February.[41]

Abdominal problems were apparently widespread, for on December 18, 1909, Frederic Remington — who by then was nearing four hundred pounds — began complaining of stomach pains and constipation.[42] On December 23, a surgeon finally cut him open on the kitchen table of his upstate New York home and discovered that his appendix had burst and peritonitis had set in. Remington died the day after Christmas. He was forty-eight years old.

Not that Nancy or Charlie ever acknowledged it, but the coincidence of their 1910 trip to the East and Remington's death could not have been more fortuitous. In his last years, Remington had been moving away from depicting violent scenes. His paintings were more studies of atmosphere than action, more in tune with Monet, the Impressionist, than Muybridge, the influential motion-study photographer of the day. "I am no longer an illustrator," Remington pronounced in 1908, around the time of a very successful show at New York's Knoedler Gallery.[43] Some of Remington's paintings were no longer even Western, but of the pastoral East.

At the same time Remington had been remaking his image, he was taking a licking in the popular press. The December 19, 1908, issue of *Collier's* carried an essay, "Wild West Faking," by Emerson Hough, in which he complained that the "Wild West boom" was engineered, and distorted, by Easterners. And while acknowledging that Remington was the leading Western artist, he panned the Westchester cowboy as an unreliable and somewhat overbearing authority: "[I]f Mr. Remington to-day wanted to add a cubit to the tail of the American bison, or to establish a Western horse with five legs, he certainly could make it stick." Hough felt it was time to banish the pretenders. Who should take Remington's place? "My artist is Charlie Russell," Hough declared. (Charlie had in fact illustrated Hough's *Story of the Cowboy* in 1897.)

Right on cue, less than two months after Remington's passing, Charlie Russell rode out of the West once again. First stop, as usual, was St. Louis. During a monthlong stay, Charlie had two different exhibits, in which he showed major pieces (*Jerked Down, Smoke of a .45, Bronc to Breakfast.*)[44] It would take a while for the public to accept the new prices, but when it came to showering attention on its native son, St. Louis was anything but stingy. "Is He Remington's Successor?" was the headline over a richly illustrated feature in the *St. Louis Republic.* "The curtain is being lowered on the old life," the article opined.

A few more years and it will be history and tradition dimmed in the perspective. Even now, to many people, a hazy mist is gathering over the Golden West of that other day and enveloping its stirring scenes.

The records are being preserved in the prints and in the paintings. The question is, which is the more accurate portrayal of the former frontier existence, that of the historian who gets his data from books, and the painter who draws his inspiration from the same source, or that of the man who has lived the life he depicts? And will it fall to the lot of a native of St. Louis to preserve in art for succeeding generations the true picture of those scenes of romance and adventure?[45]

The debate was fanned by three different St. Louis papers throughout the month of March. The consensus was, yes, Charlie was the "logical successor" to the great Remington. Some praised him for his extreme realism; others praised him for the opposite, his poetic sentimentalism. They liked him for his action and his "alkali dust rising from the sun-baked earth." They noted his eccentric dress and his energetic wife. "Nobody ever did think much of me," Charlie told the *Post-Dispatch,* "until my wife began telling people about me."[46]

Yet in the face of so much adulation, he came across almost gruff. When a reporter suggested that he had been born in St. Louis (true), Charlie said he been born in nearby Oak Hill. "Of course, St. Louis is home to me, and I manage to come here every year," he elaborated, "but these tall buildings which have grown up since my boyhood days don't appeal to me at all. Somehow I like the needle pines of the Montana mountains best. There is more nature in them." Then, as a final show of his discomfort, he took the city fathers to task, fully aware of his own family's ongoing role in the development of St. Louis: "I notice you have a Million Population Club here, too. [St. Louis was always competing with Chicago.] A million is what St. Louis is after. I suppose it doesn't make any difference whether it is a million people, good, bad or indifferent, outlaws, thugs, or thieves, so [long as] the million mark is reached."[47]

The next stop was New York. Little is known of Nancy and Charlie's doings there that spring, except that it was probably the year he firmed up his friendship with a group of other talented Western souls who had drifted far from their home range. Their favorite hangout was the Forty-second Street studio of Ed Borein.

Borein was cut from the same colorful cloth as Charlie.[48] The son of a government bureaucrat in California, he too had dreamed of becoming a cowboy, and though scrawny, he eventually hired on as a vaquero on one of the vast Spanish land-grant ranches near Santa Barbara. Among his other exploits, Borein rode on a trail drive from California to New Mexico and explored the Baja on horseback, sketching all the while. In 1901, he and another talented California artist, Maynard Dixon, set out from Oakland on a horseback journey across the Sierras, the Great Basin, and the Rockies, with the aim of recharging their Western spirits and filling their sketchbooks. By 1906, Borein was settled in San Francisco, working for a newspaper and placing cowboy drawings in various publications. The devastating earthquake of April 18, 1906, drove Borein and Dixon, as well as many other artists, out of the Bay Area, and by 1908 they both had set up studios in New York.

Borein shared his third-floor loft with another illustrator, Jimmy Swinnerton. It was right down the street from Will Crawford and John Marchand's old studio. Next door was the Knickerbocker Hotel, the home away from home of theatrical luminaries such as Enrico Caruso, as well as a watering hole for the notorious hustlers then lurking at the fringes of the Great White Way. By contrast, Borein's "owl's nest" was a "veritable museum of Indian and Mexican curios," recalled one visitor. It was filled with "everything imaginable — blankets, rugs, costumes, hats, ropes, saddles, etc. and pictures and clay models galore."[49] A kettle of cowboy beans simmered perpetually on the stove.

Actor Leo Carrillo wrote in his autobiography that on his first visit to Borein's, "I was almost instantly asphyxiated by the pleasant odor of California frijoles cooking, a smell which I certainly didn't expect to find in the stone jungles of New York." Carrillo knew Borein from their California ranch days and had since made a name for himself in vaudeville (in a routine that eventually won him the part of Pancho in the *Cisco Kid* TV series). He was so glad to see his old friend Borein that at first he didn't pay much attention to the other men in the studio. "Then I saw a fresh-faced man with skin that looked as if his mother had just washed him with kitchen soap. He was busy modeling an Indian girl who stood in native costume on a little raised stand in one corner. . . . 'What is that?' I asked, pointing to the sculpture of the Indian girl. The fresh-faced man turned to me and drawled, 'Prairie chicken.' " Borein quickly introduced Carrillo to Charlie.[50]

No one recalls exactly when Charlie and Will Rogers first became acquainted. It could have been as early as the St. Louis World's Fair, though neither ever made note of any such meeting. It could have been on Charlie's second or third trip to New York, when Rogers was performing his rope tricks on the vaudeville stage. Most likely it was at Borein's.

The similarities between Charlie Russell and Will Rogers were uncanny.[51] With their broad faces, lantern jaws, and undisciplined forelocks, they even looked alike, though Rogers was fifteen years younger. People always claimed Charlie looked part Indian; Rogers actually was: one-quarter Cherokee. Like Charlie, Rogers was from a prominent and prosperous family, had washed out of military school, and had left home to work on a ranch. Eventually Rogers found his creative calling, as a trick roper. However, it was his down-home stories and his easy Western persona that ensured his beatification as an American icon. Will Rogers's message was always commonsensical; he spoke for the little person, yet somehow managed to be the darling of the grandees and stuffed shirts he lampooned. He never forgot his cowboy days and never snubbed his cowboy cronies.

Over the next three decades, Rogers would become the most popular man in America; he was even mentioned as a presidential candidate in 1928 and again in 1932. Because Rogers wrote the introductions to both *Trails Plowed Under* and *Good Medicine* and bought several pieces of Charlie's art, it has been assumed that he and Charlie were the closest of friends. They were indeed soulmates and mutual admirers, but the fact of the matter was, their lives were filled with so much travel, and so many glad-handers, that they never did spend as much time together as they would have liked. The bean-eating days in New York were probably some of the best. After that, they shared only occasional dinners in California, or Charlie was invited to drop by one of Rogers's movie sets. Rarely did they find a moment to let their hair down. Yet each meeting was a special occasion, for in their own low-key way, they both knew that the other was special. Eventually Charlie would immortalize Rogers in bronze. Rogers reciprocated with a eulogy in *Good Medicine*. Charlie "wasn't just 'Another Artist,' " Rogers said. "He wasn't 'just another' anything. In nothing that he did was he 'just another.' "[52]

IN 1910, CHARLIE'S talent paid off in a steady stream of commercial successes. Calendar business with Brown & Bigelow was brisk; the firm was buying the reproduction rights to half a dozen Russell originals a year. The

Ridgley Company was likewise moving a sizable inventory of prints, including *Roping a Grizzly, The Hold Up,* and *A Rainy Morning in Cow Camp.*[53] And Charlie's illustration work was steady. That year, he completed a drawing for George Pattullo's Texas story "Corazon," published in *McClure's;* a pair of paintings for the Life Saver Seat Lock Company of Minneapolis depicting an automobile scaring a horse-drawn wagon off the road; and seventeen paintings and sixty-eight pen-and-inks for *Fifteen Thousand Miles by Stage,* the picaresque memoir of Carrie Adell Strahorn, wife of a publicist hired by the Union Pacific to explore and promote the West. Last but not least, the Macmillan Company hired him to do forty-two line drawings for an edition of *The Virginian* that also included illustrations by Remington. The publisher chose one of Charlie's watercolors for the frontispiece and cover.

By the time Charlie and Nancy returned to New York the following year, his ascendancy was all but assured. No longer would he show in paint stores, basements, or parish halls. Charlie was about to enter a period of prominence and prosperity that would continue till his dying day.

11

"THE WEST THAT HAS PASSED"

C HARLIE'S 1911 EXHIBITION in New York was the most significant of his career to that point. He titled it, appropriately, "The
West That Has Passed." For three weeks in April, thirteen oils, twelve
watercolors, and six bronzes were on display in the well-regarded Folsom
Galleries on Fifth Avenue, across the street from Tiffany's. Because patrons
had been slow to pay Nancy's pumped-up prices, the Folsom show was in
effect a collection of Charlie's best — though unsold — work of the past
four years, beginning with *Jerked Down,* the 1907 oil, and ending with
Nature's Cattle, a new bronze of buffalo.

Reviews were indulgent. Arthur Hoeber, writing in the *New York Evening Globe* the day after the show opened, singled out *The Medicine Man*
as Charlie's "most important offering." Today *The Medicine Man* is still
considered one of his finest. Willis Sharpe Kilmer, the businessman from
Binghamton, New York, who paid $1,000 for it, certainly thought so.[1] As
a sort of thank-you note to his new patron, Charlie wrote a three-page explanation of the canvas. Judging by the letter's formality and syntax, it was
probably edited by Charlie's self-improved wife:

> "The Medicine Man" I consider one of the best pieces of my work and
> these few words may give you some idea of the meaning of the pic-
> ture[.] The medicine man among the plains Indians often had more to
> do with the movements of his people than the Chief and is supposed
> to have the power to speak with spirits and animals. . . . The landscape

was taken from a sketch I made on Loan Tree creek in the Judith Basin and I remember when this was a game country. The mountain range in the background is the Highwood with Haystack and Steamboat Butts to the right. . . . This country to day is fenced and settled by ranch men and farmers with nothing but a few deep worn trails where once walked the buffalo but I am glad Mr. Kilmer I knew it before natures enimy the white man invaded and marred its beauty.[2]

The Medicine Man was one of Charlie's only sales from the 1911 show. Nevertheless, the trends were favorable: Mr. Kilmer had paid a higher price than any previous buyer, and the reviews suggested that the painting was worth every cent. "Comparison with the late Frederick [sic] Remington is inevitable," opined the *Evening World,* "so we may as well have it over at once, and say that Russell is slightly in the lead and still going strong."[3]

Being taken seriously by serious critics marked Charlie's arrival as an artist. But he had to accept a few bitter pills with the sugar. Hoeber of the *Globe* was one of the first critics to observe that Charlie's bronzes were his "greatest strength,"[4] then added that his watercolors were less convincing and more uneven than his oils.

The greatest amount of attention came from the *New York Times.* The paper had previewed Charlie's show with an interview on March 19. In characteristic modesty, Charlie had begun his question-and-answer session with "rough words rapped out beneath scowling brows." But before the *Times* reporter "pocketed his pencil in despair," Charlie managed to enchant him with a few of his harmless fibs: an erroneous birth date, his life as an Indian in Canada, and a claim that he did most of his painting in the open air. Charlie dismissed Impressionism as "smeary." Questioned on the value of foreign instruction, he chimed, "I can't see how a Dutchman or a Frenchman can teach me to paint things in my own country."[5]

The *Times* picked on Charlie's naïveté in its review of the Folsom show a month later. With all due respect, the paper complained that Charlie's obsession for detail tended to "get in the way of the general impression and the interest is more or less scattered over the different parts of the picture." Yet in the final analysis, the critics were willing to move beyond his shortcomings and appreciate his energy and specificity. "It is . . . as historical documents that [his paintings and sculpture] demand our praise," the *Times* concluded, "and in putting it thus it is necessary to remember that historical documents in art mean the record not merely of facts and incidents but of the spirit of a vanished time."6

Nancy was quick to distribute the big-city reviews to the papers back home, though Charlie never joined in any such chest-thumping in his letters to the Central Avenue crowd. When he wrote to Bill Rance from Savannah, Georgia, where he and Nancy had gone for a vacation after the Folsom show closed, he mentioned the weather and real-estate boosters, but kept quiet about having one of his wildlife bronzes, *The Lunch Hour,* selected for that year's International Exposition in Rome.7

By the time Charlie and Nancy had arrived back in Great Falls in early June, word of his New York and Rome success had reached the right ears. On June 22, Montana governor Edwin L. Norris wrote to Charlie, inviting him to appear in Helena. The state was commissioning a large mural to be mounted in the new House of Representatives wing of the capitol. Initially the preference had been for an artist of broad renown, someone of the caliber and experience of John Alexander, the National Academy artist who had painted a mural for the Library of Congress. But thanks to Charlie's recent jump in status — and some effective lobbying by friends Paris Gibson and Frank Linderman, who was deputy secretary of state at the time — Charlie had jumped to the top of the list of candidates. He met with state officials in Helena on June 30, telling them (according to Austin Russell), "If you want cupids and angels and Greek goddesses, give the New Yorker [Alexander] the job. If you want a western picture, give it to me." By July 24, he had received a contract to pay him $5,000 for the capitol mural.8

Charlie did not get around to painting the mural until the following year. He and Nancy spent the summer of 1911 at Bull Head Lodge, hosting Bent Russell and family, among others. Glacier had become an official national park the year before, a mixed blessing in Charlie's opinion. Because Charlie and Nancy had purchased Bull Head before 1910, they were guaranteed an "in-holding" within the park's boundaries. Charlie was glad to have hunting banned in the park. But national-park status also meant more tourists.

Back in Great Falls, Charlie still did not begin the big mural right away, allowing one distraction after another. He and Nancy deliberated and agreed finally to sell their interest in the Ridgley printing company.9 The briskness of his business with Brown & Bigelow had a lot to do with the decision, as did the death of Ridgley co-owner and president Charles Schatzlein. The main reason Charlie hesitated on the capitol mural, however, was the overwhelming scope of the undertaking. The commission called for a painting twenty-five feet wide and twelve feet tall. A canvas that size would not even fit in his low-slung studio.

Charlie had submitted two ideas: a wagon train under attack by Indians, or Lewis and Clark trading with a band of Indians. The governor chose the latter, stipulating a scene that explicitly depicted the explorers on Montana soil. And in contrast with the wagon-train idea, it stressed peace, not war.[10]

In September 1805, Lewis and Clark had encountered a group of "33 Lodges about 80 men 400 total and at least 500 horses." The Indians called themselves "Eoote-lash-Schute" (Oat-la-shoot, meaning "those down below," members of the Flathead tribe). Lewis and Clark found them friendly and noted their stout physiques and light complexions. They made careful inventory of the Indians' hairstyles and garments: "the men Cewed with otter skin on each Side falling over the Sholrs forward, the women loose promisquisly over the Sholdrs & face[,] long Shirts which Coms to the anckles & tied with a belt about their waste with a roabe over." The explorers were impressed by the quality of the Indian horses and negotiated the purchase of eleven before breaking camp two days later.[11]

On January 26, 1912, six months after he had received the commission, Charlie, still in a muddle, wrote to Philip Goodwin. "I got the job of the capital an as the picture is onley 25 feet long and 12 wide its got me thinking some," he joked uneasily. "[T]his is some jump for me an I am liabel to have to call for help send for all my New York forends an put them to worke." At the top of his letter, Charlie drew a small caricature of himself suspended before a large canvas by block and tackle.[12] The mural he is working on in the sketch is only vaguely similar to the composition he actually painted, indicating that he had yet to settle on a final image.

Instead of bearing down, he and Nancy packed up and made another trip east. His second show at the Folsom Galleries, thirteen oils and four watercolors, hung for two and a half weeks.[13] This time Nancy had no big sales to brag about.

Shortly after the show came down on March 25, Charlie and Nancy paid a visit to Charlie's father and stepmother, who had retired to Florida. To Charlie, Florida was "the home of all crawling swimming an flying things" and a "land of flowers where things grow with out the help of man." But while he was admiring the natural beauty, the impact of the real-estate boom was not lost on him. He sketched a Seminole Indian and, in the accompanying letter to Sid Willis, observed sarcastically that "the whites are always kind to these people an they let him have all the lande thats under water."[14]

The boys at the Mint may have been glad to hear of Charlie's doings in Florida, but Governor Norris was anything but amused when he learned that Charlie had not even begun the capitol mural. Two of Montana's other prominent artists, Edgar Paxson and Ralph DeCamp, had completed commissions for other parts of the building. Where was Charlie? The governor wanted the mural done by September — no excuses.[15]

Charlie met the challenge. Over the winter, workmen had raised his studio walls by four logs to accommodate the mural's twelve-foot height. And while Charlie never did have to call on his New York friends to help him paint, he did solicit their counsel. At some point he apparently even talked to John Alexander, who, according to Nancy, advised Charlie "not to think of it being unusual but go right on and handle it like it was an ordinary size canvas."[16]

At the end of May, Charlie and Nancy traveled to Ross' Hole, not far from where the east fork of the Bitterroot enters the main river. Nancy wrote years later that Charlie had made the trip simply to sketch the background.[17] For descriptions of the actual historic meeting, he had his trusty, dog-eared copy of the Lewis and Clark journals. In Great Falls, he holed up in the studio and finished the canvas in two months, though his anxiety over completing the biggest job of his career — the biggest art commission ever awarded in the state — occasionally got the better of him. His friend Frank Linderman described Charlie's turmoil in his book *Recollections of Charley Russell:*

> While Charlie was at work upon the painting the weather was exceptionally warm and dry. An electric fan was set up to keep him comfortable as he painted. One day when I had been watching him paint for several hours the shack was as quiet as a cemetery. An occasional passage of words between us and the hum of the fan were the only noises. Yet I grew vaguely conscious of a laborer's work on the street in front of the studio. The blows of his pick against the hardpan reached me. I had seen him as I arrived, but I had become absorbed in watching Charley paint and had forgotten him.

"Hear that, Frank?" Charley asked. He moved out of the fan's draft to roll and light a cigaret. "Shut that damn thing off," he said, nodding toward the fan. When he spoke again I realized that he too had been hearing the blows of the laborer's pick and that they had bothered him. "Things ain't fair by a damn sight," he said more to himself than to me. Then he turned to face me, "That poor devil out there in the hot sun with the sweat runnin' down his back can't save as much as I'm gettin' for this picture in his whole lifetime, not if he works every day. He's probably got a woman and some kids, too. Here I am sittin' in the shade with an electric fan blowin' on my neck gettin' five thousand dollars for this thing. An' I didn't make the canvas, an' I didn't make the paint, an I didn't make the brushes. I didn't make a damn thing I'm usin' to make that money with. I just bought 'em with money I made by usin' stuff that other men made for wages — an' damn poor wages, too. By God, that man out there ought to hate me. I wouldn't blame him a damn bit if he walked in here an' killed me with his pick."[18]

Charlie delivered *Lewis and Clark Meeting Indians at Ross' Hole* to Helena by early July. It was quickly hailed as a masterpiece — "his best and most finished product," exclaimed the *Minneapolis Sunday Journal* — though in later years various know-it-alls would pick at details of authenticity.[19] (For instance, Charlie had dressed the Indians in blanket capotes and cloth leggings; Lewis and Clark had observed no cloth garments on the Flatheads.)[20] A half-dozen braves on horseback command the central foreground; majestic mountains and pressing clouds span the top half of the mural. Only after the eye has studied the landscape and admired the clutch of Indians does it come to Lewis, Clark, Sacagawea, and York, as they enter stage right in the middle distance. The scene is as heroic as any painted by Emanuel Leutze or his Düsseldorfian protégés.

Moreover, Charlie had managed to count subtle coup on the entire state of Montana. From 1912 forward, every legislator to appear on the floor of the House of Representatives, every lobbyist who worked the aisles, every citizen who gawked from the gallery would be greeted by a twelve-by-twenty-five reminder that Montana had once belonged to someone else. That Charlie would be honored for his accomplishment with a special proclamation at a special joint session of the legislature in March 1913 is proof of the mural's irrefutable grandeur. If any irony was implicit in the composition, then no local O. Henry stepped forward to spell it out.

⁓

ONE REASON CHARLIE had worked so feverishly to complete the capitol mural — other than the whipcrack of the governor — was so he could attend the annual Fourth of July powwow on the Blackfeet reservation in Browning, Montana. He had received a special invitation through Frank Linderman. Linderman was five years younger than Charlie, and one more example of a headstrong, barely educated youth who had come to Montana and then grown up with the country.[21] He had worked as a trapper, hunter, guide, prospector, assayer, newspaperman, insurance salesman, and politician. Like Charlie, he was a keen student of Indian culture, half-wishing that he had been born a different color himself. He collected Indian stories the way Charlie collected artifacts. Linderman ultimately made a huge contribution to American history by interpreting the folktales and life stories of various Native Americans.

If there was a difference between Linderman and Russell, it was that Linderman made an effort to understand the mind and soul of Indians, while, relatively speaking, Charlie seemed more content to observe their outward actions and customs. "I have always studied the wild man from his picture side," he once admitted.[22] He probably never spent much time talking with Indians — not serious, penetrating exchanges, anyway — due to his extremely limited native vocabulary. For Charlie, acting Indian never entirely lost its Mayne Reid boyishness. Grown men who darkened their faces, dressed up like braves, and struck cigar-store poses, as Charlie did regularly at Lake McDonald, were paying tribute more to the tradition of the Anglo-Saxon house party than that of a dignified and complex indigenous people. That did not mean that Charlie did not care about Indians; he cared about them deeply, incessantly. He simply was never really close to many as individuals.

The trip to the Blackfeet reservation that summer was a graphic example of Charlie's Indian awareness, if Frank Linderman's recollection of the event can be counted on. With the opening of Glacier Park, the Great Northern had begun promoting the romance of its "High Line" route by hiring Indians to congregate in full regalia at stations and in hotel lobbies. Tourists stepped from their Pullmans to watch groups of Blackfeet dance, smoke, and tell stories with their hands, usually with a jaded sidekick singsonging a translation. Powwows, still rich with religious, social, and economic tradition, had begun to attract curious whites as well.[23]

The summer of 1912, a number of other artists besides Charlie had come to observe the Browning powwow, including Frank Tenney Johnson, illustrator Joe Scheurle, and portrait painter William Krieghoff.[24] Not everyone took to the powwow with the same zeal, or had the same access as Linderman and Charlie. In 1909, the United States government, struggling over what to do with the 150 (some put the number as high as 400) homeless, wandering Cree-Chippewa in Montana, had decided to assign them to the Blackfeet reservation. But the Cree-Chippewa were long-standing rivals of the Blackfeet. Understandably, only a small group of 50 or so, led by the Chippewa chief Rocky Boy, had stuck it out among the Blackfeet. Many more preferred to squat near the slaughterhouses east of Helena or in squalid camps outside Great Falls and Havre.[25]

Frank Linderman had been an outspoken advocate for the Cree-Chippewa cause. Charlie had been sensitized to the Indians' plight by his Cree friend Young Boy. During one of the Cree-Chippewa's darkest hours during 1909, Charlie had published a letter in the *Tribune* scolding his fellow Montanans:

> Lots of people seem to think that Indians are not human beings at all and have no feelings. These kind of people would be the first to yell for help if their grub pile was running short and they didn't have enough clothes to keep out the cold, and yet because Rocky Boy and his bunch are Indians, they are perfectly willing to let them die of hunger and cold without lifting a hand.[26]

In the spring of 1912, Linderman had persuaded a group of Indians living near Helena to comply with a government order to give the Blackfeet reservation another try; they trusted Linderman enough to move. When Charlie and Linderman visited Browning that July, they were the honored guests of Little Bear, the Cree leader who had been harassed and pilloried by the governments of both Canada and the United States ever since his participation in the Riel Rebellion thirty-five years before.

At the powwow, the Indians put Charlie and Linderman up in their own tent. Linderman relates that in the middle of the night, they were awakened by the sound of drums a mile or so away. When a mixed-breed tent mate informed them that it was a Cree sun dance, the two threw off their blankets and slipped through the night in the direction of the sacred and secret ceremony. "The sun lodge was now in sight," Linderman wrote, "and little lances of firelight were darting through its sagebrush-covered sides. A voice deep and stern, nearly angry in tone, was haranguing the dancers. The whistles were quiet, the drums silent when we reached the entrance. Charley hesitated, his hand on my arm, 'By God, I don't know about this butting in,' he said."

The sun dance was indeed a private affair, and strong medicine. Doubtless many of the Indians were in trances, experiencing the supernatural shapes and voices of animals mixing with the drumbeats, smoke, and shadows. Rather than being expelled from the magical proceedings, Charlie and Linderman were recognized by Little Bear and invited to stay. "The shrill eagle-wing whistles, the drumming, the singers, the painted faces, the weird headdresses fascinated Charley," Linderman recalled, and Linderman had to suppress his friend's urge to take out his sketchbook and draw.

The two spectators stayed all night. "I wouldn't have missed seeing that for a thousand dollars," Charlie told Linderman the next morning. "The dancin' in that firelight was great."[27] If Charlie had felt or understood the underlying medicine of the sun dance, as Linderman clearly had, he never expressed it in pictures or words. He had been a keen and compassionate observer, but much of the mysticism of the evening had flown right over his head.

CHARLIE WAS AN honored guest a second time that summer. In 1912, Guy Weadick, a former trick roper for the famous Miller Brothers 101 Ranch Wild West Show, masterminded the first Calgary Stampede. Calgary was by then a booming Canadian commercial center of sixty thousand. The Calgary Exhibition was the region's annual exercise in pomp and self-promotion, and in 1911 it had drawn ninety thousand to its horse races, trade booths, airplane demonstrations, and agricultural and livestock fair. Backers of the 1912 Exhibition figured that the addition of a rodeo — or stampede, as the Canadians call such affairs — would only make the weeklong festivities that much more attractive.[28]

Guy Weadick's Stampede was rodeo showmanship writ large. He promised roping and bucking events for both men and women. Winners would receive $1,000, a silver belt buckle, and a new saddle. There would be stage-coach races, wild horse races, "fancy" and trick riding, and an Indian relay race. He hired a hundred Indians to parade around the Stampede grounds in war paint. And he invited every cowboy he had ever known to come to Calgary. That included Charlie Russell, as well as Ed Borein, whom he solicited to exhibit artwork.

Charlie was initially skeptical about Weadick's extravaganza. "Glory riders" he called rodeo contestants, and he had no kinder words for rodeo audiences. "The big half of the folks that take in ridin' contests never rode nothin' but cushions," Charlie's alter-ego Rawhide Rawlins groused, "so if Mister [bronc] Buster gets unloaded, they say he couldn't ride; if he stays and scratches his bronc [with his spurs — a measure of a good ride] they say the hoss didn't buck."[29]

Nancy, on the other hand, saw opportunity in Calgary. There were many wealthy landowners in Alberta, some of them English gentry; the Calgary Exhibition was also known to attract some of the most prominent people from the eastern provinces. Nancy made sure that twenty of Charlie's best paintings arrived in Calgary in time for the Stampede's opening on September 2.[30] She and Charlie were booked into a downtown hotel, all expenses paid.

"Ive seen som good wild west showes but I wouldint call what you pulled off a show, it was the real thing an a whole lot of it," Charlie wrote to Weadick after his return to Montana.[31] Charlie's sunny mood was un-doubtedly encouraged by the warm reception his work was given in a downtown exhibition hall. Thirteen of the twenty paintings sold — an unprecedented run at unprecedented prices. Henry Pellatt, the Toronto hydroelectric and railway financier, bought five: *Heads and Tails, When Horse Flesh Comes High, In Without Knocking, Moving Camp,* and *Scouts.* Guy Weadick's claim that Charlie had brought $100,000 worth of art was wildly exaggerated, but correspondence later that fall indicates that Pellatt had paid $3,500 for a single oil.[32]

As gilt on the lily, Charlie and Nancy were given a royal audience at the end of the week. "The exhibition gallery was cleared Saturday after-noon," the *Albertan* reported, "while the Duchess [of Connaught, wife of Queen Victoria's son Albert, governor general of Canada] and Princess Patricia [their daughter] and other members of the vice-regal party viewed the pictures, and the artist and Mrs. Russell were presented to Their Royal Highnesses." Ballie Buck, one of Charlie's old puncher friends, was with him as the royal party arrived: "When the Duke's outfit came in instead of Charlie making a big ado over them he kind of got closer to me and then Princess Patricia came over to where we were and she asked Charlie if he did the things the riders and ropers [in his paintings] were doing. 'Oh, no, I was just a common dub cowpuncher,' he said and she savvied what he ment and got a big laugh out of it."[33]

Humility aside, this was heady stuff — with considerable residuals. Newfound English fans urged him to bring an exhibition to London.[34] Selling well and selling high made it easier for Nancy to persuade galleries in other American cities to show Charlie's work. Commissions began rolling in. For George Lane, one of the Canadian ranchers who had financed the Stampede, Charlie painted *Camp Cook's Trouble*. Lane came to Great Falls in person to pick up the finished oil. "When it was finished he was well pleased except for one thing," Nancy reminisced. Lane, for all his wealth and royal connections, considered himself an unreconstructed cowman and a bit of a skinflint besides. "You know, Charlie, no outfit ever had an axe without a broken handle," Lane said, picking on a minor detail in the canvas. "They always kept me broke buying new ones." Charlie obliged his patron, dabbing some white paint on the ax in the picture so it appeared to have been mended. Lane approved and reached for his checkbook. "How much do you want for it?" he asked. "Charlie knew perfectly well," Nancy asserted, but he turned to Lane and said, "My wife is the hold up in the family."[35]

Nancy's files do not record what she held Lane up for, but it was probably in the neighborhood of $2,000. That same fall, she had driven a similarly hard bargain with Malcolm Mackay, a New York investment banker who owned a large ranch near Roscoe, Montana.[36] Mackay and his wife, Helen, would loom large in the lives of Charlie and Nancy Russell, becoming huge patrons and perhaps even more generous friends. (Today the Mackay Collection at the Montana Historical Society in Helena is one of the four largest and most important collections of Russell's art.)

Mackay first met Charlie and Nancy in 1908, most likely in New York, and started acquiring Russell paintings and sculpture.[37] By the fall of 1912, however, with the state capitol and Calgary successes behind her, Nancy was showing no favoritism to Charlie's most loyal followers. Mackay commissioned a three-foot-by-five-foot oil, expressly requesting a roundup scene, and offered to pay $1,000. Nancy dug in, and when *The Roundup* was completed the next year (at slightly reduced dimensions), Mackay met her price of $1,800. Mackay did send the painting back so Charlie could paint Mackay's Lazy EL brand on one of the cows. It was the only concession Nancy would grant.[38]

~~~~~

MACKAY WAS IN many ways the quintessential Russell patron. Not surprisingly, the typical collector was male. Not all were self-made men — many were heirs — but all revered the strenuous life. They liked action and open space, an antidote to the claustrophobia of their drawing rooms and desk jobs. They saw themselves as captains of capitalism, men of re-flex and decision, corporate cowboys of sorts. Western art spoke to them in a way that "modern" art did not. In fact, the rise in popularity of Western art curiously paralleled the rise of the Modern movement.

On February 17, 1913, a week after Malcolm Mackay sent Nancy Russell his check for *The Roundup,* the International Exhibition of Modern Art opened at the 69th Regiment Armory in New York. The Armory Show, as it came to be called, had been organized by a small group of rebels from the National Academy who called themselves the Association of Ameri-can Painters and Sculptors. The larger goal of the exhibition was to trace the development of Modern art from its classical roots, through Real-ism and Impressionism, to the present. The smorgasbord of twelve hun-dred works included such European masters as Corot, Daumier, Delacroix, Goya, Manet, Monet, Renoir, Rodin, and Vuillard, as well as Ameri-cans George Bellows, Solon Borglum, Albert Pinkham Ryder, Cassatt, Glackens, Hassam, Henri, Hopper, Luks, Inness, Twachtman, and Whistler. The artists who created the biggest stir, however, were the Cubists.[39]

In the monthlong run at the Armory, roughly seventy thousand people paid to see what the uproar was all about. There was a constant crowd around *Nude Descending a Staircase,* Marcel Duchamp's Cubist-Futurist oil inspired by stop-action photography. *Nude* was variously described as "a lot of disused golf clubs and bags," an "orderly heap of broken violins," or, the jab most often repeated, "an explosion in a shingle factory." Soon the critical waggishness became an art form all its own. Brancusi's *Mlle. Pogany* was sent up as a "hardboiled egg on a cube of sugar." The entire Cubist room, which included two Légers, three Braques, four Picabias, and eight

Picassos, was labeled a "Chamber of Horrors." Even Cézanne, Van Gogh, and Gauguin came under fire, and Matisse took the worst drubbing of all for his "gauche puerilities" and "essentially epileptic" art.[40]

The most conservative detractors viewed the show with millennialist outrage. The center was not holding, in art as in most other facets of civilization. The Fauves, Cubists, and Futurists were seen as a vanguard of "European extremists" and "artistic anarchists" who presented a "grave danger to public morals." "They have abolished the representation of nature and all forms of recognized and traditional decoration," lamented American painter Kenyon Cox in *Harper's Weekly.* "Two years ago I wrote: 'We have reached the edge of the cliff and must turn back or fall into the abyss.' Deliberately and determinedly these men have stepped over the edge."[41]

Charlie and Nancy were in town for another exhibition of his art at Folsom and made sure to take in the Armory Show. "Yes, I saw the cubist and futurist exhibit in New York, but can't savvy that stuff," Charlie said to a reporter later. "It may be art . . . but I can't savvy it. Now, I may paint a bum horse, but people who know what a horse looks like will know that I tried to paint a horse, at least. Most people can't savvy all this dreamy stuff."[42]

Charlie's standards were unwavering. Admiring a painting by Rosa Bonheur, the disciplined French animal artist, Charlie once commented, "By God, I can smell the cows that gal painted." Of Ralph DeCamp, the Montana landscape painter, Charlie remarked, "That boy can sure paint the wettest water of anybody I know. You can hear his rivers ripple." Contrarily, when he was taken by a cousin to see an exhibit of paintings by George Inness, the American Impressionist, Charlie was unhesitatingly acerbic: "I have rolled out of my blankets in a heap of country," he told Fergus Mead, the relative who accompanied him, "but I never saw the world all squit over with tobacco the way this fellow did."[43]

In the extremely rare instances when Charlie's own work wandered off track, he was his own harshest critic. Frank Linderman recalled entering Charlie's studio one day and seeing a very uncharacteristic painting: "The picture was unlike anything that had ever come from his brush. . . . The coloring was strange; the landscape was dim; the figures were scarcely discernible." Linderman indicated his disapproval. "Uh-huh, you don't like the picture," Charlie said to his friend.

That's because you *cahn't* appreciate true *aht*. . . . Look — these are cows, an' that's a water hole, and this is a cowpuncher. Yeah, I know, but dust *obscuahs* 'em so's you wouldn't know what they are. . . . It's an impressionistic *pictuah*. . . . Know why painters are impressionistic? 'Cause they can't draw an' they know they can't. So they blur their paintin' an hide their bum drawin'. Just let your eyes try to follow a man's leg that they draw; start from the boot — the leg's as likely to run into his belly as anywhere else. Hell!

At which point Charlie turned and kicked a hole in the canvas. "That's an ordered picture," he spat. "A man wants it, but he ain't goin' to get it."[44]

There were plenty of people who did not like Modernism any more than Charlie did and took refuge in "genre" art — marine, military, or Western. Malcolm Mackay collected only Russells, and both Mackay and Sir Henry Pellatt eventually added "Russell rooms" to their otherwise re-fined manors. Decorated with Indian blankets, animal skins, and Charlie's art, these dens were smoky sanctuaries where novelty was turned away at the door.[45]

Charlie's art became more and more conspicuous wherever men gath-ered. In the summer of 1913, Guy Weadick orchestrated a second stampede, this one in Winnipeg. Charlie exhibited seventeen oils, seven watercolors, and nine bronzes. The following year, the Montana Club, Helena's bastion of male movers and shakers, commissioned Charlie to paint a picture to hang over the mantel in the club's reading room; the result was *When the Land Belonged to God,* a three-foot-by-six-foot oil masterpiece of a herd of buffalo emerging from the Missouri River at sundown. Another men's club, the Duquesne in Pittsburgh, paid $2,000 for *When Shadows Hint Death,* a tense scene of two white men trying to slip through Indian country unde-tected. "Pittsburghers . . . may not be so strong on art," Charlie said, "but they are real men and they like real life."[46]

Perhaps the only pitfall to painting for real men was that they expected macho images; for that reason, after his 1912 showing at Calgary secured cli-ents such as Pellatt, Lane, and Mackay, Charlie turned out fewer and fewer sensitive scenes of Indian women and domestic life and more and more scenes of derring-do and machismo. A list of some of his titles beginning in 1913 sums up the trend toward "predicament" subject matter: *Wild Horse Hunters, Crippled But Still Coming, The Toll Collectors, Caught with the Goods,*

Whose Meat?, Jumped, Loops and Swift Horses Are Surer Than Lead, The Challenge, The Marauders, Meat for Wild Men, A Bad One, Men of the Open Range, The Bluffers.

Charlie accepted the masculine pigeonhole, and never tired of all-male company. When in Great Falls, he was still a regular at the Mint and Silver Dollar. (In 1914, Sid Willis finally consented to closing the Mint one afternoon a week so that women could admire his considerable Russell collection.)[47] And each year Charlie seemed to find an excuse to disappear into the backcountry with a group of men. In October 1913, he joined Frank Linderman, Linderman's father, and a fourth man identified as "Doc Nash" on a two-week, four-hundred-mile boat trip down the Missouri. Linderman and Charlie had become best friends through their visit to the Blackfeet reservation, their work to help the Cree-Chippewa, and Linderman's lobbying on behalf of the capitol mural. This outing, however, promised to be purely for pleasure. The plan, Linderman wrote Charlie, was to put a small scow in the river at Fort Benton and "let her drift," except in the flat stretches, where they would employ a small outboard motor. Charlie, six months shy of his fiftieth birthday, showed up with pillow, bedroll, air mattress, change of clothes, and his Lewis and Clark journals.

They did little carefree floating. The boat struck a rock and sprang a leak. Gasoline seeped into their grub box; they ran aground in the low water of autumn and had to drag their heavily laden boat through gumbolike mud; they were snowbound for three days; and Charlie's pillow caught fire. Nevertheless, they managed to keep their spirits up. Linderman shot a mule deer and "we got lots of duck and grouse," Charlie reported. Periodically, Charlie would read aloud from Lewis and Clark. "His reading was like that of a small boy," Linderman remembered. "He frequently spelled out words for our pronunciation. 'Them old boys could go up this river with a load an' we can't even go down the damned thing without getting stuck forty times a day,' " Charlie joked to his fellow adventurers.[48]

BY NOW, CHARLIE should have been used to shifting back and forth between the rough and the refined. But none of his experiences on the Missouri prepared him for his next boat trip. In March 1914, after another New York show, Charlie and Nancy boarded the liner *Oceanic* and steamed to England, where his latest collection of "The West That Has Passed" was scheduled for exhibition in the Doré Galleries in London. Charlie was horribly seasick on the crossing, complaining to Central Avenue friends that the "wave wagon," as he called the ship, "dun the tango[,] hesitaton waltz an all the late snakey dances all the way a cross."[49]

The English had a long-standing love affair with homespun Americans, particularly Western Americans, having been smitten successively by the likes of John James Audubon, George Catlin, Bret Harte, Mark Twain, and Buffalo Bill over the years. Even so, the reviews of Charlie's art were as tough as or tougher than some of his New York notices. The London *Observer* allowed that Charlie was a "surprisingly competent draughtsman," but ghettoized him as an illustrator whose paint had "no quality." Other reviewers, though, were willing to overlook the rough edges. The *Globe,* while declaring his drawing "uncertain" and his color "unpleasant," forgave his technical defects in light of "so much suggestion of movement and vigorous action, so much life and virile feeling, and so much revelation of intimate acquaintance with the world he has lived in."[50]

The Doré exhibition juxtaposed Charlie's work with that of a Futurist show in the next room. Futurists had evolved from Cubists, having found Cubism too static and lacking in ideological thrust.[51] They worshiped the speed and precision of machines, especially the motion-picture camera and the automobile. The Doré show was one of the movement's defining moments, but the jittery, multifaceted paintings in the Doré Galleries were anathema to Charlie. (Could it have been entirely coincidental that a show titled "The West That Has Past" hung simultaneously with one that codified Futurism? Surprisingly, not a single reviewer found the common denominator in the exhibitions: motion. The Futurists were trying new ways to express it, and as Frank Linderman once observed, "Everything Russ paints is a goin' some.")[52]

Charlie called his gallery mates "Futes," as if they were a lost tribe. He got as big a chuckle out of the artists as he did out of their art. One of the Italians was "bilt like a wine bottle verry lady like an wore a thin beard I think to head off regular men that might make naughty eys at him." One of the man's paintings looked like "an enlarged slice of spoilt summer sausig." Charlie gathered that another piece "represented the feeling of a bad stomach after a duck lunch." In the end, he did find some measure of value in the Futurist effort. "I'd like to shut some of the old 'punchers up in here when they're on a big drunk," he said, "an' let 'em wake up with all them things all 'round 'em. It'd either cure 'em of drinkin', or the shock'd kill 'em."53

As for the rest of his trip to England, Charlie seemed to be of two minds. He was well aware of his own English heritage and had a soft spot for English ways. He liked the sheer age of England, describing it to a Great Falls neighbor as a "historical range." In a letter to Frank Linderman he wrote, "This is an old old land with more people under the sod than there is on top." He visited Buckingham Palace and the Tower of London. "Il say this much for the English," he wrote Linderman, "they have worked hard to save a fiew things God made. . . . The English ar a slow but nature loving people who have kept there small country beautiful."54

But even while Charlie admired England's scenery and history, he stopped short of endorsing his own escutcheon. Like most men of his time, he took note of the nationality of his friends and acquaintances and was more than a little xenophobic — he did not hesitate to make Limburger jokes about the Germans, kilt jokes about the Scottish, and drinking jokes about the Irish — but usually his jabs were light, and he was just as quick to turn the brickbat on himself. "Nobody is important enough to be important" was one of Charlie's favorite sayings, and on his visit to the executioner's chamber in the Tower of London he was tickled to learn that a "Sir Sombody Russell" had had "the upper end of his back bone removed by the Kings ax man." While noting that "the Russells were pritty plenty in this land," Charlie concluded that "the Russell tree was a scrub."55

The Doré show, for all the splash it made, produced only three or four sales. The remaining paintings were invited to hang at the Anglo-American Exposition in London after the Doré show closed, but that honor did not cure Charlie's homesickness. "[T]his is shure a cold bread country," he complained, adding that "tea and muffins aren't my kind of fodder."56

Toward the end of the trip, Charlie and Nancy took a three-day junket to Paris, apparently guided by an art buyer for a calendar company. The most notable aspect of the visit was that it made practically no positive impression on Charlie. In fact, about the only descriptive record of the trip is a mention at the end of a letter he wrote to painter Bill Krieghoff: "Wev been to Paris stayed onely three days[.] Saw Seven hundred miles of pictures [the Louvre] about the same distance in resteronts sevarl Churches and Nepoilans Toom. Old Nepo has been a sleep a long time but judging from the size of the stone over him an the gards a round the French are taking no chances on him waking up."

Austin Russell, who called his uncle "a philistine of the first water," explained that the old masters bored Charlie. "Who in hell wants to look at miles and miles of entombments and descents from the Cross and martyrs crucified upside down," Charlie told Austin. "I'd just as soon visit the morgue."57

ALL OF EUROPE was on tenterhooks that spring of 1914. A month after Charlie and Nancy sailed for New York — aboard the soon-to-be-sunk *Lusitania* — Archduke Ferdinand was felled by a shot heard around the world. By August, the German army was marching through the streets of Brussels on its way to France. Yet in his numerous letters home, some of the lengthiest he wrote in his life, Charlie had mentioned not a single rumor of war. He had plenty to say about the Futes and "Bill Conk" (William the Conqueror), but never mentioned the Huns or the Kaiser.58

It is risky to read too much into Charlie's initial taciturnity on World War I; after all, most of his remarks were directed to Montana friends who counted on the usual chestnuts from their Cowboy Artist. On the other hand, Charlie's minimal notice of not just this war but such world-shaking events as the Spanish-American War, the Boer War, the Boxer Rebellion, the assassination of President McKinley, women's suffrage, and the nation's economic panics of 1893 and 1907 suggests that he nursed a larger ambivalence toward the major headlines of his times.

One illustration of Charlie's quirky apathy dates back to 1896, during William Jennings Bryan's populist campaign for the presidency. The anecdote is apocryphal, but the mere fact that it has been endlessly attributed to Charlie implies that the shoe fit, even if it once had belonged on someone else's foot. Charlie was living in Cascade at the time Bryan was whistle-stopping across the West, and was loafing near the station when the train from Great Falls stopped on its way to Helena and Butte. Bryan stepped down from the car for a minute to stretch his legs, making small talk with the only man on the platform. He certainly did not know Charlie, nor did Charlie recognize the great orator of the Platte. Finally, as the whistle signaled departure, Bryan asked Charlie why the town was so deserted. The story goes that Charlie looked at the famous stranger and said, "They all went to Great Falls last night to hear that windjammer Bryan."[59]

Admittedly, Charlie was less blasé about issues closer to home: land speculation, encroachment by homesteaders, mistreatment of Indians, the general taming of the West. Generally, though, his opinions were just that — sermons preached to a choir whose altar was mahogany with a brass rail attached.

To his credit, he did eventually get involved in the war effort — quite passionately, in fact. Montana, though it had a sizable population of German and Austro-Hungarian immigrants, was solidly in support of President Wilson's war. More than twelve thousand Montanans volunteered for service, and because of a gross overestimation of the state's population, one out of every ten men in Montana was drafted, a portion of the total population that was 25 percent higher than any other state's contribution.[60] At fifty-three, Charlie was clearly beyond service of any sort when the United States joined the fight in 1917. "Dad time has bar[r]ed me from this scrap," he wrote to a friend in uniform, expressing his misgivings about not wearing one himself.

> [T]hairs a lot of stay at homes like my self here that clame they want to go to the front, but I think if it came to a show down theyd need more pooshing than holdin. [M]y years have maby saved my scalp but if Uncle Sam raised the age limit I [would] go but I dont yearn for trench life[.] I am often ashamed when I see others going to fight and take chanches for me an its shame not bravory that would send me to the front.[61]

In 1918 Charlie donated two paintings that were used in posters for the Food Administration of Montana: *Meat Makes Fighters* and *Pardners*. The latter showed an old-timer making flapjacks out of his horse's oats, thereby "leavin' meat and wheat for fightin' men." Likewise, Charlie went public with his support of tobacco rationing. When the government announced it was going to divert all Bull Durham exclusively to the troops, many people predicted that most roll-your-own men, particularly cowpunchers, would greedily stock up. Charlie set an honorable example. "No, I guess I'll just take a couple of packages as usual. . . . I wouldn't feel right with a big bunch of it in the cellar and knowing that the fellows in the trenches were hungry for a 'Bull' smoke." Newspapers around the state repeated the propaganda, along with a picture of a small clay model Charlie had made of a cowboy pulling a packhorse laden with two bags of Bull Durham.[62]

Nancy got behind the war effort, too, heading a fund-raising drive for the Women's Division of the United War Work campaign. She oversaw nearly two hundred women and raised thousands of dollars, an achievement that reflected not only her patriotism but her improved standing in Great Falls society.[63]

Though Nancy would never be taken into the stuffy fold of the Maids & Matrons, by the war years she had nevertheless earned a certain degree of respect and prominence in the community. A large, very flattering photo of her appeared in the *Great Falls Tribune* society column on October 11, 1914; a headline identified her, benignly and aptly, as "One of City's Popular Social Leaders Who Enjoys the Distinction of Being the Wife of Montana's Famous Artist." Mrs. Russell, the caption elaborated, "is ever gracious as a hostess and in assisting the clubs in the city, although she is too busy to affiliate with them, as she accompanies Mr. Russell on all of his trips, and has little time to devote to club work."

Nancy did find time to attend the Episcopal Church of the Incarnation, though Charlie preferred to spend his Sunday mornings in his studio cooking dutch-oven breakfasts for his friends. Nancy helped with various fund-raising projects for the church's women's guild, including a 1916 performance of the forgettable operetta *Little Almond Eyes* at the Grand Opera House. (She recruited Charlie to paint the masks.) It was this experience, and her obvious knack for separating people from their money, that earned her the chairmanship of the war drive.

As a couple, Charlie and Nancy gave and attended dinner parties. In the winter of 1914–15, they took dancing lessons and attended the formal Fortnightly balls in the Palm Room at the Rainbow Hotel, where Great Falls society attempted the latest steps sweeping the country. Surprisingly, Charlie seemed to enjoy the occasions more than Nancy, and sometimes he showed up at Fortnightly by himself.[64]

Mostly Nancy was consumed with the task of driving Charlie's career. From her desk in the front room of the Fourth Avenue house, she handled all of his business correspondence with galleries, calendar companies, publishers, and individual patrons. In 1915, she arranged for another show at the Folsom Galleries in New York and also booked his work into Minneapolis, Chicago, and San Francisco. The following year she negotiated shows in

Chicago and New York again, as well as Duluth and Pittsburgh. The list of cities in which Charlie exhibited eventually grew to include Milwaukee, Denver, Washington, and Los Angeles. As she and Charlie became more prosperous, Nancy was able to hire steady housekeeping help and ultimately a stenographer to assist with the dozens of letters she wrote each week. Still, the job of managing their lives was immense, and she drove herself as hard as she drove her husband.

When stress mounted, Nancy was usually the first to crack. Always high-strung, she flew into rages "where a body would expect the iron skillet to come flying through the air," testified Margaret Coulter, a neighbor at Lake McDonald. "[S]he used to storm at him like an outraged sparrow." Charlie eventually came to understand that silence, or occasional retreat, was the better part of valor. "She had a very quick hot temper and had not learned to control it like I had," he once admitted. "I had learned to control mine so when differences came up I would take my hat and go down town and when I came back the clouds would have all passed away. I would come in the back door happy and whistling [and in the early days, lubricated] and she would meet me with a smile, she would be so sorry for her misdoings."[65]

Occasionally, though, Charlie would respond to her excesses by sulking conspicuously or by being mischievously contrary. In her memoirs, Nancy describes Charlie repairing to Johnny Matheson's ranch near Belt, where he would sit on a haystack and replenish his creative juices. One wonders whether these occasions were dreamy respites or willful flights from Nancy's pecking.

When he chose to peck back, his favorite place to do it was in public. Nancy "treated him like a child," claimed Lillian Huidekoper, wife of the eventual owner of *Waiting for a Chinook,* "and she was forever correcting or chiding him in front of others."[66] When it got too much, Charlie reacted the way he had toward every teacher and tutor he had ever had. He abandoned parlor etiquette and delighted in playing the little rascal.

It didn't take a scolding for Charlie to misbehave, however. He was gleefully naughty when thrown into stuffy company. When forced to don a formal morning coat or dinner jacket — he called them his "black clothes" — Charlie insisted on wearing his Métis sash as a flag of protest. He wore it in London at a dinner in his honor given by English nobles (where Charlie claims he accidentally stepped on and ripped the trailing hem of his hostess's dress) and again to the home of American plutocrat and art patron Andrew Mellon (where he stage-whispered jokes about the caviar and servants in "sateen knee pants").

At other times, when his choice of dress was not so eyebrow-raising, his choice of conversation topic was. The Western illustrator and author Ross Santee recalled meeting Charlie for the first time at one of the Folsom exhibitions. Spotting the fellow cowboy, Charlie took great pleasure in pulling Santee aside and, despite the Fifth Avenue setting, launching into a long-winded scatological joke.[67]

During another exhibition, this one at the Ambassador Hotel in Los Angeles, Nancy, with Charlie in tow, was wooing some potential buyers in the hotel dining room. Charlie, according to one account, was meanwhile in an obvious state of "great discomfort and boredom, answering only in monosyllables when spoken to." Then, out of the blue, he spotted Alberta Bair, an old friend and the daughter of wealthy Montana sheep baron Charlie Bair. Russell, a scampish gleam in his eye, seized the opportunity. "Say," he asked Alberta, "has your father heard from Pink-eye Smith lately?" Pink-eye, the other dinner guests quickly gleaned, was a Montana man of the Bairs' acquaintance who had recently been arrested for murder. For the rest of the evening, Charlie and Alberta discussed Pink-eye's innocence, Charlie warming to the topic as the wealthy buyers blanched and Nancy's glances grew chillier.[68] He committed an even more egregious faux pas one year while visiting Santa Barbara. Nancy had again corralled some ripe prospects. When Charlie could take no more, he climbed out a back window of the house and fled into the night.

These stories were the flamboyant extremes, of course, and as such are the ones most cherished by friends and memoirists. The stories of his obedience, though not as colorful, are just as telling about Charlie's relationship to Nancy and his own fame. The constant touring was becoming a dog and pony show as programmatic as any performed by an itinerant dry-goods drummer. But when it came to publicity, Charlie rarely failed to play his part in the act. As the cities changed from month to month, he could be counted on to hold forth in lobby or café, his hat tipped back on his head and a smoke clamped between ringed fingers. Invariably the news stories would mention his "open western countenance," "hearty handshake," and "bleach-blue eye." Proof that Charlie's presence and performance went hand in hand with sales came the year Nancy took an exhibition to Denver by herself. It was a "complete failure," according to Joe DeYong. She returned to Great Falls dejected. "It's no good without Charlie," she confided to DeYong. "The show just doesn't go over!"[69]

In Charlie's interviews with the press, he continued to express his gratitude to "the lady I trot in double harness with." Without her, he said, "I'd be swamping in some saloon." Nancy was just as needy. She fed off Charlie's talent, his pedigree, his success, his money, his innate self-confidence; moreover, she was bolstered by the very knowledge that he had accepted her. "I was too weak to measure up but he pretended not to see my big faults," she wrote Joe DeYong after Charlie's death. "I loved doing things for him. . . . It just seem[ed] I must have his approval."[70]

By the summer of 1916, both Nancy and Charlie were receiving plenty of approval. Their little manipulations of each other aside, the world seemed to be "wagging well," in Nancy's words. The previous July, they had enjoyed their first pack trip through Glacier Park with Howard Eaton, the Pennsylvanian who had founded the nation's first dude ranch. When Glacier became an official park, enterprising and charismatic "Uncle Howard" began leading his guests on trips from St. Mary's, on the east side of the Continental Divide, over breathtaking passes to Lake McDonald.[71] Charlie particularly relished the rigorous, albeit catered, expedition, and the fact that the fun came at no charge made the journey that much more comfortable. Eaton regarded Charlie's presence in camp and on the trail as an added treat for the paying customers and tariff enough for Charlie.

Eaton and the Russells had hit it off so well that in September 1916, Eaton asked them to join a trip he was leading to the Grand Canyon and the Navajo lands of the Southwest. Again, they had a fine time, tenting with "a good bunch," though Charlie joked that the desert was "too far betwine drinks [of water] to live in." Charlie wrote to Ed Borein, describing the Navajo: "They were not like the Indian I know but every thing on them spelt wild people and horsemen and in a mixture of dust and red sunlight it made a picture that will not let me forget Arizona."[72] Photos of Charlie on the trip show him tanned and robust. But they also reveal the wrinkled hands, snowy hair, and creased face of a cowboy who was edging past middle age.

At home in Great Falls after a whirlwind year that had included stays in Pittsburgh, Chicago, New York, Glacier, and Arizona, Charlie and Nancy took a hard look at their lives. They had created so much, and so much had come to them — yet something was still missing.

12

CAMPFIRE STAR

J OE DEYONG WAS the child Charlie and Nancy thought they would never have, and his arrival added a delightful dimension to their lives. Yet in a way, his presence also furthered the blurring of their professional and private identities.

DeYong was precisely thirty years younger than his mentor. Like Charlie, he was born in St. Louis. When he was five, his family moved to Dewey, Oklahoma, where his father Adrian DeYong opened a general store. As a boy, Joe was consumed by two passions: drawing and cowboying. He studied Remington's illustrations in *Collier's Weekly,* many of which he regarded "with impatience, and sometimes scorn." Even as an untrained artist, he knew that "Indian bucks did not ride Squaw Saddles" and that a cowboy would never "swing and throw a loop while a quirt hung from the wrist of the same arm."

DeYong claims he saw his first Russell art on a billboard at the St. Louis World's Fair. The manufacturer of a local laxative, Heptol Splits, had used one of Charlie's bucking-bronco scenes in its advertisements. (One can only surmise that it was the suggestive movement of horse and rider that made Charlie's drawing a fitting graphic for the product.) From that point forward, DeYong declared, "Charlie Russell was my ideal." Each year when the local saddle shop in Oklahoma handed out its new Russell-illustrated calendars, DeYong made sure he was first in line.[1]

DeYong was never tall — barely over five feet without boots — but on horseback he was a young man of stature and ease. He became a welcome sidekick at area roundups, and by his mid-teens was earning wages as a cowhand. A big turning point in DeYong's life came when he met a local Wild West show performer by the name of Tom Mix.

By 1910, Mix was well on his way to becoming the first full-blown cowboy idol of the silver screen. He claimed that he had been born in Texas to a cavalryman father and Cherokee mother; that he had fought with Teddy Roosevelt, with the Marines in the Boxer Rebellion, with the Boers in South Africa, and with Madero in the Mexican Revolution; that as a Texas Ranger he had survived a shot in the back and had single-handedly captured a band of desperadoes. In fact, Tom Mix had been born in Pennsylvania, in 1880, and like many young boys, had grown up idolizing Buffalo Bill and his Wild West performers. He did serve in uniform, but saw no action beyond guard duty, and went AWOL as soon as he got married. The Mixes moved to Oklahoma in 1902, where the handsome and cocky deserter found work as a fitness instructor, bartender, and ranch hand, before finally joining the Miller Brothers 101 Ranch in 1905.

With the popularity of Western movies soaring, production companies had begun tapping the Wild West shows for experienced performers. By 1911, Mix was a star for the Selig Polyscope Company, and throughout the decade he filmed in Oklahoma, Colorado, and Arizona (including *Chip of the Flying U* in 1914). It was during this period, living near Dewey, that he got to know Joe DeYong.[2]

In early 1913, when DeYong was eighteen, he hired on with Selig to help out on a Mix movie being filmed near Prescott, Arizona. If he had hopes of following in Mix's bootprints, they were dashed in February when he came down with spinal meningitis. DeYong regained most of his strength by summer, but had lost his hearing forever.

Unable to ride and barely able to walk, DeYong whiled away the months of convalescence drawing horses and cowboys, trying to mimic Russell prints. Eventually he summoned the nerve to send the famous Cowboy Artist some sketches, a photo of his first model, and a letter asking advice. DeYong's art and letter touched Charlie. Perhaps it was because he had never received a fan letter from anyone so young and earnest; upon his return from the Winnipeg Stampede, Charlie wrote Joe a two-page letter of encouragement and topped it with an illustration of a cowboy on a bucking horse. Charlie's note was mostly how-to stuff: "I use bees wax dimond brand . . . I paint with oil coler using turpentine to thin the paint."[3]

That was enough for Joe DeYong. "Nobody ever had anything happen to them that could mean any more," he recalled years later. "From then on . . . I was Hell-bent to go to Montana."[4] When his father began looking around the West for a new job, Joe urged him to take a trip north in the hope that the family might wind up near the Russells. Joe soon grew impatient waiting for his father to pick a new home, and in the spring of 1914 he set out for Montana on his own. Not long after, his father and mother, Mary (affectionately nicknamed Banty), caught up with him and settled in Choteau, forty miles northwest of Great Falls, where Adrian became proprietor of a pool hall.

Joe met Charlie in Great Falls his first summer north, but their friendship was not fully sealed until a year later, when Joe and a friend, Howard Hall, visited Great Falls a second time. DeYong's letter home in July 1915 overflowed with enthusiasm:

> Wednesday morning we were out at Russells and got a good deal of information on different dope. . . . The skunk picture of Russells [*Men's Weapons Are Useless When Nature Goes Armed,* given as a thank-you to Howard Eaton the following year] is going to be good — Two old hunters just coming to camp one got a deer over his saddle he is holding up his hand for the fellow behind him to wait a minute till these skunks move. The moon is coming up and it is sure pretty. Then he has another big one going of a group of Indians and one is holding up a looking glass and the sun hitting in it [*The Signal Glass*]. . . . Russell was working on some small pen sketches for a book [Linderman's first anthology, *Indian Why Stories*]. . . . [O]ne of the pictures was a beaver sitting up beating on an Indian drum and some skunks and other small animals were doing a war dance.[5]

The coup de grâce came when "Russell got down a big peace pipe and cut up some Indian tobacco and lit the pipe and then handed it to each one of us and we all took a puff." Never mind that the tobacco tasted like "wet hay." Joe was completely smitten. Soon, using a home-cooked sign language loosely based on the gestures he had learned from Linderman and Indians he had met over the years, Charlie was able to break through Joe's deafness. The love that Joe returned for such attentiveness was enormous and unconditional.

Charlie and Nancy had long since despaired of having their own child. In the early years of their marriage, Nancy had succeeded once in becoming pregnant, but had miscarried. She was never able to conceive again.[6] The disappointment she felt was compounded whenever she considered the importance of family to Charlie. Charlie's own childhood had been so happy, he wanted to pass the gift along. Yet it was the one worldly pleasure his wife could not provide him. "I never could be a wife to him," Nancy told a family friend after Charlie's death, "but I made it up to him in other ways."[7]

So Joe DeYong became a stand-in, though he was not the first. Charlie and Nancy had had a maid for several years, a widow named Marie Johnston. Charlie adored Mrs. Johnston's boy Delbert and nicknamed him Skookum, Indian slang for "good." Austin Russell maintained that Charlie and Nancy would have adopted Delbert in an instant, if only the boy's mother had been willing to give him up. She wasn't.[8]

Austin was another surrogate himself. He had attached himself to Charlie and Nancy after his family's first visit to Montana in 1907. Though his moods tended toward the gray and cynical, Charlie and Nancy seemed to like having him around, and kept in close contact with him. (Austin even lived in a Great Falls boardinghouse with Nancy's father for a while.) He felt he enjoyed special status in the family, and it could not have been complete coincidence that Austin left Montana for good about the same time Joe DeYong became a fixture at Fourth Avenue North.

Though twenty-one when he came to stay in January 1916, in many ways Joe was like a child. A visitor to Charlie's studio at the time underestimated Joe's age by seven years.[9] He was so small, so wide-eyed in his devotion. Joe could read lips well, and the sign language helped a great deal. In many instances, though, Charlie and Nancy found it easier to exchange shorthand notes with him. The three of them soon found themselves in a linguistic and emotional interdependence that went far beyond the strict parameters of pedagogy.

At first the idea was that Joe would apprentice in Charlie's studio in exchange for house-sitting and other duties. Nancy had scheduled exhibitions in Chicago, Pittsburgh, and New York for the winter of 1916. In the Russells' absence, Joe could feed the furnace, the chickens, and Charlie's horse Neenah. Soon, though, Joe found himself showered with favors that no amount of fetching and hauling could repay. Nancy baked Joe special sweets and treated him to the movies (which were conveniently silent in those days) and sightseeing trips in the car. She and Charlie sent him to a doctor to see whether his deafness could be cured. "These folks are treating me the finest in the world — all the time," Joe wrote to his real parents.[10]

Years later, Austin Russell joked that Charlie and Nancy would have adopted Joe, just as they had wanted to adopt Delbert Johnston, if only Joe had been an orphan. But Joe had two loving parents already, and despite his filial comportment, he was no child. Charlie and Nancy would have to look elsewhere to fill that void.

Sometime in 1916, Charlie and Nancy had asked their doctor to keep an eye out for a child they might adopt. Charlie preferred a daughter; knowing that Nancy would outlive him, he thought a girl child would keep her company. "If we adopt a boy," Charlie purportedly told Austin Russell, "he'll light out across the country as soon as he grows up, or go to jail or something; but a girl stays home till she's married."[11]

One Sunday evening in early December, the lights blazed at the Russell house. At last a baby had arrived. "[H]e's a peach," Joe wrote to his parents, though he added that the infant was "awful thin & weak." The dark-eyed new arrival was three months old and weighed only twelve pounds. Charlie held out for naming him Childe or Mason, Joe noted, "but Mrs. Russell and I hit on Jack Cooper so thats what it finally turned out to be. He's got a hold on every body here."[12]

Jack's arrival did not precipitate the exile of Joe DeYong, however. He would continue to live with the Russells and work under Charlie's tutelage on and off for the next ten years. Joe accompanied the family to Glacier Park in the summer and on at least one occasion stayed into the fall to close up Bull Head Lodge. Through Charlie and Nancy's introduction, Joe found work with dude rancher Howard Eaton and lived for a while at Eatons' Ranch in Wyoming and accompanied Eaton trips in Glacier. Also through Charlie's encouragement and entrée, Joe began to place his own illustrations in magazines and the hands of collectors. Ultimately his talent would take him to California, where he continued to sculpt and draw. Over the years, he contributed to the set and costume designs for numerous Hollywood Westerns, most notably *The Plainsman* (starring Montanan Gary Cooper as Wild Bill Hickok) and *Shane* (scripted by Montana novelist A. B. Guthrie). Joe's greatest gift to Western history, though, was not his artistic or cinematic portfolio, but rather the record he left of the last ten years of Charlie Russell's life.

Joe was never a burden, but that was not always the case with Jack. He was a handful, and a spoiled one at that. "Talk about attention," Joe kidded. "[H]e sure gets it here and you bet nothings too good for him — Every time Mrs Russ goes down town she comes back with something for him."[13] Charlie was equally obsequious. The *Tribune* took a picture of Jack bouncing on his father's knee, a grinning, bleary-eyed Charlie informing the reporter that the only lullabies he knew were old range ballads, "I'm Only a Cowboy and I Know I've Done Wrong" and "Sam Bass Was Born in Indiana."[14]

The Cowboy Artist was now the cowboy pater. "Maby you dont know it," Charlie wrote to Con Price, "but we got a boy at our house now[. H]e was a little . . . slick ere [an unbranded, un-earmarked calf] when we put our iron on him." To another friend he wrote, "[H]e's ours all right and we shure love him." At a birthday dinner for Charlie at the Rainbow Hotel, a group of Charlie's men friends, led by Frank Linderman, Robert Vaughn, and cowboy poet Johnny Ritch, presented Charlie (and Jack) with a baby buggy decorated with two silver buffalo skulls. A year later Charlie would make a rocking horse for Jack, customizing it with his own brand.

By his first birthday, Jack was plump and garrulous in a language his parents could not comprehend. He "cant crawl on his hind legs yet," Charlie wrote Linderman in November 1917, "but all four feet down he can dam near loap and it keeps us both busy range hearding him."[15] Charlie and Nancy didn't travel east that year, and Charlie did not get a lot done in the studio either. His most noteworthy accomplishment was a series of illustrated "Historical Recollections by Rawhide Rawlins," published in syndicated inserts in small-town Montana papers. This was the beginning of an extended engagement with the Montana Newspaper Association, headed by his friends Bill Cheely and Percy Raban, and all eight of the stories that appeared that winter — including "How Pat Discovered the Geyser," "Where Highwood Hank Quits," and "When Pete Sets a Speed Mark" — would wind up in the Rawhide Rawlins books and eventually *Trails Plowed Under.* In addition, Charlie completed *Buffalo Bill's Duel with Yellowhand,* the first of a series of oils commissioned by Thomas F. Cole, a mining executive from Duluth. Buffalo Bill had died in January, and Charlie was moved to pay tribute.[16]

Several other deaths affected Charlie in 1917. In February, he traveled to Chico Hot Springs to say good-bye to Johnny Matheson, who was paralyzed and fading fast. In April, Albert Trigg cut his hand and died of blood poisoning. Then in August, while the Russells and Joe were at Lake McDonald, they received a telegram that C. S. Russell was dead from a stroke. Charlie did not attend the funeral. "Father did not care for mourning you know," his sister Sue wrote from St. Louis. Charlie's efforts to honor the sentiment were not entirely successful. "He never batted an eye," Joe DeYong wrote, "but he's been Injun'en off alone all day." His sorrow was acute, but cumulative as well. "[R]ight now I know more dead men than live ones," he wrote that summer to Kid Price, one of the old Hungry Seven from the free-range days. "[T]hirty seven years Iv lived in Montana, but Im among strangers now."[17]

Nancy's spirits were no better. Joe DeYong's letters home describe a succession of lows: "Mrs. Russell has a head ache. . . . Mrs. R. keeled over twice in the past two days." Despite having Marie Johnston, Joe, and Charlie to help out with Jack, occasionally she had to draw the curtains and retreat to her bed. Even on good days she was a notoriously slow riser. It fell to Charlie to start the fires every morning and make breakfast, which he usually served to her in bed. Most mornings, recounted DeYong, "she don't show up downstairs till Jacks all bathed and dressed."[18]

Eventually, though, like most new parents, Charlie and Nancy began to reclaim a cautious equilibrium. Margaret and Josephine Trigg were only three doors away. Josephine was the children's librarian in Great Falls and, divorced and childless, a fawning babysitter. As Jack grew older she read to him constantly, and he began keeping a separate toy box at the Triggs' house.[19] Joe, too, was a reliable sitter, and soon Charlie and Nancy felt comfortable enough to attend dinners, theater, and the movies.

Entertaining resumed that summer at Bull Head. The privacy screen for 1918 was decorated with the signatures of the George Calverts (the prosperous contractor who had built Charlie's studio); the Triggs; sister Sue Portis and her husband, Tom; Joe DeYong; and two young girls to help with cooking, housekeeping, and babysitting. Since the official opening of Glacier Park, Lake McDonald had put on an Adirondack air. The few private homes scattered around the lake were owned or rented by affluent doctors, lawyers, and industrialists, some of whom came from as far away as the East Coast to enjoy the mountain summer. In 1914, John Lewis, who previously had worn the hats of professional baseball player, fur trader, and land speculator, completed construction of a new hotel at the north end of the lake. An astute promoter, Lewis vowed not to be outdone by the grand log palaces that had been erected by the Great Northern at the other side of the park.[20]

Glacier Hotel was built in the style of a European chalet, the timber porches of its one hundred rooms affording views of the glistening lake and snowcapped mountains. The hotel's centerpiece was a three-story lobby decorated with an immense hearth, stuffed heads, bearskin rugs, Indian lanterns, hickory furniture, and framed scenes of the park. Along with a roof garden, dancing pavilion, and separate guest cabins, Lewis's resort offered riding stables, boating excursions, a formal dining room, and a platoon of uniformed bellboys. As final filigree, Lewis offered his guests the chance to rub shoulders with authentic local characters — Charlie Russell being the celebrity everyone wanted to meet.

Lewis did everything to make the Russells welcome and conspicuous. He sent the hotel launch to pick them up at Bull Head Lodge. He had Charlie and Nancy announced as they entered the hotel dining room, and he paid for their meals. He hung Charlie's art prominently in the lobby and ultimately dedicated a guest cabin as a gallery from which Nancy could wheel and deal with the well-heeled tourists, many of them still chuckling over a yarn told by Charlie. One such vacationer describes an interlude on the second-floor gallery: "[B]efore we realized it, 'Charlie' had said a pleasant word or two to everybody and silently slipped out of sight. Mrs. Russell, however, was a most charming entertainer. In the gallery she was busily engaged in explaining the high points of her husband's pictures to all who might be in the least interested."[21]

Even if Nancy did not always close a sale at the hotel, the Glacier admirers often turned up at later Russell shows on the East or West Coast. Churchill Mehard, a Pittsburgh attorney who summered with his family at Lake McDonald, helped Charlie make the right contacts in Mehard's hometown and became a collector himself. Another Lake McDonald patron was James Bollinger, a judge in Davenport, Iowa, and law-school chum of John Lewis's. Bollinger's in-laws had known Charlie in the Judith days. He, Lewis, and Charlie got along famously, and soon established a ritual fall hunting trip for which they hired guides and packed into the mountains (outside the park) in quest of deer, elk, and relaxation.[22]

Crow indian in war dress

22. Boyhood sketch (*Collection of Mr. and Mrs. Lyle Woodcock, St. Louis*)

23. Cowboy Camp During the Roundup, c. 1885-87 (*Amon Carter Museum*)

24. Waiting for a Chinook, 1887 (*Montana Historical Society, Owned by the Montana Stockgrowers Association*)

25.

25. Not a Chinaman's Chance, c. 1893
(*Amon Carter Museum*)

26. Contrast in Artist's Salons — Charlie
Painting in His Cabin, c. 1894
(*Amon Carter Museum*)

27. Cowboy Bargaining for an Indian
Girl, 1895 (*Hood Museum of Art,
Dartmouth College*)

26.

27.

28. Letter with self-
    portrait, November
    14, 1903 (*Stark
    Museum of Art,
    Orange, Texas*)

29. Smoking Up, 1904
    (*Amon Carter Museum*)

31. When I Was a Kid,
    1905 (*Collection of*
    Frederic G. and Ginger K. Renner)

30. Buffalo Hunt, 1905 (*Amon*
    Carter Museum)

32. Jerked Down, 1907 (*Gilcrease*
    Museum, Tulsa)

33. In Without Knocking, 1909
(*Amon Carter Museum*)

34. Lewis and Clark Meeting Indians
at Ross' Hole, 1912 (*Montana
Historical Society*)

35. Charlie Himself, c. 1915
(*Amon Carter Museum*)

36. Running Buffalo, 1918
(*Gilcrease Museum, Tulsa*)

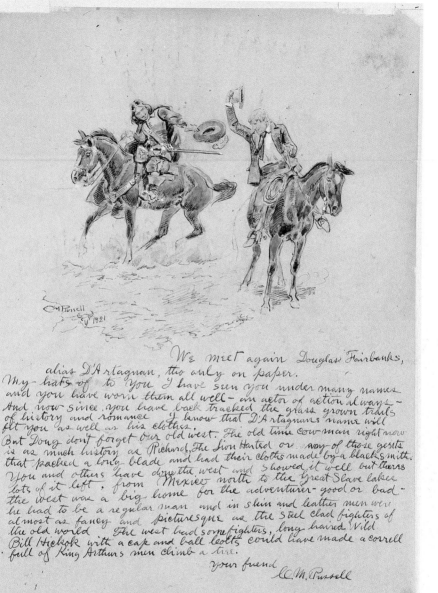

We meet again Douglas Fairbanks, alias D'Artagnan, tho only on paper.

My hats of to You I have seen you under many names and you have worn them all well — an actor of action always — And now since you have back tracked the grass grown trails of history and romance I know that D'Artagnans name will fit you as well as his cloths.

But Doug dont forget our old west. The old time cow man right now is as much history as Richard, The Lion Harted or any of those gents that packed a long-blade and had their cloths made by a blacksmith. You and others have done the west and showed it well but theres lots of it left, from Mexico north to the Great Slave lakes the west was a big home for the adventurer good or bad — he had to be a regular man and in skin and leather men were almost as fancy and picturesque as the steel clad fighters of the old world The west had some fighters, long haired Wild Bill Hickok with a cap and ball colts could have made a corell full of King Arthurs men climb a tree.

your friend
C M Russell

37. Letter to Douglas Fairbanks, May 1921
(*C. M. Russell Museum*)

38. Salute of the Robe Trade, 1920
   (*Gilcrease Museum, Tulsa*)

39. Charles M. Russell and His Friends,
   1922 (*Montana Historical Society, Mackay
   Collection*)

The trips were also a chance for Charlie to replenish his larder of images. More and more of Charlie's clients were asking for hunting scenes; Philip Goodwin had helped make hunting and fishing art its own genre with his work for firearm and fishing gear calendars and ads. Charlie responded over the years with *Whose Meat?*, *Meat's Not Meat Till It's in the Pan, Crippled But Still Coming, When Mules Wear Diamonds,* and many others. The narrative content of these canvases was often fictional, but their settings came from sketches and memories collected on Charlie's forays into the backcountry.

Nancy was more than willing to allow Charlie to disappear with Bollinger and Lewis on these manly outings. They were gentlemen of standing, unlike some of Charlie's owlhoot chums of old. Bollinger was also a loyal adviser to Nancy, and Lewis and she enjoyed a special rapport. "John was money-minded. So was Nancy," Bollinger reflected. "I always thought he taught her much that way."[23]

Charlie understood his role at Lake McDonald, and he seemed to enjoy the attention paid to him. He accepted more invitations to accompany Eaton pack trips, knowing his personality was what paid his way. Writer Mary Roberts Rinehart was on one such trip with Charlie. "The pine and balsam [of the campfire] crackled and burned, and overhead, often rising in straight walls around us for thousands of feet, were the snow-capped peaks of the Continental Divide," she recounted. As darkness fell and the wranglers would unravel their tales, it was Charlie who was "the campfire star," his delivery creating an unduplicatable magic. "To repeat one of his stories would be desecration," Rinehart declared. "No one but Charley Russell himself, speaking through his nose, with his magnificent head outlined against the firelight, will ever be able to tell one of his stories."[24]

Even in years when Charlie did not ride with the Eaton group, he was frequently on hand to greet them as they came off the trail at Glacier Hotel. One summer Nancy and Charlie had the entire Eaton party over to Bull Head Lodge for lunch. Another time, when Frank Linderman was visiting, he, Charlie, and Joe DeYong entertained the Eaton dudes with a sign-language skit, with Nancy playing the translator.[25] Performances such as these, with Charlie signing, Nancy translating, led many observers to assume that Charlie was fluent in Indian sign language. His vocabulary was indeed large and grew larger after Joe DeYong came into his life. But the reality was that these public displays (before tourists, high school students, ladies' clubs) were carefully scripted and rehearsed; Charlie knew exactly what he would sign, and Nancy knew exactly how she would translate. It was a routine copied from hotel-lobby Indians.

Some mornings at Bull Head, Charlie would set up an easel indoors under the cabin's skylight or on the front porch. But the light was not great at Bull Head — too shady, with mountains blocking the sun early in the morning and late in the afternoon. These conditions gave Charlie the perfect excuse to do other things. He took particular pleasure in teaching Jack how to ride. "My Father loved saddle horses more than any other animal and wanted me to love them also," Jack wrote years later, "so he would take me . . . in front of him and ride around with me holding the bridle reins and tell me I would be a cow boy some day."[26]

In the afternoons, there were fish-fries on the outdoor barbecue, and in the evenings, trips to John Lewis's hotel. Charlie considered himself a fair hoofer; he enjoyed the dance bands at the hotel and liked to crank up the Victrola at Bull Head. His signature step remained the fox-trot; more than one wag has suggested that Charlie believed he was impersonating the creature for which the dance was named.[27]

NANCY WAS FOREVER trying to be businesslike in social settings and social in business settings. The result was that she made money, but often at the expense of friendship. Such was the case in 1919, when she pressured Charlie to choose between Frank Linderman and the next Stampede to be held at Calgary.

In the spring of 1919, Linderman was negotiating with Charles Scribner's Sons over the publication of another volume of Indian folktales, this one to be called *Indian Old-Man Stories*. Scribner's was happy to publish the stories "as they are," Linderman said, but only if he could assure the publisher that the tales would again be accompanied by Charlie Russell's illustrations. Linderman had not prospered in recent years; he had failed as a candidate in the Republican primary for U.S. House of Representatives in 1916 and had made little money from his writing since the publication of *Indian Why Stories* in 1915. Charlie was only too willing to help out his good friend, and he set to work on illustrations and "marginal" drawings for the new book. Linderman was counting on publication in the fall.[28]

Shortly after making his promise to Linderman, Charlie broke his right wrist in a riding accident. He was obliged to wear a cast for six weeks and fell behind in his work. Then in August, a forest fire swept down the shore of Flathead Lake and nearly destroyed Linderman's house at Goose Bay; the flames burned his Indian lodge on the point and stopped only when they reached the water, even consuming the line that moored Linderman's sailboat, which was set mercifully adrift. Adding to Linderman's misery and anxiety was a telegram from Scribner's only a few days after the inferno. It read succinctly: WE HAVE NOT YET RECD DRAWINGS INDIAN OLD MAN STORIES.

Three days later Linderman wrote a panicky note to Charlie at Lake McDonald: "They are pounding me on the back for those illustrations. . . . If they don't get them right away they won't publish my book this season[.] I need the money. . . . I've been over two years earning nothing. . . . Will you PLEASE send all you have done direct to them and save time? . . . Make any old thing in any old way just so I get bye this one time."

Despite the desperate tone of Linderman's letter, Charlie was not able to come to his friend's rescue. With Nancy hovering, he instead had spent the summer preparing for the trip to Canada and did not complete the book illustrations until the end of October, long after Scribner's had decided to postpone the publication date. Linderman was bereft. "If there is anything that can happen [to] a damned fool that hasn't happened to me this year," he wrote Charlie, "I'd like to know what it can be." Charlie eventually patched up his relationship with his friend, but Linderman never completely forgave Nancy for putting the book assignment on the back burner.29

Around this time, Charlie and Nancy passed through a rocky interlude of their own. In February 1919, Nancy had taken the train to Minneapolis for a spell of rest and recuperation from whatever was ailing her. She "looks like 'nerves,' " Joe DeYong observed before Nancy left Great Falls.30 By that he probably meant neurasthenia, a common complaint of the day.

Neurasthenia was truly a modern syndrome, believed to be brought on by all the social uncertainties and pell-mell mobility of a new century. Symptoms included insomnia, hysteria, hypochondria, sick headaches, rashes, and hot and cold flashes.31 It was a stylish malady, and Nancy Russell, beneath her misery, may have been ever so slightly proud to have a fancy name for her long-standing condition.

The standard treatment for neurasthenia was peace and quiet, so Nancy went to stay with Granville and Margaret Bennett, an Episcopal minister and his wife who once had lived in Great Falls. Her absence made Charlie downright lovelorn. Likely both Nancy's and Charlie's nerves had been jangled in the days before she had left; the conciliatory tone of his letters suggest that they may even have had a row of some sort. "Dear Mame," he began his letter of February 6, "its a week to night you left and it seems like longer to me." After a few sentences of small talk about Jack, the DeYong family, and the egg output of their chickens, he quit beating around the bush:

> [W]e shure had a good time at Lethbridge [a rodeo they had attended in Canada the previous summer] and if you could rest more we cold be that way all the time[. I]f the hive was all drones thaird be no huney[. I]ts the lady bee that fills the combe with sweetniss[. I]ts the same with humans[. I]f the world was all hes it would sour and spoil[. T]he flowers have some times been far apart in your flight so rest your wings and when you spred them you will bring me honey.

Three days later, he pined again:

> Im afraid if you would drop in now you wold get smothered with XXXX[;] dont show my letters to aney body they might think I am spooney but I feel that way[. Y]ou going away has don me good and when you come back Il proove it. . . . I guss you think Im locoed writing love letters to you but I think wed both do better by using more of that stuff an from now on Im going to try it[. M]aby Iv falling [in] love the second time I guess its all right if its the same woman and it is.

By the end of two weeks, his ardor was unabashed:

> Il admit it must seem funny after beeing married over 22 years [to] start writing love letters but it dont seem like I ever wanted you like I do now. . . . [I]t is ten past elevon and I guess Il bed down[. T]hairs one Girl I know I wish was here with her cold feet in my back[. W]ith love and XXXXXXX[.] I could make more of these but the ink is getting low.[32]

Nancy returned to Montana as restive as ever. She had not sat still during much of her stay in Minneapolis. Instead, she had used the time to book a show at the Minneapolis Institute of Art for the fall and, via letter, had tried to coax Charlie into traveling to New York for an exhibition there.[33] He talked her out of the New York junket, but by March she had her sights set on Calgary, the scene of their great achievement seven years earlier. Their old friend Guy Weadick was still in charge; this year's extravaganza was billed as a Victory Stampede, to celebrate the Armistice. Dignitaries and deep pockets were expected to attend in force.

Once again, Charlie's exhibition in Calgary was a whopping success. Nancy had shrewdly included three different paintings saluting the Royal Canadian Mounted Police: *When Law Dulls the Edge of Chance* (1915), *The Queen's War Hounds* (1914), and *Whiskey Smugglers Caught With the Goods* (1913). The Mounties had impressed Charlie ever since he had first seen them on his ride into Canada thirty-one years earlier. He had admired them again during his Calgary exhibition in 1912 and over the next four years had completed a series of four paintings of the red-coated knights. Only one (*Single Handed*) had sold by 1919. Now the time and place were right. Canadians held their Mounties in the highest esteem — and western Canadians in particular had a comparable regard for Montana's Cowboy Artist. Former Mountie Ralph S. Kendall knew as much when he published the first of his wildly popular adventure novels, *Benton of the Royal Mounted,* a year earlier. In his description of a typical Mountie post, Kendall was careful to mention the "unframed copies of famous pictures" by Charlie Russell hanging on the walls.[34]

Perhaps the most salient of the three Mountie paintings Charlie showed at Calgary was *Whiskey Smugglers.* It depicted the days of the late nineteenth century when liquor from Fort Benton had been sold illegally to Canadian Indians. Its theme also happened to be extremely up to date. Montana had gone "dry" at the end of 1918 (one year ahead of the national Volstead Act), and Mounties were once again pressed to stop whiskey smuggling across the international border, though this time the flow was from north to south.

An estimated thirty thousand people came to see Charlie's exhibition in Calgary. *Whiskey Smugglers* was bought by Patrick Burns of the "Big Four" cattlemen of Alberta, who had sponsored both the 1912 and 1919 Stampedes. He was one of ten buyers. Another of Charlie's oils — the record is unclear, but perhaps it was *When Law Dulls the Edge of Chance* — sold for the astronomical sum of $8,000.[35] After returning to Great Falls, Nancy boasted to the *Tribune* that Russell paintings were now on their way to Chicago, Montreal, and New York. The biggest coup, though, had been the presentation of two paintings to English royalty. George Lane, another member of the Big Four and the owner of *Camp Cook's Trouble,* had hosted Albert, Prince of Wales, on his visit to western Canada that summer. Along with showing the prince his ranch near High River, Alberta, Lane was keen to have His Royal Highness see the work of his favorite Western artist. Prince Albert caught up with the exhibition in Saskatoon. Charlie and Nancy were presented to the prince by the mayor and spent half an hour discussing Charlie's paintings. Prince Albert returned to England with *When Law Dulls the Edge of Chance,* a scene of two Mounties arresting horse thieves, a gift from George Lane and the citizens of High River. The prince carried a second Russell painting, *A Doubtful Handshake,* a gift from the Big Four to be passed along to the prince's uncle, the Duke of Connaught, who had admired Charlie's work during his 1912 visit to Canada.[36]

Charlie was now the darling of dollar-a-day cowboys and kings-to-be. In December he and Nancy showed the same pieces that had toured Canada (minus the ones that had sold) at the Minneapolis Institute of Art.[37] Reviews were predictably friendly, and thanks to Nancy's promotional work, the press was eager to celebrate Charlie's personality and fame. He made a token try at fending off the attention with his patented modesty, but was not entirely successful.

The *Minneapolis Tribune* found him in his hotel wearing "a soft flannel collar turned back from the neck, his high boots crossed one over the other, his broad brimmed hat lying on a chair beside him, his coat opened to show his brightly colored bead belt." He griped about the local streetcars, while rolling cigarettes and doing his just-an-old-cowhand bit. To another paper he was more expansive. "They know my work in the east as much as they do in the west," he said almost cockily. "From little thumbnail sketches I am trying to make real western masterpieces." He then made sure his audience was aware of the high prices these self-proclaimed "masterpieces" now fetched.[38]

In a *Minneapolis Journal* article, a rare show of egotism came across as a rebuke of his home state. "Most millionaires 'drather buy beefsteak than paintings, especially in Great Falls," he reproved. "Now my friends out there, they like my pictures, but they can't afford to buy them, while the rich fellows would rather buy something to eat or to have a good time with. They don't care for pictures. If I depended on my home state, I would starve." This said at a time when many in his home state were indeed starving. After a wartime boom, Montana had fallen into a severe depression, due to brutal drought and an abrupt decline in the demand for the state's raw materials. Just when Charlie and Nancy's fortunes were soaring, banks and homesteads were boarding up and Montana was actually losing population. Charlie compounded his gaffe by going on to say that even those Montanans who did want to own his art could manage only small pieces. "I never paint big pictures now. People haven't homes large enough. They haven't room for paintings. They haven't room for anything."[39]

In all fairness, though, it was not Montana that was running out of room for Charlie. Rather, it was Charlie who was finding less and less room in his life for Montana, especially Great Falls. Between summers at Glacier National Park, fall hunting forays, and art trips to Canada, Minneapolis, Chicago, Pittsburgh, and New York, he was not exactly a fixture in his hometown anymore. Beginning in 1920, he was a virtual absentee. That February, Charlie and Nancy joined the snowbirds flocking to Southern California.

CALIFORNIA

SOUTHERN CALIFORNIA IN 1920 was irresistible. Seemingly overnight, missions and fruit groves were giving way to bungalows and highways. Between 1910 and 1920, the population of Los Angeles had doubled to more than half a million, and it would double again over the next decade. "This steady, speedy growth," reported the *New Republic* magazine, "is the most important thing to understand about Los Angeles. . . . Anything seems possible; the future is yours, and the past? — there isn't any."[1]

For Charlie, the logic of his move to California was as perverse as it was consistent: First he had built a house in the least Western of Montana cities; then he had built a summer cabin in the least cowboyish quarter of the state; now he had chosen to spend his winters in the least nostalgic city in America.

According to a joke of the time, Los Angeles was the second capital of Iowa. Starting at the end of the nineteenth century, farm family after farm family, weary of the cold, wind, drought, and the sheer uncertainty of raising and selling crops, had succumbed to the come-ons of Southern California boosters. Los Angeles had solved its biggest transportation problem with the arrival of the Southern Pacific and Santa Fe railroads in the 1880s; its harbor problem with the development of San Pedro at the turn of the century; and its water problem with the diversion of the Owens River in 1913. After these hurdles had been surmounted, the region's climate made growth inevitable. An article published in *Harper's* a few months after

Charlie and Nancy's first arrival on the West Coast described the seduction in near-Edenic terms:

> [T]he sun shines, a faint breeze blows gently, the hills lie in the clear light as if nothing on them had stirred since they were first chiseled in brown or green. There is nothing wayward or mysterious about the landscape. The air is too crystalline to bear upon it tangs and odors. You have moments of thinking there *is* no air; that all California is broad, kindly vacancy filled with sunlight and no more.[2]

By the mid-1920s, only one out of four Angelenos could claim a decade of residency there. Midwesterners predominated, but they shared the sunshine with New Englanders, New Yorkers, and frostbitten refugees from Montana and other northern states. "Home-state picnics," sponsored by the Federation of State Societies, were a huge part of the Los Angeles social fabric. On nearly every Saturday of the year, Sycamore Park was jammed with emigrants from the American heartland. Montana had one a year, traditionally on Washington's Birthday. In 1918, two years before the Russells first visited Los Angeles, thirty-five hundred Montanans attended their home-state picnic.[3]

But Los Angeles was more than simply "Gopher Prairie de luxe." Despite the lip service paid to sun-drenched egalitarianism, wherein every workingman earned a decent wage and lived in a handsome bungalow, Los Angeles was as quick and eager to stratify as any other emerging city. It was still a city of Mexican flavor, perhaps the largest Mexican metropolis outside Mexico itself. But as white Americans poured into the Los Angeles Basin, Mexicans and Mexican-Americans found themselves relegated to a role of cheap labor, and their culture reduced to quaintness. Historian Kevin Starr has discerned three tiers in the social structure of white Los Angeles in the 1920s: the Oligarchs, the Babbitts, and the Folks. The Folks were the Midwestern masses; the Babbitts were the bourgeois real-estate salesmen in checked suits; the Oligarchs were the wealthy elite, most of whom had been ensconced for a decade or more.[4]

In a city so new, the rich were easy to identify. They included the big land developers and the lawyers and bankers who backed them. They included the fruit growers who controlled millions of acres. They included the Otises, owners of the *Los Angeles Times*. They included railroaders, like

Henry E. Huntington, and heirs, like Jean Paul Getty, who built palatial homes in Pasadena and a freshly minted development called Beverly Hills. Los Angeles was an oil boomtown, too, a fact often forgotten today. By 1920, the annual production of oil in the Los Angeles area was valued at more than $80 million.

At the top of Southern California's golden pyramid, however, was a caste that had no equivalent anywhere else in the world: the movie crowd. Beginning in 1909, dozens of studios moved to, or started up in, Los Angeles. They were pirates fleeing the patent restrictions of Edison-owned "flicker" technology and sunseekers in an era when nearly all movies were filmed under natural light. By 1920, the movie industry in California was huge, employing nearly ten thousand people and distributing hundreds of single- and multi-reel "pictures." The pioneers of the medium, many of whom were European-born Jews, were already millionaires; the actors, who as yet were not required to speak, were the country's tacit royalty.[5]

This was the California that lured Charlie and Nancy. They knew several Montanans who had already resettled there for reasons of health or other gain. Cut Bank Browne, former proprietor of the Maverick saloon in Great Falls, had gone into real estate in Los Angeles. Cowboy poet Wallace Coburn, whose *Rhymes from a Round-up Camp* Charlie had illustrated in 1899, was now making movies in Hollywood. Charlie and Nancy had their own reasons for eschewing Montana winters: she with her habitual headaches and nerves, he with his stiffening joints from years bouncing on horseback and bedding in damp cow camps. A lifetime of smoking had taken a toll on his lungs, and a goiter, which he'd been aware of for two or three years already, began pressing against the left side of his windpipe. Out of stoicism and vanity, he never talked about his affliction, but its persistence made it easier for him to acquiesce when Nancy suggested they head south for the winter.

They rented a house in Pasadena, northeast of downtown Los Angeles. Redolent of flowers and set against a gorgeous backdrop of mountains, Pasadena had been a popular vacation spot for American gentility since the 1880s. Pasadenans were conservative and proud of their patronage of the so-called Arroyo Culture, named for the narrow canyon linking Pasadena and Los Angeles and consisting of a group of writers, poets, artists, actors, and impresarios who mingled there.[6]

If Charlie was skeptical about throwing in with the "picknickers,"

boosters, and "bungaloo" dwellers, he was cheered by the prospect of seeing his old friends William S. Hart and Will Rogers, both of whom had
settled in Southern California. Rogers, who had bought one of Charlie's buffalo-hunt paintings in 1919, was making movies for the Goldwyn
studio and living in Beverly Hills. In the eighteen years that had elapsed
since Bill Hart had first met Charlie in Montana, he had become one of
Hollywood's biggest stars, playing the "good badman" in such Westerns
as *On the Night Stage, The Passing of Two-Gun Hicks, The Dawn Maker,* and
*Hell's Hinges.*7

Bill Hart was not simply a devoted friend to Charlie Russell, he was also
very much a student of Charlie's work and philosophy. In his cowboy roles,
Hart resisted the urge to dress in the gaudy getups favored by Wild West
show cowboys. He preferred realistic costumes — the right spurs, the right
kerchiefs — similar to those he saw in paintings by Russell or Ed Borein.
Likewise, Hart pushed for gritty, believable sets. Those who followed in
Hart's footsteps — Tom Mix, Hoot Gibson, Neal Hart, Tim McCoy, Ken
Maynard, Gene Autry — did not hew so assiduously to realism, but thanks
to the precedent set by Hart, they never entirely abandoned it either. One
imagines Hart worrying less about the approval of his fans and more about
the critical eye of his friend the Cowboy Artist.

Indeed, Charlie was quick to judge all he saw in California. He complained about the weather, which was typically sunny but cool in the winter due to the prevailing Pacific breezes. Pasadena, he wrote to friends in
Great Falls, was "the warmest looking and coldest feeling" place he'd ever
been. "[I]f flowers tell warme this country is a lyer . . . thair are flowers
blooming every where but that dont mean you wont need an overcoat[.]
Its like standing in a foot of snow looking through a window at a painting
of the tropicks[. T]he picture shows heat but it dont warme your feet."8

The conspicuous modernity of Los Angeles annoyed him as well. By
1920, a hundred thousand automobiles were registered in Los Angeles
County, more than in most eastern states. "[E]very street and road is crouded
with hawnking cars," Charlie said, wincing. In another letter, this one to
Philip Goodwin, he summed up his disdain in a trails-plowed-under sermon, California style:

Im down among the roses[. T]his is a beautiful country all right but its
strictly man made[.] I think in early days it was a picture country before

the boosters made real estate out of it but Im about 100 years late. . . . Phil if I was painting frute flowers automobils ore flying mashines this would be a good country but nature aint lived here for a long time and thats the old lady Im looking for.9

Much of Charlie's grousing was pro forma, however. The last thing he wanted was for his friends in Montana to think he had been won over by the Golden State, but the truth was that he enjoyed "this over-sophisticated town," and like the rest of America, he was taken with Hollywood. "[A]s there is [no] more real [cowboys]," he wrote to Wallace Coburn, "I myself play off quite a little coin [spend considerable money] at them screen round ups." Familiarity with the moviemaking process only increased his fascination. Both Bill Hart and Will Rogers invited Charlie to watch their movies being shot; on Hart's location, Charlie had the added pleasure of meeting Tom Mix and Neal Hart (no relation to Bill).10

Westerns, though very much the slave of new technology, were nonetheless a link to the old days. Most were set in the past, and once the film industry had moved to California, Western movies began celebrating, overtly or subtly, classic Western backdrops. The actors themselves were living legacies. William S. Hart was an exception, but he had a good mentor in Charlie Russell. Tom Mix was an Easterner, but had earned his spurs with the Miller Brothers 101 Ranch. Indeed, the Miller Wild West show, which had moved to Santa Monica, California, in 1912, had served as Central Casting for many of the Westerns shot in the early teens. Miller alums Hoot Gibson, Neal Hart, and Mix were all expert horsemen who performed many of their own stunts.

The work of the "Hollywood posse," as the pool of cowboy extras was often called, was seasonal in the early years and patchy even in the best years. A rider might join a Wild West show in the spring, pick up a movie part in the summer, and then work a roundup in the fall. He brought his regional customs and costume with him when he came to Los Angeles, down to the crease of his hat and the drawl of his "Howdy." When idle, the posse congregated at a saloon known as the Waterhole on the corner of Cahuenga Avenue and Hollywood Boulevard. On the job, they ate their meals at a chuck wagon and took many risks that old-time punchers would not have dared. In barroom fights, the chairs were "breakaway" and the

punches pulled, but in many of the early gunfight scenes, the bullets rico-
cheting off of the sandstone were real. "In those days," recalled director John
Ford, "if you had to have a glass shot out of somebody's hand, Pardner [Ed
"Pardner" Jones, a Ford regular] would actually shoot it out." The riding
escapades were dangerously authentic as well. Before the Humane Society
stepped in, a typical fall was done with a "Running W" or "Stationary W,"
in which a galloping horse literally had its forelegs jerked from underneath
it. Animals died; the bones of many riders were broken.[11]

In the six winters Charlie spent in California, he never tired of visiting the movie sets, and his respect never wavered for the daring, talented,
hardworking performers who pieced together the grand illusion of cinema.
"Suddenly from a grove of live oak trees thair bursts a band of riders," he
wrote after his first round of visits — probably to the sets of Bill Hart's *The
Toll Gate* and Tom Mix's *The Daredevil* — in February 1920. "[F]or looks
thair shure scary all heeled to the teeth and spuring dow[n] the slope with
guns smoking. . . . [T]he leader of this band is . . . to[o] fancyfull to be real
but to an old romance loving boy like me its the best thing Iv seen in Calif
[. A]t least they were live men with living horses under them."[12]

Charlie took great pleasure in explaining the tricks of the trade to his old
cowboy friends back home. "I take back aney thing I ever said with my
hat in my hand about moove [movie] cow boys[. T]hair good riders and
hard to scare," he wrote after one location visit. To Teddy Blue Abbott
he reported, "It takes sevral kinds to make a hero on the screen[. T]he
beautiful cow boy that makes love till reformers want to burn the picture
houses aint the same man that spures his horse of[f] a thirty foot rim rock
into the water and swims three miles to save his sweet hart from a band
of out laws." Charlie, though, was always quick to add that even the stars
who "sat back of the camra man in a coushened catalack smoking a camal"
during these perilous shots were "good fellers" for the most part.[13] Mere
access to their magical world fostered tolerance. And it did not hurt that
most of the stars were huge Charlie Russell fans.

Other Western legends had mingled with the movie crowd before
Charlie. Dodge City lawman William Tilghman had become a producer.
Emmet Dalton, the only surviving member of the Dalton gang, had ap-
peared in a three-reel "documentary" about his family's larcenous exploits.
After cleaning up Tombstone, Wyatt Earp had retired to California and be-
come a friend of Bill Hart, Tom Mix, and others. He even appeared as an

extra in the 1916 Douglas Fairbanks film *The Half-Breed*. But Charlie was valued by Hollywood as more than a relic. He was a celebrity in his own right, a man with both a romantic past and a convivial presence.

Moreover, Charlie's stories and paintings possessed a natural cinematic verve. Bill Hart was not the only person inspired by Charlie's detail and perspective. John Ford, who began directing silent movies in 1917, freely admitted to borrowing from compositions by Russell (and Remington, too) throughout his career. On at least one occasion, a studio expressed interest in having Charlie direct his own picture. It was not a serious offer, but the fact that the notion was even fleetingly discussed is evidence of the high regard that the Western-movie industry had for Charlie and his art.[14]

In Los Angeles, Charlie eventually met many more actors — Harold Lloyd, Wallace Beery, Fred Stone — and most of the other artists in the area, including Western painters Carl Oscar Borg, Clyde Forsythe, Frank Tenney Johnson, and the venerable Thomas Moran, who was closing out his life in Santa Barbara. Perhaps the most kindred of all the spirits Charlie became acquainted with in California was Charles Lummis.

Charles Fletcher Lummis was born in Massachusetts in 1859, the son of a minister.[15] He was a scrawny, sickly kid; at Harvard, he befriended another scrawny kid, Theodore Roosevelt; unlike Roosevelt, Lummis left Cambridge without a degree. He headed west, seeking his own version of the strenuous life. He set out from Cleveland, Ohio, in September 1884; fourteen months later he arrived in Los Angeles, having endured mountain snow, desert heat, robbery, an attack by a wildcat, and a broken arm. He had walked the entire way. By prearrangement, the *Los Angeles Times* paid Lummis $5 apiece for the weekly dispatches he had filed during the journey. The day after his arrival, the newspaper named him city editor.

After a stroke paralyzed his left side in 1887, Lummis quit the *Times* and embarked on a five-year ramble through the American Southwest. He immersed himself in the language, art, religion, and archaeology of the Indians he encountered in New Mexico and Arizona, and produced a number of articles and books, including the rhapsodic *The Land of Poco Tiempo*. Upon his return to Los Angeles in 1893, Lummis threw himself into various causes, all of which were aimed at preserving the life and culture of the Southwest. In 1894, he took over editorship of *The Land of Sunshine,* a promotional mouthpiece of the Los Angeles Chamber of Commerce (soon changing the name to *Out West*). Under Lummis's stewardship, *The Land of Sunshine/Out*

West abandoned crass boosterism and began publishing the more elegant musings of John Muir, Emerson Hough, Joaquin Miller, and Jack London. Lummis also had an eye for young Western talent. Robinson Jeffers and Mary Austin were two of his protégés. Lummis was the first to publish Ed Borein's illustrations and the short stories of another cowboy, Eugene Manlove Rhodes.

By the time Charlie and Nancy Russell found themselves in Lummis's gravitational field, he was ensconced at El Alisal, the eccentric hacienda he had built with Indian labor out of river rock and rough-hewn timbers in the sycamore groves of Arroyo Seco. Lummis was sixty-one in 1920, but as flamboyant as ever. He never quit drinking, smoking, or womanizing. He dressed every day in a baggy green corduroy Mexican suit and, like Charlie, wore a sash, never a belt. Life at El Alisal was one long succession of "noises" — Lummis's name for his free-for-all salons. No telling who would show up: over the years, the guest book garnered the signatures of Clarence Darrow and Carl Sandburg and the doodles of artists such as Remington and Borg. "The place seems to be real Bohemian," Joe DeYong said of one of the later noises, "and some of the men wore flannel shirts while others were in evening clothes." Often at the center of the crowd were Lummis, Gene Rhodes, Will Rogers, and exiled Spanish novelist Vicente Blasco Ibañez, author of *The Four Horsemen of the Apocalypse*. They dubbed themselves "the Four Horsemen of the Eucalyptus."[16]

Charlie and Lummis hit it off instantly. Lummis came to the Russells' rented house in Pasadena and was deeply moved by Charlie's art — "so virile, so true, so full of imagination as well as fact, and of poetry as well as sanity." Soon Charlie and Nancy were regulars at El Alisal, and they were a big hit with their sign-language routine. One guest recalls that in the middle of a story, Charlie "would make a certain sign and [Nancy] would blush furiously, saying, 'Charlie, I'm not going to say that.' Wooden faced he would repeat the gesture. 'Now, Charlie, you stop. I won't say it and if you keep on talking like that I won't come here any more!' "[17]

Nancy, though, was anything but a tagalong on such occasions. She had her own designs on local society. Through Lummis, Will Rogers, and Bill Hart, she had gained entrée to the cream of Southern California. The first year was a trial run; she exhibited only a few of Charlie's pieces at the Pasadena house and did not sell many, if any, by the time she and Charlie headed north in the late spring. Next year, however, she vowed, she would take California by storm.

Back in Great Falls, Charlie made the rounds downtown, assuring his old friends that the high life on the coast had not gone to his head. Central Avenue could boast little high life of its own that year. Prohibition had closed Bill Rance's Silver Dollar on New Year's Day 1919 and turned Sid Willis's Mint into a virtual soda parlor (with a card room in the back). Willis was a survivor, unlike his competitor. Rance never really got back on his feet after shutting the Silver Dollar. Most of his Russell artwork eventually found its way into the Mint collection, including the peep show, *Joy of Life*. Rance finally committed suicide in 1932, swallowing poison on the fire escape of a Central Avenue hotel.[18]

Nancy, in contrast to Charlie, did little to play down her season in the California sun. Great Falls women might still malign her behind her back, but now they were just as likely to be gossiping about all the fancy people she knew. A few weeks after their return home, Nancy bought a membership in the newly opened Meadow Lark Country Club in Great Falls. All the good families were joining. Nancy, having been impressed by the myriad beach clubs, polo clubs, and country clubs that had sprung up in Southern California, was not going to be kept out of her hometown's pale equivalent. In the early years, the Meadow Lark greens were not green at all, but made of hard-packed tailings carted in from the copper smelter. Nancy played occasionally with Joe DeYong; Charlie took no interest in golf, yet he was never one to deny Nancy her spoils.[19] In the prosperous years of the 1920s, Nancy rarely returned from a trip without new dresses, hats, or a fur coat. Her taste in automobiles ran to Cadillacs, Lincolns, and Pierce Arrows.

⤳

AFTER LITTLE MORE than a month in Great Falls, Charlie and Nancy were off again to Lake McDonald. In the fall, Charlie hunted on the south fork of the Flathead River with Judge Bollinger and John Lewis. Then in January, he and Nancy headed east for exhibitions in Pittsburgh and New York. In Pittsburgh, they were the guests of the Mehards, whom they had seen at Lake McDonald the previous summer. During their tour of New York, they were guests of the Mackays.[20]

In 1920, Malcolm and Helen Mackay had just completed a new Dutch colonial house in Tenafly, New Jersey and wanted to commission a special piece to hang over the hearth of their new Russell room. When Charlie and Nancy visited Appledorn, as the twenty-acre estate was called, the Mackays' chauffeured limousine would pick them up as they disembarked from the Hudson River ferry. Mackay kept a small bunch of Jersey cows at Appledorn, as well as a couple of cow ponies he had imported from Montana. On several occasions, he was able to coax Charlie into the saddle, and artist and investor would chase the cows around the estate for an hour or so before dinner.

Charlie did not seem to mind indulging the Western fantasies of his patron and friend. On a visit a year later, he and Nancy dressed in their Indian garb for a special dedication of the Russell room. Charlie, Nancy, and Malcolm and Helen Mackay sat around on the floor while a set of branding irons heated in the fire. Charlie talked with his hands; Nancy translated. When the irons were red hot, they solemnly burned Charlie's old Lazy KY beef brand and $\frac{3}{E}$ horse brand into the ax-hewn mantelpiece.[21]

Between his various trips in 1920, Charlie found time to paint two marvelous oils: *A Tight Dally and a Loose Latigo* and *Salute of the Robe Trade*. *Tight Dally* is a classic hell-popping composition of cowboys roping wild cattle in a central Montana coulee. *Robe Trade* leans just as heavily on the tried and true. A group of Indians descend the hill above Fort Benton, emptying their guns in "salute" to make clear their friendly intentions as buffalo-robe traders. The log stockade around the post indicates the era is mid–nineteenth century. The Missouri River winds toward the horizon; a golden sunset drenches the Indians, their horses, the river, and the Montana badlands in the distance.

It is a moment that Charlie could only imagine — and a scene he lifted directly from Carl Wimar's 1859 oil *Indians Approaching Fort Union*.[22] Wimar's Indians pause on a similar bluff, and in both paintings, the river bisects the canvas horizontally, the fort is at the lower right, and the sunset lends a romantic glow. The only difference between the two canvases is one of message: Wimar's comes across as a recognition of man's small place in the grand tableau of nature; in Charlie's treatment, men loom larger, but he implies that the time of noble freedom for such people was as fleeting as twilight on the Missouri Breaks.

Charlie and Nancy took *Salute of the Robe Trade* and several more paintings with them to California in the winter of 1921. This time around, Nancy had arranged for an exhibition at a proper venue. Through the first two decades of the twentieth century, most public exhibitions in Los Angeles had been sponsored by art clubs. But with the increase of hotels and retail enterprise downtown, a handful of legitimate art galleries began courting the new wealth. Nancy chose the most established one, the Kanst, located on Hill Street. She did not regret her decision. Shortly after the show opened, millionaire oilman William M. Armstrong bought *Salute of the Robe Trade* for $10,000, one of the highest prices paid for a painting by a living American artist. Nancy, needless to say, was ecstatic; Charlie, for the record at least, was dumbstruck. "Charlie looked so funny the day we got home after closing the bargain," Nancy wrote home to Great Falls. "I said, 'It's kind of nice for a real, live, kicking artist to enjoy some of the fruits of his own work.' "²³

The fruit kept ripening. Shortly after the sale to Armstrong, Nancy sold a $3,500 oil, *The Navajos,* to Douglas Fairbanks and Mary Pickford.²⁴ In 1921, Fairbanks and Pickford were the acknowledged king and queen of Hollywood, both earning salaries of well over $1 million a year. Pickford, "America's Sweetheart," had startled her adoring public by divorcing her first husband the year before and marrying the swashbuckling Fairbanks, who was ten years her senior and also divorced. The newlyweds held court at Pickfair, their renovated hunting lodge atop a remote canyon of Beverly Hills. Between movies — they were making four or five films a year in those days — they entertained a circle of guests as diverse and eclectic as any assembled by their friend Charles Lummis. They saw a great deal of Hollywood chums, including Charlie Chaplin and director D. W. Griffith, their two partners in a newly formed studio, United Artists. And on any given weekend, royalty mixed with brains, brawn, and money. Lord and Lady Mountbatten were photographed pushing a lawn mower. Albert Einstein explained physics by moving knives and forks around on the dinner table. The incurably acrobatic Fairbanks showed Henry Ford how to climb to the roof of Pickfair. Fairbanks particularly liked to entertain celebrity athletes and always challenged them at their own game, playing tennis with Bill Tilden, knocking a baseball around with Babe Ruth, sparring with Jack Dempsey.²⁵

To be granted an audience with the Fairbankses was the ultimate anointment. Unfortunately, Nancy Russell's copious records do not reveal how she and Charlie first met them; the Russells should not have been surprised, however, that the First Couple of Hollywood would take a shine to

Charlie's artwork. Fairbanks had grown up in the West (Denver) and had starred in his share of Western movies, including *The Man from Painted Post, Arizona,* and *The Knickerbocker Buckaroo.* The energy, romance, and detail of Charlie's painting and sculpture had much in common with Fairbanks's approach to moviemaking.

According to one published account, Fairbanks and Pickford each tried secretly to buy *The Navajos* for the other. Pickford was working on a ten-reeler, *Little Lord Fauntleroy,* that winter, and Fairbanks was equally consumed by his role as D'Artagnan in *The Three Musketeers.* Pickford took Nancy aside and purchased the painting; a few minutes later Fairbanks took Charlie aside and did the same. A Montana newspaper blurb, whose details presumably were furnished by Nancy Russell, reported that the mix-up, once discovered, had caused "considerable merriment."[26]

Charlie and Nancy visited Fairbanks on the set of *The Three Muske-teers,* where Charlie struck a wooden, almost truckling pose in a photograph of himself and Fairbanks. "We are both picture makers," Charlie told Fairbanks, but there was no doubt who was the chief of the tribe. Shortly after the studio visit, Charlie sent an unusually saccharine letter to Fairbanks. In the accompanying illustration, they are both on horseback — Fairbanks still as D'Artagnan — doffing their hats to each other. "We meet again Douglas Fairbanks, alias D'Artagnan," Charlie wrote, his improved syntax and spelling suggesting that his first draft had been edited by Nancy and then rewritten. "I have seen you under many names and you have worn them all well — an actor of action always. And now since you have back tracked the grass grown trails of history and romance I know that D'Artagnans name will fit you as well as his clothes." As a final measure of ingratiation, Nancy had Mary Pickford send Charlie some publicity stills of Fairbanks for a painting he was considering. He never completed it — perhaps because neither Fairbanks nor Pickford ever gave the go-ahead for the commission — but he eventually presented them with a bronze of Fairbanks as D'Artagnan.[27]

Charlie still dashed off drawings, letters, and models with abandon — to him, a half-day devoted to a smart-alecky sketch for an old roundup companion was as worthwhile as one spent on a $5,000 oil. But with increasing frequency, his creativity was freighted with a shrewder purpose. Nancy understood that every one of his tangible whimsies had measurable, negotiable value. What she could not sell, she would use to win favors or to repay them. John Lewis got a special letter for the perquisites he had showered on Charlie and Nancy at Lake McDonald. Justin Bootmakers of Texas got one for the complimentary boots they had sent to Charlie and Nancy. The head of the Montana Stockgrowers Association got one for extending a special (presumably all-expenses-paid) invitation to the group's annual convention.[28] In the spring of 1921, Charlie made an extraordinary gift to his extraordinary patron, William Armstrong.

Shortly after the sale of *Salute of the Robe Trade*, Charlie was a guest at the home of its new owner. Having made his fortune in Wyoming, Armstrong cherished his collection of Western Americana, including a two-volume, gold-embossed, morocco-bound deluxe edition of Francis Parkman's *The Oregon Trail*. That Frederic Remington had illustrated this 1892 edition of one of Charlie's favorite books was undoubtedly a source of low-grade irritation and jealousy. Perhaps Charlie hinted as much to his host, for he left Armstrong's house that day with the deluxe Parkman volumes under his arm and did not return them for several weeks. In the open space at the beginning and end of chapters, Charlie had painted forty-nine intricate watercolors. His absorption in the task was boundless, almost childlike. He had shown (to himself, anyway) how Parkman's text ought to have been illustrated, and he had delivered a heartfelt thank-you to the man who had paid an unprecedented price for his work.[29]

Not all of Charlie's gift-giving in California had to do with business or social advancement, however. When he made a bronze of Will Rogers, he did it out of simple friendship, not as a way to curry favor. And when Charlie visited Rogers on the movie set of *A Poor Relation* in 1921, there was none of the stiffness of the Fairbanks interlude. They hunkered down, eye to eye, on a studio doorstep and conducted a meeting of their mutual admiration society. Rogers called Charlie "Old Hand"; Charlie called Rogers "Chewing Gum Bill."

The other Hollywood figure with whom Charlie struck up a close friendship was Harry Carey. Carey was a dozen years younger than Charlie, but their similar backgrounds helped explain the kinship.[30] Carey had grown up spoiled in White Plains, New York. His father had been a Tammany-appointed judge who had made a fortune off of the horsecar line he had built from the suburb of Pelham Park to nearby City Island. Carey learned to ride his father's dray horses, dreams of Wild West shows dancing in his head. Later, as a law student, Carey wrote a play called *Montana*.

Friends dared him to quit his legal studies, and casting himself as leading man, he took *Montana* on the road. By the age of thirty, he had made a quarter of a million dollars from the melodrama. A second play was not so successful, and by 1915, he had gravitated to Hollywood Westerns, first working with director D. W. Griffith, and then John Ford.

Carey was the logical successor to William S. Hart. He possessed a rugged handsomeness, and while he did wear stylish Western clothes, they had none of the jinglebob flashiness of, say, Tom Mix. Carey never reached Mix's level of stardom, either, or even that of Bill Hart. But in Hollywood Western circles, he was highly admired and considered a charismatic hub of professional and social activity. In particular, much of Carey's vision of what a Western hero should be — especially his tough rectitude — rubbed off on John Ford, who later would coach Hollywood's most famous Western actor, John Wayne, to talk, walk, and act like his old silent-movie pal Harry Carey.

If one of John Wayne's big influences was Carey, then one of Carey's big influences was Charlie Russell. Carey and his wife, Olive, owned a ranch in the San Francisquito Canyon northwest of Los Angeles, which became a hangout for the movie-cowboy crowd. Charlie, Nancy, and Jack Russell were among the regulars in the early 1920s. Carey, in his passion for the true West, had imported a community of Navajo families from Arizona to live and work on the Carey property. The Indians looked after the sheep, cattle, and horses. They also made silver jewelry and wove rugs, which they sold at the ranch's own trading post. Their other duty was to stage Navajo rodeos for the benefit of the Careys' weekend guests. Primed with bootleg booze that Carey's hands kept buried in the desert, the Hollywood posse would perch on corral rails while the Navajo presented their interpretation of the cowboy craft. "I never enjoyed a rodeo as much in my life," Charlie opined. "This is the first time I ever saw the Injuns get an even break."[31]

With friends such as the Careys, as well as the Rogerses and Charles Lummis, Charlie began to feel more at home in California. He continued to play the outlander in his letters, but the very fact that he spent so much time on movie sets and at the beach gave the lie to his professed distaste for the California lifestyle. "[Y]ou know all artists should know the human form," he wrote to John Hagerson, the proprietor of a Central Avenue cigar store, "so a fiew days ago I went to Long Beach to study anitamay[.] Thairs all kinds of it out thair all sises and shapes both hes and shes[.] I seen Ingunes waring onley paint and a clout[,] I seen naked canabals in the moovies[,] but its a sinch bet that for vari[e]ty in shape the whites have got all other humans on this Earth skined to the dew claws."[32] This was hardly a condemnation; Charlie merely wanted to share the mildly risqué scenery with his buddies.

In the winter of 1922, the Russells returned to Southern California, the guests of Nancy's father. A few months before their arrival, James Cooper had purchased a lot and begun building a house in a new subdivision in Pasadena.[33] The setting was ideal. Five-year-old Jack could romp out-of-doors, and Charlie could breathe more easily. Lately his goiter had become so prominent that he had begun wearing custom-made shirts to hide the bulge on the side of his neck.[34]

Nancy, too, breathed more easily in California, though for different reasons. In March she arranged another show at the Kanst Galleries. William Armstrong bought another oil, *When Guns Speak, Death Settles Disputes*, a Remingtonesque night scene of three armed cowboys fleeing a saloon scrape. At the same time, several developments back home were making it possible for Charlie to earn money in Montana even while he was away.

The previous autumn, Bill Cheely and Percy Raban's Montana Newspaper Association had gathered together Charlie's Rawhide Rawlins stories and illustrations, which had run in the association's Sunday supplements intermittently since 1916, and published them in book form. *Rawhide Rawlins Stories* — eighteen of Charlie's homespun yarns and thirty-five drawings — sold for a dollar a copy. "These are hard times with a lot of folks," Charlie remarked in an accompanying promotional piece. "If this book is going to give anyone a laugh and make him forget his troubles for a while, I want the price low enough so that people to whom a dollar means a dollar will feel that they're getting their money's worth."[35]

Despite the bleak economy, Raban and Cheely were optimistic about the sales of *Rawhide Rawlins* and had another scheme they hoped would be just as lucrative. On March 5, 1922, the Cheely-Raban Syndicate began publishing a series of historical pieces in the Sunday inserts under the rubric "Back-Trailing on the Old Frontiers." Each week's segment described the adventures of a notable Western character — trapper, voyageur, conquistador, priest, outlaw, prospector, rustler, settler, soldier, or Indian. And each segment was illustrated by a Russell pen-and-ink. The idea was that Charlie would provide a drawing a week, and then at the end of each year, Cheely and Raban would publish the "Back-Trailing" collection as a book.³⁶ Granted, the series would not circulate beyond the seventy or so papers that subscribed to the syndicate's inserts, but the project meant steady money for not much work. The real beauty was that Charlie did not have to do any writing, and he could do his drawings anywhere, including California.

≫

NINETEEN TWENTY-TWO was very much a year of back-trailing for Charlie. Old friends loomed large at every turn. In January, after a year of procrastination, Charlie finally completed the painting that Malcolm Mackay had requested for over the hearth in his Russell room. Mackay had asked for a "poster" version of an illustration Charlie had done of various Western types, called *I Savy These Folks*. Charlie responded with a for-givably vain oil, *Charles M. Russell and His Friends*. The scene is the Missouri River between Cascade and Great Falls, with Square Butte, his favorite landmark, anchoring the horizon. In the foreground, Charlie painted a younger, trimmer version of himself on horseback. His right hand grips the reins, while his left is extended, palm up, in a gesture of introduction to the groups of cowboys and Indians galloping toward the viewer. Charlie has cast himself (at Mackay's request) not as a mere witness to history, but as a virtual gatekeeper. Mackay was apparently quite pleased with the canvas, and Charlie's implicit solipsism did not seem to register; three years later, Mackay would complete a self-published memoir titled *Cow Range and Hunting Trail* (illustrated by Russell).³⁷

Shortly after the Kanst show, Charlie and Nancy drove up the coast to see Ed Borein and his wife, Lucile, who had moved to Santa Barbara the year before. Like Los Angeles, Santa Barbara was flourishing in the 1920s, the quaintness and beauty of the tiny mission town attracting some of the country's wealthiest families. A colony of artists then followed the sun and the money; Thomas Moran, Carl Oscar Borg, Frank Tenney Johnson, Alexander Harmer, Fernand Lungren, and a score of lesser, but distinctly Western, talents had taken up studio space in the district of adobe and stucco buildings that flanked De La Guerra Plaza or on the mesa overlooking the sea. The well-staffed Santa Barbara School of Arts opened in 1920; by the time Charlie and Nancy came to visit, Santa Barbara was recognized nationally as an "artist's paradise." At an open house hosted by Alexander

Harmer, Borein introduced Charlie to the Santa Barbara colony, and he and Nancy repaid the welcome with an Indian-sign routine.[38] They liked Santa Barbara immediately — for the collegiality, but also for the old-timiness. The Spanish architecture, cobblestone streets, and vast ranches surrounding the city were flavorful vestiges of the old vaquero days.

At the same time Charlie was getting reacquainted with Ed Borein, a ghost sprang up from another corner of his past: Jake Hoover. On April 13 an attorney representing Hoover sent Charlie a telegram. Charlie had not seen his friend in years. Hoover had left Montana at the turn of the century to follow the Alaska gold rush. Luck did not follow him, and he drifted south again, eventually taking a job as a fishing guide and boat-dock proprietor in Seattle. In April 1922, Hoover was seventy-three years old, a fact that made the content of the telegram all the more shocking. JAKE HOOVER WHO KNOWS YOU WELL IS IN JAIL HERE CHARGED WITH INTIMACY WITH A GIRL, the lawyer announced with Western Union bluntness. HE WANTS YOU TO ASSIST HIM FINANCIALLY IN THE CASE HE HAS NO MONEY WILL YOU HELP HIM.

The wire had been sent to Great Falls, but caught up with Charlie in California. Despite Hoover's request that Charlie "wire answer immediately," Charlie chose to answer by letter instead. If the pokiness of a mailed envelope hinted at ambivalence, the message within verged on betrayal of the man who, by Charlie's own accounts, had nurtured him during his first tough years in Montana. "I am verry sory to here that my old friend is in trouble," Charlie wrote to Hoover's lawyer, "and am more sorry I cant do any thing for him[.] I have no money and a broke friend is mighty little comfort to a man in Jakes fix." Charlie then tried to soften his refusal with bromides: "I have known Jake 42 years and in days gon I camped with him maney years[.] Every western man knows that camp fires and wether make men acquainted and Iv camped with Jake when it was 50 below and the sky was our roof [.] Iv seen him tryed out and I dont think he wronged aney girl[. T]he big hills dident make that kind of men and Jake was a mountain made man."[39]

Charlie's plea of poverty was a lie, of course. Three weeks earlier, Montana newspapers had reported the sale of a painting to William Armstrong and another to the former president of Cadillac Motors, each for $10,000.[40] Nancy and Charlie were living the good life, driving a new car, dining in fine restaurants.

The most likely explanation for the cold shoulder seems to be Nancy. In her view, she and Charlie had come too far to sully themselves by helping an uncouth geezer who had been thrown in jail on a morals charge. Perhaps she even had urged Charlie to ignore Hoover's SOS altogether, and a character reference was the best he could muster. He could not very well write that his wife would not let him part with funds he had earned himself. Hoover eventually did work his way out of the jam and died of heart disease in 1925. Still, the episode is a measure of how far Charlie had come since his days as a teenage camp-tender.

Frank Linderman was another case of a friendship gone awry, but by 1922 he was "in the good graces of the Russells again," observed Joe DeYong.[41] Linderman had continued living on Flathead Lake after the 1919 fire. *Indian Old-Man Stories* had been published, albeit belatedly, in 1920. Scribner's had been pleased enough with the result to publish two more books by Linderman the following year. In 1922, Linderman's first novel, *Lige Mounts, Free Trapper,* came out; he did not wish to risk any more ruffled feathers by asking Charlie to do the artwork, so he got the next best thing: Joe DeYong.

DeYong had been picking up more and more illustration work, ranging from a cover for the *Literary Digest* to an advertisement for Powerized Gasoline, though he still depended on the Russells, Eatons' Ranch, and his parents for support. In August 1922, DeYong was dude-wrangling in Glacier with Howard Eaton when Linderman came to the park for a visit. In a letter to his parents, DeYong noted that Charlie and Linderman were once again putting on joint performances of Indian sign language at John Lewis's hotel. Their duets must have gone well enough, because a month later, after closing up Bull Head Lodge for the season, Charlie and Nancy, along with Jack, Josephine Trigg, and her mother, Margaret, made a special detour to the Lindermans' place on Flathead Lake. The stopover was to all appearances like old times: the women picked elderberries, Charlie danced the fox-trot with the Lindermans' grown-up daughters, Norma, Verne, and Wilda, and he and Frank sat by a tepee a short distance from the house and swapped yarns of the good old days.[42]

At either Glacier or Flathead, Charlie and Nancy learned that the Lindermans had made plans to winter in Santa Barbara. Linderman was not in great health himself — high blood pressure was one symptom — and his doctor had urged him to seek respite at a lower elevation; in October, he and his family moved into a bungalow on the ocean. The Russells had also been thinking of Santa Barbara, ever since their pleasant visit the previous

winter. Still, it came as quite a surprise to the Lindermans when Charlie
and Nancy rented the beach house right next door. For Charlie, it was a
chance to be near his good friend. For Nancy, the decision to winter in
Santa Barbara, instead of Los Angeles or Pasadena, smacked of her compul-
sive urge to avoid being bested, especially by the Lindermans. The Russells
could afford to pay twice as much rent as the Lindermans, doubtless a point
of pride for Nancy.[43]

Nancy would never feel entirely at ease among the Linderman family.
The cold war took the form of mutual condescension: she pitied them for
their lack of wealth because she felt they looked down their educated noses
at her wayward past. "Gosh its offel to be poor and so darned high class
you cant hardly keep your feet on common soil," Nancy griped in a letter
to Joe DeYong.

> I do wish some good thing in the shape of an oil lease [oil exploration
> was under way throughout Montana] would come their way and leave
> them 25 or 30 thousand. It would make a very happy family. I feel they
> are off on us and its becaus we are so *common* I guess you know our
> lives are so close to Old Mother earth that at times there is mud on our
> shoes. . . . I feel they would hate me if they knew I ever thought such
> a thing so you burn this scribble after you have read it.[44]

After attending to all the details that absence from Montana and a trip
south demanded, Nancy was exhausted. Joe DeYong, even while he was
playing the role of Nancy's loyal confidant, was telling his own parents about
her jangled condition. "[S]he has no more system at times than a dish full of
noodles or spaghetti," he commented. "[She] just does the most important
things and has to let the others slide." But to suggest to Nancy that she get
a more sensible grip on her affairs "would be worth our life," Joe added
cattily.[45]

Yet once she had settled in Santa Barbara, Nancy made an effort to pull
herself together. Her letter to Joe on January 31, 1923, several weeks after
her arrival, reads like an entry in the diary of a sanitarium patient who has
finally faced up to her neurosis:

> I feel something like a rock abandone[d] in Mid Ocean with a great
> storm about to break but in the hart of this rock there is a whispered

promis that when the storm has passed and all the waters calm the foundation under the abandon[ed] rock will be firm and Chas and I will
be there for the boat to land on. . . . We are so nicely located and the
house is most comfortable[. T]he waves washing on the sands sound like
a heavy wind and I am just beginning to sleep and to wonder why this
house dont shake when the wind is blowing so hard[. T]hat old Ocean
is so restless and so beyond the human understanding.[46]

Gradually, the storm within her did subside, at least temporarily. There
were several reasons for the change in her spirits. First, of course, was the lovely
setting; she also claimed some benefits from the newfangled treatments
she was receiving. California in the 1920s was already a mecca for mystics,
quacks, and other panacea peddlers. In Santa Barbara, Nancy tried some
sort of "electric" therapy, which called for her to "sit in a chair connected
to a machine of some weard vibration stuff for one to two hours daily."[47]
She never described the physical symptoms that led her to this experi-
mental treatment, but presumably she suffered from her usual headaches,
nerves, and constitutional frailty. A placebo might have been just what she
needed.

Not to be discounted was the boost Nancy got from knowing she was
among the right people. She and Charlie — especially Charlie — were received as celebrities among the circle of artists and their patrons. What is
more, the unabashed snobbishness of the place enveloped her like a man-
tilla. "As I sit here," Verne Linderman wrote to Joe DeYong from their
beach house on Cabrillo Boulevard, "I can see ships riding at anchor, smart
people riding beautiful horses along the edge of the surf, and an endless
stream of cars, — mostly luxurious, with chauffeurs and fine ladies and
dogs."[48] Nancy's view from next door was no different.

Eventually Nancy's mood improved to the point that she even negotiated
her own cautious rapprochement with the Lindermans. "It is fun having
the Russells next door," Verne wrote to Joe. "Mrs. Russell takes us down
town almost every afternoon. Wilda is tutoring Jack in mornings and Babe
[Norma] does her stenography." Mah-jongg was all the rage in those days,
and when Charlie's stepmother, Florence, came to visit, she taught Nancy
and the Linderman women how to play. Having spent so much time with
Nancy, Verne Linderman was pleased to discern that Nancy was "much
more solid underneath than one might guess."[49]

All the while, Frank Linderman and Charlie continued to enjoy each other's company. It was to Linderman's house that Charlie fled after climbing out the bathroom window to escape a particularly dull party. It was Linderman, fanatical about boats, who wangled an invitation for them to tour the battleship *Oklahoma,* anchored offshore. And only Linderman could have cajoled Charlie into a mackerel-fishing expedition aboard a small dory they had found washed up on the beach. The fish were biting, but Charlie was too seasick to care, not even appreciating the school of porpoises that passed nearby.[50]

Bouts of claustrophobia and mal de mer aside, the Santa Barbara trip had a positive effect on Charlie. "I haven't see[n] Chas look so well in a long time," Nancy observed. Indeed, Frank Linderman reflected some years later, "That winter . . . was kind to us all."[51]

Instead of socializing with the idle rich in Santa Barbara, Charlie, often with Linderman in tow, preferred to make the rounds of the other artist studios. A favorite hangout was La Barranca, the Boreins' Spanish-style house on the mesa. Lucile Borein recalls an evening when Charlie and her husband were joined by Will Rogers.

They told stories before dinner, during dinner and after dinner . . . far into the wee hours of the morning. There was no drinking and no off-color stories. They were just like little boys. I went up to bed, and at 3 A.M. came down to find out if Ed intended to sleep at all. The three were amazed to learn what time it was — they had lost themselves completely in their story-telling. They smoked Bull Durham, rolling their own . . . and next morning the tobacco was inches thick on the rugs.[52]

In March, Charlie and Nancy traveled to Los Angeles for a major exhibition of his work that she had set up at the Stendahl Galleries, located in the new and extravagant Ambassador Hotel on Wilshire Boulevard. Of all the nostrums Nancy had tried that winter, nothing perked her up like the astounding success in Los Angeles. The city was full of nouveaux riches in 1923, cash apparently burning a hole in their pockets. Before the Stendahl show had closed, a "retired Kansas City capitalist," a "Denver oil magnate," a "Pittsburg[h] manufacturer," and a "Pittsburg[h] capitalist" had snapped up six paintings for a total of $20,000, the *Los Angeles Times* reported.[53]

News of the buying frenzy traveled fast, gathering embellishment with time and distance. "My God, Charlie, how many pictures did you sell?" wrote Judge Bollinger. "Met a fellow on the train who said you were 'lousy rich now.' . . . Said you had sold thirty pictures." Charles Lummis dispatched an effusive congratulation, giving credit where credit was due: "I'm delighted beyond expression on news of the big Surround & Killing — you corraled pretty near the Whole Herd! The people that haven't any money are the ones that are safe from that Insatiable Nancy! No little coyote about her — she's the real timberwolf that can pull down the old Bull himself! You've shown 'em an American artist can get European — or Dead Men's — prices."54

Charlie and Nancy were feeling very much alive by the time they left California at the end of May for the long drive north. Just before leaving, Nancy had purchased the lot next to her father's in Pasadena with the notion that they would soon build a house there.55 Meantime, she and Charlie looked forward to another summer at Bull Head Lodge. Jack would start his second year of school in the fall, and Charlie was already hatching plans for an elk-hunting trip with Bollinger and some others.56 Little did either of them realize that their world was about to close in, and that after the summer of 1923, the jokes about dead men's prices would cease to be funny.

TRAIL'S END

I N THE SUMMER of 1923, America again had its eye on Montana. And as with so many big moments in the state's history, Charlie Russell seemed to slip into the corner of the picture. At the end of June, President Warren G. Harding detrained in Butte during a tour of the western United States. (He would die of a cerebral hemorrhage in San Francisco four weeks later.) The whistle-stop was only the third visit by a president to Montana, and as coincidence would have it, both previous visitors, Theodore Roosevelt and William Howard Taft, were proud owners of Russell art. Harding soon joined the club: the Shriners of Butte presented him with the bronze *Where the Best of Riders Quit,* which had been cast earlier that year.[1]

Unlike the occasion nearly thirty years earlier when Charlie had seemed indifferent to the hoopla surrounding William Jennings Bryan's visit to Montana, this time he could not resist the big event. He rode the train down to Butte, and though he was neither a Shriner nor a Republican, he gave the day his blessing. There is no solid proof that he actually met the President at the time the bronze was presented; more likely he never got much closer than a nearby soda shop. "I've got no business here [in Butte]," he told the press. "I'm a black-hearted [D]emocrat myself, but here's looking at 'em all," he toasted, raising a glass of malted milk.[2]

Another big event drew Charlie's attention that summer.[3] On July 4, heavyweight boxing champion Jack Dempsey was scheduled to defend his title in, of all places, Shelby, Montana, ninety miles north of Great Falls.

The match is still celebrated as one of the most improbable events in sporting history. Shelby had recently become an oil boomtown and suddenly
boasted a population of one thousand. Its mayor and chief promoter, James
A. Johnson, entertained visions of logarithmic increase. But first he had to
make the name of his town a household word.

Dempsey's name already was. The "Manassa Mauler" was the most famous athlete in the country (except maybe for Babe Ruth, who had hit
fifty-six home runs in 1921). By offering Dempsey and his manager enough
cash — $300,000 — Johnson and his associates were able to schedule a
fight against Tommy Gibbons, a solid but smaller journeyman who had
the twin attributes of being white and from the Northwest (St. Paul). The
promoters predicted that a minimum of forty thousand fans would attend
the match and leave behind more than a million dollars, even though no
paved roads led to Shelby in 1923. The majority of the spectators would arrive by special trains. The open-air bleachers to seat the anticipated throng
took a million and a quarter board feet of pine and two carloads of nails.
By May, scores of new buildings, with an emphasis on hotels and dance
halls, were under construction. The proximity of dry Shelby to wet Canada
obviated any concerns about refreshments.

Charlie remained a teetotaler, but he did have a keen interest in boxing.
Bill Rance of the Silver Dollar had sponsored a series of local fighters over
the years, and his enthusiasm for the sport had rubbed off on his good friend.
Charlie even finessed an invitation to meet Dempsey, who was living and
training in an old roadhouse on the outskirts of Great Falls.

Despite the collective enthusiasm for the fight, it quite nearly fizzled.
Backers had trouble coming up with the $300,000, and as the date neared
and public skepticism increased, the Great Northern canceled many of its
trains. In the end, the money, or most of it, was raised, and the fight did
come off on time, but fewer than eight thousand fans paid full price for
tickets. Another seventeen thousand paid far less, and some gate-crashers
nothing at all. Gibbons withstood the hot July sun and Dempsey's pounding
for all fifteen rounds (losing by decision), but the fight's promoters took it
on the chin.

In California, Charlie and Nancy had learned that Douglas Fairbanks and
Mary Pickford were considering coming to Shelby to root for their friend
Dempsey. Nancy dashed off a letter, urging them to visit Lake McDonald
as well. Fairbanks and Pickford ultimately decided against the Montana

trip, so Charlie went to Shelby in the company of Joe DeYong. After the fight, their train did not arrive at the Belton station in Glacier Park until well after dark. They were exhausted by the time they finally reached Bull Head Lodge, and Charlie's back, which had nagged him for some time, was extremely sore. The path from the road to the house was unlit and steep. Feeling his way down the wooden walkway in high-heeled boots, Charlie slipped and landed in a heap. The next morning he awoke in agony, barely able to get out of bed.[4]

The injury, presumably to one or more discs in Charlie's spine, left him with an excruciating case of sciatica, an inflammation of the nerve that runs from the lower back down the thigh. "[T]he medison man says I spraned my syatic nerve," Charlie wrote to Frank Linderman. "[I]f thats what it is I got more nerve than I thought I had." Six weeks after the accident, he was still "on the bum" and being treated three times a day by a doctor who happened to be vacationing at Lake McDonald. In early September, Nancy was able to get Charlie home to Great Falls, and by early October he was able to move around the house on crutches, but still could not sit up straight enough to work. "His back is so bent over and his legs crooked not being able to put any weight on the right one," Nancy wrote to Percy Raban.

By early December, a full five months after the accident, Charlie was able to hobble out to the studio under a nurse's care, but could not work much, and finally had to retreat to a bed that had been made up for him on the first floor of the house. Adding to the gloom, Nancy suddenly fell seriously ill herself. She claimed it was "a combination of spoiled oysters and intestinal flu," but perhaps the strain put on her by Charlie's injury had had an exacerbating effect. On December 21, she was obliged to write Olive Carey, declining an invitation to spend Christmas at the Carey ranch:

> [T]his family is a mess. Chas. is still on crutches and really little bet-
> ter. . . . Then to make things more interesting I have been flat in bed
> going on four weeks so the house is full of trained nurses. . . . Just think
> how we are stranded; Chas down stairs and cant get up; while I am
> upstairs and cant get down. It now looks as if it will be the middle of
> January before we can travel south.[5]

Slowly Charlie and Nancy began to recover from their dual decline, though he could not get around without "riding a cane" or crutches for most of the winter. By early February, they were back in California, along with Jack and Joe DeYong. But they were not the same pair who had gadded about Los Angeles with abandon in previous seasons. Whereas a year earlier the Santa Barbara paper had marveled at Charlie's "rebellious" (though graying) hair, "piercing" gaze, and the "free, indolent looseness" of his cowboy posture, now an old acquaintance was shocked to see Charlie "suffering and handicapped," his overall manner "so aged and tired."[6]

Throughout the ordeal of sciatica, Charlie had not lost his sense of humor, but he was clearly not as breezy with his jokes. "I have been near enough Hell to smell smoke," he wrote a friend. "[T]heires fiew men in this old world that I dont care much about but thair aint non that I hate bad enough to wish siatica on." Having glimpsed his own mortality, his trademark nostalgia had turned inward and even more somber. "Old Dad Time trades little that men want," he wrote Josephine Trigg that spring. "[H]e has traded me wrinkles for teeth[,] stiff legs for limber ones."[7]

The year before, increasing wealth and improving health had made Nancy cocky and optimistic. Now, with the unexpected arrival of hardship, she appeared anxious and as fragile as "a bit of Dresden china," according to a *Los Angeles Times* column. Charlie had done virtually no painting or modeling since leaving California the previous June. Their income from art in that period had been next to nil. "It sure don't pay to be sick," Nancy complained.[8] Even the publication of the first *Back-Trailing* anthology in the autumn of 1923 had been a bust, forcing Cheely and Raban to abandon plans for future volumes. Meanwhile, the expense of the Russells' fancy lifestyle, not to mention medical care, was sizable. They were not destitute by any means, but memories of childhood poverty haunted Nancy.

Instead of panicking, she grew shrewder. Rather than pay cash to a Great Falls doctor, she settled the bill with a watercolor.[9] She wrote to offer likely patrons Charlie's paintings at a discount. In Los Angeles, she severed ties with the Stendahl Galleries, after the owner insisted on raising his commission from 25 to 33⅓ percent, and she aligned with another gallery, located in Los Angeles's newest, grandest hotel, the Biltmore. The Biltmore Salon had been started in 1923 by Western artists Clyde Forsythe, Jack Wilkinson Smith, and Frank Tenney Johnson. In late March, Charlie exhibited fourteen oils and twelve bronzes there, most of them recycled from previous shows. Sales were good enough that shortly after the show closed in April, Nancy was able to begin paying back a $1,000 loan from Joe DeYong's mother. "Don't worry about the Russells and their money," Joe wrote Banty DeYong some weeks later. "[O]ne sale will wipe out their debts and they are not really broke you know."[10]

As the spring progressed, Charlie was feeling much better, his morale boosted by the overwhelming attentiveness of fans and acquaintances. "[T]he Doctors showed me the wagon marks but my Friends cleared the trail for me," he wrote Linderman, thanking him for the cheery poetry — "medicon virs" — Linderman had sent. In Los Angeles, where the Russells had decided to stay instead of Santa Barbara, Harry Carey was particularly generous. He had Charlie out to the movie studio for lunch and took him to the circus. When the Russells grew uncomfortable staying at the home of old friend W. C. Tyler — whose embarrassing outbursts of lunacy eventually landed him in an institution — Carey offered to shift them to a house he and Olive owned in Los Angeles and even offered to build Charlie a studio there. (Instead, they spent the rest of their stay in Pasadena with Nancy's father.) Carey also was one of the ringleaders of a surprise birthday party for Charlie, attended by some of his favorite people.[11]

For some reason, Charlie was usually a year behind in his age. On March 19, 1924, he turned sixty, but as far as he and the rest of the world were concerned, he was only fifty-nine. Nevertheless, Nancy went all out, inviting thirty guests, including the Careys, Charles Lummis, Ed and Lucile Borein, and a variety of actors and artists. Percy Raban and his wife, new California residents, joined the family circle of Joe DeYong and Nancy's half-sister Ella Allen Ironside, who had also settled in Southern California. Will Rogers served as master of ceremonies, leading the stories and laughter into the small hours of the morning.

Despite the sunshine and hospitality of California and the increasing likelihood that he and Nancy might one day own their own house there, Charlie itched for Montana. At the end of May, he and Nancy took a car trip up the coast to Monterey, Carmel, and then to Yosemite National Park. Charlie was impressed, though as one more tourist, he felt like a stranger in a strange land. "California is all right," he wrote to the Great Falls bunch, "but I cant see [B]elt or [S]quar[e] [B]utte from here."[12]

For the car trip home to Montana in June, they hired a driver and chose a route through Death Valley and Nevada. They paid a visit to author B. M. Bower, who had moved to the tiny desert town of Las Vegas with her husband, Bud Cowan. A letter written by Bower describes driving out to meet the Russells' Cadillac as it crossed the California state line: "We had just crossed the dry lake . . . when we met them buzzing down that long, sandy slope, Mame in the front seat beside the driver with a green veil over her face, and Charlie tucked back among the grips etc. I suppose he was perfectly comfortable, but he looked tucked, if you get my meaning."[13]

Bower suggested they all stop for a picnic, but Nancy "threw up both hands in horror" and complained of a blinding headache. Bower swore at herself "for having forgotten that one mustn't plan things for Mame Russell. . . . Of course it never occurred to Mame to lower the shades in that big sedan and sit back out of the glare. Instead she must perch in the front seat, stare at the desert and curse the sun." As soon as they reached their Las Vegas hotel, Nancy collapsed into bed. "She wouldn't let Jack out of the room . . . and the child persisted in breathing occasionally which made it worse for the child. Charlie couldn't do a thing for Mame, and she wouldn't have him near her, nor let him go on off somewhere."

In an hour or so, Nancy had proved her resilience once again, though Bower hints vaguely that Nancy accepted some sort of medication:

Mame told me her troubles, decided she would get up, brushed her long, beautiful hair and powdered her nose, got into a cool dress and became human. . . . So "Everything passed off pleasantly." She went to Doolittle's [where Bower's friends were gathered], and everybody was nice to her and she was once more queen. Charlie managed to say to me afterwards, "God, I sure was glad when you come and got Mame out of that hot room! She wouldn't do it for me — but now she's all right. . . ."

That's all there was to it. They came, tarried tumultuously and went. The desert swallowed them — and I'm glad they arrived home all right. I know I helped Mame, and by that means Charlie also. I wish she might learn how to go at life, but until she does learn she will go on being "edgy" and hurried and worried and insincere. It's her eagerness for life and her driving energy and ambition that are wearing her and everyone else to ribbons. She doesn't know how to go at it, is all.

But go at it she did, and with renewed intensity. Charlie's tender back kept him from hunting in the fall of 1924, but Nancy had big plans for the coming winter: an exhibition in Duluth in December, New York in January, Washington, D.C., in February, and Los Angeles in March. Was she making up for lost time, or did she sense that Charlie did not have much time left? Either way, Nancy could not have been more manic, and she was pushing Charlie harder than ever.

At the end of October, Joe DeYong and his mother had settled into the Great Falls house to look after eight-year-old Jack, while Nancy and Charlie geared up for another winter of campaigning. As Jack grew from toddler to gangly boy, he found himself lost in the shuffle of his parents' lives. Charlie, old enough to be his grandfather, was characteristically laissez-faire with his son; Nancy was characteristically impatient. Their come-and-go, hot-and-cold style of child-rearing eventually gave Jack a case of emotional whiplash. His parents pulled him out of school in Great Falls every winter and stuck him in another in California. They never took him on their trips east, but would shower him with gifts when they got back. Even the kindest of the Russells' friends acknowledged that the boy was becoming a brat. "Jack has never done worth a damn in school," Joe DeYong wrote to Frank Linderman in November, "so I've just naturally hammered hell out of him. . . . If they leave him to me I can make or break him."[14]

At the time, Charlie and Nancy were off in Los Angeles. Nancy had been courting oilman Edward Doheny and his wife, Estelle, all year, and finally, through the help of the Biltmore Salon, she and Charlie had been invited to California to discuss a special commission. The very hint of working for the immensely wealthy Dohenys was worth a cross-country dash.

Edward and Estelle Doheny lived in a three-story mansion in down-town Los Angeles. Across the street they maintained a private deer park, and at the back of the house an enormous glass conservatory covered a swimming pool, palm trees, and five thousand orchids. Their Pompeian Room, ornamented with Tiffany glass and Siena marble, could seat more than a hundred dinner guests. Estelle Doheny's taste in collecting ran to glass paperweights, rare books, and Barbizon paintings. Her husband, however, reserved one room as a shrine to the West. He installed a fireplace made of petrified wood and an upright piano decorated with Indian scenes. On the walls he hung paintings by Frederic Remington and W. R. Leigh. From Charlie's 1924 Biltmore show he bought *The Wolf and the Beaver*, an oil depicting an outlaw on the run (the "wolf") who is enviously eyeing the snug cabin of an honest, hardworking settler (the "beaver").

Doheny was in trouble himself in 1924, mired deep in the Teapot Dome scandal. A congressional committee had accused him and fellow oil millionaire Harry Sinclair of bribing Interior secretary Albert Fall to gain the rights to lucrative, government-owned oil fields in Wyoming. Despite all the turmoil in Doheny's life at that point, he somehow had found time to discuss the possibility of Charlie painting a frieze that would chronicle the "history of the west."[15]

The meeting in Los Angeles went well enough, for Charlie returned to Montana with orders to paint watercolor studies for two walls of the Dohenys' Western room. The other two walls had been painted years earlier by German-born Detlef Sammann and depicted a variety of Indian scenes: Indians greeting Pilgrims, Indians hunting buffalo, Indians competing at games, Indians spying on a wagon train.[16] In December, while Nancy rushed to Duluth to oversee the exhibition there, Charlie stayed home to work on the Doheny studies. Sammann's Indians prevented Charlie from painting them in his own graphic history of the West. (One cannot imagine him leaving Indians out for any other reason.) Instead, he proposed scenes of the white man's impact: a cattle roundup, a stagecoach, hunting, and prospecting.

Despite Charlie's prompt completion of the studies, the Dohenys took five months to make up their minds. Nancy was understandably keen to bag a commission so plump — but she had no choice but to wait the Dohenys out. She and Charlie spent Christmas in Great Falls; two days later they were on a train to New York to open an exhibition at the Arthur H. Harlow Galleries on Fifth Avenue.

The New York show went well. "We surely have had a successful trip so far," Nancy wrote to Joe DeYong, "and I am still hoping to land a few more before Thursday."[17] During the day, she and Charlie worked the gallery, and at night they hobnobbed with Bill Hart, Will and Betty Rogers, and Fred Stone, who all happened to be in town that January. By the time they boarded a Washington-bound train, the Russells were exhausted. Nancy managed to keep a stiff upper lip, but Charlie nursed a runny nose and a low-grade uneasiness toward yet another exhibition in yet another city. "Chas has a very sad face because we are not bound for home, but I cant help that," Nancy wrote from the train. "[H]e does not feel very well

[and] has had a cold almost two weeks[,] not a down and outer but enough to make him feel bum." That was all the sympathy she would allot him, however. "I have kept quite well in deed when I think of the things I have done in the past four weeks with so little rest," she boasted. "Success is the tonic."[18]

And so they rolled into Washington, the first visit for either of them. Fourteen paintings and fourteen sculptures were on display at the Corcoran Gallery of Art for three weeks. The cheapest bronze was priced at $75, the most expensive oil $10,000. The *Washington Post* reviewer was overcome by "the desire to gallop across the plains with the men of daring."[19]

Charlie, however, felt anything but invigorated and was never so relieved to leave "the big Camp" and get back home to Great Falls. He was so worn-out that he and Nancy decided not to take a house in California for the winter, the first time in five years they did not migrate to "the oringe belt." Charlie's exhibition at the Biltmore Salon in April was one of the rare occasions neither he nor Nancy was on hand to promote the work.

Nancy did make a quick trip to Los Angeles in May to meet with Estelle Doheny. After cooling her heels in the Biltmore Hotel for several days, she finally got the call she had hoped for: Mr. Doheny had approved the studies for the frieze, with one amendment. He insisted that Charlie update his history of the West by including several oil wells in one of the panels. Nancy was not about to protest — not when Doheny promised to pay $30,000 for Charlie's effort. She raced back to Montana, brimming with satisfaction.[20]

The Russells had precious little time to savor the windfall. Now that Charlie was a venerable, high-profile celebrity, the demands on his time were extraordinary and neverending. On June 15, the University of Montana awarded him an honorary doctorate for "his attainments and his services to Montana in preserving her early history." In presenting the degree — only the fourth in the university's twenty-eight-year history — university president Charles Clapp offered an encomium that Charlie had heard a hundred times before:

> Charles Marion Russell, or just plain Charlie Russell, as he is widely and fondly called, came to Montana forty-five years ago — a mere lad of sixteen years, but a real cowboy. He has lived intimately and intensely

the life of the early Montana plainsman and mountaineer. This life he has pictured in his stories, drawings, modelings and paintings; not for us as Montanans alone but for the entire world, for the world has recognized and claimed him; and rightly so, for no other has so well interpreted Montana life.[21]

Those who were not honoring Charlie that summer wanted him to honor them with his presence. It seemed as if every rodeo in the Northwest had extended an invitation for Charlie and Nancy to ride in their parade and grace the VIP seats in the grandstand. Charlie was tempted, but he simply could not say yes to everyone. He did travel to the Pendleton Round-Up in Oregon that summer, but turned down an invitation from his cowboy friend Guy Weadick to attend the Calgary Stampede. Weadick's old-time's-sake offer conflicted with a more opulent one from Ralph Budd, president of the Great Northern Railway. The railway's latest publicity extravaganza was the Upper Missouri Historical Expedition, a special trainload of "educators, jurists, historians, . . . rail executives, bankers, steel men, directors of great flour corporations, [and] editors" who intended to roll across Minnesota, the Dakotas, and Montana in mid-July, dining at every major depot and christening monuments to the explorers, road builders, and military men who had helped open the country for the aforementioned grandees.[22]

Charlie and Nancy joined the group at Fort Union, near the Montana–North Dakota line. When the expedition stopped at Glacier National Park on July 22, Charlie hosted a banquet for his fellow passengers at John Lewis's hotel. Seated at Charlie's table were General Hugh L. Scott, who had participated in the capture of Chief Joseph and his band of Nez Percé, and John F. Stevens, the engineer–explorer whose discovery of the Marias Pass had guaranteed the settlement and development of northern Montana. As dinner speaker, Charlie had recruited his new friend, popular Southern humorist Irvin S. Cobb, who was vacationing that summer at Lake McDonald.[23]

Despite such diversions, Charlie still managed to see his old chums. He kept up with cowmen Con Price, Teddy Blue Abbott, Henry Keeton, and Bob Thoroughman; Kalispell taxidermist Harry Stanford; Ed Nietzling, his favorite hunting guide; and Young Boy, the Cree. He loved to kill an hour or two in one of the cigar stores in Great Falls or slip away from fancy dinners in Glacier Park and join the dude wranglers, packers, and other wage earners who lived apart from the park tourists. And in August 1925, when a forest fire threatened Apgar — and briefly forced the Russells to evacuate Bull Head Lodge — Charlie and Nancy were quick to roll up their sleeves and help out in the fire-camp kitchen.[24]

But for each newspaper mention of Charlie helping feed a fire crew, there seemed to be two that placed him at a dinner with an Irvin Cobb, a movie star, senator, judge, or business leader. Maybe he did not like some of the things these men stood for, but he liked them as men and liked the fact that they liked him.

In October, Charlie joined a group of well-heeled Montanans on a hunting trip on the Little Thompson River, southwest of Glacier Park. It was his first trip since hurting his back. "The big game of western Montana had better watch out," began an October 24 article in the *Anaconda Standard*. "This morning there will depart from Butte an aggregation of hunters the likes of which has seldom sought the bear and the wildcat." If the newspaper was poking fun, it was not poking very hard, for the guest list included some of the state's most powerful men: Con Kelley, chairman of Anaconda Copper; Jim Hobbins, vice president of Anaconda; Sam Stephenson, president of the First National Bank of Great Falls; plus John Lewis, Judge Bollinger, George Calvert, and a half-dozen other affluent businessmen.[25] Hunting with this group was a far cry from the days when Charlie had batched with Jake Hoover. These city dwellers traveled with a retinue of guides and a caravan of pack animals and lived like pashas. Given Charlie's physical condition, he could not have managed the trip under conditions any more strenuous. Breathing was difficult, especially at high altitude, and he stayed close to camp during the ten-day outing.

While Charlie was away, Nancy was in Great Falls, firming up plans for another trip to New York. This time she wanted to organize her own private exhibition, without gallery affiliation, and Irvin Cobb helped them find an apartment — "parlor suits," Nancy called their accommodations — on Gramercy Park. She devoted much of her time to courting two fresh, and keenly acquisitive, patrons. One was George Sack, a New Yorker whose wealth seems to have been tied to perfume, but whose taste for art ran toward Western sculpture. "No, Mr. Charles M. Russell, I am not surrounded by Russell bronzes, only about half," Sack had written in mock indignation when he had learned that Charlie and Nancy were coming to

New York. "[W]hat I want to know is, what you are going to do about it." Sack was champing at the bit, and Nancy was eager to see that he got all the Russell bronzes his heart desired.[26]

The other patron was Dr. Philip Cole, who in 1925 was fast becoming one of the leading collectors of Western art in the country. Cole was a silver-spoon Easterner; his father had lived in the West, but then had made a fortune in Brooklyn as the holder of the patent on the pressure valve for automobile tires. After college, Cole had decided to make his own way, moving west to practice medicine in Helena. But after World War I, he acceded to his father's wish and joined the family auto-parts business. He never again lived anywhere other than the East Coast, though he never thought of himself as anything other than a Western man. "He always told us we were 'Montana blood' and reared us to be just 'simple Montana folks,' " his daughter explained. "None of us had ever seen Montana, though, and living in surroundings something like Buckingham Palace it was sometimes difficult to achieve."[27]

Zeeview, the Cole estate on the Hudson, was indeed palatial, though Cole's driving ambition was to fill it from floor to ceiling with images of cowboys and Indians. Eventually his collection would include significant pieces by a wide array of Western artists: Remington, Schreyvogel, Sharp, Borein, Johnson, Leigh, and Montanan Olaf Seltzer. Cole reserved a special passion for Russells. The first piece he owned, one of Charlie's buffalo-hunt oils, had been a wedding gift from his father in 1919. In 1925, Charlie did his first commission for Cole, *The Discovery of Last Chance Gulch,* of prospectors discovering gold on the site of present-day Helena. It was the beginning of a demanding and rewarding relationship. Nancy had met her match in Philip Cole; he was forever bargaining for a better deal and trying to swap older paintings (which he considered inferior) for newer ones. Nancy met most offers with counteroffers of her own, and through the course of her life sold Cole nearly four dozen oils and watercolors.

Nancy had one further reason for coming to New York that winter. In December, Percy Raban and Bill Cheely had published the second volume of Rawhide Rawlins stories, *More Rawhides.* Neither volume had circulated much beyond Montana, and the anthologies had not made either Charlie or his publishers rich. Meanwhile, cowboy artist Will James was enjoying huge national success with his stories and books. Charlie and Nancy had known James, or at least known of him, for a decade, ever since the ex-convict/ex-cowboy had beseeched Charlie for advice on how to break into the illustration business. James and the Russells saw each other that winter in New York — and Charlie treated the lanky Canadian warmly. Nancy, however, was predictably reserved and jealous. James's 1924 book, *Cowboys North and South,* had been a hit for Scribner's. He had published a second book, *The Drifting Cowboy,* in 1925, and when the Russells saw him in New York, he was about to publish a third, *Smoky the Cowhorse,* which would become one of the best-selling children's books of all time.[28]

As Nancy hated to be surpassed by anyone, the ascendancy of Will James added impetus to her visit with Harry Maule, editor of *Frontier* magazine, published by Doubleday, Page and Company. Maule, as it happened, had been on a "dude trip" to Glacier the previous summer and needed little introduction to the charm and commercial potential of Charlie's work. Together he and Nancy hatched an idea for a "reminiscen[ce] book" by Charlie — "somewhere between *Rawhide Rawlins* and Will James," Maule suggested.[29]

Although the trip east had been good for business, it had done nothing for Charlie's health. He had seen doctors in New York about his goiter, but had found no relief. By the time he and Nancy returned to Great Falls in late December, he was in miserable shape. The decision to head for California was made not so much for business or friends or fun, but for comfort, even survival.

Charlie was experiencing "terrible choking" and dizzy spells, as his enlarged thyroid continued to squeeze his windpipe and his overtaxed heart struggled to pump fresh blood through his system.[30] Meanwhile, the two Doheny friezes, twenty-nine inches tall and twenty-plus feet long, loomed like an Augean chore. He plugged away throughout the winter and early spring, but the result was an uninspired, shopworn montage. How many times had he painted a composition of cowboys closing in on a bunch of longhorns? How many times had he painted a swarthy mountain man, rifle raised, and body turned just so in the saddle? And how many times had he painted a backdrop of Montana mountains at sunset or a cow camp at mealtime?

Charlie took little pride in the Doheny project, and he put very little energy into it. The prospectors panning for gold in one of the Doheny panels were borrowed from Philip Cole's *Last Chance Gulch* commission. In 1918, Charlie had thrown a fit when a pushy client had demanded he paint over something so minor as the slobber on a buffalo's tongue; now he dabbed in Doheny's derricks without protest, though he placed them where they would be hidden by the room's stairwell. He did much of the work in the guest house at the Carey ranch, and when the canvases were finally rolled up and delivered, the Dohenys happily paid the $30,000.[31]

ONE OF THE first things Nancy did was buy a new Lincoln. But when it came time to drive home in early June, even the ride in a comfortable new sedan was too much for Charlie. Nancy had to put him on the train in Salt Lake City. Lying down was too uncomfortable, so Charlie sat up the entire trip to Great Falls.[32]

Work was almost out of the question, though Nancy was loath to admit it. Throughout the spring, she had been corresponding with Harry Maule about the prospect of a book. Maule had some of the original illustrations for *More Rawhides* and was proposing a merger and extrapolation of the two Rawhide books that would include an additional fifty drawings and ten thousand words of narrative. He was anxious to get the book out so Doubleday could cash in on the current cowboy-literature craze. "Western things of this sort are very much to the fore now," Maule wrote to Nancy, "and Mr. Russell's book ought to come along while the vogue is at its height." Concerned about Charlie's health and his ability to write another ten thousand words on time, Maule suggested a ghostwriter. Nancy resisted, assuring Maule, if not herself, that Charlie could get the job done. She wrote Maule back, asking what sort of royalty Will James was getting from his publisher. She wanted the same, or better, for Charlie.[33]

The truth was, Charlie had not done much since finishing the Doheny frieze, save for writing and illustrating a few letters. At the same time that Nancy was allaying Maule's worries about Charlie's ability to work, she was sending a contradictory message to trusted friends. Malcolm Mackay had agreed to lend his Russell painting *Jerked Down* to *Country Life* magazine, which planned to include a reproduction in an upcoming profile of Charlie. Unfortunately, the painting was damaged in shipment to the magazine. The Mackays were highly upset by the accident, and after collecting

$6,000 from *Country Life,* asked Charlie whether he could paint a copy of the injured oil. Nancy was forced to write back: "Charlie is not very well and he has a great deal of work ahead of him and it would likely be a year before he could even touch Mr. Mackay's picture." (Charlie never did get around to replacing *Jerked Down,* and it was sold to Philip Cole.)[34]

Unable to work and barely able to breathe or sleep, Charlie finally had to embrace the inevitable. Both his physician and his osteopath had been urging him to have the goiter removed. They knew of surgeons in Rochester, Minnesota, who were making dramatic progress in the treatment of conditions exactly like Charlie's. Doc Edwin, the osteopath, took Nancy aside and leveled with her: If Charlie didn't have an operation, he would die. "Charlie belongs to the world," Edwin counseled, "so take him to Mayo."[35]

CHARLIE RUSSELL WAS not alone in his fear of being treated by an unfamiliar doctor. The notion of entering a hospital for safe and successful care was only beginning to gain currency. Babies were delivered at home; many surgical procedures, including complicated ones, were performed in a doctor's office. Hospitals were still stigmatized as institutions for the poor or the insane.

The Mayo brothers helped to change that perception.[36] As pioneers of modern surgery, they were among the first to keep careful medical records and to rely on diagnostic technology such as the electrocardiograph. Most significantly, their hospital was a forerunner in the application of anesthesia and antiseptic procedures. Such advances opened up a whole world of surgical possibilities. In 1910, Mayo surgeons had performed eight thousand operations. In 1925, they did three times that many.

Mayo had practically invented goiter surgery, known more properly as thyroidectomy. Goiter, an enlargement of the thyroid, was a widespread problem until the 1920s; so prevalent was the affliction in certain regions, such as the Great Lakes, upper Midwest, and Missouri River valley, that they were known as "goiter belts." Conventional wisdom held that goiters, like gout or neurasthenia, were brought on by modern stresses. Dr. Israel Bram, one of the acknowledged thyroid experts in the 1920s, linked goiters not only to " 'jazz' music," but " 'jazz' thinking." Writing in a textbook on thyroid conditions, Bram argued that life in general has lost considerable of its wholesome simplicity, and has become artificial, strained, and self-consuming. Relaxation that is really relaxing has become a rare event in a goodly percentage of humanity; stage plays are tense with mystery, suspense, and exciting sex appeal; movies are likewise of a sort calculated to unearth the worst rather than the best from our inner makeup. Sleep, already abbreviated by this strenuosity incident to earning more dollars and taking in more entertainment, has become deficient in quantity and quality, and the mind in many of us is in more or less of a daze in waking hours.[37]

If the new age was catching the blame for goiters, it responded by coming up with a cure. Mayo doctors were among the first to fully understand the relationship of iodine to the treatment and prevention of goiters, and by 1926, they had thyroid surgery nearly down pat, performing more than two thousand thyroid operations that year, with a 99 percent survival rate. Such statistics were of a little consolation to Charlie, however. His fear of surgery had not abated since his appendectomy in 1907. Nor had his disdain for newfangled inventions and procedures. He agreed to go to Rochester only if Doc Edwin would accompany him and oversee every step of the ordeal. It would take the constant assurances of friends, he admitted, for him to summon "nerve to go up aganst the knife."[38]

Charlie, Nancy, and Edwin arrived in Rochester on June 29 and checked into the Kahler Hotel, where Mayo patients and their families stayed before and after surgery. Everywhere they looked — lobbies, sidewalks, restaurants — they saw people with gauze wrapped around their necks "where a woman's beads might rest." Charlie's mood did not improve in such company, and he grew edgier as the day of his surgery approached. To boost his morale, Nancy and Doc Edwin had him visit Jack Flannery, a smelter employee from Great Falls who had recently undergone a Mayo thyroidectomy. Charlie was impressed that Flannery was sitting up in bed the day after surgery. Nobody chose to tell Charlie that regardless of how a patient felt, he was made to sit up so that his incision could drain more easily.[39]

Charlie's surgery on July 3 was routine. It took Dr. William Plummer thirty-six minutes to remove a noncancerous goiter measuring four inches by four and a half inches. The only irregularity in the procedure was the presence of Doc Edwin in the operating room. The Mayo normally banned "osteopaths or other cultists" from its facilities, but because Charlie was deemed an "exceedingly nervous patient," Edwin was allowed to don a coat and mask and sit with a group of observing interns. Since Charlie's operation was done under a local anesthetic, which meant he was awake for much of the procedure, the Mayo felt that Edwin's calming presence was worth a breach in policy. "I took a local anasthic," Charlie wrote while convalescing. " '[L]ocal' means 'nearby' and it was so near by I dident miss much. The feeling wasent bad but my eres were tuned up till I could here a bug whisper and the nois of the nife was plane."[40]

The surgery, as it turned out, was the least of Charlie's worries. He came through it well, though slowly. As part of his preparation for the operation, he had undergone a battery of tests and examinations. Doctors learned, for instance, that Charlie had a hernia on his right side — which might explain why he had never given up wearing his sash. (He claimed it made him look slimmer; functioning as a truss, it undoubtedly did.)[41] The worst news, though, related to his heart and lungs. Blood tests, not to mention his history of smoking, indicated he probably had emphysema, and his enlarged heart indicated that he probably had suffered a heart attack at some previous date. Worse still, tests also detected "coronary sclerosis with myocardial degeneration."

In other words, Charlie's heart was shot. The Mayo doctors estimated he had only "a year or so" to live.[42]

One of the most commonly accepted Russell stories is that Charlie and Nancy learned of his life expectancy separately, and out of love and stoicism, each kept the information from the other.[43] But given the procedural discipline of the Mayo, this seems unlikely, and there is no documentation to support the account of mutual silence. More likely, Charlie and Nancy shared the grim prognosis and then chose not to discuss it.

Charlie, Nancy, and Doc Edwin left Rochester on July 16, just in time to hook up with the Columbia River Historical Expedition, the Great Northern's follow-up of the previous year's Upper Missouri excursion. In the cushioned company of railroad president Ralph Budd and other captains of industry, Charlie and Nancy were able, however briefly, to take their minds off the uncertain future. They left the expedition when it stopped in Great Falls two days later, choosing to skirt the brass band and the thousand expedition enthusiasts who crowded the train station. They spent only one night at Fourth Avenue North, departing the next day for Lake McDonald.[44]

≈

NANCY HAD TWO tasks that summer: to heal Charlie and to extract from him the work she had promised Harry Maule. She had Banty DeYong and Margaret and Josephine Trigg join her at Bull Head as nurses and comforters. She wrote letters to many of Charlie's old friends, urging them to cheer him up with get-well letters. And she wrote Maule on July 27 to report that "Mr. Russell is working on the stories and drawings . . . and that is all he will do until it is ready for publication. . . . [W]e will have the new manuscript ready . . . by the first part of Sept." She assured Maule that Charlie was "on the road to health again" and though he was "weak of body," his mind was "keen so the stories are growing as well as the illustrations for them."[45]

In August, Maule had a chance to find out for himself. In Montana for another horseback-riding vacation, he visited Charlie and Nancy at Bull Head Lodge. He was clearly upset to see Charlie so wan and helpless.[46] To complicate matters, the biggest forest fire in the history of Glacier National Park was bearing down on Lake McDonald. It eventually changed course before reaching Bull Head Lodge, but burned nearly a mile of lakefront just north of them. For most of August, smoke stung the eyes and clung to clothing. What had begun as a window of rest and recuperation had turned into a cloud of tension and deadline.

As soon as Maule returned to New York, he wrote Nancy, suggesting that they postpone the book until Charlie was in better shape. Nancy protested, insisting that the stories and illustrations were nearly done. And finally they were. Having closed up Bull Head for the season, Nancy wrote Maule from Great Falls to report that nine new stories were ready to be typed and that Charlie had completed fourteen full-page illustrations and thirty-five smaller drawings. Maule responded by sending a contract for the book. He liked the title Charlie and Nancy had suggested: *Trails Plowed Under*.[47]

Charlie had other unfinished business that fall. Philip Cole, his new, insatiable patron, had been pestering him all summer to send an illustrated letter. Unaware of Charlie's medical problems, Cole had written Nancy on July 1, complaining, "I am frankly much disappointed that Charley has not seen fit to send me the water color illustrated letter that was promised. I have received this courtesy from all of my other artists friends." Charlie finally got around to writing the letter on September 26. The illustration was of a group of elk set against a backdrop of mountains and fall foliage. In his letter, after describing the damage that horned animals could inflict on predators, Charlie concluded on a personal note: "Iv got no kick coming[.] Iv been trimed my self but the medicine men at Rochester onely took from me things I dident need and was glad to get rid of [.] I look and feel better but Im still very weak."[48]

Not so weak that he could not make it out to the studio. He had told Con Kelley, his hunting companion the year before, that he would do a painting to hang over the mantel at Kelley's hunting lodge. He was also plugging away on another one of his historical oils, *Father DeSmet's First Meeting with the Flathead Indians.*

In recent years, Charlie's painting had lost little of its authentic intent, but his palette had become increasingly romantic as he came under the influence of the commercial artist Maxfield Parrish. "Maxfield Parrish, I reckon, is my favorite painter," he had told a reporter as early as 1919. "I like his bright colors. My own colors are kind of stout."[49]

Parrish, who lived and worked in New Hampshire, was perhaps the most popular illustrator of his day.[50] His sweet images of gossamer-draped nymphs and smooth-cheeked fairy-tale characters appeared in *Century* and the *Ladies' Home Journal* and in ads for products ranging from tires to gelatin. It was a rare house that did not have a Parrish print on the wall. Charlie, like the rest of America, was taken by Parrish's rich blues, deep purples, and golden yellows, which enhanced the idyllic mood of the subject matter. A Parrish picture described a past that was pure and innocent — and contrasted dramatically with the raucous reality of the twentieth century. Defending Parrish from a Western perspective, Charlie commented: "Lots of people say he paints too vivid. Say, did you ever go out in these hills in Montana . . . in Indian summer, did you? Well, if you can see color you know there's not fine enough colors in the tubes to exaggerate them."[51]

Charlie was clearly echoing Parrish in his final painting for the Mackays, *Laugh Kills Lonesome.* Completed in 1925, it shows a group of cowpunchers circled around a campfire. Their saddles and gear are strewn about; the cook is cleaning pots at the chuck wagon; the stars are out and the moon is rising. Charlie — a much younger, nighthawking Charlie — stands at the edge of the firelight in boots, spurs, chaps, and slicker. His hat is pushed back so that his entire profile, like that of his cow-camp companions, is washed in bright orange light. If *Laugh Kills Lonesome* is a scene from memory, its colors are from a dream. The arcadian mood is what matters: The free range may have passed, but the feeling of freedom and friendship of those days can never be lost.

As Charlie was growing more sentimental, Nancy was becoming more practical. During the months leading up to Charlie's surgery and in the weeks of recovery, she had put on hold the plans for a new house in Pasadena. But once she and Charlie had left Lake McDonald and were contemplating another chilly Montana winter, her attention turned to California once again. The house, clearly influenced by Charles Lummis, was to have a Hopi feel, with stucco walls, exposed beams, flat roof, and protruding vigas. The living room would double as a gallery for Charlie's work. Their plan was to spend as many winters there as they had left. In the summers, Nancy's father could keep his eye on the place. On September 10, Nancy wrote the contractor, urging him to begin construction on Trail's End, the name they had chosen for the new house.[52]

Charlie approved of her decision. He had always known that he would die first, and he wanted her to lead a life of her choosing. He also went along with her plan for Great Falls: Three weeks after Nancy had initiated construction on the Pasadena house, she had a contractor begin expanding the log-cabin studio. The new room, twenty-eight by thirty-eight, would be the counterpart to the parlor gallery in Pasadena.

In her letter to the Pasadena contractor, Nancy acknowledged that Charlie was "not getting strong as fast as he thinks he should." By the end of October, he sensed that he was, if anything, getting weaker. His response was to reach out to those he cared about. He drew one more of his celebrated Christmas cards, this one of two cowpunchers passing a bottle of holiday cheer on a snowy trail. The accompanying toast, in Charlie's unimproved hand, was a reflection of his own grim straits:

> Heres hoping the worst end of your trail is behind you
> That Dad Time be your friend from here to the end
> And sickness nor sorrow dont find you.[53]

On Friday, October 22, Charlie ran into Ed Cooney, editor of the *Great Falls Leader,* on Central Avenue. Charlie asked after Horace Brewster, the roundup boss who had first hired him in the Judith Basin forty-four years earlier. Brewster had recently stayed with Cooney while visiting Great Falls. "Charley was much interested [in learning how the aging Brewster was faring] and, something unusual, thanked me very feelingly for having taken care of Horace while he was here," Cooney recalled. "He also expressed the wish that he could see Horace again, but didn't expect to."[54]

Charlie did something else noteworthy that day. He persuaded Cooney to accompany him around the corner to the studio of a promising but unknown young artist, Charles Beil. Beil had been a cowboy and guide, but had recently taken up sculpting full-time. Charlie urged Cooney to "kinder help him along." As they climbed the stairs to Beil's second-floor studio, Charlie had to stop and fight for breath. "The old pump ain't working," he reportedly confessed to Cooney between gasps. "I am weak as a cat, and the doctor says I can't even ride a horse." When Cooney asked Charlie how long before he might ride again, Charlie whispered, "Never. I have throwed my last leg over a saddle, the old pump is about to quit."

＞

TWO DAYS LATER, Sunday, October 24, the weather was sunny and crisp. Fall in Montana could be glorious — the hills golden, the sky and river bluer than at any other time of year. In the afternoon, Nancy bundled Charlie and Jack into the new Lincoln and had her young chauffeur, Ted Taylor, take them for a ride in the countryside.[55] Great Falls had changed greatly since they had arrived there in 1897. Horses no longer waited at the hitchracks on Central Avenue; saloons no longer served liquor; the most conspicuous landmark, visible from twenty miles away, was the five-hundred-foot-tall stack of the Boston & Montana smelter.

That night, Joe and Effie Thoroughman, ranching friends from near Cascade, came to Fourth Avenue North for supper. After the meal, Charlie took his customary glass of warm milk and went to bed. Sometime after 11 he awoke, complaining he could not breathe. Nancy rushed downstairs to the phone and called Doc Edwin, who lived eight blocks away. When Edwin arrived minutes later, he found Charlie sitting on the commode in the small bathroom at the top of the stairs. A froth of blood was on Charlie's lips, and as Edwin reached the landing, Charlie lunged forward into his arms. Edwin put the time of death at 11:30.

Doc Edwin was duty-bound to call the undertaker, but prevailed on the man not to contact the newspaper, which would have rushed the news into the Monday edition. Nancy wanted time to notify their closest friends. At daybreak, she woke ten-year-old Jack, who blessedly had slept through the night, and broke the news. "A terrible thing happened last night," she began. Then she went down the block to tell Josephine and Margaret Trigg.[56] By mid-morning, all of Great Falls knew of the death of Charlie Russell. By the end of the day, the entire country knew. Charles Marion Russell, the Cowboy Artist, was dead at sixty-two.

EPILOGUE

O N **TUESDAY, OCTOBER 26,** two days after Charlie's death, his casket lay in state in the parlor at 1219 Fourth Avenue North. Funeral and burial were scheduled for the following afternoon.

First came the telegrams of condolence — from the governor of Montana, William S. Hart, Will Rogers, and a mix of Charlie's wealthy patrons. Next came the letters. The least sentimental was from Dr. Plummer of the Mayo Clinic, who expressed his surprise at "the unfortunate termination in Mr. Russell's case." More typical notes leaned on worn Westernisms: hearts were "on the ground" at the news that Charlie had "crossed the Great Divide." The most ambitious letters sought to enthrone Charlie. "I can think of no man who has filled so large a niche as he in the world of art, and one equally large in the field of history," declared George Bird Grinnell. Joseph Henry Sharp concurred: "His pictures will remain a record of inestimable value and truth, when all future work of the kind will have to be done from hearsay, literature and photographs."

The task of rooting Charlie firmly in his times was left to Frank Linderman. "There can never be another Charley Russell for the same reason that there can never come another Abe Lincoln," Linderman wrote to Nancy. "American environment has been changed, and Ellis [I]sland, the blood-channel which is flowing into our country, has been to blame for many things besides crime-waves. The blood of the original stock is being bred out, and only where it still lives can there be any real appreciation of American ideals, or early American life."

If Linderman was trying to pay Charlie a high compliment, his message came across as harsh and ignoble when compared with the note from Young Boy, whose "original stock" was indisputable. "I am going to talk to you not to think so hard you wont be so lonesome you lost your husband," Young Boy wrote to Nancy. "[G]od made our life. [W]e cant live all the time. . . . [H]e was a good man every place. I sure think of him and feel sorry for him just like my own relation. [T]hats all I could tell you to day."[1]

The funeral at the Church of the Incarnation on Wednesday was packed. Alice Calvert, daughter of neighbors George and Minnie Calvert, sang "I Go Where You Want Me to Go." The Russells had always been Episcopalian, but even while Charlie had acknowledged his denominational heritage and enjoyed the company of Anglican ministers, he rarely darkened the doors of their sanctuaries. When one of his less-than-angelic friends did break down and attend, he accused him of "taking out fire insurance."[2]

Yet he was not without religion. Perhaps the best endorsement of Christianity can be found in his letter to "Brother Van," W. W. Van Orsdel, Montana's famed pioneer Methodist minister. "I have met you maney times . . . sometimes in lonely places," Charlie wrote on the occasion of Van Orsdel's birthday in 1918.

> [B]ut you never were lonsum ore alone, for a man with scar[r]ed hands and feet stood beside you and near Him there is no hate. . . . Be good and youl be happy is an old saying which many contradict and say goodniss is a rough trail over dangiros passes, with wind falls and swift, deep rivers to cross[.] I have never ridden it verry far myself, but judging from the looks of you, its a sinch bet that with a hoss called 'Faith' under you its a smooth, flower-grone trail with easy fords.[3]

The procession from the church to Highland Cemetery was signature Russell. Charlie had let it be known that he did not want to be carried to his grave in a "skunk wagon." But by 1926 there were no more horse-drawn hearses to be found in Great Falls. One had to be brought up from Cascade, and a pair of black horses were fitted to harness. To drive the hearse, Nancy chose Ed Vance, a friend with years of stagecoach experience. Charlie Beil, one of Charlie's newest friends, rode behind the hearse, leading a riderless horse that wore Charlie's saddle and bridle. As an added flourish, Charlie's Colt six-guns and holsters were strapped behind the cantle. Horace Brewster, Charlie's old roundup boss, rode alongside Beil. Completing the cortege was a long line of automobiles, at the front of which were Nancy and Jack in the chauffeured Lincoln.

The procession of horses and autos wound through downtown Great Falls. All schools, courtrooms, and city offices had closed for the afternoon, and thousands of solemn faces — children, old-timers, cowboys, Indians, merchants, smelter workers — lined the curbs. In its story the following day, the *Great Falls Tribune* contrived to find a bright spot in the dreary march: As the hearse eased out of town, "a cloud off to the north emitted a sprinkle of rain, through which the sun steadily shone. Then for a moment there was a rainbow, in late October!"

Highland Cemetery is located on a gentle rise two miles south of the city. Will Rogers had wired money and directions for a graveside flower arrangement shaped like a saddle. And when the mourners raised their heads from prayer, they gazed across a rolling prairie, golden brown according to the season. In the distance, east and south, they could make out the timbered Highwood and Little Belt mountains, two guardians of Charlie's Judith Basin.

NANCY BUCKED UP well in the days following Charlie's death. On November 19, four weeks after the funeral, she wrote Harry Maule, matter-of-factly advising him that the name on the *Trails Plowed Under* contract needed to be changed from Charlie's to hers.[4] On December 4, she sent Maule the stories and illustrations that Charlie had completed before his heart attack. Then she mailed the Christmas cards that Charlie had finished that fall. She and Jack were in California in time to spend the holidays with her father. From there she could oversee the completion of Trail's End and set up a January show in Santa Barbara, the first of a series of memorial exhibitions she was already planning.

Charlie's will, drafted in November 1924, was two sentences: "I Charles M Russell Do here by Devise and bequath all of my real and pursonal property to my wife Nancy C Russell[.] I am not providing for my Son Jack C Russell because I know my wife will provide for all his needs[.]" Charlie probably had no idea of his net worth at the time of his death, but he need not have worried. Nancy and Jack were well fixed, and Nancy had their financial affairs in hand. Aside from real estate and various investments, including stock in Parker-Russell, she had a sizable inventory of Charlie's paintings and sculpture in her possession. The list of forty-two oils and watercolors included *Roping Fresh Mounts, Bruin Not Bunny Turned the Leaders, Romance Makers,* and *When Mules Wear Diamonds;* she had multiples of at least a dozen bronzes. Her aim was to sell them — at posthumously high prices — through exhibitions and directly from the galleries she was establishing at Trail's End and the Great Falls studio.[5]

The imminent publication of *Trails Plowed Under* would be a big boost, a good start, in Nancy's campaign to preserve Charlie's reputation. In January, shortly after receiving Nancy's signature on the new contract, Harry Maule wrote to suggest that Owen Wister contribute an introduction to the book. Perturbed by Maule's choice of the dandified Easterner, Nancy lobbied hard for Will Rogers and soon got her way. "I always did say that [Charlie] could tell a story better than any man that ever lived," Rogers lauded in his rambling introduction.[6] The first copies rolled off the press on September 8.

Nancy had not waited for *Trails Plowed Under* to be published before undertaking a second book. In the spring of 1927, she hired Dan Conway, a young writer for the Montana Newspaper Association, to prepare a biography of Charlie. She had Conway up to Lake McDonald for the summer, and by the first of October he had completed a draft, titled "A Child of the Frontier." Nancy paid Conway $780 and sent the manuscript off to Maule at Doubleday.[7]

Maule wasted little time in turning down the book; Scribner's and at least one other house also rejected it. It offered too much sentiment, not enough substance. Nancy was disappointed; worse, for years she had to put up with Conway's incessant hounding, as he became increasingly paranoid and volatile with each new rejection. Nancy would have liked to dismiss him from her life, but Conway had wangled his way onto the committee organized to turn the Great Falls studio into a museum. (Years later, when Conway turned up on the streets of Los Angeles, Nancy refused his appeal for a handout. He died nearly destitute.)[8]

Meantime, Nancy was making a new life for herself in Pasadena. After the autumn of 1926, she and Jack spent little time in Great Falls. It was no longer home. They continued to spend summers at Lake McDonald, but after the collapse of her health and a spate of burglaries at Bull Head, they quit coming north entirely after 1935. In Pasadena, they were scarcely ever alone. James Cooper and his brother Lafayette lived next door. Late in life, Nancy's father had married Julia Johnson, one of Nancy's housekeeper-babysitters. The extended family also included thirty-eight-year-old Ted Taylor. He had driven Nancy and Jack to California in December 1926, but with Charlie gone, he became much more than a chauffeur. Taylor pitched in on the construction of Trail's End and lived in the garage apartment behind the house for long stretches. Rumors persist that he and Nancy became lovers. In October 1938, after Taylor fell off the roof of his garage on Flathead Lake and broke his neck, Nancy wrote to William S. Hart, "I have lost one of the strongest, kindest friends and I feel so weak and helpless."9

Likewise, gossipmongers have speculated that Nancy had a twilight romance with Hart. Evidence of this is even more circumstantial. It is true that Hart kept a photo of Nancy in the bedroom of his ranch house in Saugus, California, and they did write, phone, and visit frequently. But those who knew Hart well describe him as a gentleman bachelor who lived quite primly with his sister throughout his retirement years.10 He and Nancy could not have been more than loyal friends. For one thing, by 1935 Nancy was no spry bird. That was the year of her first heart attack. She recovered fairly well, only to suffer a stroke in 1937. From then on, she was often in a wheelchair or bedridden, dependent on nurses and housekeepers, though still active in her correspondence and art dealings.

Ted Taylor and Bill Hart stood by her through the bad times. Jack, however, was not the comfort that she and Charlie had hoped he would be. Nancy looked at her adopted son and saw a stranger. Naturally, he did not resemble Charlie; he was dark-haired with big feet and had mushroomed into a lean six-footer by the age of eighteen. He had no interest in art; he preferred cars and electrical gadgets. If he had anything in common with his father, it was a dislike of classrooms and a taste for liquor. He was in and out of boarding schools and lasted only one year at the University of Southern California. He married young, joined the Army, and never looked back. After military service, he chose a career in highway construction and spent more than twenty years building freeways across the California desert — his own legacy to the West. Jack Cooper Russell eventually retired to a trailer park in Oceanside, south of Los Angeles. His memories of his father, never voluminous, grew dim with age. Nancy had given him one of Charlie's paintings as a wedding present, but he sold it a couple of years later. It was the only original of his father's work that he ever owned.[11]

If Jack was not Charlie's artistic heir, there were others who were eager to take his place. Joe DeYong was attending art school in Santa Barbara at the time of Charlie's death and never quite forgave himself for missing the funeral. Thereafter, he saw it as his bounden duty to repay Charlie for the decade of special attention he had given him. DeYong designated himself guardian of Russell's sacred image, leaving the role of promoter to Nancy. DeYong always vowed that he would one day write his own book about Charlie, but never did. Instead, he hoarded his notes and memories and tried to dissuade others from undertaking the story.[12]

One of the most frequent targets of DeYong's protectionism was the Great Falls artist Olaf Seltzer. The spirit of the West, and his exposure to Charlie Russell, inspired Seltzer, a Danish immigrant, to strive to be more than a railroad worker. His machinist hands made him an excellent draftsman, but precision could take him only so far. Seltzer painted hundreds of Western portraits and scenes, though he had no cow-camp or hunting-trail experiences to work from or old rawhide chums to stir his imagination. Dozens of his paintings and drawings, in fact, were direct copies of Russell compositions, without much narrative zest.

Seltzer nonetheless enjoyed a certain amount of prominence. After Charlie's death, Philip Cole latched onto Seltzer as the next best thing. In the late 1920s and early 1930s, Cole bought nearly everything Seltzer painted, ultimately commissioning portraits of eighty-five "Western Characters." (The collection is now preserved at the Gilcrease Museum in Tulsa.) For his part, Seltzer did not hesitate to cast himself as Charlie's understudy. Charlie, no doubt, had been flattered by the earnest sycophancy of the young Dane and had given Seltzer occasional pointers. Seltzer later led the public to believe that he and Charlie were inseparable buddies who had spent days, even weeks, together in a free exchange of their mutual genius.

Joe DeYong had a different story to tell. DeYong considered Seltzer a drunken "blow hard," maintaining that under Philip Cole's patronage, Seltzer had become a "keg-carrying, artistic St. Bernard." DeYong resented the fact that Seltzer's work hung alongside Charlie's in Great Falls saloons and forever refuted the claim that Charlie and Seltzer had been close friends. On the contrary, DeYong asserted that Seltzer had not been above taking the occasional shot at Charlie's back. When Charlie returned from his trip to Europe in 1914, DeYong recalled, Seltzer was "so ruffled" by Charlie's success that he refused to speak to him on the street. Charlie, in turn, was taken aback. "I don't care if [Seltzer] copies my pictures," he purportedly said, "but I do wish he'd treat me decent."[13]

Nancy, too, was wary of Seltzer, and her mistrust only intensified after Charlie's death. She wished good things for DeYong, but did not want any of Charlie's light to illuminate Seltzer's career. The ultimate transgression came in 1928, when Philip Cole hired Seltzer to put the finishing touches on the incomplete *Father DeSmet's First Meeting with the Flathead Indians*. Nancy was livid, but had to choose her words of protest carefully. Cole was still a good customer; she could not afford to alienate him. "I feel when anybody puts a brush with paint on it on that canvas it is not Charlie's any longer," she wrote to Cole. "I feel you will be damaging and lessening the value of your picture — but Gee whiz I can't tell you for sure as it may be just my own feelings." Seltzer had no such qualms and was quick to please Cole by touching up *Father DeSmet* and several other Russell paintings. Charlie had been "a worthy, though not faultless artist," Selzter told a scholar some years later.

Throughout the 1930s, Nancy found herself more and more at the mercy of the market. To succeed, she taught herself to invoke Charlie's charm even while she was stoically minding the store. The most extraordinary example of her new (and awkward) role was her relationship with New York collector George Sack.

Sack was keen to collect one of every Russell bronze, as well as a representative group of paintings. Apparently he considered the bronzes as something more than art; Sack truly believed that he was able to reach Charlie's ghost through his collection. Half of Sack's letters to Nancy in 1929 were business discussions of availability, price, delivery; the other half were transcriptions of conversations that Sack and his wife had had with Charlie during evening seances. "He asked me to give you and Jack his love, & he is trying to get in communication with you," Sack wrote in March. "Won't you give him the chance, Nancy?" As with Cole, Nancy had to endure these powerful tugs on her widow's emotions while keeping her eye on the prize. "I'm always happy to know you are in communication with Charlie," she wrote back to Sack. Then, as deftly as a tea-party hostess, she changed the subject: "Now, regarding 'The Waterhole' . . ."[14]

Nancy held her ground more confidently when it came to dealing with the people of Great Falls. The city had never quite lived up to Paris Gibson's prophecy that it would reach a half-million population and exceed the industrial clout of St. Paul. The 1920s and 1930s hit Montana hard, and Great Falls was not exempt. Many of the blocks platted by Gibson for residential development at the turn of the century remained prairie thirty years later. In search of a new image, Electric City looked to its most famous citizen and, by extension, to his widow. The city council briefly considered changing the name of the city's main street from Central Avenue to Russell Avenue. The chamber of commerce formed a committee (with Dan Conway aboard) to turn the Russell studio into a museum and tourist attraction. Nancy's stiff posture toward the project spoke volumes about her relationship with Great Falls. She generously sold Charlie's studio to the city for one dollar, but would not turn the property over until the Charles M. Russell Memorial Committee had raised $20,000 to buy the house and land around it. The money was raised — the gifts ranging from Will Rogers's $500 to fifty cents from an Indian, Joe Bull Shoe — and the city took over the property in August 1928.[15]

Nancy's nature worked against her on at least two occasions. After the debacle of the Conway biography, she played with the idea of converting the flawed manuscript into her own memoir. Doubleday instead steered her to compile a collection of Charlie's illustrated letters; it was accompanied by a nine-page "Biographical Note" from Nancy and a second Will Rogers introduction.[16] Nancy had cast her net wide and employed every inveiglement in her arsenal. Still, *Good Medicine* went to press in 1929 with Charlie's letters to Frank Linderman, Sid Willis, and Bill Rance conspicuously absent. They owed Nancy no particular favors.

Her other confrontation came in 1931. The Montana Legislature had voted to place a statue of Charlie in the National Statuary Hall in the Capitol in Washington, D.C. Nancy had initially welcomed the submission of a model by Great Falls neighbor Jesse Lincoln Mitchell, but when more discerning friends declared Mitchell's likeness of Charlie too "weak" and "crumbling," Nancy put her foot down. She coaxed letters of protest from every important person she could think of. As a result, the statue project came to a screeching halt. Not until 1959 did a seven-foot bronze by Jack Weaver of Butte finally join George Washington, Thomas Jefferson, Sam Houston, Robert E. Lee, Brigham Young, William Jennings Bryan, and Will Rogers in the national hall. Charlie Russell is the only artist in the lot.[17]

Nancy did not live long enough to see the statue installed. Nor was she alive in 1952 to witness the sale of the extensive "Mint collection" of Russell art to Texas millionaire Amon Carter or the purchase that same year of the almost-as-fabulous "Mackay collection" by the Montana Historical Society. Many Russellophiles viewed the Carter deal as a crime against the state, a plundering of Montana's crown jewels. The Mackay family's low asking price of $50,000 made it possible for Montana to claim at least one substantial collection of Russell art. With Josephine Trigg's bequest of her private collection (she died in 1951) and the subsequent opening of a new gallery next to Charlie's log-cabin studio, his visual legacy to his adopted state was ensured.[18]

꒜

NANCY RUSSELL DIED on May 24, 1940, after another stroke and kidney failure. She was sixty-one years old. Her last years had been a struggle: Her inventory of art had dwindled; Jack had moved away; she was a virtual invalid. She continued to work on her memoir right up to the end, but it was too much, too late. She kept up with her friends — Bill Hart, Joe DeYong, James Bollinger, Malcolm and Helen Mackay — and they helped her through the hard times of national and personal depression. Most everyone who visited Nancy at Trail's End in the late 1930s remarked on how dignified she was, even when propped up in her wheelchair and nagged by nurses.

Occasionally, though, she lifted her veil of stoicism. Fred Barton, an old friend of Charlie's, recalled a visit to Pasadena shortly before she died. Nancy dismissed her nurse, leaned forward in her wheelchair, and, according to Barton, said, "I want to tell you something private." She then commenced to overflow with guilt and regret. "I know now that I ruined the last years of Charlie's life," Barton recalls her confessing. "We had plenty, but I always wanted more and drove him to make more, keeping him from idling with the friends he enjoyed. Now for three years I have been using up everything we made. . . . Life for me is torture and I made Charlie's life a torture."[19]

She was being too hard on herself. There is no question that she loved him, and he her. She had been the agent of his success; she had taken care of him. "Mrs. Russell you deserve credit," Teddy Blue Abbott consoled. "[Y]ou saved Charlie."[20]

If there had been pain in their marriage, it is not clear who had inflicted it first. Above all, Nancy had regretted not being able to give Charlie children and blamed herself. The cause of her infertility, according to a routine autopsy conducted by Huntington Memorial Hospital in Pasadena, was "bilateral salpingitis with pelvic adhesions." Today this is known as pelvic inflammatory disease, the leading cause of which is gonorrhea. Had Nancy been infected as a teenager when she was running with the "wrong crowd" in Helena? Had Charlie picked up a dose during his sporting days and passed it on to Nancy? The answer will never be known. But the likelihood that they shared this venereal disease — and endured its penalty — explains much about the private dynamic behind their outward lives. Indeed, the temptation to review their entire marriage through this pathological lens is almost overwhelming. Was Charlie's obedience to Nancy his way of atoning? Was her commitment to his career a form of compensation for an irreversible error of youth?

Speculation works as a bridge over gaps in knowledge, but as a foundation, it is unstable. The goal of this chronicle has been to establish — in some cases, reestablish — the facts of Charlie Russell's life and to set them in useful context. But after all is said and done, no one will ever know the real Russell again. His true identity died with him, leaving only glimpses, moments, memories. Even Charlie, who considered himself a scrupulous documentarian, knew that re-creating the past completely and objectively was a shaky proposition.

On May 20, 1927, seven months after Russell's death, another Charles — Charles Lindbergh — set out across the Atlantic aboard the *Spirit of St. Louis*. The aviator had eclipsed the cowboy as the new Lochinvar. Five months later, on October 6, 1927, Americans began lining up to see their first talking picture, *The Jazz Singer*, starring Al Jolson. The culture of storytelling had changed forever. But somehow Charlie Russell's story has endured, myth acting as a natural preservative, his paintings and sculpture as talismanic artifacts. "[C]inch your saddle on romance," Charlie once advised Frank Linderman, employing yet another of his hooved metaphors. "[H]es a high headed hoss with plenty of blemishes but keep him moovin an theres fiew that can call the leg he limps on and most folks like prancers."[21] Charlie Russell was one part St. Louis thoroughbred, one part Montana bronc. More than that, he was one of the world's marvelous prancers.

NOTES

Abbreviations Used in the Notes

AB	Ramon F. Adams and Homer E. Britzman, *Charles M. Russell, the Cowboy Artist: A Biography* (Pasadena: Trail's End Publishing, 1948). Trail's End Publishing was owned by Britzman, the collector who purchased NCR's house and much of its contents after her death.
AR	Austin Russell, *C.M.R.: Charles M. Russell, Cowboy Artist* (New York: Twayne Publishers, 1956)
BBHC	Buffalo Bill Historical Center, Cody, Wyoming
BC-CSFAC	Helen E. and Homer E. Britzman Collection, Taylor Museum for Southwestern Studies of the Colorado Springs Fine Arts Center
CMR	Charles M. Russell
CMRM	Charles M. Russell Museum Archives, Great Falls, Montana
FBL	Frank Bird Linderman
FBL-RCR	Frank Bird Linderman, *Recollections of Charley Russell* (Norman: University of Oklahoma Press, 1963)
FBL-UM	Frank Bird Linderman Collection, K. Ross Toole Archives, University of Montana, Missoula
GFT	*Great Falls Tribune*
JBR	James Brownlee Rankin
JBR-MHS	James Brownlee Rankin Research Collection, Montana Historical Society, Helena. From 1936 till 1940, JBR conducted scores of interviews

and wrote and received hundreds of letters with the aim of compiling a CMR biography and catalogue raisonné. He never completed his project.

JDY   Joe DeYong

JDY-NCHF   Joe DeYong Collection, National Cowboy Hall of Fame and Western Heritage Center, Oklahoma City

JFD   J. Frank Dobie

JFD-UT   J. Frank Dobie Collection, Harry Ransom Humanities Research Center, University of Texas, Austin

MHS   Montana Historical Society Archives, Helena

MMWH   *Montana: The Magazine of Western History*

NCR   Nancy Cooper Russell

NCR-MS   Nancy Cooper Russell, unpublished typescript and manuscript, BC-CSFAC (unfinished biography of CMR begun in 1928)

TPU   Charles M. Russell, *Trails Plowed Under* (Garden City, N.Y.: Doubleday, Page, 1927)

WP   Brian W. Dippie, ed., *Charles M. Russell, Word Painter: Letters 1887–1926* (Fort Worth and New York: Amon Carter Museum and Harry N. Abrams, 1993)

[1]
INTRODUCTION

1. NCR to Malcolm Mackay, August 6, 1926, BC-CSFAC; *Superintendent's Annual Report,* 1926, George C. Ruhle Library, Glacier National Park, 1; Alan S. Newell, project director, "Historic Resources Study, Glacier National Park, and Historic Structures Study," 1975, George C. Ruhle Library, Glacier National Park.

2. C. W. Buchholtz, *Man in Glacier* (West Glacier, Mont.: Glacier National History Association, 1976), and Warren L. Hanna, *Montana's Many-Splendored Glacierland* (Grand Forks: University of North Dakota Foundation, 1987).

3. NCR-MS.

4. NCR to Malcolm Mackay, August 6, 1926, BC-CSFAC; CMR's medical records are summarized in a letter written to Jack Russell by Dr. R. M. Tucker of the Mayo Clinic, September 24, 1973, copy in possession of the author.

5. Jack Russell, interview by the author, Oceanside, California, January 20, 1993.

6. Harry Maule to NCR, April 17, 1926, BC-CSFAC; NCR to JDY, May 20, 1926, BC-CSFAC; NCR to Maule, May 28, 1926, BC-CSFAC.

7. AR, 208.

8. NCR to Maule, October 8, 1926, BC-CSFAC.

9. TPU, xix–xx.

10. John Riddell, "Last of His Line," *Vanity Fair* 29:4 (December 1927), 146.

11. Indeed, there is no catalogue raisonné of Russell's work. Ginger Renner of Paradise Valley, Arizona, who has undertaken an inventory of known Russell artwork, told the author in 1993 that the total might be closer to three thousand.

12. CMR to Josephine Trigg, verse accompanying clay sculpture *Romance,* n.d., CMRM.

[2]
ST. LOUIS

1. James Neal Primm, *Lion of the Valley: St. Louis, Missouri,* 2nd ed. (Boulder, Colo.: Pruett Publishing Co., 1990); William Barnaby Faherty, *St. Louis: A Concise History* (St. Louis: Masonry Institute of St. Louis, 1989).

2. Bernard DeVoto, *Across the Wide Missouri* (Boston: Houghton Mifflin, 1947); Stanley Vestal, *The Missouri* (New York: Farrar & Rinehart, 1945).

3. Mary Joan Boyer, *The Old Gravois Coal Diggings* (Festus, Mo.: Tri-City Independent, 1954); Lyle S. Woodcock, "The St. Louis Heritage of Charles Marion Russell," *Gateway Heritage* 2:4 (Spring 1982), 2–15; William Hyde and Howard L. Conrad, eds., *Encyclopedia of the History of St. Louis* (St. Louis: Southern History Co., 1899); Lyle S. Woodcock and George Ward Parker, interviews by the author, St. Louis, April 20–21, 1993.

4. David Lavender, *Bent's Fort* (Garden City, N.Y.: Doubleday, 1954); Allen H. Bent, *The Bent Family in America* (Boston: David Clapp & Son, 1900).

5. Deborah J. Binder, *St. Louis Silversmiths* (St. Louis: St. Louis Art Museum, 1980); Ruth Hunter Roach, *St. Louis Silversmiths* (St. Louis: self-published, 1967).

6. AR, 15.

7. *St. Louis Post-Dispatch,* February 16, 1910.

8. Susan Portis to NCR, n.d., BC-CSFAC.

9. CMR to Albert J. Trigg, November 10, 1903, in WP, 56–58.

10. William Barnaby Faherty, *Henry Shaw: His Life and Legacies* (Columbia: University of Missouri Press, 1987).

11. Basil Rudd, "Idol of the Cowboys: Russell of Montana, Master Painter of the Old West," unpublished typescript, 1954, copy in possession of the author, 11.

12. AR, 34.

13. NCR-MS.

14. AR, 28.

15. Philip Durham, "Dime Novels," introduction to *Seth Jones,* by Edward S. Ellis, and *Deadwood Dick on Deck,* by Edward L. Wheeler, ed. Philip Durham (1860, 1878; reprint, 2 vols. in 1, New York: Bobbs-Merrill, 1966), vi; Christine Bold, *Selling*

the Wild West: Popular Fiction, 1860 to 1960 (Bloomington: Indiana University Press, 1987), 10–11.

16. NCR-MS; TPU, 177. (*Rawhide Rawlins* and *More Rawhides* materials are cited throughout as TPU, which contains all but one of the stories first printed in the *Rawhide* collections.)

17. Captain Mayne Reid, *The Boy Hunters; or, Adventures in Search of a White Buffalo* (New York: Thomas R. Knox & Co., 1885, reprint), 16–17.

18. Harry Castlemon, *Frank on the Prairie* (Philadelphia: John C. Winston Co., 1893, reprint), 15–16, 24, 27.

19. Woodcock, "The St. Louis Heritage of Charles Marion Russell."

20. "The Ghost Horse," TPU, 91.

21. Mrs. T. R. Thorn to JBR, December 6, 1937, JBR-MHS; AB, 16–17.

22. Archie Douglass to NCR, July 8, 1929, JBR-MHS.

23. Mary Lovey Wood, *Language Disorders in School-Age Children* (Englewood Cliffs, N.J.: Prentice-Hall, 1982).

24. JDY, "Charlie and Me . . . We Run Together Fine," *Persimmon Hill* 11:3/4 (1982), 75.

25. NCR to C. H. Clapp, September 20, 1922, BC-CSFAC.

26. R. D. Warden, *C. M. Russell Boyhood Sketchbook* (Bozeman, Mont.: Treasure Products, 1972).

27. Susan Portis to NCR, n.d., BC-CSFAC; Mab Mulkey, "History of the St. Louis School of Fine Arts, 1879–1909," master's thesis, Washington University, May 1944, 8–9; *St. Louis Republic,* October 3, 1876.

28. Rick Stewart et al., *Carl Wimar: Chronicler of the Missouri Frontier* (Fort Worth and New York: Amon Carter Museum and Harry N. Abrams, 1991); Brian W. Dippie, "Two Artists from St. Louis: The Wimar-Russell Connection," in *Charles M. Russell: American Artist* (St. Louis: Jefferson National Expansion Historical Association, 1982); AR, 40–41.

29. Donelson F. Hoopes, *The Düsseldorf Academy and the Americans* (Atlanta: High Museum of Art, 1972).

30. CMR to Charles Reymershoffer, August 23, 1907, Missouri Historical Society Archives; CMR to JDY, studio note, n.d., JDY-NCHF.

31. *St. Louis Star,* March 12, 1910; Susan Portis to NCR, n.d., BC-CSFAC.

32. Mulkey, "History of the St. Louis School of Fine Arts," 31; Kathryne Wilson, "An Artist of the Plains," *Pacific Monthly* 12:6 (December 1904), 343.

33. Archie Douglass to NCR, July 8, 1929, JBR-MHS.

34. NCR-MS; Harold McCracken, *The Charles M. Russell Book* (Garden City, N.Y.: Doubleday, 1957), 27.

[3]
MONTANA

1. *Travelers Official Guide of the Railway and Steam Navigation Lines in the United States and Canada* (Philadelphia: National Railway Publication Co., March 1880). There is a possibility that he took a slightly different route — perhaps the Missouri Pacific to Kansas City, connecting with the Kansas Pacific, and then boarding the Union Pacific at Denver; or he could have taken the Atchison & Northern from Kansas City to the Union Pacific at Columbus, Nebraska. But the most direct, and by far the most convenient, route was the Wabash, St. Louis & Pacific, direct to the Union Pacific at Omaha.

2. Miller did not last long in the Judith Basin. By 1883 he had leased his ranch, and by March 1884 had sold it and left Montana. The Minneapolis city directory for 1885 lists him clerking in a hardware store there.

3. Merrill G. Burlingame, *The Montana Frontier* (Helena: State Publishing Co., 1942); Joseph Kinsey Howard, *Montana: High, Wide, and Handsome* (New Haven, Conn.: Yale University Press, 1943); Michael P. Malone, Richard B. Roeder, and William L. Lang, *Montana: A History of Two Centuries* (Seattle: University of Washington Press, 1976); K. Ross Toole, *Montana: An Uncommon Land* (Norman: University of Oklahoma Press, 1959).

4. AR, 45.

5. NCR-MS; NCR, "Biographical Note," introduction to Charles M. Russell, *Good Medicine* (Garden City, N.Y.: Doubleday, 1929), 16; AR, 48–49.

6. Quoted in Al J. Noyes, *In the Land of Chinook* (Helena: State Publishing Co., 1917), 119.

7. JBR, notes of interview with William Wallace, n.d., JBR-MHS.

8. NCR-MS.

9. Gary E. Moulton, ed., *The Journals of the Lewis & Clark Expedition,* vol. 4 (Lincoln: University of Nebraska Press, 1987), 215–20.

10. John C. Ewers, *The Blackfeet: Raiders on the Northwestern Plains* (Norman: University of Oklahoma Press, 1958).

11. Col. William D. Pickett, *Forest and Stream,* Feb. 1, 1908, 168–69, typescript in MHS; Stephen M. Voynick, *Yogo: The Great American Sapphire* (Missoula, Mont.: Mountain Press Publishing Co., 1985), 10–11.

12. Paul C. Phillips, *Forty Years on the Frontier: The Reminiscences and Journals of Granville Stuart,* vol. 2 (Cleveland: Arthur H. Clark, 1925), reprinted as Stuart, *Pioneering in Montana: The Making of a State, 1864–1887* (Lincoln: University of Nebraska Press, 1977).

13. Interview with John H. Newton et al., January 11, 1941, Montana Writers' Project, United States Work Projects Administration, MHS.

14. *Butte Inter Mountain,* January 1, 1903.

15. Unidentified newspaper clipping, 1903, BC-CSFAC. According to Dan R. Conway ("A Child of the Frontier," unpublished typescript, 1927, MHS), Monte's price was $90.

16. Reid, *Boy Hunters,* 36–37.

17. John R. Barrows, *Ubet: A Greenhorn in Montana* (Caldwell, Idaho: Caxton Printers, 1934), 49; Barrows to JBR, April 20, 1938, JBR-MHS; E. P. Chandler, May 10, 1887, quoted in Anna Zellick, "A History of Fergus County, Montana, 1879–1915," master's thesis, University of Chicago, 1945.

18. Lyle Woodcock, interview by the author, April 21, 1993; Laura Edgar Whittemore to JBR, March 14, 1938, JBR-MHS.

19. CMR, "A Slice of Charley Russell's Early Life," *Roundup Annual* (yearbook of Great Falls High School), June 1919, 48–49.

20. Jake Hoover, interview transcription, October 10, 1924, Montana Pioneers Collection, MHS; Montana Newspaper Association Insert, March 7, 1921.

21. Ibid. A grub-line rider moved from place to place, cadging free meals.

22. JDY, "Modest Son of the Old West," MMWH 8:4 (Fall 1958), 92.

23. FBL-RCR, 104.

24. AR, 56–57.

25. NCR-MS; FBL-RCR, 18–22.

26. John Barrows to JBR, March 9, 1938, JBR-MHS; JDY, unpublished manuscript, JDY-NCHE.

27. James W. Bollinger to JBR, September 30, 1938, JBR-MHS.

28. Anna Williams Lee to JBR, July 15, 1937, JBR-MHS.

29. Laura Edgar Whittemore to JBR, March 14 and 31, August 17, September 12, 1938, JBR-MHS.

30. JDY, "Modest Son of the Old West," 92; Mrs. Charles A. Belden to Don A. Myrick, Stanford, Mont., April 5, 1940, Montana Writers' Project, United States Work Projects Administration, MHS.

31. Sarah Glasgow Willcockson, interview by the author, Webster Groves, Missouri, April 22, 1993. Photos of "the Club" and the diary of Club regular Nellie Miller Glasgow are in the private collection of Mrs. Willcockson, who is the granddaughter of Nellie Glasgow.

32. CMR, *Good Medicine,* vii.

[4]
"LAST OF FIVE THOUSAND"

1. Account book, J. D. Weatherwax Store, Utica, Montana, CMRM.

2. NCR, "Biographical Note," *Good Medicine,* 18; AB, 49.

3. CMR to Harry T. Duckett, July 1901, transcript in BC-CSFAC; original partially reproduced in WP, 44.

4. *Butte Inter Mountain,* January 1, 1903.

5. Boyer, *Old Gravois Coal Diggings,* 18; AR, 59. Several independent sources corroborate CMR's story, putting the date of Fulkerson's death as spring 1882. However, Boyer asserts that the year was 1883; likewise, a notation in a Fulkerson family Bible in the possession of Ward Parker of St. Louis states that "James W. Fulkerson died in Billings, Montana May 28, 1883."

6. *Butte Inter Mountain,* January 1, 1903.

7. Brian W. Sindelar, interview by the author, Judith Basin, Montana, June 10, 1993; Robert L. Ross et al., "Soil and Vegetation Inventory of Near-Pristine Sites in Montana," U.S. Department of Agriculture, Soil Conservation Service, Bozeman, Montana, July 1973.

8. Con Price, *Memories of Old Montana* (Pasadena, Calif.: Trail's End Publishing Co., 1945), 103.

9. James S. Brisbin, *Beef Bonanza; or, How to Get Rich on the Plains* (Philadelphia: Lippincott, 1880), 15.

10. John Clay, *My Life on the Range* (Chicago: privately printed, 1924), 13, 74, 131.

11. *Great Falls Leader,* October 27, 1926.

12. JDY to NCR, August 15, 1927, BC-CSFAC.

13. Ross Santee, *Lost Pony Tracks* (New York: Scribner's, 1953), 167.

14. Belknap "Ballie" Buck to JBR, March 27, 1938, JBR-MHS; C. J. Ellis to JBR, August 16, 1938, JBR-MHS.

15. E. C. "Teddy Blue" Abbott and Helena Huntington Smith, *We Pointed Them North: Recollections of a Cowpuncher* (New York: Farrar & Rinehart, 1939), 191.

16. John Barrows to JBR, April 20, 1938, JBR-MHS.

17. *Great Falls Leader,* October 27, 1926.

18. C. J. Ellis to JBR, August 16, 1938, JBR-MHS.

19. Joseph Kinsey Howard, *Strange Empire; A Narrative of the Northwest* (New York: Morrow, 1952).

20. C. J. Ellis to JBR, August 16, 1938, JBR-MHS; John Barrows to JBR, March 21, 1938, JBR-MHS.

21. C. J. Ellis to JBR, August 16, 1938, JBR-MHS.

22. Al Andrews to JBR, August 15, 1938, JBR-MHS; Frank "Doc" Nelson to JBR, June 2, 1937, JBR-MHS.

23. E. C. "Teddy Blue" Abbott to NCR, January 3, 1937, BC-CSFAC; John Barrows to JBR, October 24, 1938, JBR-MHS.

24. John Barrows to JBR, June 12, 1938, JBR-MHS; JDY, "Modest Son of the Old West," 96.

25. Eliza Walker to JBR, December 17, 1936, JBR-MHS; Laura Edgar Whittemore to JBR, March 14, 1938, JBR-MHS.

26. AB, 65; Eliza Carr Young to JBR, n.d., JBR-MHS.

27. Frederic G. Renner, *Charles M. Russell; Paintings, Drawings, and Sculpture in the*

Amon Carter Museum (Austin: University of Texas Press, for the Amon Carter Museum, 1966), 21; Brian W. Dippie, *Remington & Russell* (Austin: University of Texas Press, 1982), 60; AB, 84.

28. Renner, *Charles M. Russell*, 47; Rick Stewart, *Charles M. Russell: Masterpieces from the Amon Carter Museum* (Fort Worth, Tex.: Amon Carter Museum, 1992), 10.

29. Theodore Roosevelt, *Ranch Life and the Hunting-Trail* (New York: Century, 1888), 21–22.

30. Howard, *Montana: High, Wide, and Handsome*, 156; Burlingame, *Montana Frontier*, 283.

31. Abbott and Smith, *We Pointed Them North*, 143; Abbott to NCR, August 15, 1930, BC-CSFAC.

32. H. P. Brooks to Thomas C. Power, May 23, 1886, Thomas C. Power Papers, MHS, quoted in Barbara Fifer Rackley, "The Hard Winter, 1886–1887," MMWH 21:1 (Winter 1971), 54; Robert S. Fletcher, "That Hard Winter in Montana, 1886–1887," *Agricultural History* 4:4 (October 1930); Howard, *Montana: High, Wide, and Handsome*, 157–63.

33. Lincoln A. Lang, *Ranching with Roosevelt* (Philadelphia: Lippincott, 1926), 239–42; Abbott and Smith, *We Pointed Them North*, 175; Howard, *Montana: High, Wide, and Handsome*, 157; *Yellowstone Journal and Live Stock Reporter*, November 20, 1886, quoted in Leland E. Stuart, "The Winter of 1886–1887 — The Last of Whose 5,000?" MMWH 38:1 (Winter 1888), 34.

34. Abbott and Smith, *We Pointed Them North*, 176.

35. Henry Bierman, "From Butcher Boy to Buffalo Hunter; Excerpts from the Unpublished Journals of Henry Bierman," MMWH 11:1 (Winter 1961), 48; H. P. Kennett to Samuel T. Hauser, January 29, 1887, S. T. Hauser Papers, Montana Historical Society Archives, quoted in Rackley, "The Hard Winter, 1886–1887," 56.

36. Abbott and Smith, *We Pointed Them North*, 176.

37. TPU, 159.

38. Clay, *My Life on the Range*, 80, 116.

39. AB, 75–76. CMR gave a very similar rendition to GFT on December 21, 1902; see also Wallis Huidekoper, "The Story Behind Charlie Russell's Masterpiece: 'Waiting for a Chinook,' " MMWH 4:3 (Summer 1954); (Helena) *Montana Record-Herald*, July 12, 1939.

40. I. F. "Finch" David to Bill Arnold, n.d., *The Bill Arnold Collection of the Works of Charles M. Russell* (Austin: Pemberton Press, 1965).

41. AB, 76.

42. Wallace Stegner, *Wolf Willow: A History, a Story, and a Memory of the Last Plains Frontier* (New York: Viking Press, 1962), 222; Burlingame, *Montana Frontier*, 284; Howard, *Montana: High, Wide, and Handsome*, 160.

43. Abbott and Smith, *We Pointed Them North*, 184.

[5]
CANADA AND BACK

1. Stuart, *Pioneering in Montana*, 237.

2. TPU, 15.

3. Stewart, *Charles M. Russell*, 12.

4. *Helena Weekly Independent,* May 5, June 16, 1887.

5. *Helena Weekly Herald,* May 26, 1887, 7.

6. Walter Lehman to JBR, February 9, 1939, JBR-MHS.

7. TPU, 31.

8. TPU, 55–56.

9. Barrows to JBR, October 24, 1938, JBR-MHS.

10. W. H. Hutchinson to JFD, November 7, 1956, JFD-UT; Coburn F. Maddox to JBR, March 5, 1937, JFD-UT.

11. Allis Stuart to JBR, April 4, 1937, JBR-MHS.

12. Paula Petrik, "Capitalists with Rooms: Prostitution in Helena, Montana, 1865–1900," MMWH 31:2 (Spring 1981), 28–41; Rex C. Myers, "An Evening of Sin: Chicago Jo and Her Hurdy Gurdy Girls," MMWH 27:2 (Spring 1977), 24–33.

13. AR, 62.

14. Phil Weinard to JBR, October 3, 1938, JBR-MHS; WP, 388.

15. Phil Weinard to JBR, January 4, 1938, JBR-MHS.

16. Noyes, *In the Land of Chinook,* 121.

17. Brian W. Dippie, *The Vanishing American: White Attitudes and U.S. Indian Policy* (Middletown, Conn.: Wesleyan University Press, 1982); Dippie, "The Moving Finger Writes: Western Art and the Dynamics of Change," in Jules David Prown et al., *Discovered Lands, Invented Pasts: Transforming Visions of the American West* (New Haven, Conn.: Yale University Press, 1992), 89–115; Alex Nemerov, "Doing the 'Old America': The Image of the American West, 1880–1920," in William Truettner, ed., *The West as America: Reinterpreting Images of the Frontier, 1820–1920* (Washington, D.C.: Smithsonian Institution Press for the National Museum of American Art, *1991),* 285–343.

18. Brian W. Dippie, *Catlin and His Contemporaries: The Politics of Patronage* (Lincoln: University of Nebraska Press, 1990); William H. Goetzmann and William N. Goetzmann, *The West of the Imagination* (New York: Norton, 1986).

19. George de Forest Brush, "An Artist Among the Indians," *Century Magazine* 30:1 (May 1885), 55.

20. Peggy Samuels and Harold Samuels, *Frederic Remington: A Biography* (Garden City, N.Y.: Doubleday, 1982). Blackfeet refers to tribal members living in the United States. The Blackfoot are Canadian.

21. Phil Weinard to JBR, February 14, 1938.

22. Phil Weinard to JBR, January 4, 1938, JBR-MHS.

23. Hugh A. Dempsey, "Tracking C. M. Russell in Canada, 1888–1889," MMWH 39:3 (Summer 1989), 2–15.

24. AB, 95.

25. CMR to Charles M. Joys, May 10, 1892, in WP, 25.

26. Con Price to JFD, August 9, 1946, BC-CSFAC.

27. B. J. Stillwell to CMR, February 8, 1915, CMRM.

28. Nellie Miller Glasgow diary, private collection of Sarah Glasgow Willcockson, Webster Groves, Missouri.

29. GFT, December 19, 1954.

30. Samuels and Samuels, *Frederic Remington.*

31. Brian W. Dippie, *Looking at Russell* (Fort Worth, Tex.: Amon Carter Museum, 1987); Peter H. Hassrick, *Charles M. Russell* (New York: Harry N. Abrams, in association with the National Museum of American Art, Smithsonian Institution, 1989), 32–33.

32. *Fergus County Argus,* May 23, 1889.

33. Mildred Taurman et al., *Utica, Montana* (Stanford, Mont.: Judith Basin Press, 1968), 203; I. F. "Finch" David to JBR, February 3, 1937, JBR-MHS; patent records, U.S. Bureau of Land Management Archives, Billings, Montana; AR, 77–78.

34. Huidekoper, "The Story Behind Charlie Russell's Masterpiece," 38.

35. Charles Hallock, "Notes from Montana," *Nature's Realm* 2:4 (April 18, 1891), 151.

36. CMR to William W. "Pony Bill" Davis, May 14, 1889, in WP, 16–17.

37. Wilford J. Johnson to JBR, April 20, 1937, JBR-MHS; AB, 113.

38. John Barrows to JBR, October 24, 1938, JBR-MHS.

39. *Butte Inter Mountain,* January 1, 1903; AR, 82.

40. (Fort Benton) *River Press,* November 30, 1892; Noyes, *In the Land of Chinook,* 123–26.

41. CMR to Edward "Kid" Price, June 1, 1917, in WP, 235–36.

42. AB, 126.

43. Abbott and Smith, *We Pointed Them North,* 145.

44. CMR to Edward C. "Teddy Blue" Abbott, May 13, 1919, in WP, 279–80.

[6]

THE WHITE CITY

1. CMR to Albert J. Trigg, February 24, 1916, in WP, 225; TPU, 5.

2. Alan Trachtenberg, *The Incorporation of America: Culture and Society in the Gilded Age* (New York: Hill and Wang, 1982); Dave Walter, *Today Then: America's Best Minds Look 100 Years into the Future on the Occasion of the 1893 World's Columbian*

Exposition (Helena: American & World Geographic Publishing, 1992); William Cronon, *Nature's Metropolis: Chicago and the Great West* (New York: Norton, 1991), 341–56; Carolyn Kinder Carr et al., *Revisiting the White City: American Art and the 1893 World's Fair* (Washington, D.C.: Smithsonian Institution, 1993).

3. Hamlin Garland, *A Son of the Middle Border* (New York: P. F. Collier & Son, 1914; reprinted Macmillan, 1924), 460.

4. Herbert Bancroft, *The Book of the Fair*, vol. 5 (Chicago: Bancroft Co., 1893), 830.

5. David C. Huntington, *The Quest for Unity: American Art Between World's Fairs, 1876–1893* (Detroit: Detroit Institute of Art, 1983), 13.

6. A. E. Ives, "Talks with Artists: Mr. Childe Hassam on Painting Street Scenes," *Art Amateur* 27 (October 1892), 116, quoted in H. Barbara Weinberg et al., *American Impressionism and Realism: The Painting of Modern Life, 1885–1915* (New York: Metropolitan Museum of Art, 1994), 4.

7. Peggy Samuels and Harold Samuels, *Samuels' Encyclopedia of Artists of the American West* (1976; reprint, Secaucus, N.J.: Castle, 1985), 77.

8. Ray Allen Billington, *Frederick Jackson Turner: Historian, Scholar, Teacher* (New York: Oxford University Press, 1973), 108–31; Frederick Jackson Turner, *The Frontier in American History* (1920; reprint, Tucson: University of Arizona Press, 1986).

9. Richard Slotkin, *Gunfighter Nation: The Myth of the Frontier in Twentieth-Century America* (New York: Atheneum, 1992), 63–87; Don Russell, *The Lives and Legends of Buffalo Bill* (Norman: University of Oklahoma Press, 1960); Joseph Rosa and Robin May, *Buffalo Bill and His Wild West* (Lawrence: University of Kansas Press, 1989).

10. CMR to Percy Raban, May 3, 1907, in WP, 86.

11. Renner, *Charles M. Russell*, 22.

12. *Helena Weekly Herald*, January 11, 1894.

13. Howard Mumford Jones, *The Age of Energy: Varieties of American Experience, 1865–1915* (New York: Viking Press, 1970); Arthur M. Schlesinger, *The Rise of the City, 1878–1898* (New York: Macmillan, 1933); T. J. Jackson Lears, *No Place of Grace: Antimodernism and the Transformation of American Culture, 1880–1920* (New York: Pantheon Books, 1981); Robert H. Wiebe, *The Search for Order, 1877–1920* (New York: Hill and Wang, 1967).

14. Quoted in Billington, *Frederick Jackson Turner*, 110.

15. Quoted in Roderick Nash, ed., *The Call of the Wild (1900–1916)* (New York: George Braziller, 1970), 83.

16. Ben Merchant Zorpahl, *My Dear Wister: The Frederic Remington–Owen Wister Letters* (Palo Alto, Calif.: American West Publishing Co., 1973); Robert Murray Davis, ed., *Owen Wister's West: Selected Articles* (Albuquerque: University of New Mexico Press, 1987).

17. Lela Roberts to Marguerite Greenfield, affidavit in Charles Diggs Greenfield,

Jr., Family Papers, MHS. CMR was not one to save correspondence, even from his mother. But NCR, who came into his life in 1895, saved everything. Even so, the estate papers, which survive today as the Britzman Collection (BC-CSFAC), include only a handful of letters from Russell family members in St. Louis. This is surprising, considering how devoted CMR's family was to him. Unfortunately, there is little hope that any of the meager correspondence from CMR to family members in the 1880s and 1890s will ever surface.

18. Barrows's remarks are knit together from three separate letters to JBR: January 3, 1934, April 3 and 20, 1938, JBR-MHS.

19. AR, 84.

20. Conway, "Child of the Frontier."

21. "Historical Art Exhibition of Works by St. Louis Artists of the Last 50 Years," 1895, MHS.

22. Dippie, *Looking at Russell,* 7.

23. Larry Barsness, *The Bison in Art: A Graphic Chronicle of the American Bison* (Flagstaff, Ariz.: Northland Press in cooperation with the Amon Carter Museum, 1977); Dippie, *Looking at Russell,* 54–55.

24. CMR, studio note, JDY-NCHE

25. NCR-MS.

[7]
NANCY

1. Joan Stauffer, *Behind Every Man: The Story of Nancy Cooper Russell* (Tulsa: Daljo Publishing, 1990).

2. NCR to Josephine Trigg, August 28, 1936, CMRM.

3. WP, 29; JBR to Daisy Rankin, July 24, 1937, JBR-MHS; JFD, notes of interview with Mrs. Charles L. Sheridan, July 27, 1947, JFD-UT.

4. Arthur T. "Punk" Ward, "Montana Reminiscences," oral history recording, MHS.

5. JFD, notes of interview with Mrs. Charles L. Sheridan (née Hebe Roberts), July 27, 1947, JFD-UT.

6. McCracken, *The Charles M. Russell Book,* 167.

7. Fred Barton to JFD, July 5, 1963, JFD-UT.

8. Frederic G. Renner, "Rangeland Rembrandt: The Incomparable Charles M. Russell," MMMW 7:4 (Autumn 1957), 25.

9. Clarence J. Rowe, ed., *Mountains and Meadows: A Pioneer History of Cascade, Chestnut Valley, Hardy, St. Peter's Mission, and Castner Falls, 1805 to 1925* (self-published, 1970), 170; *Cascade County Directory and Register, 1896–1897* (Great Falls, Mont.: W. T. Ridgley, 1896).

10. JFD, notes of interview with Mrs. Charles Sheridan, July 27, 1947, JFD-UT.

11. AB, 135.

12. NCR-MS.

13. Ibid.

14. AB, 135.

15. CMR to NCR, August 20, 22, 1896, in WP, 29, 30.

16. AR, 87.

17. NCR medical records, Huntington Memorial Hospital, Pasadena, April 15, 1937, copy in possession of the author.

18. NCR-MS. Chivareeing is the tradition of pestering newlyweds with serenades and lighthearted pranks.

19. GFT, September 9, 1896.

20. CMR to Ed Borein, c. July 1921, in WP, 316; TPU, 135.

21. AB, 137; NCR-MS.

22. Wedding-present tags and cards, BC-CSFAC; NCR-MS.

23. NCR-MS.

24. Ibid.

25. CMR, "Early Days on the Buffalo Range," *Recreation* 6:2 (April 1897), 231.

26. Receipt, D. Appleton & Co., BC-CSFAC.

27. William Bleasdell Cameron, "The Old West Lives Through Russell's Brush," *Canadian Cattlemen* 13:1 (January 1950), 11.

28. Ibid.

29. William Bleasdell Cameron, "Russell's Oils Eye-Opener to the East," *Canadian Cattlemen* 13:2 (February 1950), 26.

30. McCracken, *The Charles M. Russell Book,* 182.

31. AR, 91.

32. NCR-MS.

33. Dippie, *Remington & Russell,* 102.

34. AR, 209.

35. NCR-MS.

36. Ibid.

37. *New York Telegram,* March 11, 1925.

38. Partially identified clipping, BC-CSFAC.

[8]
GREAT FALLS

1. Quoted in William J. Furdell and Elizabeth Lane, *Great Falls: A Pictorial History* (Norfolk, Va.: Donning, 1984), 24.

2. Moulton, ed., *Journals of the Lewis & Clark Expedition,* vol. 4, 284.

3. Richard B. Roeder, "Paris Gibson and the Building of Great Falls," MMWH 42:4 (Autumn 1992); W. Thomas White, "Paris Gibson, James J. Hill & the 'New Minneapolis,' " MMWH 33:3 (Summer 1983); William H. Bertsche, Jr., *The Building of a City* (Great Falls: Dufresne Foundation, n.d.); Paris Gibson, *The Founding of Great Falls, Montana, and Some of Its Early Records* (Great Falls, n.p., 1914), 7.

4. C. M. Webster, "Great Falls of Yesterday," *Montana Illustrated,* March 1895, 8.

5. H. B. Mitchell, ed., *Reclamation Edition of the Great Falls Leader* (Great Falls: Leader Co., 1907), 1; C. K. Cunningham, ed., *Gazetteer to the City of Great Falls and Neihart and Barker, Montana for 1892* (Great Falls, Mont.: Industrial Printing Co., 1892), 40–41.

6. Walt Coburn, *Western Word Wrangler: An Autobiography* (Flagstaff, Ariz.: Northland Press, 1973), 17–18. Walt Coburn is Wallace Coburn's half-brother.

7. Ellan R. Yuill, *A Centennial Celebration* (Great Falls: self-published, 1984), 143–84.

8. Ethel Calvert and Joe Wolff, interviews by the author, Great Falls, June 17, 18, 1993.

9. JDY, unpublished manuscript, n.d., JDY-NCHF.

10. AR, 147–49; JDY to Mary DeYong, c. 1917, JDY-NCHF; FBL-RCR, 13; NCR-MS.

11. The two-finger admonition is one of the most universally accepted CMR stories; see AB, 150; McCracken, *The Charles M. Russell Book,* 181; Renner, *Charles M. Russell,* 25. It has even been immortalized in "The Gift," a song about CMR written and recorded by Ian Tyson (Slick Fork Music, 1986).

12. Stewart, *Charles M. Russell: Masterpieces,* 26; Hassrick, *Charles M. Russell,* 66.

13. JDY, unpublished typescript, n.d., JDY-NCHF.

14. GFT, July 4, 1932.

15. Paul T. Devore, "Saloon Entrepreneurs of Russell's Art and the Pilgrimage of One Collection," MMWH 27:4 (Autumn 1977), 34–53; GFT, September 4, 1955, November 8, 1935; JDY, "Charlie and Me," 78.

16. GFT, April 12, 1987.

17. Carter V. Rubottom, "I Knew Charles M. Russell," MMWH 4:1 (Winter 1954), 19; Santee, *Lost Pony Tracks,* 168.

18. JDY to Mary "Banty" DeYong, January 27, 1918, JDY-NCHF; Dawson's Book Shop (Los Angeles), catalogue 152, February 1941; inventory of books in CMR studio, typescript, n.d., CMRM.

19. Wallace D. Coburn, *Rhymes from a Round-up Camp* (Great Falls: W. T. Ridgley Press, 1899).

20. Unidentified newspaper clipping, BC-CSFAC.

21. AR, 91.

22. NCR-MS.

23. C. S. Russell to William Macbeth, November 17, December 9, 1898,

January 16, March 6 and 8, August 21, 1899, Macbeth Gallery Correspondence, Archives of American Art, Smithsonian Institution.

24. C. S. Russell to NCR, November 15 and 27, December 15 and 19, 1899, BC-CSFAC.

25. NCR-MS.

26. GFT, August 30, 1900.

27. *Helena Independent,* May 13, 1901, reprinted from *St. Louis Post-Dispatch,* n.d.; AR, 91.

28. AR, 92.

29. Reprinted in *Helena Independent,* May 13, 1901.

30. Forest Crossen, *Western Yesterdays: Charlie Russell — Friend* (Fort Collins, Colo.: Robinson Press, 1973), 74.

31. AR, 103.

32. NCR, introduction to *Good Medicine,* 23.

33. JDY, unpublished manuscript, n.d., JDY-NCHF.

34. NCR, introduction to *Good Medicine,* 23.

35. *The Log Cabin Studio of Charles M. Russell, Montana's Cowboy Artist* (Great Falls, Mont.: Russell Memorial Committee, n.d.).

36. JDY, unpublished manuscript, n.d., JDY-NCHF.

37. GFT, March 1, 1914; JDY, unpublished manuscript, n.d., JDY-NCHF; JFD, notes of interview with Mrs. Roy Waller (née Norma Linderman), July 12, 1954, JFD-UT.

38. CMR to JDY, Joe DeYong–C. M. Russell Notes, Flood Permanent Collection, CMRM; JDY, unpublished manuscript, n.d., JDY-NCHF; John Young-Hunter, *Reviewing the Years* (New York: Crown, 1963), 81.

39. JDY, unpublished manuscript, n.d., JDY-NCHF; approximate text published in JDY, "Charlie and Me," 80.

40. Wallace Stegner, "Finding the Place," in Clarus Backes, ed., *Growing Up Western: Recollections* (New York: Knopf, 1990), 174.

41. L. E. Falk to JBR, March 6, 1937, JBR-MHS.

42. NCR, introduction to *Good Medicine,* 24.

43. CMR to Great Falls Elks Club, in WP, 260–61.

44. Helen M. Clark, "Johnny Matheson — Freighter, Philosopher," *Montana Parade,* GFT, July 31, 1960, 3–5, 12; NCR-MS. The jerkline was a means of controlling a team of twelve to twenty horses by means of a single, continuous rein attached to the bit of the lead horse.

45. Larry Burt, "Nowhere to Go: Montana's Crees, Métis, and Chippewas and the Creation of Rocky Boy's Reservation," *Great Plains Quarterly* 7 (Summer 1987), 195–209; Verne Dusenberry, "The Rocky Boy Indians: Montana's Displaced Persons," Montana Heritage Series No. 3, MHS, 1954; Celeste River, "A Mountain in His Memory: Frank Bird Linderman, His Role in Acquiring the Rocky Boy Indian

Reservation for the Montana Chippewa and Cree, and the Importance of That Experience in the Development of His Literary Career," master's thesis, University of Montana, 1990; Thomas R. Wessel, *A History of the Rocky Boy's Indian Reservation* (Bozeman, Mont.: self-published, 1975).

46. GFT, October 27, 1926; unidentified newspaper clipping, BC-CSFAC. On a visit in August 1903, Sumner Matteson reported Monte "still on the premises and well taken care of" (Matteson, "Charles M. Russell, the Cowboy Artist," *Leslie's Weekly,* March 3, 1904, 204).

47. William S. Hart, *My Life East and West* (Boston: Houghton Mifflin, 1929); Kevin Brownlow, *The War, the West, and the Wilderness* (New York: Knopf, 1979), 263–74; George N. Fenin and William K. Everson, *The Western: From Silents to the Seventies* (New York: Penguin Books, 1977, revised edition), 75–78, 104–07; Kalton Lahue, *Winners of the West: The Sagebrush Heroes of the Silent Screen* (New York: A. S. Barnes, 1970), 148–58; John Tuska, *The Filming of the West* (Garden City, N.Y.: Doubleday, 1976), 81–86, 115–22.

48. William S. Hart to CMR, February 26, 1902, BC-CSFAC.

49. CMR to William S. Hart, in WP, 53–54.

50. William S. Hart to CMR, July 23, 1902, BC-CSFAC.

51. Owen Wister, "Preface — An Introduction," c. 1929, reprinted in Wister, *The Virginian: A Horseman of the Plains* (New York: Penguin Books, 1988), xxxvii.

52. Forrest Fenn, *The Beat of the Drum and the Whoop of the Dance: A Study of the Life and Work of Joseph Henry Sharp* (Santa Fe, N.M.: Fenn Publishing Co., 1983); James D. Horan, *The Life and Art of Charles Schreyvogel* (New York: Crown, 1969), 23.

53. Reprinted in *Denver Times,* July 13, 1902.

54. William Macbeth to NCR, October, December 19, 1902, BC-CSFAC.

55. Matteson, "Charles M. Russell, the Cowboy Artist," 204.

56. NCR to William Macbeth, March 7, 1903, Macbeth Gallery Correspondence, Archives of American Art, Washington, D.C.; NCR to Charles Kurtz, March 7, 1903, Richardson Memorial Library Archives, St. Louis Art Museum.

57. Charles Kurtz to NCR, March 12, 1903, ibid.

58. Antoinette Spanos Johnson, *Vision of the West: The Art of Will Crawford* (Birmingham, Ala.: Birmingham Museum of Art, 1986); Lila Marchand Houston to JBR, December 4, 1936, JBR-MHS; Homer E. Britzman to JBR, March 22, 1939, BC-CSFAC; GFT, October 9, 1903.

[9]

TALL TEPEES

1. Primm, *Lion of the Valley,* 357; Dorothy Daniels Birk, *The World Came to St. Louis: A Visit to the 1904 World's Fair* (St. Louis: Bethany Press, 1979), 13.

2. Primm, *Lion of the Valley,* 367–84; Alexander Scot McConachie, "The 'Big Cinch': A Business Elite in the Life of a City, Saint Louis, 1895–1915," Ph.D. dissertation, Washington University, 1976, 1–9.

3. David R. Francis, *The Universal Exposition of 1904* (St. Louis: Louisiana Purchase Exposition Co., 1913), 71, 401; Lyle S. Woodcock, "Charles M. Russell and His St. Louis Heritage," transcript of speech presented to C. M. Russell Auction, Great Falls, March 26, 1982, Missouri Historical Society.

4. NCR to Halsey C. Ives, November 5, 1903, Louisiana Purchase Exposition Archives, St. Louis Art Museum; *World's Fair Bulletin* 5:2 (December 1903), 7.

5. Entry form, St. Louis World's Fair of 1904, Louisiana Purchase Exposition Archives, St. Louis Art Museum.

6. "Cowboy Artist Who Has Lived Among the Indians for Twenty-Three Years Will Exhibit Studies at the World's Fair," *St. Louis Post-Dispatch Magazine,* December 6, 1903.

7. Stewart, *Charles M. Russell, Sculptor,* 32. Karl Theodore Bitter, "Sculpture for the St. Louis World's Fair," 165–83; Robert T. Paine, "How the Sculpture Is Enlarged," 184–89; "List of Sculpture Commissions — A Record," 191–98; Lorado Taft, "Sculptors of the World's Fair," 199–236; "Casting of Bronze Statuary," 237–39. All in *Brush and Pencil* 13:3 (December 1903).

8. CMR to Albert J. Trigg, November 10, 1903, in WP, 56.

9. "Cowboy Artist Is Now in St. Louis," *St. Louis Star Sunday Illustrated Magazine,* December 27, 1903; John W. Leonard, ed., *The Book of St. Louisans* (St. Louis: St. Louis Republic, 1906), 500; Primm, *Lion of the Valley,* 400–01.

10. CMR to William H. Rance, December 17, 1903, in WP, 63–64.

11. AR, 109.

12. *Helena Independent,* May 13, 1901, reprinted from *St. Louis Post-Dispatch.*

13. NCR to CMR, n.d., BC-CSFAC.

14. AR, 111.

15. GFT, October 9, 1903.

16. Conway, "Child of the Frontier"; FBL-RCR, 69; Lila Marchand Houston to JBR, December 4, 1936, JBR-MHS. The $12 rate is estimated from receipts later in the year (BC-CSFAC).

17. Susan E. Meyer, *America's Great Illustrators* (New York: Harry N. Abrams, 1978), 8–37; Frank Luther Mott, *A History of American Magazines, 1885–1904,* vol. 4 (Cambridge, Mass.: Belknap Press, 1957), 1–11.

18. Quoted in Homer Saint-Gaudens, *The American Artist and His Times* (New York: Dodd, Mead, 1941), 162–63.

19. Meyer, *America's Great Illustrators,* 211–31; Arthur Lubow, *The Reporter Who Would Be King: A Biography of Richard Harding Davis* (New York: Scribner's, 1992), 127.

20. Samuels and Samuels, *Frederic Remington,* 249–50; Lubow, *Reporter Who Would Be King,* 142–44.

21. GFT, February 16, 1904; Lila Marchand Houston to JBR, December 4, 1936, JBR-MHS; Raymond Wemmlinger et al., *Edwin Booth's Legacy: Treasures from the Hampden-Booth Theatre Collection at The Players* (New York: Hampden-Booth Theatre Library, 1989), 57.

22. William S. Hart to NCR, January 22, 1929, Seaver Center for Western History Research, Natural History Museum of Los Angeles County.

23. Hart, *My Life East and West,* 347.

24. Ibid., 348.

25. GFT, February 16, 1904; Conway, "Child of the Frontier"; FBL-RCR, 70; Homer E. Britzman to JBR, March 22, 1939, JBR-MHS; CMR to JDY, studio note, n.d., Flood Permanent Collection, CMRM; Johnson, *Vision of the West,* 14; AR, 97. CMR even hung a Crawford drawing in his house (JDY to Branson Stevenson, September 3, 1967, CMRM).

26. C. Wellington Furlong to JBR, May 7, 1938, JBR-MHS.

27. GFT, February 16, 1904.

28. Ibid.

29. Horan, *Life and Art of Charles Schreyvogel.*

30. Samuels and Samuels, *Frederic Remington,* 301, 314, 341–44, 416; Horan, 31–40.

31. *New York Herald,* April 28, 1903.

32. Calling card, Jack "Doc" Sahr Collection, MHS.

33. AR, 95–96; McCracken, *The Charles M. Russell Book,* 192; Joseph Keppler to JBR, April 17, 1939, JBR-MHS; JDY, "Modest Son of the Old West," 95–96; GFT, February 16, 1904; Renner, "Rangeland Rembrandt," 24.

34. GFT, February 16, 1904.

35. C. S. Russell to Halsey C. Ives, March 15, 1904; Ives to C. S. Russell, March 22, 1904, Louisiana Purchase Exposition Archives, St. Louis Art Museum.

36. John Marchand to CMR, April 8, 1904, BC-CSFAC.

37. Walter Parker to CMR, May 9, 1904, BC-CSFAC; L. R. Myers to CMR, February 20, 1905, Jack "Doc" Sahr Collection, MHS.

38. John A. Sleicher to NCR, September 16, 1904; invoice, September 3, 1904, Jack "Doc" Sahr Collection, MHS.

39. NCR to H. Behrens, October 14, 1904, BC-CSFAC.

40. Birk, *The World Came to St. Louis;* Francis, *The Universal Exposition of 1904;* Mark Bennitt, ed., *History of the Louisiana Purchase Exposition* (St. Louis: Universal Exposition Publishing Co., 1905).

41. Ben Yagoda, *Will Rogers: A Biography* (New York: Knopf, 1993), 70–81.

42. CMR to Albert J. Trigg, January 29, 1905, in WP, 65.

43. Transcription of speech, *Contributions to the Historical Society of Montana,* vol. 5 (1904), 103.

44. Stewart, *Charles M. Russell, Sculptor,* 36–37; "The Roman Bronze Works Collection," Guernsey's auction catalogue, New York, September 17, 1988.

45. CMR to Albert J. Trigg, January 29, 1905, in WP, 65.

[1 0]

BULL HEAD AND BUFFALO

1. *New York Evening World,* February 2, 1921; Helen Raynor Mackay, "Charles M. Russell," *The Cattlemen* 35:10 (March 1949), 33–34; Samuels and Samuels, *Frederic Remington,* 357–58; *Helena Independent,* March 18, 1905.

2. McCracken, *The Charles M. Russell Book,* 195–96; *Butte Evening News,* n.d., clipping in BC-CSFAC; Stewart, *Charles M. Russell, Sculptor,* 52; Samuels and Samuels, *Frederic Remington,* 358.

3. *Helena Independent,* March 18, 1905; Theodore Roosevelt to CMR, December 14, 1904, BC-CSFAC.

4. Stanley R. Davison, "The Author Was a Lady," MMWH 12:2 (Spring 1973), 2–15; Noyes, *In the Land of Chinook,* 121; B. M. Bower to JBR, May 28, 1937, JBR-MHS.

5. B. M. Bower to JBR, May 17, 1937, JBR-MHS; B. M. Bower to Ella Ironside, July 25, 1924, Jean Ironside Papers, MHS.

6. W. T. Ridgley to CMR and NCR, January 9, 1905, October 23, 1906, BC-CSFAC.

7. WP, 72.

8. Genevieve Walsh Gudger, May 6, 1951, quoted in Leona Harrington, ed., "History of Apgar," unpublished collection of letters, George C. Ruhle Library, Glacier National Park.

9. Marcus J. Gruber, January 5, 1957, in Harrington, "History of Apgar"; Michael J. Ober, "Enmity and Alliance: Park Service–Concessioner Relations in Glacier National Park, 1892–1961," master's thesis, University of Montana, 1973, 17.

10. WP, 72.

11. Fergus Mead to JBR, August 5, 1938, JBR-MHS.

12. Sally Hatfield (granddaughter of Frank Linderman), interview by the author, Flathead Lake, Montana, June 27, 1993; Philip R. Goodwin to his mother, August 2, 1907, Philip R. Goodwin Collection, Harold McCracken Library, BBHC; CMR to Philip R. Goodwin, May 26, 1908, in WP, 98–100; Philip R. Goodwin to CMR, July 14, 1908, in Patricia Johnston, "In Search of Philip Goodwin," *Persimmon Hill* 8 (1988), 53.

13. CMR to Robert J. Benn, August 15, 1908, in WP, 104; NCR-MS.

14. CMR to Edgar I. Holland, September 4, 1908, in WP, 106.

15. Agreement between CMR and Con Price, January 1, 1906, BC-CSFAC.

16. (Mexico City) *Daily Record,* March 24, 1906.

17. Clee Woods, "The World's Greatest Cattleman," *True Magazine,* December 1944, 38–41, 86.

18. CMR to JDY, studio note, n.d., JDY-NCHF.

19. CMR to Robert Stuart, January 16, 1907, in WP, 78.

20. *St. Louis Post-Dispatch,* February 16, 1910.

21. Walter Lehman to JBR, November 25, 1936, JBR-MHS; McCracken, *The Charles M. Russell Book,* 95, 204–05.

22. NCR to C. W. Lawrence, October 4, 1907, BC-CSFAC.

23. Price, *Memories of Old Montana,* 148.

24. CMR to William H. Rance, April 7, 1912, in WP, 166.

25. AR, 150.

26. WP, 93.

27. CMR to Philip R. Goodwin, May 26, 1908, in WP, 98.

28. Agreement between Brown & Bigelow and CMR, May 1, 1908, BC-CSFAC.

29. Hubert H. Bigelow to NCR, April 25, 1908, BC-CSFAC.

30. WP, 95; Alvin J. Schmidt, *Fraternal Organizations* (Westport, Conn.: Greenwood Press, 1980), 100–01.

31. Fergus Mead to JBR, August 5, 1938, JBR-MHS; Austin Russell to JDY, February 25, 1956, JDY-NCHF; AR, 118, 133.

32. Tom McHugh, *The Time of the Buffalo* (New York: Knopf, 1972), 16–17; "Montana Has the World's Largest Buffalo Herd," *Anaconda Standard,* October 23, 1904; John Kidder, "Montana Miracle: It Saved the Buffalo," MMWH 15:2 (Spring 1965), 52–67; David A. Dary, *The Buffalo Book: The Full Saga of the American Animal* (Chicago: Swallow Press, 1974), 222–25; Jim Jennings, *Qua Quei, or How the Buffalo Were Saved* (St. Ignatius, Mont.: Mission Valley News, 1974); Velma R. Kvale, *Where the Buffalo Roamed* (St. Ignatius, Mont.: Mission Valley News, 1976); Paul Fugleberg, *Buffalo Savers: The Story of the Allard-Pablo Herd* (Polson, Mont.: Treasure State Publishing, 1991); Newton Mactavish, "The Last Great Round-Up," two parts, *The Canadian Magazine,* vol. 33 (October and November 1909), 6, 7; Sumner Matteson, "Doom of Extinction Averted from the American Bison," *Leslie's Weekly,* February 27, 1908; M. O. Hammond, diary, April 30–June 14, 1909, MHS.

33. GFT, March 1, 1914, 4.

34. *Dillon Tribune,* n.d., clipping in MHS.

35. Mactavish, "Last Great Round-Up," November 1909, 26.

36. CMR to Philip R. Goodwin, January 1909, in WP, 112–13.

37. GFT, March 1, 1914.

38. CMR to Philip R. Goodwin, January 1909, in WP, 112–13.

39. Mactavish, "The Last Great Round-Up," November 1909, 33.

40. GFT, September 8, 1909; CMR to Philip R. Goodwin, September 7, 1909, in WP, 120; John H. Raftery, "Art in Montana," *Treasure State,* October 10, 1908, 4.

41. CMR to Howard Douglas, January 12, 1910, in WP, 128; CMR to Con Price, January 1910, in WP, 127.

42. Samuels and Samuels, *Frederic Remington,* 438.

43. Ibid., 418.

44. *St. Louis Star,* March 12, 1910.

45. *St. Louis Republic,* March 6, 1910.

46. *St. Louis Post-Dispatch,* February 16, 1910; *St. Louis Star,* March 12, 1910.

47. *St. Louis Republic,* March 6, 1910.

48. Harold G. Davidson, *Edward Borein, Cowboy Artist: The Life and Works of John Edward Borein, 1872–1945* (Garden City, N.Y.: Doubleday, 1974).

49. Ibid., 63, 82; Frederic G. Renner, *Paper Talk: Illustrated Letters of Charles M. Russell* (Fort Worth, Tex.: Amon Carter Museum, 1962), 72.

50. Leo Carrillo, *The California I Love* (Englewood Cliffs, N.J.: Prentice-Hall, 1961), 236–38.

51. Donald Day, *Will Rogers: A Biography* (New York: David McKay, 1962); Yagoda, *Will Rogers.*

52. Quoted in CMR, *Good Medicine,* 11.

53. Agreement with Brown & Bigelow, May 1, 1908, BC-CSFAC; Auguste Beste to NCR, July 23, 1910, BC-CSFAC.

[1 1]
"THE WEST THAT HAS PASSED"

1. This price is a guess. The Niedringhaus catalogue of 1910 listed *The Medicine Man* at $900; Nancy surely raised the asking price in New York; *New York Evening Globe,* April 13, 1911.

2. CMR to Willis Sharpe Kilmer, April 24, 1911, in WP, 152.

3. *New York Evening World,* April 15, 1911.

4. *New York Evening Globe,* April 13, 1911; the *St. Louis Post-Dispatch,* March 13, 1910, preceded Hoeber, remarking that "Russell is stronger at modeling than he is at painting."

5. *New York Times,* March 19, 1911.

6. Ibid., April 23, 1911.

7. CMR to William H. Rance, May 23, 1911, in WP, 155; unidentified newspaper clipping, BC-CSFAC; invitation, Roman Exposition, April 22, 1911, BC-CSFAC.

8. Gov. Edwin L. Norris to NCR, June 22, 1911, CMR Microfilm, MHS; AR, 226–27; contract with State of Montana, July 24, 1911, BC-CSFAC.

9. GFT, November 16, 1911.

10. Gov. Edwin L. Norris to CMR, November 9, 1911, CMR Microfilm, MHS.

11. Moulton, *Journals of the Lewis & Clark Expedition,* vol. 5, 187.

12. CMR to Philip R. Goodwin, in WP, 162.

13. Catalogue, Folsom Galleries, March 5–23, 1912, BC-CSFAC.

14. CMR to William H. Rance, April 7, 1912, in WP, 166; CMR to Albert J. Trigg, April 7, 1912, BC-CSFAC; CMR to Sid A. Willis, April 7, 1912, in WP, 165.

15. Gov. Edwin L. Norris to CMR, April 30, 1912, CMR Microfilm, MHS.

16. NCR to JDY, May 2, 1939, JDY-NCHE.

17. NCR to R. H. Fletcher, November 14, 1936, BC-CSFAC. Austin Russell states that CMR and NCR traveled to Ross' Hole in the fall (AR, 226), but NCR wrote to Governor Norris on May 21, 1912, alerting him that "Mr. Russell goes to Ross' Hole this week for the mountain backdrop" (NCR to Governor Edwin L. Norris, May 21, 1912, CMR Microfilm, MHS).

18. FBL-RCR, 98–99.

19. *Minneapolis Sunday Journal,* July 28, 1912.

20. John C. Ewers, *Artists of the Old West* (New York: Promontory Press, 1982), 233. In another instance, CMR was accused of portraying an Indian wearing beads not representative of his tribe. "He couldn't help it," CMR reportedly replied. "His squaw wasn't [of that tribe] either." CMR's 1909 oil *When Horseflesh Comes High* has a rider dismounting from the uncustomary right side of his horse. The explanation, of course, was that the rider is a half-breed; Indians dismount differently from whites.

21. Frank B. Linderman, *Montana Adventure: The Recollections of Frank B. Linderman* (Lincoln: University of Nebraska Press, 1968).

22. CMR to Harry Stanford, December 13, 1918, BC-CSFAC.

23. Hanna, *Montana's Many-Splendored Glacierland,* 83; Anne Farrar Hyde, *An American Vision: Far Western Landscape and National Culture, 1820–1920* (New York: New York University Press, 1990), 287–88; Irvin S. Cobb, *Exit Laughing* (Indianapolis: Bobbs-Merrill, 1941), 413.

24. Harold McCracken, *The Frank Tenney Johnson Book: A Master Painter of the Old West* (Garden City, N.Y.: Doubleday, 1974); Thornton I. and Margo Boileau, "Joe Scheurle: Modest Man with Friendly Palette," MMWH 21:4 (Autumn 1971), 39–58; WP, 169.

25. Wessel, *A History of the Rocky Boy's Indian Reservation,* 6, 33–35; River, "A Mountain in His Memory," 72.

26. GFT, January 10, 1909.

27. FBL-RCR, 53–56.

28. James H. Gray, *A Brand of Its Own: The 100 Year History of the Calgary Exhibition and Stampede* (Saskatoon: Western Producer Prairie Books, 1985).

29. TPU, 165.

30. "Special Exhibition, Paintings by Charles M. Russell at 'The Stampede,' Calgary 1912," BC-CSFAC.

31. CMR to Guy Weadick, October 13, 1912, in WP, 172.

32. "Special Exhibition, Paintings by Charles M. Russell at 'The Stampede,' " BC-CSFAC; Guy Weadick to JBR, February 6, 1937, JBR-MHS; Henry Mill Pellatt to NCR, October 31, 1912, BC-CSFAC.

33. Typescript of unidentified article in the *Albertan,* BC-CSFAC; Belknap "Ballie" Buck to JBR, March 27, 1938, JBR-MHS.

34. GFT, September 25, 1912.

35. NCR-MS.

36. NCR to Malcolm Mackay, October 15, 1912, BC-CSFAC.

37. Numerous sources give 1911 as the date of Mackay's first meeting with CMR. The first correspondence between Mackay and CMR begins in the winter of 1908 (BC-CSFAC). This was shortly after Mackay married his wife, Helen, and began buying art for their new home. Perhaps Mackay had seen CMR's art in New York or Montana before actually meeting him in person.

38. NCR to Malcolm Mackay, September 24, October 15, 1912, BC-CSFAC; Vivian A. Paladin, *Malcolm Mackay: C. M. Russell: The Mackay Collection* (Helena: Montana Historical Society, 1979), 11; William Mackay, interview by the author, Roscoe, Montana, October 1, 1993.

39. Milton W. Brown, *The Story of the Armory Show* (New York: Joseph H. Hirshhorn Foundation, 1963).

40. Ibid., 110, 112, 142.

41. Theodore Roosevelt, "A Layman's View of an Art Exhibition," *Outlook* 103 (March 29, 1913), 718; Brown, *Story of the Armory Show,* 138; Kenyon Cox, "The 'Modern' Spirit in Art," *Harper's Weekly,* March 15, 1913, 10.

42. *Chicago Evening Post,* March 6, 1914.

43. FBL-RCR, 84, 93; Fergus Mead to JFD, October 24, 1949, JFD-UT. Mead repeated this anecdote almost verbatim in a letter to JBR (May 10, 1938, JBR-MHS).

44. FBL-RCR, 92–93.45.

45. Mackay, "Charles M. Russell," 33; Sir Henry Pellatt to NCR, August 11, 1919, BC-CSFAC.

46. Rex C. Myers, "The Montana Club: Symbol of Elegance," MMWH 26:4 (October 1976), 30–51; FBL-RCR, 94–96; NCR to FBL, January 27, February 16, 1914, FBL-UM; author's correspondence with Duquesne Club, January 19, 1993; NCR to W. B. Walker, May 20, 1916, BC-CSFAC; Donald J. Howard to JBR, April 21, 1937, JBR-MHS; *Minneapolis Journal,* December 14, 1919.

47. GFT, May 3, 1914.

48. FBL-RCR, 58–66; FBL to CMR, August 24, 1913, BC-CSFAC; CMR to Charles S. King, January 2, 1914, transcript in BC-CSFAC.

49. AB, 203; NCR to FBL, February 16, 1914, FBL-UM; CMR to James R. Smith, March 30, 1914, in WP, 192.

50. (London) *Observer,* April 12, 1914; (London) *Globe,* April 8, 1914.

51. Robert Hughes, *The Shock of the New* (New York: Knopf, 1981), 40–56;

Marianne W. Martin, *Futurist Art and Theory, 1909–1915* (Oxford, England: Clarendon Press, 1968); Marjorie Perloff, *The Futurist Moment: Avant-Garde, Avant Guerre, and the Language of Rupture* (Chicago: University of Chicago Press, 1986), 80–115.

52. FBL-RCR, 88.

53. CMR to William G. Krieghoff, May 4, 1914, in WP, 202; AB, 205.

54. CMR to Edgar I. Holland, May 14, 1914, in WP, 203; CMR to FBL, April 25, 1914, in WP, 201.

55. JDY, "Modest Son of the Old West," 96; CMR to Edgar I. Holland, May 14, 1914, in WP, 203.

56. Renner, *Charles M. Russell,* 28; CMR to Albert J. Trigg, April 12, 1914, in WP, 197; *New York Morning Telegraph,* March 7, 1916.

57. AB, 205; CMR to William G. Krieghoff, May 4, 1914, in WP, 202; AR, 141.

58. CMR to Percy Raban, April 20, 1914, in WP, 200.

59. Rudd, "Idol of the Cowboys," 55.

60. Malone et al., *Montana,* 269–70.

61. CMR to Churchill B. Mehard, October 22, 1918, in WP, 263.

62. JDY to his parents, May 11, 1918, JDY-NCHF; GFT, June 15, 1918; Montana Newspaper Association Insert, July 15, 1918.

63. GFT, November 10, 1918; JDY to his parents, c. December 1917, JDY-NCHF.

64. FBL-RCR, 136; Lew L. Callaway, "Visits with Charles M. Russell," MMWH 38:3 (Summer 1988), 73; JFD, notes from interview with Hugh and Josephine Harrell, Hollywood, California, April 14, 1956, JFD-UT.

65. Margaret Coulter Verharen, quoted in (Kalispell) *Inter Lake,* March 21, 1954; unidentified typescript, n.d., BC-CSFAC.

66. JFD, notes of interview with Lillian Huidekoper, n.d., JFD-UT.

67. Churchill Mehard to JBR, April 27, 1937, JBR-MHS; Noyes, *In the Land of Chinook,* 121; FBL-RCR, 71–72; AB, 201–02; Ross Santee to JFD, October 9, 1946, JFD-UT.

68. Grace Stone Coates to JBR, December 16, 1936, JBR-MHS.

69. JFD, notes of interview with Fred Barton, Los Angeles, February 22, 1956, JFD-UT; *Chicago Evening Post,* March 6, 1914; JDY, unpublished manuscript, n.d., JDY-NCHF.

70. Unsigned typescript, n.d., BC-CSFAC; JDY, unpublished manuscript, JDY-NCH; NCR to JDY, June 11, 1929, JDY-NCHF.

71. Hanna, *Montana's Many-Splendored Glacierland,* 151; Mary Roberts Rinehart, *Through Glacier Park: Seeing America First with Howard Eaton* (Boston: Houghton Mifflin, 1916), 41–42.

72. CMR to Churchill Mehard, October 1916, in WP, 229; CMR to Edward Borein, February 13, 1918, in WP, 247.

[12]
CAMPFIRE STAR

1. Montana Newspaper Association Insert, January 16, 1922; GFT, July 3, 1927; JDY, "Glory Hunters," unpublished manuscript, n.d., JDY-NCHF.

2. Tom Mix, *The West of Yesterday* (Los Angeles: Times-Mirror Press, 1923); Brownlow, *The War, the West, and the Wilderness,* 300–12.

3. CMR to JDY, September 12, 1913, in WP, 180–81.

4. GFT, July 3, 1927; JDY, unpublished manuscript, August 18, 1964, JDY-NCHF.

5. JDY to his parents, July 2, 1915, JDY-NCHF.

6. NCR medical records, Huntington Memorial Hospital, Pasadena, June 10, 1937, copy in possession of the author. Dr. R. C. Olmsted noted "one child that died; no other preg," but specified no date for the miscarriage.

7. JFD, notes of interview with Charles Beil, July 11, 1954, Banff, Alberta, JFD-UT.

8. AR to Delbert Johnston, June 8, 1957, carbon copy in JDY-NCHF; AR to JDY, April 26, 1957, JDY-NCHF.

9. Noyes, *In the Land of Chinook,* 122.

10. JDY to his parents, January 17, 1916, JDY-NCHF.

11. AR, 207.

12. JDY to his parents, December 1916, JDY-NCHF.

13. Ibid.

14. GFT, March 30, 1917.

15. CMR to Con Price, "October 32" [sic], 1917, in WP, 245; CMR to Alexander "Tex" McLeod, June 5, 1918, in WP, 254; CMR to FBL, November 5, 1917, in WP, 246.

16. Sam Gilully, *The Press Gang: A Century of Montana Newspapers, 1885–1985* (Great Falls: Montana Press Association, 1986), 20; Dippie, *Remington & Russell,* 154; AB, 279–80; Noyes, *In the Land of Chinook,* 122.

17. JDY to his parents, February 16, March 1, April 17, August 30, 1917, JDY-NCHF; "Passing of Johnny Matheson," Montana Newspaper Association Insert, June 25, 1917; *St. Louis Globe-Democrat,* August 31, 1917; Sue Portis to CMR, September 1917, BC-CSFAC; CMR to Edward "Kid" Price, June 1, 1917, in WP, 235.

18. JDY to his parents, n.d. and July 2, 1917, JDY-NCHF.

19. Jack Russell, interviews by the author, Oceanside, California, January 20, 1993, July 25, 1994.

20. Ober, "Enmity and Alliance," 18, 30–31; Churchill Mehard to JBR, May 3, 1937, JBR-MHS.

21. JDY to his parents, August 7, 26, 1916, JDY-NCHF; "Lewis Glacier Hotel," promotional brochure, n.d., MHS; Charles G. Jenness, quoted in *Rochester Courier,* October 20, 1922.

22. Mehard to JBR, April 27, 1937, JBR-MHS; JDY to his parents, August 4, 1920, JDY-NCHF; James W. Bollinger to JBR, February 18, June 15, 1937, July 13, August 16,

September 30, 1938, JBR-MHS; Bollinger to John E. Lewis, October 2, 1919, BC-CSFAC; Bollinger, *Old Montana and Her Cowboy Artist* (Shenandoah, Iowa: World Publishing Co., 1963).

23. James W. Bollinger to JBR, July 13, 1938, JBR-MHS.

24. Rinehart, *Through Glacier Park,* 41–42.

25. JDY to his parents, n.d. and August 14, 1922, JDY-NCHF.

26. Jack Russell, unpublished manuscript, n.d., BC-CSFAC.

27. Philip R. Goodwin to his mother, n.d., BBHC; Norma Linderman Waller, in FBL-RCR, 136. "One felt that it wasn't a dance to him," Mrs. Waller explained, "but a ritual to the stealth of the fox and that he danced his partner into the land of the fox."

28. CMR to FBL, May 19, 1919, FBL-UM.

29. GFT, July 27, 1919; FBL-RCR, 50; Charles Scribner's Sons to FBL, telegram, August 30, 1919, FBL-UM; FBL to CMR, September 2, October 26, 1919, BC-CSFAC; CMR to FBL, September 22, 1919, FBL-UM.

30. JDY to his parents, January 28, 1919, JDY-NCHF.

31. Tom Lutz, *American Nervousness, 1903: An Anecdotal History* (Ithaca, N.Y.: Cornell University Press, 1991).

32. CMR to NCR, February 6, 9, 12, 1919, BC-CSFAC.

33. WP, 272; CMR to NCR, February 9, 1919, BC-CSFAC.

34. Ralph S. Kendall, *Benton of the Royal Mounted: A Tale of the Northwest Mounted Police* (New York: Grosset & Dunlap, 1918), 55.

35. GFT, September 21, December 7, 1919; partially identified clipping, Minneapolis, December 1919, BC-CSFAC. CMR is quoted, "I can get as high as $8,000 now for my canvases." A more contemporary source states that *When Law Dulls the Edge of Chance* was sold for $10,000 (*Charles M. Russell, 1864–1926* [Edmonton, Alberta: Edmonton Art Gallery, 1967]).

36. F. R. MacMillan to CMR and NCR, September 10, 1919, BC-CSFAC; Montana Newspaper Association Insert, December 1, 1919; Duke of Connaught to Arthur Lane, December 6, 1919, BC-CSFAC.

37. GFT, December 7, 1919.

38. *Minneapolis Sunday Tribune,* December 14, 1919; partially identified clipping, Minneapolis, December 1919, BC-CSFAC.

39. *Minneapolis Journal,* December 14, 1919; Malone et al., *Montana,* 280–83.

[13]

CALIFORNIA

1. Bruce Bliven, "Los Angeles: The City That Is Bacchanalian — in a Nice Way," *New Republic,* July 13, 1927, 197.

2. Harrison Rhodes, "Is There a West?" *Harper's,* June 1920, 70.

3. Work Projects Administration, *Los Angeles: A Guide to the City and Its Environs* (New York: Hastings House, 1941), li; Montana Newspaper Association Insert, March 18, 1918.

4. George W. West, "California the Prodigious," *The Nation,* October 4, 1922, 327; James A. B. Scherer, "What Kind of a Pittsburgh Is Los Angeles?" *World's Work* 41 (February 1921), 382–92; Kevin Starr, *Material Dreams: Southern California Through the 1920s* (New York: Oxford University Press, 1990), 120–36.

5. WPA, *Los Angeles,* 74; Scherer, "What Kind of a Pittsburgh Is Los Angeles?" 389.

6. Nancy Dustin Wall Moure, "Impressionism, Post-Impressionism, and the Eucalyptus School in Southern California," in Ruth Lilly Westphal, ed., *Plein Air Painters of California: The Southland* (Irvine, Calif.: Westphal Publishing, 1982), 4–15; Kevin Starr, *Inventing the Dream: California Through the Progressive Era* (New York: Oxford University Press, 1985), 107–18.

7. Diane Kaiser Koszarski, *The Complete Films of William S. Hart: A Pictorial Record* (New York: Dover Publications, 1980); Fenin and Everson, *The Western,* 75; Brownlow, *The War, the West, and the Wilderness,* 267–68.

8. CMR to Berners B. Kelly, February 22, 1920, in WP, 288.

9. Ibid.; CMR to Philip R. Goodwin, April 10, 1920, in WP, 298.

10. CMR to Henry Herbert Knibbs, January 11, 1921, BC-CSFAC; CMR to Wallace Coburn, January 27, 1915, in WP, 213; CMR to JDY, March 30, 1920, in WP, 295.

11. Brownlow, *The War, the West, and the Wilderness,* 290–300; Diana Serra Cary, *The Hollywood Posse: The Story of the Gallant Band of Horsemen Who Made Movie History* (Boston: Houghton Mifflin, 1975); Peter Bogdanovich, *John Ford* (Berkeley: University of California Press, 1968), 39.

12. CMR to Berners B. Kelly, February 22, 1920, in WP, 288–89; Koszarski, *Complete Films of William S. Hart,* 121; M. G. "Bud" Norris, *The Tom Mix Book* (Waynesville, N.C.: World of Yesterday, 1989), 164.

13. CMR to W. W. Cheely, May 3, 1924, in WP, 351; CMR to Edward C. "Teddy Blue" Abbott, April 14, 1926, in WP, 389; CMR to Guy Weadick, July–August 1922, in WP, 324.

14. Bill Libby, "The Old Wrangler Rides Again," *Cosmopolitan,* March 1964, 21, cited in William C. Howze, "The Influence of Western Painting and Genre Painting on the Films of John Ford," Ph.D. dissertation, University of Texas, Austin, August 1986, 26–27; Dan Ford, *Pappy: The Life of John Ford* (Englewood Cliffs, N.J.: Prentice-Hall, 1979), 228; Tag Gallagher, *John Ford: The Man and His Films* (Berkeley: University of California Press, 1986), 254; Percy Raban to CMR, September 27, 1923, BC-CSFAC.

15. Turbesé Lummis Fiske and Keith Lummis, *Charles F. Lummis: The Man and His West* (Norman: Southwest Museum in association with the University of Oklahoma Press, 1975); Robert E. Fleming, *Charles F. Lummis* (Boise, Idaho: Boise State University, 1981); Daniela A. Moneta, ed., *Chas. F. Lummis: The Centennial Exhibition Commemorating His Tramp Across the Continent* (Los Angeles: Southwest Museum, 1985);

David Roberts, "A Tough Little Guy Became the Original Southwest Booster," *Smithsonian* 21 (May 1990), 116–26.

16. JDY to his parents, March 3, 1924, JDY-NCHF; Fiske and Lummis, *Charles F. Lummis,* 161.

17. Charles F. Lummis to CMR, February 26, 1920, BC-CSFAC; Fiske and Lummis, *Charles F. Lummis,* 163.

18. GFT, July 4, 1932.

19. NCR investment and income record, July 8, 1920, CMRM; William Bertsche, interview by the author, Great Falls, September 16, 1993; JDY to his parents, October 29, 1923, JDY-NCHF; CMR to Mose Kaufman, June 5, 1926, in WP, 395–96.

20. NCR to James W. Bollinger, September 29, 1920, BC-CSFAC; CMR to NCR, October 11, 1920, in WP, 303; NCR to Malcolm Mackay, December 1920, BC-CSFAC; JDY to his parents, August 4, 1920, JDY-NCHF.

21. William Mackay, interview by the author, Roscoe, Montana, October 1, 1993; Helen Raynor Mackay, "Charles M. Russell," 33–35.

22. Hassrick, *Charles M. Russell,* 133.

23. Westphal, *Plein Air Painters of California,* 29; *Los Angeles Times,* October 22, 1933; NCR to Percy Raban, April 13, 1921, BC-CSFAC.

24. NCR to Mary Pickford, May 19, 1921, BC-CSFAC.

25. Gary Carey, *Doug & Mary: A Biography of Douglas Fairbanks and Mary Pickford* (New York: Dutton, 1977); Booton Herndon, *Mary Pickford and Douglas Fairbanks: The Most Popular Couple the World Has Ever Known* (New York: Norton, 1977).

26. Montana Newspaper Association Insert, May 23, 1921.

27. CMR to Douglas Fairbanks, June 15, 1921, BC-CSFAC; CMR to Fairbanks, May 1921, in WP, 313; Mary Pickford to NCR, June 14, 1921, BC-CSFAC.

28. CMR to John E. and Olive Lewis, August 11, 1918, in WP, 256; CMR to H. J. Justin and Sons, December 28, 1921, in WP, 320; CMR to George W. Farr, March 12, 1919, in WP, 277.

29. Ginger Renner, *A Limitless Sky: The Work of Charles M. Russell in the Collection of the Rockwell Museum* (Flagstaff, Ariz.: Northland Press, 1986), 29–30; Louis D. Lighton to Homer E. Britzman, April 17, 1941, BC-CSFAC.

30. Harry Carey, Jr., interview by the author, Durango, Colorado, October 15, 1993; Ford, *Pappy,* 20; Gallagher, *John Ford,* 17–25; Lahue, *Winners of the West,* 43–52; Glenn Shirley, "Harry Carey, Western Natural," *True West* 21 (June 1974), 6–11, 46–48; Tuska, *Filming of the West,* 77.

31. CMR to Harry Carey, February 25, 1921, BC-CSFAC; W. C. Tuttle, quoted in a letter from Jack Reynolds to JFD, May 21, 1960, JFD-UT.

32. CMR to John F. Hagenson, April 8, 1921, in WP, 307.

33. Agreement between California-Michigan Land & Water Company and J. A. Cooper, November 26, 1921; deed dated December 1, 1921; Los Angeles County Recorder's Office, Norwalk, California.

34. Hilda Josephson to JBR, n.d., JBR-MHS.

35. Montana Newspaper Association Insert, October 31, 1921.

36. Percy Raban to NCR, August 6, 1922, BC-CSFAC; William W. Cheely and H. Percy Raban, *Back-Trailing on the Old Frontier* (Aurora, Colo.: John Osterberg, 1990), foreword by John Osterberg.

37. NCR to Malcolm Mackay, January 24, 1922, BC-CSFAC; Malcolm Mackay to NCR, October 29, 1921, BC-CSFAC; Malcolm S. Mackay, *Cow Range and Hunting Trail* (New York: G. P. Putnam's Sons, 1925).

38. Davidson, *Edward Borein,* 101–02; William H. Gerdts, *Art Across America: Two Centuries of Regional Painting, 1710–1920,* vol. 3 (New York: Abbeville Press, 1990), 293–98; Michael James Phillips, *History of Santa Barbara County, California, From Its Earliest Settlement to the Present Time,* vol. 1 (Chicago: S. J. Clarke Publishing Co., 1927), 355–56; Southern California Writers' Project, Work Projects Administration, *Santa Barbara: A Guide to the Channel City and Its Environs* (New York: Hastings House, 1941); L. W. Wilson, "Santa Barbara's Artist Colony," *American Magazine of Art,* December 1921, 412; *Santa Barbara Daily News,* April 22, 1922.

39. Benton Embree to CMR, photographic reproduction of telegram, April 13, 1922, JFD-UT; Jake Hoover, transcript of interview, October 10, 1924, MHS; Montana Newspaper Association Insert, March 7, 1921; Hoover death certificate, City of Seattle Department of Health, April 14, 1925, BC-CSFAC; CMR to Benton Embree, photographic reproduction of letter, April 15, 1922, copy in possession of the author.

40. *Billings Gazette,* March 22, 1922.

41. JDY to his parents, August 4, 1921, JDY-NCHF.

42. Ibid.; Linderman guest book, Flathead Lake, private collection of Sally and Bob Hatfield; Sally Hatfield, interview by the author, Flathead Lake, June 26, 1993.

43. JDY to his parents, September 23, 1922, JDY-NCHF; FBL to CMR, c. November 1922, BC-CSFAC.

44. NCR to JDY, April 4, 1923, JDY-NCHF.

45. NCR to JDY, December 5, 1922, JDY-NCHF; JDY to his parents, December 9, 1922, JDY-NCHF.

46. NCR to JDY, January 31, 1923, JDY-NCHF.

47. NCR to JDY, April 4, 1923, JDY-NCHF.

48. Verne Linderman to JDY, October 22, 1922, JDY-NCHF.

49. Ibid., January 31, 1923, JDY-NCHF.

50. FBL-RCR, 74–76; CMR to George B. Calvert, April 4, 1923, in WP, 331.

51. NCR to JDY, April 4, 1923, JDY-NCHF; FBL-RCR, 76.

52. Quoted in Davidson, *Edward Borein,* 111.

53. *Los Angeles Times,* March 18, 1923; Margaret Tante Burk, *Are the Stars Out Tonight?: The Story of the Famous Ambassador and Cocoanut Grove, Hollywood's Hotel* (Los Angeles: Round Table West/Ambassador Hotel, 1980).

54. James W. Bollinger to CMR, May 19, 1923, BC-CSFAC; Charles Lummis to CMR, March 29, 1923, BC-CSFAC.

55. Agreement between Meyering Land Company and NCR, signed May 15, 1923; deed dated June 5, 1923; Los Angeles County Recorder's Office, Norwalk, California.

56. CMR to James W. Bollinger, April 24, 1923, in WP, 333.

[14]
TRAIL'S END

1. *Butte Daily Post,* June 29, 1923; GFT, October 17, 1911; James K. Ballinger, ed., *Charles M. Russell: The Frederic G. Renner Collection* (Phoenix: Phoenix Art Museum, 1981), 60.

2. Stewart, *Charles M. Russell, Sculptor,* 237; *Butte Daily Post,* June 29, 1923.

3. Tony Dalich, "Shelby's Fabled Day in the Sun: Fourth of July 1923," MMWH 15:3 (Summer 1965), 2–23; James W. (Body) Johnson, "The Fight That Won't Stay Dead," *Sports Illustrated,* July 4, 1966, 64–73; John Lardner, "That Was Pugilism: Shelby, 1923," *New Yorker,* June 19, 1948, 52–67.

4. NCR to Mr. and Mrs. Douglas Fairbanks, June 21, 1923; Mary Pickford to NCR, July 2, 1923, BC-CSFAC; Elsie Gabrielson Fowler, unpublished notes, October 2, 1981, CMRM.

5. CMR to FBL, August 5, 1923, FBL-UM; NCR to JDY, August 13, 1923, JDY-CMRM; NCR to C. F. Kelley, October 8, 1923, BC-CSFAC; NCR to Percy Raban, November 7, 1923, BC-CSFAC; JDY to his parents, December 2, 1923, JDY-NCHF; NCR to JDY, December 10, 1923, JDY-CMRM; NCR to Ella Ironside, December 22, 1923, stenographer's notebook, CMRM; NCR to Mrs. Harry Carey, December 21, 1923, stenographer's notebook, CMRM.

6. CMR to Con Price, February 29, 1924, in WP, 341; *Santa Barbara Morning Press,* January 21, 1923; William Bleasdell Cameron, "Charlie Russell Comes Home," *Canadian Cattlemen* 13:4 (April 1950), 46.

7. AB, 261; CMR to Josephine Trigg, March 27, 1924, in WP, 345.

8. *Los Angeles Times,* March 30, 1924; NCR to Percy Raban, October 8, 1923, BC-CSFAC.

9. Ballinger, ed., *Charles M. Russell: The Frederic G. Renner Collection,* 41; the painting was *Mexican Buffalo Hunters* (1924).

10. NCR to C. F. Kelley, November 21, 1923, BC-CSFAC; JDY to his mother, February 27, June 26, 1924, BC-CSFAC; *Los Angeles Times,* December 23, 1923; Westphal, *Plein Air Painters of California,* 110; McCracken, *The Frank Tenney Johnson Book,* 171; Karl Yost and Frederic G. Renner, *A Bibliography of the Published Works of Charles M. Russell* (Lincoln: University of Nebraska Press, 1971), 43.

11. CMR to FBL, April 24, 1924, in WP, 347; JDY to his mother, April 21, 1924, JDY-NCHF

12. *Los Angeles Times,* March 30, 1924; JDY to his mother, March 20, May 22, 1924, JDY-NCHF; CMR to Frank B. Brown, May 4, 1924, in WP, 352.

13. B. M. Bower to Ella Ironside, July 25, 1924, Jean Ironside Papers, MHS.

14. CMR to Ed Neitzling, November 9, 1924, in WP, 358; JDY to FBL, November 25, 1924, FBL-UM.

15. NCR to E. G. Furman, November 2, 1926, telegram book, CMRM; Dan La Botz, *Edward L. Doheny: Petroleum, Power, and Politics in the United States and Mexico* (Westport, Conn.: Praeger Publishers, 1991), 3–6, 10–11, 15, 35; Lucille V. Miller, "Edward and Estelle Doheny," *Ventura County Historical Society Quarterly* 6:1 (November 1960), 5–6, 16–17; Ward Ritchie, *The Dohenys of Los Angeles* (Los Angeles: Dawson's Book Shop, 1974), 18–19, 21–23, 37–38; Robert O. Schad, "The Estelle Doheny Collection," *New Colophon* 3 (1950), 229–42; WP, 360; Eliza C. Robert, "Russell Is Here Tonight," unpublished manuscript, n.d., BC-CSFAC.

16. CMR to NCR, December 1 and 2, 1924, in WP, 360; NCR to Mrs. Edward Doheny, December 15, 1924, telegram book, CMRM; Edan Milton Hughes, *Artists in California, 1786–1940* (San Francisco: Hughes Publishing Co., 1989), 489; *Los Angeles Times,* September 4, 1910; *Graphic,* March 11, 1911.

17. *Duluth News Tribune,* December 7, 1924; CMR to NCR, December 1, 3, 6, 1924, in WP, 360–61; NCR to JDY, January 27, 1925, CMRM.

18. NCR to JDY, January 27, 1925, CMRM.

19. "Special Exhibition of Paintings and Bronzes by Charles M. Russell," Corcoran Gallery of Art, February 3–27, 1925, catalogue with NCR's handwritten price list, BC-CSFAC; *Washington Post,* February 8, 1925.

20. NCR to CMR, May 8, 12, 1925, telegram book, CMRM; NCR to CMR, May 12, 1925, BC-CSFAC; M. Hal Sussmann, "Russell Murals Unveiled," *Southwest Art* 18 (May 1989), 62; WP, 360.

21. Commencement program, State University of Montana, Missoula, June 15, 1925, BC-CSFAC.

22. JDY to his mother, September 28, 1925, CMRM; Guy Weadick to CMR, September 10, 1925, BC-CSFAC; Agnes C. Laut, *The Blazed Trail of the Old Frontier* (New York: Robert M. McBride, 1926), 9; NCR to Ralph Budd, May 27, 1925, and Ralph Budd to NCR, June 2, 11, 30, 1925, Great Northern Railway President's Subject Files, Minnesota Historical Society.

23. GFT, July 23, 1925.

24. JDY, "Charlie and Me," 78; unidentified clipping, August 23, 1925, MHS; photo from unidentified newspaper, dated September 20, 1925, BC-CSFAC.

25. Bollinger, *Old Montana and Her Cowboy Artist,* 23; *Anaconda Standard,* October 24, 1925; James W. Bollinger to CMR, December 10, 1926, BC-CSFAC.

26. NCR to Malcolm Mackay, October 27, 1925, BC-CSFAC; NCR to George Sack, November 25, 1925, BC-CSFAC; George Sack to CMR, November 11, 1925, BC-CSFAC. Information on Sack's background and source of wealth is sketchy at best;

his ties to the perfume industry are deduced from his various letters to NCR in BC-CSFAC.

27. David C. Hunt, "The Old West Revisited," *American Scene* 8:4 (1967); Mildred D. Ladner, *O. C. Seltzer: Painter of the Old West* (Norman: University of Oklahoma Press, 1979), 51–54; David C. Hunt, "Curator's Report on the Philip Cole Collection," unpublished typescript, Gilcrease Institute of American History and Art, Tulsa, June 14, 1967, 6.

28. Will James to CMR, c. 1920, BC-CSFAC; William Gardner Bell, *Will James: The Life and Works of a Lone Cowboy* (Flagstaff, Ariz.: Northland Press, 1987); Jim Bramlett, *Ride for the High Points: The Real Story of Will James* (Missoula, Mont.: Mountain Press Publishing, 1987), 118–19; Will James, *Lone Cowboy: My Life Story* (New York: Scribner's, 1930), 283–85; J. M. Neill, ed., *Will James: The Spirit of the Cowboy* (Casper, Wyo.: Nicolaysen Art Museum, 1985), 1–20; WP, 399–400, 425; NCR to JDY, December 5, 1925, JDY-NCHE.

29. Harry Maule to CMR, June 4, December 7, 1925, BC-CSFAC.

30. NCR to George Sack, July 9, 1926, BC-CSFAC.

31. NCR to Thomas F. Cole, July 17, 1918; AB, 282; JBR to his fiancée, c. 1940, JBR-MHS; Harry Carey, Jr., interview by the author; Sussmann, "Russell Murals Unveiled," 62.

32. Philip Cole to NCR, May 27, 1926, BC-CSFAC; N. B. Holter to JBR, August 3, 1938, JBR-MHS.

33. NCR to JDY, May 20, 1926, CMRM; Harry Maule to NCR, May 28, October 2, 1926, BC-CSFAC; Harry Maule to NCR, March 1, April 8, 1926, BC-CSFAC.

34. NCR to Malcolm Mackay, October 2, 1926, BC-CSFAC; Frank M. Chapman, Jr., "The Man Behind the Brush," *Country Life* 50:4 (August 1926), 35–40; Helen Mackay to CMR, August 6, 1926, BC-CSFAC; NCR to Reginald Townsend, September 24, 1926, BC-CSFAC.

35. Dr. Russell Edwin, interview by the author, Great Falls, June 17, 1993.

36. Willard Bartlett, *The Surgical Treatment of Goiter with Foreword by Dr. Charles H. Mayo* (St. Louis: C. V. Mosby Co., 1926); Helen Clapesattle, *The Doctors Mayo* (Minneapolis: University of Minnesota Press, 1941); Gunther W. Nagel, *The Mayo Legacy* (Springfield, Ill.: Charles C Thomas, 1966); Lucy Wilder, *The Mayo Clinic* (New York: Harcourt, Brace, 1936).

37. Israel Bram, *Goiter Prevention and Thyroid Protection* (Philadelphia: F. A. Davis Co., 1928), 6–7, 169–70.

38. Dr. Edward S. Edwin, tape recording of speech to the Junior League of Great Falls, April 8, 1971, copy in possession of the author; CMR to Isabel Brown, July 30, 1926, in WP, 401.

39. R. M. Tucker to Jack Russell, September 24, 1973, copy in possession of the author; Nagel, *The Mayo Legacy*, 54; Edward S. Edwin, Junior League of Great Falls, April 8, 1971.

40. R. M. Tucker to Jack Russell, September 24, 1973; CMR to Charles D. Eliot, July 9, 1926, BC-CSFAC.

41. CMR to JDY, studio note, n.d., CMRM.

42. William A. Plummer to NCR, November 12, 1926, BC-CSFAC.

43. AB, 317; AR, 242; G. Renner, *A Limitless Sky,* 22.

44. *Great Falls Leader,* July 19, 20, 1926.

45. NCR to Harry Maule, July 27, 1926, BC-CSFAC.

46. Harry Maule to NCR, September 14, 1926, BC-CSFAC.

47. Ibid.; NCR to Harry Maule, October 8, December 4, 1926, BC-CSFAC; Memorandum of Agreement between CMR and Doubleday, Page & Co., October 21, 1926, BC-CSFAC.

48. Philip Cole to NCR, July 1, 1926, BC-CSFAC; CMR to Philip Cole, September 26, 1926, in WP, 404–05.

49. Dippie, *Looking at Russell,* 120–28; *Minnesota Journal,* December 14, 1919.

50. Alma Gilbert, *The Make Believe World of Maxfield Parrish and Sue Lewin* (San Francisco: Pomegranate Artbooks, 1990); Coy Ludwig, *Maxfield Parrish* (New York: Watson-Guptill, 1973).

51. *Rocky Mountain News,* November 21, 1921.

52. NCR to J. W. Theisen, BC-CSFAC.

53. CMR and NCR, Christmas card, December 1926, JDY-NCHE

54. GFT, November 15, 1926.

55. AB, 319; Conway, "Child of the Frontier"; Stauffer, *Behind Every Man,* 247.

56. Edward S. Edwin, Junior League of Great Falls, April 8, 1971; Russell Edwin, interview by the author; Jack Russell, interview by the author.

[15]

EPILOGUE

1. GFT, October 26, 27, 28, 1926; William A. Plummer to NCR, November 12, 1926, BC-CSFAC; George Bird Grinnell to NCR, October 26, 1926, BC-CSFAC; Joseph Henry Sharp to NCR, November 6, 1926, BC-CSFAC; FBL to NCR, November 16, 1926, BC-CSFAC; John Young Boy to NCR, December 5, 1926, BC-CSFAC.

2. John C. Frohlicher to JFD, January 1945, JFD-UT.

3. CMR to William W. Van Orsdel, March 20, 1918, in WP, 251.

4. NCR to Harry Maule, November 19, 1926, BC-CSFAC.

5. CMR will, November 8, 1924, Cascade County District Court, Great Falls, Montana; Woodcock, "The St. Louis Heritage of Charles Marion Russell"; appraisal of NCR estate, 1940, Los Angeles County Courthouse; inventory with appraised values, Huntsberger-Givens Company, Great Falls, January 24, 1927, BC-CSFAC.

6. Harry Maule to NCR, January 7, September 8, 1927, BC-CSFAC; NCR to Harry Maule, January 19, 1927, BC-CSFAC; TPU, xiv.

7. GFT, June 30, 1927; NCR to Dan R. Conway, April 2, September 1, 1927; Conway to NCR, October 9, 1927; NCR to Wade H. George, January 4, March 1, 1937; BC-CSFAC.

8. Harry Maule to Dan R. Conway, November 23, 1927; Owen Culbertson to NCR, January 9, 1928, BC-CSFAC; Conway to NCR, November 23, December 1, 1927, April 7 and 16, August 23, October 18, 1928, December 30, 1932, BC-CSFAC; NCR to Conway, January 9, 1933, BC-CSFAC.

9. NCR medical records, Huntington Memorial Hospital, Pasadena, April 15, 1937, copy in possession of the author; NCR to U.S. Senator Burton K. Wheeler, January 31, 1936; NCR to Rodney Houston, May 15, 1937; NCR to Bill Taylor, May 20, 1939, BC-CSFAC; Jack Russell, interviews by the author; NCR to J. W. Theisen, December 7, 1926, BC-CSFAC; Stauffer, *Behind Every Man,* 220–21, 300–01; Van Kirke Nelson to Joan and Dale Stauffer, April 8, 1983, copy in possession of the author; GFT, October 6, 1938; NCR to William S. Hart, October 8, 1938, BC-CSFAC.

10. Hart's ranch house and all its original contents have been preserved as the William S. Hart Museum, Newhall, California; the photo of NCR remains on the bedside table to this day.

11. Jack Russell, interviews by the author; NCR to Philip Cole, May 22, 1933, BC-CSFAC.

12. JDY to his mother, September 18, 1926, JDY-NCHF; JDY to NCR, November 4, 1926, BC-CSFAC; JDY to Branson Stevenson, March 2, 1945, November 11, 1949, September 18, 1956, January 13, 1964, CMRM; JDY to NCR, October 7, 1928, BC-CSFAC.

13. Ladner, *O. C. Seltzer;* JDY, "Charlie and Me," 79–80; JDY, unpublished manuscript, n.d., JDY-NCHF.

14. George Sack to NCR, May 30, 1928, March 15, May 23, November 23, December 16, 1929, BC-CSFAC; NCR to George Sack, March 19, 1929, BC-CSFAC.

15. NCR to I. W. Church, May 1, 1928, BC-CSFAC; Dan R. Conway to Ed Borein, April 7, 1928, BC-CSFAC; Conway to NCR, January 1, August 23, 1928, BC-CSFAC.

16. Harry Maule to NCR, February 3, 1928, BC-CSFAC; NCR to JDY, January 15, 1929, BC-CSFAC.

17. NCR to Charles Beil, September 25, 1931, BC-CSFAC; NCR to John Lewis, April 18, 1931, BC-CSFAC; GFT, March 20, 1959.

18. GFT, August 27, October 3, 1952; GFT, January 6, 1951.

19. JFD, notes from interview with Fred Barton, Los Angeles, March 22, 1956, JFD-UT.

20. Edward C. "Teddy Blue" Abbott to NCR, December 21, 1926, BC-CSFAC.

21. CMR to FBL, January 18, 1919, in WP, 269.

INDEX